LOTUS® NOTES™ 4
ADMINISTRATOR'S SURVIVAL GUIDE

Andrew Dahl

SAMS
PUBLISHING

201 West 103rd Street
Indianapolis, Indiana 46290

PUBLISHER AND PRESIDENT	Richard K. Swadley
ACQUISITIONS MANAGER	Greg Wiegand
DEVELOPMENT MANAGER	Dean Miller
MANAGING EDITOR	Cindy Morrow
MARKETING MANAGER	John Pierce
ASSISTANT MARKETING MANAGER	Kristina Perry

ACQUISITIONS EDITOR
Grace Buechlein

DEVELOPMENT EDITOR
Dean Miller

SOFTWARE DEVELOPMENT SPECIALIST
Cari Skaggs

PRODUCTION EDITOR
Robin Drake

TECHNICAL REVIEWERS
Randy Davison
Marcia R. Thomas
Scott J. Hertz

EDITORIAL COORDINATOR
Bill Whitmer

TECHNICAL EDIT COORDINATOR
Lynette Quinn

RESOURCE COORDINATOR
Deborah Frisby

Formatter
Frank Sinclair

Editorial Assistants
Carol Ackerman
Andi Richter
Rhonda Tinch-Mize

COVER DESIGNER
Tim Amrhein

BOOK DESIGNER
Alyssa Yesh

COPY WRITER
Peter Fuller

PRODUCTION TEAM SUPERVISOR
Brad Chinn

PRODUCTION
Mary Ann Abramson, Stephen Adams, Carol Bowers, Georgiana Briggs, Gina Brown, Charlotte Clapp, Jeanne Clark, Jason Hand, Sonja Hart, Mike Henry, Clint Lahnen, Donna Martin, Beth Rago, Erich Richter, Bobbi Satterfield, Laura A. Smith, SA Springer, Andrew Stone, Mark Walchle

Overview

Contents

PART III   INSTALLING NOTES

PART IV   ADMINISTERING NOTES

Acknowledgments

A book of this scope is never written by a single person. I would like to thank all the people who added suggestions and tips, reviewed the manuscript, and generally made this book a true resource for administrators. You know who you are. Thanks to Rob Wunderlich for contributing the chapter on using Notes with the Internet. I would also like to thank Leslie Lesnick, without whom this book would not have been possible.

Rob Wunderlich, CLP/CLI, is an instructor and Notes consultant for ENTEX Information Services in Bloomfield Hills, Michigan, formerly The LEAD Group. He is the author of numerous articles on groupware in general and Lotus Notes in particular. In addition to consulting and development work with Notes, Rob is ENTEX/Michigan's Webmaster and has "grown to love" the InterNotes products by employing them on ENTEX/Michigan's Web page (`http://web1.leadgroup.com`).

About the Author

Andrew Dahl is a co-founder of L3Comm, a consulting firm that specializes in Lotus Notes and the World Wide Web. Andrew is a graduate of MIT and has more than 10 years' experience working with networks and client/server systems. Before founding L3Comm, as part of CompuServe's Enterprise Connect for Lotus Notes team, Andrew designed and developed network-management tools for an international Notes network. He has also worked as an IBM consultant, specializing in user interface development for client/server systems. His previous author credits include *Internet Commerce*, *Connecting NetWare to the Internet*, and *Inside OS/2*. He lives in Columbus, Ohio and can be reached at `102174.2004@compuserve.com`.

Foreword

Since 1989, Lotus Notes has made the global business world a much smaller, more manageable place and the business of business less daunting. Lotus Notes has achieved this by systematically tumbling the barriers to sharing, managing, and distributing business information, and helping customers automate strategic business processes that improve their bottom lines.

Simply put, Lotus Notes makes the process of communicating, collaborating, and coordination easier and more productive. Notes combines a replicated document database, an enterprise-scalable messaging infrastructure, and a cross-platform client/server application development environment. The software is built on a client/server backbone that not only supports all of the major operating systems and network architectures, but also masks the underlying complexities and incompatibilities among systems.

Since day one, we've continued to enhance and modify Notes to incorporate support for new technologies and forms of business information—from standards such as DDE and OLE to multimedia objects such as images, video, and audio.

Today, more than 8,000 companies and 4.5 million individuals have incorporated Lotus Notes solutions into their strategic business operations.

We're extremely excited about the recent release of Lotus Notes Release 4, a major upgrade of the software featuring hundreds of new capabilities and enhancements. Release 4 was developed over the course of several years with input from thousands of customers and Lotus Business Partners. It addresses some important customer hot buttons.

Of particular interest to system administrators are:

◆ *Integrated Enterprise Management:* Lotus Notes servers are now scalable up to 1,000 users. In addition, in Release 4, system administrators will find enhanced administration and management tools, enabling you to more efficiently manage mission-critical, enterprise-wide Notes applications.

◆ *Ease of Use:* Notes Release 4 features a greatly enhanced user interface, based on the award-winning cc:Mail UI, in addition to intuitive new tools, such as intelligent agents, that make it easier for users to store and navigate information.

◆ *Integrated Client / Server Messaging:* Release 4 features a greatly enhanced user interface and world-class, robust client/server e-mail and messaging, opening up a world of new messaging applications possibilities for your company.

- *Enhanced Support for Mobile and Remotely Connected Users:* Notes Release 4 makes it easier for mobile and remotely connected workers to tap into Notes, and gives them new tools for managing information remotely.

- *Internet Integration:* InterNotes Web Navigator and InterNotes Web Publisher are integrated with Release 4, allowing users to seamlessly access the Internet from within Notes and integrate Internet resources into their Notes environments.

- *Application Development and Programmability:* Building Notes applications is easier in Release 4 with LotusScript 3.0, a cross-platform, BASIC-compatible, object-oriented programming language, in addition to some new advanced Notes programming tools.

We are continuing to enhance Notes. In the future, look for:

- *More Internet Integration:* By mid-1996, the Notes Release 4 server will include native support for HTTP, HTML, and Java technology. By building on the InterNotes Web Navigator and InterNotes Web Publisher products, we'll enable users with Notes clients or Web browsers to benefit from the full range of Notes team-oriented applications. For example, Notes users surfing the Web will be able to click on an object, download Java applets from the Web, and integrate the applets with Notes applications, rather than being restricted to programs resident on their PCs.

  Notes will provide a best-of-breed Web development and application-hosting environment, with features such as an integrated search engine based on the industry-leading Verity technology, rich forms capabilities, and database navigation via views.

- *Lotus Components:* These new, task-focused modules will extend the applications possibilities for Release 4. Your end users will find it easier and faster to complete everyday business tasks—such as creating a chart or performing a data query—while remaining in the familiar Notes environment. Developers will find that Lotus Components will reduce Notes applications development time because the components are reusable, customizable, and programmable.

- *Notes eApps:* This set of Notes-based "electronic applications frameworks" will let you more rapidly deploy Web-enabled applications. Notes developers will have a set of building blocks and tools for easily extending your company's publishing, marketing, customer service, or electronic commerce applications to the Internet.

◆ *Calendaring and Scheduling:* Future versions of Notes clients will feature integrated enterprise-wide calendaring and scheduling capabilities, as well as full interoperability with Lotus Notes Organizer clients. Notes and Organizer users will be able to schedule meetings with each other via Notes, cc:Mail, or IBM OfficeVision, extending Notes' calendaring and scheduling across the enterprise.

◆ *Notes NIC, the Notes Network Information Center Site:* To make your life easier, we're creating a new Web site (http://www.notes.net) with the latest, most complete Release 4 technical support information, maintenance resources, and early adopters' releases of our products, offering a sneak peak at forthcoming functionality.

Exciting times are ahead. This edition of *Lotus Notes 4 Administrator's Survival Guide* should help system administrators stay at the top of their form in making Notes work hard for their organizations.

Regards,

Steve Sayre
Vice President of Marketing
Lotus Development Corporation

Introduction

Managing a Lotus Notes installation poses many unique problems. Notes is a combination database tool, application development tool, and security tool customized for groupware applications—an area in which few organizations have experience. When properly done, a groupware project can significantly change jobs and the flow of information within a company. Project managers and administrators not only must deal with new technology, but with egos and corporate culture.

Lotus Notes Release 4.0 includes features that significantly reduce the time and cost associated with administrating a Notes network. With a little planning, you can position yourself to make the best use of these features. This book discusses each of these features in detail.

More than with any other product currently available, Notes requires a close working relationship between project managers, application developers, and administrators. Mistakes made by application developers or project managers can have a significant impact on administration costs. This book is intended to help project managers, application developers, and network administrators work together to reduce the costs associated with administering Notes.

WHY READ THIS BOOK?

Lotus Notes 4 Administrator's Survival Guide was written to help companies plan, install, and maintain Notes. This book goes beyond the references currently available and explains

- ◆ The most common errors made when deploying Notes
- ◆ The type of applications best suited to Notes
- ◆ How Notes works with the World Wide Web
- ◆ How to configure your Notes network to maximize performance and minimize problems
- ◆ The real story on the strengths and weaknesses of Lotus Notes

Whether you're just thinking about installing Notes, migrating to Release 4 from Release 3.x, or maintaining a current Notes installation, this book can help you reach your goal faster with fewer problems.

WHO SHOULD READ THIS BOOK?

This book is primarily targeted at project managers and administrators responsible for Notes, although some application development issues are covered. Issues for small, medium, and large organizations are discussed. You should have some background with client/server systems and/or network administration before reading this book. Because this book spends very little time introducing the Notes interface, you should spend some time using Notes as you read the text.

CONVENTIONS USED IN THIS BOOK

This book uses the following conventions:

◆ Menu names are separated from menu options by a vertical bar (I). For example, "File I Open" means "Select the File menu and choose the Open option."

◆ New terms appear in *italic*.

◆ Text that you should type (for example, in a text box) appears in `monospace boldface`.

◆ Placeholders (words that stand for what you actually type) in regular text appear in *italic*.

◆ All code appears in `monospace`.

◆ Placeholders in code appear in *`italic monospace`*.

◆ When a line of code is too long to fit on only one line of this book, it is broken at a convenient place and continued to the next line. The continuation of the line is preceded by a code continuation character (➥). You should type a line of code that has this character as one long line without breaking it.

PART I

Understanding Notes

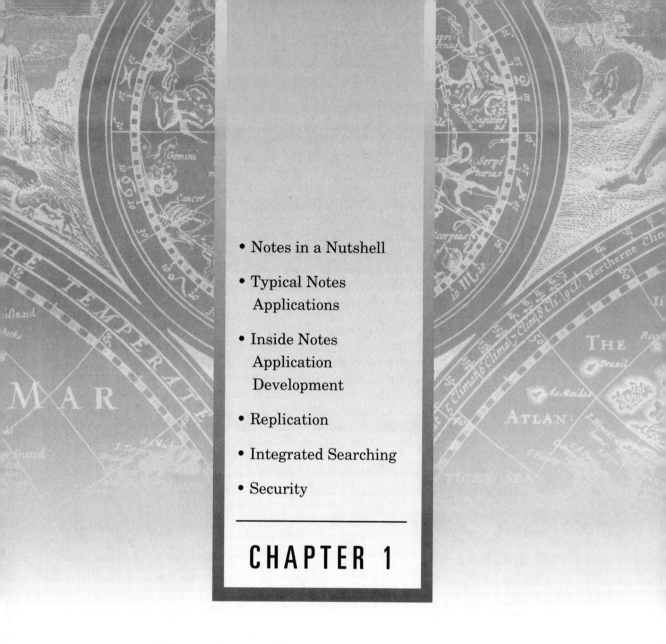

- Notes in a Nutshell

- Typical Notes
  Applications

- Inside Notes
  Application
  Development

- Replication

- Integrated Searching

- Security

CHAPTER 1

Describing Notes

Describing Notes to most information systems (IS) professionals is like describing an elephant to blind men. At first, most IS people see only one small part of Lotus Notes, ignoring the power of the overall package. This is natural. Lotus Notes is a unique product. It is a blend of various technologies including messaging (e-mail), a database engine, robust security, an application development environment, and network management (for Notes resources). If your background is database development, it's natural to focus on Notes' database components and compare it to other, higher-performance platforms. There are many other database engines available that can handle more data, but this doesn't mean that Notes is a useless database engine. It means that Notes has been specialized for a class of applications that don't require huge data flows. The same can be said for each of Notes' components. They have been specialized for a class of applications that have come to be known collectively as *groupware*.

Groupware such as workflow applications and discussion databases provides automated support for teams. Notes supports teams of any size, spread out over the entire globe. For some applications, your team could be the entire corporation—including traveling sales staff, international headquarters, and hundreds of remote offices. Notes contains all the functionality you need to support this environment. There is no need to cobble together products from multiple vendors—a practice that inevitably leads to an unstable platform.

This chapter presents an overview of Notes and applications typically implemented using Notes. Specifically, this chapter discusses

- ◆ Describing Notes to different audiences
- ◆ Typical Notes applications
- ◆ Basic Notes architecture

This chapter doesn't discuss any specific technical issues about Notes. Chapter 2, "Using Notes," conducts a more detailed discussion of Notes.

NOTES IN A NUTSHELL

Lotus has tried for years now to come up with a single 25-word explanation for Notes that will make sense to everyone involved in the implementation and use of Notes. A list of features doesn't suffice, and a general description of groupware just leads to the question, "What is groupware?" It might not be possible to come up with a single set of 25 words that accurately describes Notes to all the different audiences (executives, application developers, administrators, users). This book will leave the short descriptions to salespeople. Instead of coming up with a description, this chapter examines the different concerns each Notes audience will have, and how you might consider addressing them.

DESCRIBING NOTES TO EXECUTIVES

Executives have specific goals and problems they need to address. If you want to build support among the executive suite for a Notes deployment, you must show them how Notes can help them reach their current list of goals. When describing Lotus Notes to managers and executives, it is useful to lead them through a short list of questions like these:

◆ Do you have mobile users who need access to their data while they are out of the office?

◆ Do you have departments that need to share data?

◆ Do you need to develop applications faster than in the past?

◆ Do you want to protect your investment in legacy systems?

◆ Do you need a solution that can grow with your business?

If the answers are yes, Lotus Notes is right for their business.

The executive needs all employees to work cooperatively toward the strategic direction of the organization. She sees her organization needing a strategic tool to help the staff work together in attaining corporate goals. An executive sees Notes as a solution to building a more efficient organization. Here are some examples of improvements to an organization's capabilities that might interest an executive:

◆ Reduce product development time

◆ Enhance relationships with customers

◆ Foster interdepartmental cooperation

An executive who must decide whether to back a full-scale, organization-wide deployment of Notes will need to be convinced of the power of using a single integrated package to accomplish these goals.

DESCRIBING NOTES TO APPLICATION DEVELOPERS

Application developers must understand all of Notes' features, how they interact, and how to use them to best advantage. Most application developers need to unlearn some lessons before they can develop truly powerful applications using Notes. This isn't to say that developing applications with Notes is *difficult* (although this has been said about previous releases of Notes). Developing applications with Notes is *different*. Notes will be the first time many application developers will be faced with a database this flexible. Part of the learning curve involves coming up to speed on groupware applications. There is no doubt that Notes is the cheapest way to develop custom groupware concepts.

While talking to application developers, it is useful to emphasize what Lotus Notes is not. For example,

◆ Lotus Notes is not a relational database management system (RDBMS).

   ◆ An RDBMS organizes data into tables or fields. In Notes, data is structured into non-structured objects.

   ◆ An RDBMS efficiently processes millions of records in a single database. Notes databases rarely exceed 100,000 objects.

   ◆ RDBMS data structures are inflexible. Care must be taken to design data structures carefully. Notes objects are extremely flexible; Notes lends itself well to rapid-application-development methodology.

   ◆ An RDBMS doesn't easily support disconnected, mobile, or geographically dispersed users. Notes is designed specifically to handle these types of users.

◆ Notes is not a general-purpose application builder.

Many applications—but not all—naturally fit into the Notes interface paradigm. The simplicity of the Notes interface aids the rapid development of applications.

◆ Notes is not an e-mail system.

Being a groupware application, Notes includes an e-mail system, but goes much further. Notes is a platform for mail-enabled applications. All applications developed with Notes are mail enabled, unless the developer specifically disables this capability (in other words, by default any database can receive mail without any changes to the database). Compare this to a vanilla e-mail system or a custom application with e-mail features. This is one more way Notes shortens application development cycles.

By first eliminating these spurious ideas (which seem to be quite common among new Notes developers), you can move on to the next stage, where an application developer sees Notes as a specialized development tool that nicely solves several problems unique to groupware.

An application developer might initially view Notes as a rapid-application-development tool with a lousy database engine. However, as he digs deeper he sees the Notes database engine as a container capable of managing and distributing unstructured business information.

Notes databases integrate data and application code in a single database (often in a single document). This simple fact removes one of the biggest headaches of client/server systems: code distribution. Keeping application code and databases in sync for a worldwide network is easy for Notes. It's even easier for smaller networks.

DESCRIBING NOTES TO ADMINISTRATORS

The capability of Notes to support a wide variety of platforms and networking protocols is challenging for the administrator as he gets started with Notes. Notes networks often involve multiple operating systems and network protocols, making problem resolution difficult. The capability of Notes to be used as an inter-enterprise-wide solution presents challenges to Notes administrators that can be very different from the challenges of enterprise-wide systems:

◆ Naming conventions for users, servers, and groups become critical.

Notes uses names for security and mail routing. Keeping names accurate as people and servers come and go can take considerable time if you don't plan ahead.

◆ Learning about problems before users is difficult.

Administrators avoid heartache when they fix problems before users notice them. How does an administrator accomplish this when supporting disconnected and mobile users?

◆ Application developers can mess up a working network more easily.

Notes requires a very close working relationship between application developers and administrators. More than with any other product (that the author is aware of), application developers and administrators overlap responsibilities.

The message for administrators is not all doom and gloom. Notes Release 4 includes major advances to reduce the cost of administering Notes that also make life more pleasant for Notes administrators. These features include

◆ Use of SNMP-compliant systems to help monitor and troubleshoot disparate environments

◆ Scalable servers from single-processor to multi-processor environments

◆ Use of intelligent agents to warn the administrator of impending problems

When describing Notes to administrators, emphasize the tools available as well as the challenges of supporting a wide area network.

TYPICAL NOTES APPLICATIONS

The best way to describe Notes to most people is to completely avoid feature/function discussions and focus on how other organizations are using Notes. Notes is widely used to build workflow applications, provide searchable databases, support remote and mobile users, and hold discussions. Notes is an ideal platform for automating the collection, processing, and distribution of unstructured data common in many day-to-day business processes.

Many day-to-day business processes are unstructured and have little or no control. Decisions are made and there is little or no record of how or why they were made. It may not be possible to know ahead of time what information will be needed by a specific person. Supporting these processes requires a very flexible database and application builder along with a powerful search engine.

INSIDE NOTES APPLICATION DEVELOPMENT

Workflow is the generic term used to describe a structured flow of information through an organization. Virtually all organizations have some predefined processes for handling critical documents. Documents are created and routed through departments. Each person along the way will add to or check/correct the information in the document.

A Notes workflow application electronically accomplishes the important task of maintaining control over daily business processes. Notes is able to automate and control tasks that cannot be supported efficiently any other way. Notes workflow applications actively route documents to the next person (or group) in the workflow, enforcing time limits and restricting access to sensitive data.

Examples of workflow applications include

- ◆ Employee compensation and benefits management
- ◆ Requisition approvals
- ◆ Travel authorization
- ◆ Conference room scheduling

Workflow applications typically have all of the following elements:

- ◆ *Tasks or transitions.* These are the various activities that must be performed to complete a business objective.
- ◆ *Roles.* Each person may have one or more roles in a single workflow. Each role has a set of privileges and restrictions that enable a person to accomplish only the specific task at hand. Security is critical in workflow applications because sensitive information is often involved.
- ◆ *States.* The condition of the workflow at any given point in time.
- ◆ *Data.* The information used to complete the work. This information may be in the form of documents, images, and so on.
- ◆ *Workflow monitors.* These are computerized agents that ensure that a workflow doesn't stop or get gridlocked. Typically, these are routines that send reminders if the state remains constant past a predefined period of time.

Application developers, administrators, and users all must understand these elements. Application developers must understand these concepts before designing workflow applications. Administrators need to understand how data is flowing through the system. Users need to understand the specifics of each application they use.

There are three types of workflow models:

◆ *Send model.* This model uses the messaging features of Notes in supporting workflow applications. Documents are sent automatically from one person to the next. Figure 1.1 shows the structure of a workflow application that actively routes data. The send model is not widely used because it is difficult to build and maintain and provides no extra benefit in most situations. For example, the send model requires administrators to maintain e-mail addresses for each role in each application.

Figure 1.1.
Some workflow
applications actively
route information to
individuals.

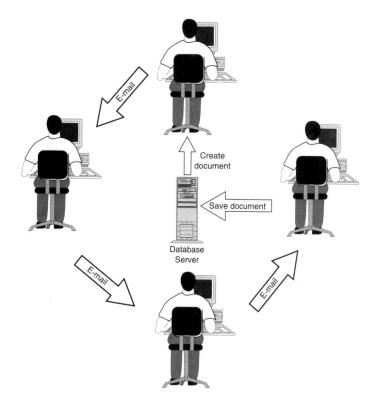

◆ *Share model.* Instead of sending documents by using mail, you can have people browse a shared database that stores the document. Here the document is on a central server, usually in a read-only form. Figure 1.2 shows the structure of a workflow where users access a shared database.

Figure 1.2.
Some workflow
applications require
users to browse a
database for doc-
uments requiring
their attention.

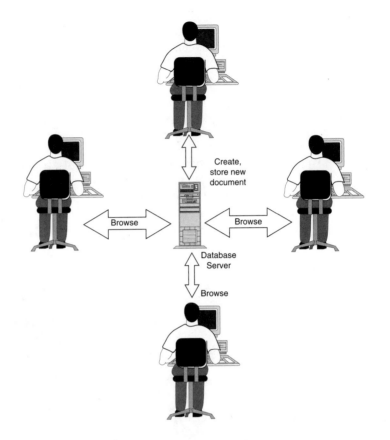

◆ *Client/server model.* This model uses a combination of the send and share
models of workflow. Some information, such as notices, is actively sent via
e-mail, and the bulk of the information is stored in a central database for
users to browse.

The type of connection your users have can influence the model you should use.
Users who are continuously connected (via LAN/WAN connection) can use the
second or third model effectively. Browsing a shared database takes little effort and
incurs no phone charges. Workflow applications supporting infrequently connected
users may need to use the first model.

The model you use for your workflow applications is less important than identifying
the correct roles and enforcing security. Chapter 3, "Understanding Security," and
Chapter 4, "Advanced Security Issues," provide a full overview of Notes security.

MOBILE/REMOTE USER SUPPORT

Mobile and remote workers are becoming commonplace. A system that supports mobility has to make working from "anywhere," "anytime" a reality.

These features of Notes enable mobile computing:

◆ *E-mail* is the umbilical cord connecting mobile users to headquarters. Notes enables users to mail any Notes document from any database, not just those stored in mailboxes. This flexibility enhances the ability of mobile users to keep in touch.

◆ *Replication* is the means by which multiple copies of databases are kept synchronized. Replication enables mobile users and remote offices to have their own copies of a database with minimal impact on Notes administrators and application developers.

◆ *Robust security.* You can use Notes to encrypt data being sent over public networks and databases stored on laptops. The availability of encryption makes it easier to support mobile users by giving them the option of storing data on their laptops, and by protecting e-mail.

◆ *Pager and fax gateways.* Pager and fax gateways add flexibility to your Notes network. Administrators should investigate the use of a pager gateway as a way to have Notes automatically notify them of problems.

Administrators and application developers cannot completely ignore the fact that Notes databases might be copied onto different servers and laptops. Applications must be crafted to ensure that remote copies of databases will work correctly. Notes integrates the widest range of features to support mobile users of any package available today.

DISCUSSION DATABASES

The most important asset of a corporation is the knowledge possessed within the individuals working for an organization. This information is of little use except when shared with others within the organization. A discussion database is the means of conducting collaborative discussion between individuals, without having to assemble at the same time and place. Lotus Notes provides the means of conducting discussions as a means of facilitating teamwork and problem-solving.

If you've participated in an Internet Usenet discussion, you have seen a basic example of a discussion database. Notes discussion databases have far more capabilities than the Internet Usenet. Notes discussion databases support multiple categorized views, threaded discussions, searchable archives, and more.

Common examples of discussion databases include

◆ Customer Support.

Use discussion databases to track problems and solutions. Lotus uses a modified discussion database to track problems and issues for Notes.

◆ Feedback and Opinion.

Why waste an hour of everyone's time when each person may only contribute one or two sentences? Create a discussion database, post the item of interest, and gather feedback without a meeting.

◆ Brainstorming.

Discussion databases let people post their ideas whenever they have them.

Some organizations that started using discussion database to post meeting minutes soon found that they could eliminate the whole meeting. Notes discussion databases can be used to eliminate routine meetings, such as status meetings.

REFERENCE DATABASES

Sometimes you just want to publish information and let users do what they want with it. Notes reference databases are useful for distributing information to a large audience. Reference databases differ from most Notes databases in that information is pushed out to users rather than collected or routed to users.

Not all reference information comes neatly packaged. You might have incomplete information on some items and special notes about others. The unstructured nature of Notes databases combined with Notes full-text search capability makes it a great tool for a reference database. Notes allows users to create ad hoc searches, using individual words or phrases. Notes sorts documents matching the search criteria so that the most relevant documents are listed first.

Examples of reference databases include

◆ Standards and Procedures.

Human Resources departments can publish information on the company's standards and procedures within a reference database, for easy access by all connected users.

◆ Reference Libraries.

Journals, magazines, and internal newsletters can be stored in a database for quick retrieval on demand.

◆ Résumés.

Consulting firms use reference databases to list the résumés and skills of their personnel. Notes' built-in search engine lets them quickly find the right person for the job.

The Notes database is an object store containing semi-structured and routing information in a common container. A database usually contains information related to some common interest. Because Notes is generally used in a team programming environment, it is usually shared.

The database consists of multiple documents stored within it. These documents could be compared to records in a traditional database.

Unlike typical records, Notes documents can contain any number of data types. These data types are stored in the Notes document as *fields*. Examples of data that can be stored in a document include

◆ Graphics

◆ Linked or embedded objects

◆ Video

◆ Voice/sound

◆ Tabular data

◆ Formatted text

◆ Scanned images

Notes comes with an easy-to-use development environment that makes it possible for novice programmers to build and implement a Notes application. The basic application development toolset consists of

◆ *Forms.* Forms are programmable filters used to view and create documents. A form is used to display fields contained in documents. You can include code in forms to search databases, perform calculations, or do just about anything else you want. Forms contain all the formatting information for individual documents.

A form need not display all the fields in a document. The form can display different subsets of the information, based on criteria programmed into the form.

◆ *Views.* A view is a filtered listing of the documents available in a database. Views are useful for scanning related documents and for displaying relationships between documents. Notes users can create their own peronal views of a database if desired. Administrators commonly set up their own personal views of key Notes databases.

◆ *Templates.* Templates enable application developers to split the management of application designs from the management of production data. Templates are Notes databases that store design elements only (no data). Design changes are made in the template and then propagated to production databases. Templates enable application developers to make design changes in one place and have multiple nonreplica databases inherit those changes. For example, you could change the personal mailbox template and have those changes propagated to all personal mailboxes. Without templates, you would have to manually update the design of every nonreplica database.

◆ *Macros.* Macros are a set of functions designed to perform some action, such as updating the status of a document or sending reminder notices. Macro types include filter macros, search macros, execute-once macros, and macros associated with buttons to automate tasks.

◆ *LotusScript.* Behind the easy-to-use development capability comes a robust and rich language called LotusScript. Using this language, programmers can create sophisticated applications.

All these application design elements are stored within Notes databases. This makes it possible to duplicate changes to an application over the network by using replication.

You also can develop Notes applications using C, C++, Visual Basic, and other languages. These tools are generally used to build applications that cannot be built using Notes macros, forms, and views. C/C++ is typically used to build custom gateways to other database systems. Visual Basic is used when you want a highly customized user interface that accesses Notes databases. There are many additional products available to support Notes application development.

REPLICATION

Notes supports distributed environments containing multiple copies of a database. Different copies of the database all contain the same information (within a few hours, typically). The means of propagating information among databases is called *replication*.

Within Notes there is no concept of a "master" database. Rather, information is available at various places, kept synchronized by the replication process. Information isn't created at one site and distributed to other sites. Notes enables data creation, editing, and deletion at any site. By default, each copy of a database is considered equivalent (application designers and administrators can change this scheme, using security settings that force changes to flow in only one direction).

Each Notes server has one or more replication tasks. Each task can either "push" information to another client or server or "pull" information from another client or server. A Replicator also can send a request to the other server to pull or push changes to its own server. Keeping track of replication is a major part of a Notes administrator's job.

Other attributes of Notes replication are

◆ *Efficiency.* Notes replicates only documents that have changes—and specifically fields that have changed. This feature keeps the resources required for replication to a minimum. Users can choose to replicate certain documents based on dates and other characteristics. This can minimize the time required for replication. This time may be especially important, for example, when the user is dialing up from an airport, with little time to spare.

◆ *Scalability.* Notes replication can be used in environments with hundreds of servers and thousands of databases.

INTEGRATED SEARCHING

Information is useless if it cannot be located and accessed quickly. Notes enables a variety of search indexes to be created for a database. Using Notes, you can

◆ Search the contents of the document currently open.

This feature is useful if you want to search a large document. If the document is opened in Edit mode, you also can perform a search-and-replace in this manner.

◆ Search the titles of documents in views for certain words or phrases.

This feature is useful to do a quick search for specific documents. This process runs very quickly because it doesn't open each document.

◆ Search all the documents to examine the entire contents of each document.

This is the most time-consuming and also the most comprehensive search possible.

Databases that will be searched often, such as reference databases, should have full-text search indexes created. Creating a full-text index enables the following search mechanisms to be made available to the user:

◆ Use of Search Builder to help novice users create sophisticated formulas

◆ Using advanced search capabilities like proximity operators (searching for words close to each other), wild cards, and case-sensitive word searches

◆ Saving search formulas for use at another time

◆ Searching multiple databases at the same time

You don't need to decide in advance which type of searches will be made available. If you can decide in advance, however, Notes allows you to create search forms that can be used to perform complex searches without requiring users to understand anything at all about Notes searching.

SECURITY

In the Notes environment, security can be controlled at server, database, document, and field level. This strategy allows applications to be flexible enough to be a powerful team tool, yet guard against accidental or criminal misuse.

Security is of prime importance when a system is highly dependent on the network for all its functionality. Security is important when many Notes users are mobile and geographically separated. Notes provides security at various levels as follows:

◆ Server level.

Notes uses a user ID file to authenticate server-to-server security and client-to-server security. The RSA public key system is used to authenticate identities. The RSA public key system is licensed from RSA Corporation and is described in more detail in Chapters 3 and 4.

◆ Database level.

Access control lists (ACLs) are used to determine which user or groups of users have access to a database. Users who have "No access" settings will not even know that the database exists, and users with manager-level security have full access to the database.

◆ Document level.

Documents support two types of access control lists: ReaderNames fields and AuthorNames fields. These special fields are actually access control lists that are embedded within a document.

◆ Field level.

Within documents, a field or set of fields can be encrypted so that they can be restricted to only specific users.

Notes security can take considerable resources to implement. Proper planning and a reasonable set of expectations can help minimize this cost. See Chapters 3 and 4 for a more detailed overview of Notes security.

SUMMARY

What then is the answer to the question, "What is Lotus Notes?" If forced to answer in a single sentence, it is

> A scalable platform for rapidly developing and deploying applications to support workgroups, including mobile and geographically dispersed users.

But this book is not written for executives or application developers. None of them risk giving up their personal life when Notes is implemented. This book is written for Notes administrators and project managers. Administrators and project managers should feel free to consider the rest of this book as the long answer to the question, "What is Lotus Notes?"

CHAPTER 2

Using Notes

This chapter gives you a basic introduction to Notes terminology and shows you how to get around in Notes, but is not a complete introduction to the Notes interface. Other parts of the interface relevant to administrators are explored throughout the book. This chapter

- ◆ Introduces basic Notes terminology for users
- ◆ Introduces the Notes interface

By the end of this chapter, an experienced computer user should be able to find where things are in Notes.

UNDERSTANDING NOTES SPEAK

Notes includes a database engine, user-interface builder, Notes systems-management facilities, and both a server and client interface. It's inevitable that a product this large will spawn a great deal of jargon. Much of this jargon resembles concepts borrowed from other products, but with some subtle distinctions. If you want to participate in discussion groups, or even just understand the rest of this book, you must comprehend these terms:

- ◆ Database
- ◆ Document
- ◆ Form
- ◆ View
- ◆ Workspace
- ◆ Replication
- ◆ Replica

A *database* is the basic repository of information in Notes. Notes applications often use several databases in Notes rather than one large database. Administrators must make sure that they know which databases collectively form an application.

Each Notes database appears as a separate icon on your Notes desktop. Identical copies of databases are called *replicas*. A typical Notes server contains anywhere from ten to several thousand individual Notes databases.

Each Notes database is made up of a collection of *documents*. A Notes document is a general-purpose object that can be used to store information in any desired format. Documents can store bitmaps, text, files, OLE objects, voice annotations, and so on. Documents are also used to store an application's design. A single Notes database contains any number of different document types. There is no restriction enforced by Notes on the internal structure of documents stored within a single database. This capability to mix and match document types within a single database is what gives Notes a great deal of its flexibility. You can even add fields to or delete fields from documents after they have been created.

Forms are what you use to create and view documents. A form is a programmable window into a document. It specifies the format of the fields on the screen. Fields can be directly contained in a document or calculated on-the-fly. A form can be used to filter out fields that should not be displayed.

A form can also contain application code. This feature allows a form to display the result of calculations and database queries, as well as the raw data stored in a document. A form need not display all the data stored within a document. For example, a form may display only five of the ten fields stored within a document. A form also gives you the capacity to display different fields at different times. Forms are the basic building block of a Notes user interface. Figure 2.1 shows the form used to view a person record in the Name and Address Book.

Figure 2.1.
The form used to view a person document in the Notes Public Address Book.

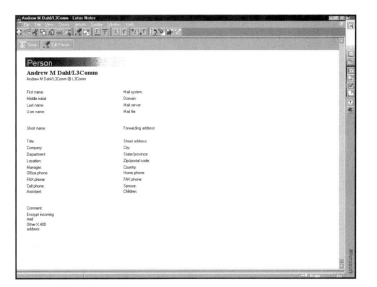

Views are a collection of documents. Views, like forms, are a user-interface feature. Each view contains a *selection formula*, which is a logical formula that determines which of the documents in a database will be displayed in a view. A view can categorize and sort the documents in a database so that they are easy to find. A typical Notes database can contain anywhere from a half dozen to thirty or more individual views. Some views are used to present information to the user; other views are hidden from the user. Hidden views are used to speed database lookups. Figure 2.2 shows a view from the Public Address Book.

Figure 2.2.
A view is a categorized /
sorted collection of
documents.

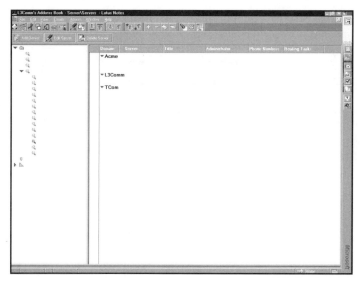

The Notes *workspace* is analogous to a desktop for an operating system. Whereas an operating system desktop gives you access to the programs and files on your computer, the Notes workspace gives you access to the databases on your Notes network. Figure 2.3 shows the Notes workspace.

Figure 2.3.
The Notes workspace.

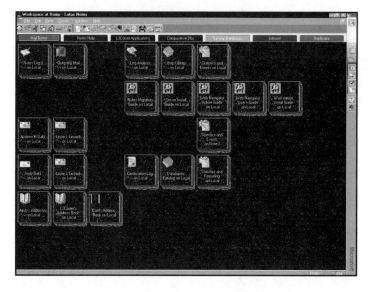

Replication is the process of updating replica copies of databases. Replicas are identical copies of databases that reside on different servers or on client workstations. Databases that are replicas of each other share a common replica ID number. Replicas need not have the same Notes file name. The Replicator server task (a *task* is a program that runs under control of the Notes server) is responsible for copying additions, deletions, and changes from one replica database to another. The Replicator is a CPU-intensive server task, and monitoring and scheduling replication is a critical part of an administrator's job.

CLIENT INTERFACE

If you've been using Notes Release 3, the new Release 4 interface may take a few minutes to get used to. If you've never used Notes before, you may want to get some basic training at some point. This section is just the briefest possible introduction to the Notes interface and how to manipulate databases. Other parts of the interface useful to administrators are explored throughout this book.

WORKSPACE

The Notes workspace is the first thing you see when you start the Notes climb. The workspace contains a menu bar, toolbar, and several tabbed pages. Tabs allow you to group databases by whatever categories make sense in your organization. In Notes Release 4, you can add or remove tabs on the workspace. The only exception is the Replicator tab, which is always on the far right.

Tasks that you can accomplish directly from the workspace include

- ◆ Adding or deleting database icons on your workspace
- ◆ Adding or removing tabs on your workspace
- ◆ Accessing dialog boxes for individual databases

The information about your workspace is stored in the DESKTOP.DSK file. Every time you add or delete a database or tab, Notes updates your DESKTOP.DSK file.

To add names to the tabs already on your workspace, follow these steps:

1. Display the Workspace Properties dialog box by right-clicking anywhere over the workspace.
2. Select Workspace Properties.

   The Workspace Properties dialog box opens (see Figure 2.4).

Figure 2.4.
The Workspace Proper-
ties dialog box.

3. Enter the name for the tab in the Workspace Page Name field.

4. Select a color for the tab.

5. Close the dialog box.

To add a new tab to your workspace, follow these steps:

1. Right-click anywhere on the workspace to display the Workspace pop-up menu.

2. Select Create Workspace Page.

    Notes adds a new workspace page to the left of the currently selected page.

To delete a workspace page, follow these steps:

1. Select the page to be deleted.

2. Right-click anywhere over the workspace to display the Workspace pop-up menu.

3. Select Remove Workspace Page.

You can remove any page except for the Replicator page.

Tip

Notes Release 4 stacks the icons of replica databases. As an administrator you sometimes will want direct access to all replica databases
on the network. To unstack replica icons, toggle the View | Stack
Replications menu option to enable/disable this feature.

The Notes workspace isn't of much use until you add database icons. To add a
database icon to the workspace, follow these steps:

1. Select the tab which will hold the database.

2. Choose File | Database | Open.

    The Open Database dialog box appears (see Figure 2.5).

Figure 2.5.
Adding a database icon
to a workspace.

3. Type the full name for the server that hosts the database you want to open, or select the server name from the pull-down list.

4. Choose Open.

5. Select the database from the list. If the database is hidden, you may need to type the file name for the database.

6. If you are going to add several databases, choose Add Icon. Otherwise, choose Open.

   Notes adds the database icon in the first open slot on the workspace page and opens the database.

The Replicator page on the workspace enables clients to configure their replication with servers, specifying a schedule as well as the specific databases to be replicated. The Replicator page must be configured for each location that the client has configured. Network-based clients will have only a single location and therefore only a single set of Replicator page settings. Mobile clients will have multiple locations configured and will need to configure the Replicator page for each location. The Notes interface automatically displays the Replicator settings for the current location. The Replicator page displays a list of servers and replicas; all replicas that have been created on the client machine are listed on each Replicator page. Figure 2.6 shows a typical Replicator page for a remote location.

You can tell that a Replicator page is for a remote location by the telephone icon next to the server name near the top of the Replicator page.

Configuring replication with the Replicator page is very straightforward. You simply place a check next to each database you want to replicate. For complete details on using the Replicator page, see Chapter 19, "Supporting Dial-Up Users."

2

USING NOTES

Figure 2.6.
A Replicator page for a
remote location.

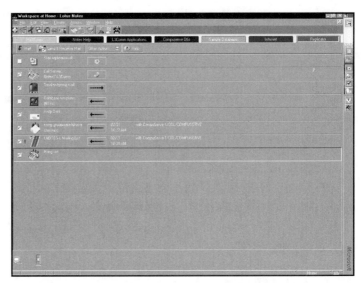

DATABASES

Each Notes database contains data, application code, and at least two Help files. One of these Help documents, the About document, is displayed automatically the first time a database is opened. (This can be changed, but it is the default.) Figure 2.7 shows the default About document for the Statistics Reporting Database (an important administrative database covered in Chapter 13, "Administrative Tools").

Figure 2.7.
The About document
should provide a basic
overview of the data-
base.

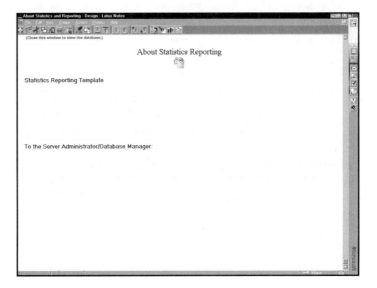

What you see when you close an About document is determined by the database designer. A typical database displays a navigator and a view. Figure 2.8 shows the display for the Public Address Book. The left pane displays all the non-hidden views in the database. The right pane shows a categorized listing of the documents in the view currently selected.

USING NOTES

Figure 2.8.
The default interface
for Notes databases is a
navigator and a view
pane.

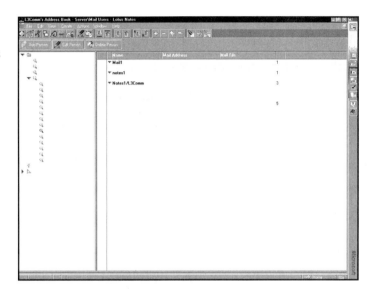

You can open an individual document by double-clicking it in the view pane. The database designer also may have added programs that can be executed. These will be listed on the Actions menu.

Administrators need to be familiar with the Database Properties dialog box (see Figure 2.9). You can display the Database Properties dialog box in several ways:

◆ From the workspace, right-click the database icon and select Database Properties.

◆ Click the Properties SmartIcon on the toolbar. The Document Properties dialog box opens. In the Properties For drop-down list box, select Database.

◆ From the menu, select File | Database | Properties.

The Database Properties dialog box is the central administrative point for viewing and configuring database settings. The tabs that concern an administrator are the Basics tab, the Information tab, and the Full Text tab. (Each of these tabs is covered later in the book.)

Figure 2.9.
All administrators
should be familiar with
the Database Properties
dialog box.

USER PREFERENCES

One other dialog box that all administrators should know is the User Preferences dialog box. The User Preferences dialog box controls

◆ Startup options for the local client

◆ The root file for the Notes data directory tree

◆ The User Dictionary

◆ User interface options, such as closing Windows with a right-double-click

◆ All international settings for the Notes client

◆ All mail settings for the local client

◆ Configuring ports for both the local client and server, if a server is installed on the local machine

Figure 2.10 displays the Basics panel of the User Preferences dialog box.

Figure 2.10.
All administrators
should be familiar with
the User Preferences
dialog box.

Each of these panels is discussed in detail later in this book.

SERVER INTERFACE

As an administrator, you will become very familiar with the server console and server administration panel. They are the primary interface to the Notes server. Chapter 13, "Administrative Tools," covers each of these in detail, as well as other administrative tools.

RELEASE 3.x MENU FINDER

Release 3 users will be lost for about 10 minutes when they first sit down in front of a Release 4 workstation. All the Release 3 menus exist somewhere in the Release 4 structure; Lotus has included a Release 3 Menu Finder that is useful in finding some of the more esoteric features. You can access the Release 3 Menu Finder through the Help menu.

SUMMARY

Notes has an integrative set of features spanning a wide range of functionality, including

- ◆ A database engine
- ◆ An application builder
- ◆ Notes systems management
- ◆ A client and server interface

Each of these areas will have some specific terminology with which a Notes administrator should be familiar. Databases and documents are the primary building blocks for the database engine. Forms, views, and the workspace are the primary user-interface tools. Replication is an important task that a server administrator has to worry about. This cursory overview of the Notes interface is far from complete. The average administrator who understands the basic terminology introduced in this chapter and spends a little time playing with the interface will quickly be able to find the correct menus to accomplish the tasks that are an everyday part of his job.

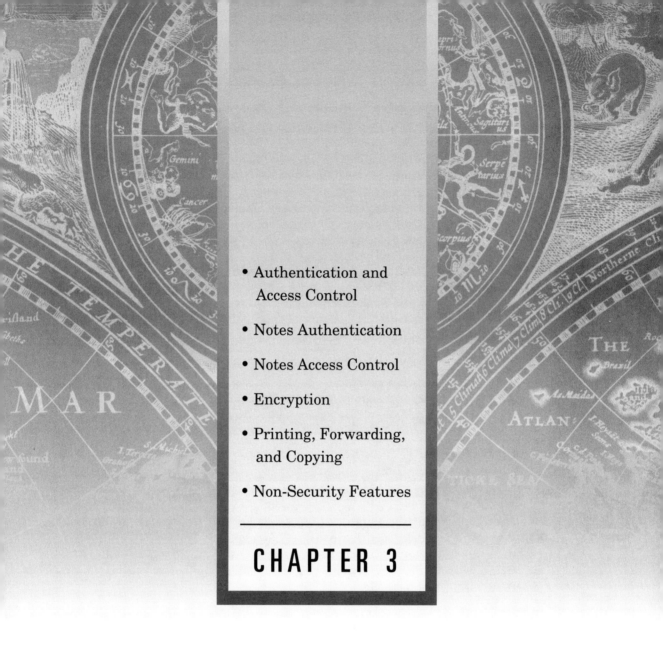

CHAPTER 3

Understanding Security

Computer and network security is a growing concern for many companies. As the amount of data transmitted over networks increases, the need for secure connections increases. No doubt about it, security will be a way of life for system administrators. In the near future, understanding basic security concepts will be a fundamental requirement for system administrators. As companies make the transition to more secure systems, some problems will arise. The military-level security integrated into Notes will be, for many companies, the feature that is least understood and causes the most problems. Before going any further, a basic introduction to network security and Notes is in order. This chapter introduces you to

◆ The concept of authentication and access control

◆ Public key encryption—the technology that forms the foundation of today's military-level security

◆ Notes' implementation of authentication and access control

◆ The various ways you can protect servers, databases, documents, and fields

Because Notes security techniques are new to most administrators, this chapter covers only the basic concepts—without discussing specific tasks required to administer Notes security. Chapter 4, "Advanced Security Issues," covers issues that are important only to specific companies. Chapter 18, "Administering Notes Security," details each of the tasks involved in maintaining a secure Notes network.

AUTHENTICATION AND ACCESS CONTROL

Authentication is the process of identifying users. Every time a user attempts to access a server, his or her identity is verified. *Access control* involves limiting what users can do once they have identified themselves. Authentication and access control are two fundamental concepts you must understand before you can administer Notes security effectively.

Authentication is the cornerstone of every security system. A weak authentication scheme cannot be overcompensated by a fancy access control system. If someone can fake an identity, it doesn't help to limit access based on identities. Passwords and ID badges are two common examples of authentication techniques. Although authentication technology can be very complex, all systems fall into one of three categories. In increasing order of security, they are

◆ Systems that rely on something you *know* (for example, passwords)

◆ Systems that rely on something you *have* (for example, a badge)

◆ Systems that rely on something you *are* (for example, thumbprints or DNA)

Most systems to date have relied on "something you know," such as passwords. There are many problems with this approach; it's just too easy to guess at things that people must remember.

Systems using passwords were built that way because there were few options. In the past, systems that relied on "something you have" were impractical, inconvenient, and expensive. But recent advances in encryption technology have made it practical to build systems that rely on something you have. Notes was one of the first major software products to integrate this level of security directly into the product. Notes uses names, encryption keys, and certificates to authenticate users. Each of these items is discussed in detail in this chapter.

Access control lists (ACLs) are the most common way of limiting access to computer system resources. Nearly every computer system built over the last two decades has used ACLs in one form or another. Access control lists are simply lists of names. Each name is associated with a set of *permissions*, which give the named user certain rights and privileges. A user who isn't listed in an access control list can't gain access to the resources protected by the ACL. Notes uses ACLs to protect documents, databases, and servers.

Notes uses a variety of names for all the ACLs it supports. Document ACLs are called *ReaderNames fields, read access lists,* or *AuthorNames fields.* Server ACLs are called *server access lists.* Only database ACLs are actually called ACLs.

PUBLIC KEY ENCRYPTION

History has seen many encryption schemes come and go. The simplest form of encryption is to simply exchange one character for another. Puzzles based on this concept are available in many Sunday newspapers. Obviously, an encryption scheme that can be cracked over danish and coffee isn't very secure. Nevertheless, advanced encryption schemes rely on this same basic concept of substituting one set of characters for another. Instead of substituting one character for another, modern encryption schemes essentially substitute one string of a hundred words for another string of a hundred words. The idea is to make it nearly impossible to guess the substitution pattern.

When most people think about encryption, they think of systems in which both the sender and receiver of a message share some common secret. This secret, also known as a *key,* is used by the sender to scramble a message and the receiver to descramble the message. *Public key encryption* uses a pair of matched keys, one public and one private, to provide privacy and authentication. Before using any public key system such as Notes, a user must generate a pair of keys. For Notes users, this process is done by an administrator when an ID file is created. (Notes can generate a set of keys in a few seconds.) The keys are stored in the ID file. In essence, the ID file becomes the user's private key.

Once generated, a public/private key pair are linked forever. One is useless without the other—a message encrypted with a public key can be decrypted *only* with the matching private key (see Figure 3.1). A message encrypted using a public key *cannot* be decrypted using the public key. This process is counterintuitive for most people. Many people's intuition is that a message encrypted using a key should be able to be decrypted using that same key. This isn't true for public key encryption.

Figure 3.1.
Public key encryption uses a pair of keys to encrypt and decrypt messages.

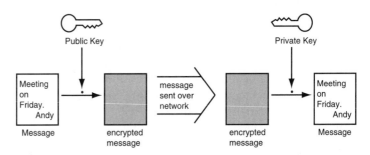

Because one of the keys is kept private, it can be used to identify a specific user. The private key is the "something you have" that Notes uses to uniquely identify a user.

All Notes security is based on the assumption that private keys are well protected. There are ways you can recover from a lost or stolen key, and Notes does help by protecting private keys with a password, but a secure Notes network cannot be maintained if private keys are easy to steal.

CERTIFICATES

Notes ACLs use names to restrict access to a server, database, or document. The preceding section describes how Notes uses private keys, which are just large prime numbers, to uniquely identify a user. In order for this to work, there must be some mechanism that connects a private key to a name. Otherwise, anyone could create a random key, attach a forged name, and gain access to any Notes resource. Notes, like all other public-key encryption schemes, uses certificates to bind a set of keys to a name. *Certificates* are electronic stamps that bind together a name, a set of keys, and the name of the certifier issuing the certificate. Notes stores certificates in ID files and in the Public Address Book.

All certificates must have a name. Certificates are commonly named after the organization that issued the certificate. Notes also enables you to create a tree structure of certificates (see Figure 3.2). Certificates that are part of a tree are known as *hierarchical certificates*. Non-hierarchical certificates are also known as *flat certificates*.

Hierarchical certificates are divided into two categories. The root certificate is known as the *organizational certificate*. Every other node in the tree represents an *organizational unit certificate*. Creating the naming scheme for your tree of certificates is a major planning step when initially deploying Notes. Each certificate in the tree can be used to stamp ID files. When a user is first stamped by a certificate, the name of the user is combined with the name of the certificate. For example, when user Leslie Lesnick is certified by Marketing/L3Comm, her full name becomes Leslie Lesnick/Marketing/L3Comm.

Figure 3.2.
You can create a tree of
certificates in Notes.

A certificate is generated by a certifier, using the certifier's private key. In Notes, the certifier's private key is contained in the CERT.ID file. The CERT.ID file is automatically generated when you install the first Notes server. Anyone with access to the CERT.ID file could use it to issue certificates. Recovering from a lost or stolen CERT.ID file can be a very large task if not properly planned beforehand. Chapter 5, "Building a Deployment Plan," shows you how to plan for this contingency. No one can afford to ignore this issue; eventually, the person in your organization who has been issuing certificates will leave, sometimes under hostile circumstances. If you haven't taken precautionary steps to minimize the risk of this former certifier getting access to your Notes network, you will have to invalidate all certificates ever issued by that certifier.

Note

Most administrators use the name of the organization for both the top-level certificate and the Notes domain. This practice has confused many administrators into thinking that there is some connection between Notes domain names and certificates. There is no connection between domain names and certificates. Domains are nothing more than a collection of servers; domain names have nothing to do with security. You can add, change, and delete domain names without having to worry about recertifying users and servers within that domain.

NOTES AUTHENTICATION

Notes provides two-way authentication. The server checks the identity of the user and the user checks the identity of the server. This second check is important when Notes is used over public networks such as the Internet. If users didn't have the ability to verify the identity of servers, someone could impersonate a server and gain access to confidential information.

When a user first contacts a server, both the server and user exchange certificates. Each party must have a certificate that is trusted by the other party. In Notes, a certificate is trusted if and only if a copy of the certificate is contained in the local ID file and the certificate is either a hierarchical certificate or is a trusted flat certificate. For example, in Figure 3.3 Leslie Lesnick is accessing the server Mail/Marketing/L3Comm. Both Leslie Lesnick and Mail have a copy of the Marketing/L3Comm hierarchical certificate. Authentication succeeds and a session is established.

Figure 3.3.
Leslie Lesnick and the
server Mail share a
certificate.

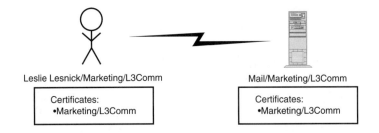

Leslie Lesnick/Marketing/L3Comm

> Certificates:
> •Marketing/L3Comm

Mail/Marketing/L3Comm

> Certificates:
> •Marketing/L3Comm

ID files don't have to contain the same certificate; they only need to have a common ancestor. This enables all the users and server within an organization to communicate. In Figure 3.4, Leslie Lesnick can contact the Server1 server, although she doesn't have the same certificate as Server1. Both Leslie Lesnick and Server1 have L3Comm as an ancestor, so each trusts the other's certificate.

ID files can hold more than one certificate. This situation arises most often when two servers from different companies need to communicate. ID files from different organizations must exchange certificates before they can communicate. A hierarchical certificate received from another organization is known as a *cross certificate*. In Figure 3.5, both Server1/Sales/L3Comm and RandD/Denver/Acme must receive a cross certificate before communicating.

Figure 3.4.
Leslie Lesnick and
Server1 share an
ancestor, L3Comm.

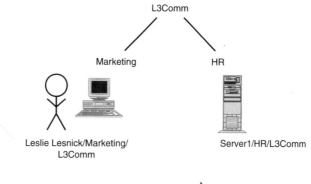

Figure 3.5.
Servers from different
organizations need
cross certificates before
communicating.

Always exchange cross certificates at the lowest level possible. This method provides the highest level of security. In Figure 3.6, Server1/Sales/L3Comm needs to communicate with Mail/HR/Columbus/Acme but shouldn't communicate with Contracts/Legal/Columbus/Acme. When creating a cross certificate, the Acme administrator should use the HR/Columbus/Acme certificate, not just the Columbus/Acme certificate. If L3Comm was cross-certified using the Columbus/Acme certificate, any ID with this certificate as an ancestor, including Contracts/Legal/Columbus, could be accessed by Server1/Sales/L3Comm.

Figure 3.6.
Server1 can access
Mail, but not Contracts.

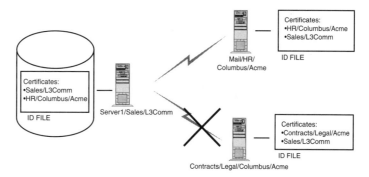

Even though the whole point of certificates is to bind names and keys together, by default Notes doesn't check that a public key stored in the local Name and Address Book is the same one in the ID file of the person or server accessing the system. Doing this check slows the system and is unnecessary. Notes uses a challenge/response sequence to authenticate users and servers. When a user (or server) contacts a server, the user sends a random number to the server. The server encrypts the number, using its private key, and returns the encrypted number to the user. The user decrypts the number using the public key of the server, which is available in the Name and Address Book. If the decrypted number matches the challenge number, the user is assured that the correct server has been reached. The process is then reversed and the server challenges the user. The certificate check is then done to validate the identities associated with the keys.

NOTES ACCESS CONTROL

Notes uses a variety of access control lists (ACLs) to control access to servers, databases, and documents. Most Notes ACLs can accept either a common name or the full hierarchical name. Providing the full hierarchical name provides better security and is the recommended approach. The following sections discuss the ways you can use Notes ACLs.

SERVER-LEVEL SECURITY

Access to servers is controlled with ACLs. Each server has many ACLs. These lists are all part of the server document in the Name and Address Book. These lists include

- ◆ An allow-access list
- ◆ A deny-access list
- ◆ A list of people able to create databases
- ◆ A list of people able to create replicas
- ◆ A list of people who can use Notes passthru (a feature that supports both dial-up users and protocol conversion between Notes servers)
- ◆ A list of servers that can be accessed through passthru
- ◆ A list of administrators for this server

Most administrators don't think of all these lists as ACLs. Many of these lists are very specialized, controlling access to a small part of Notes. No matter what they are called, these lists all function as ACLs. They are lists of names that control access to system resources.

You can allow unauthenticated access to a server. In this case, Notes bypasses the authentication challenge and accepts the name provided by the user or server. Notes keeps track of users that are unauthenticated, giving all such users the name Anonymous, and allows you to set access levels for these users. You don't leave your system completely defenseless just because you allow unauthenticated access;

unauthenticated access is useful for setting up public servers and databases. Because unauthenticated users don't need a certificate in common with the server, the server administrator doesn't need to bother with cross-certifying anyone who wants to access the server.

DATABASE-LEVEL SECURITY

You can control access to Notes databases in a variety of ways. Your options range from preventing a user from even knowing that a database exists to allowing completely open access to all parts of a Notes database. Using various techniques, you can

- ◆ Hide a database
- ◆ Restrict access to the data within a database
- ◆ Enable users to create personal agents or views
- ◆ Enable users to create shared views
- ◆ Restrict access to the database ACL
- ◆ Allow anyone to access a database
- ◆ Protect specific views and forms
- ◆ Encrypt a database
- ◆ Hide a database design

HIDING A DATABASE

You can hide the existence of a database by not listing the database's name in any catalog or in the Open Database dialog box. This method forces the user to know the full path and file name for the database. This technique isn't secure, but is often effective, and is generally used when testing a new database before making it available for production use. An administrator copies the new database to the production machine and tests it in the actual environment.

Notes allows administrators to limit access to securely hide a database. With *directory redirectors*, you can set up secure directories that can only be accessed by specific people and servers. Directory redirectors are text files with a .DIR extension. When Notes encounters a file with a .DIR extension in the Notes data path, it treats the indicated directory as a subdirectory of the current directory. The first line should give the full path of the secure directory. Other lines should list the names that are allowed to access this directory. Here is an example of a simple redirection file:

```
c:\secure\database
Andrew Dahl/Consulting/L3Comm
```

For example, if only people in Marketing should be allowed to view databases in the Marketing subdirectory, you would create a .DIR file called Marketing.DIR. In this file you would place the full path name for the location for Marketing databases. In the next line you would place `ACME/Marketing/*` and only people with names that match would be allowed to access any databases in that subdirectory.

DATABASE ACLS

The primary method of controlling access to a database is the access control list (ACL). Each name in an ACL is granted some permissions and denied others. Every Notes database has its own ACL. ACLs aren't shared across databases. Figure 3.7 shows an example of an ACL.

Figure 3.7.
A Notes access
control list.

Database access control lists control access to only a single database. They aren't shared across different databases—or replicas. Notes Release 4.0 contains features that enable an administrator to force ACLs of replicas to be identical and to keep ACLs in sync with the Name and Address Book.

The following roles and privileges can be assigned using the access control. There are several options for each access level that can be used to fine-tune access for a particular group.

◆ Manager Access

Anyone with manager access to a database can read and change all non-encrypted data, except for documents protected with ReaderNames fields. A user with manager access has full rights to update the design of a database, including all forms, agents, folders, and navigators. Most importantly, a user with manager access has the ability to update the access control lists. In fact, only a user with manager access can update the access control lists. The capacity to alter the ACL is what differentiates a manager from a designer. Designers have all the rights a manager has, except the ability to change the ACL. The only reason to give someone manager access is that his or her job requires changing the access control lists. Typically, only administrators and other servers within your domain are granted manager access.

The database administrator can decide whether a manager should be able to delete documents.

All Notes databases must have at least one manager; Notes doesn't allow you to delete the last manager in an ACL. Most databases should have two managers assigned, in case one manager is unavailable.

◆ Designer Access

A user with designer access cannot change the access control lists, but can act in every other way similar to a user with manager access. A user with designer access can add, update, and delete any non-encrypted data, and can change the design of the database.

The database administrator can decide whether to allow designers to delete documents or create LotusScript agents.

◆ Editor Access

A user with editor access can read any non-encrypted data and update or delete any data. A person with editor access cannot update the design of the database or the ACL for the database.

The database administrator can decide whether to allow editors to delete documents, create LotusScript agents, create personal views, create shared views, or create personal agents.

◆ Author Access

A user with author access cannot edit any documents in the database—not even those created by that user. The only exception is when this user is listed in an AuthorNames field in a document. A user listed in an AuthorNames field who also has author access to a database can create new documents and edit any of those documents. A user with author access cannot edit documents without being listed in a AuthorNames field. In addition, a person with author access can read any documents in the database that aren't encrypted or protected by a ReaderNames field. ReaderNames fields and AuthorNames fields are covered in the later section "Document-Level Security."

The database administrator can determine, for each author, whether to let him or her create or delete documents, create personal agents, create personal views, or create LotusScript agents.

◆ Reader Access

A user with reader access can read any documents in a database not otherwise protected by document-level security. A person with reader access cannot create, delete, or change any documents.

3

UNDERSTANDING SECURITY

The database administrator can determine, for each reader, whether to let him or her create personal agents, personal views, or LotusScript agents.

◆ Depositor Access

A user with depositor access can create documents, but cannot view documents in the database. In addition, depositors cannot change or delete any data in the database. Depositor access is most commonly used for mail routing. Users can deposit mail in a mailbox, but can't change mail after it has been deposited, and aren't allowed to read or change anyone else's mail. Therefore, depositor access is the default access on most mailboxes.

Database administrators cannot customize depositor access.

◆ No Access

You also have the option of closing out any access whatsoever to a database. No access means that the person has no capacity to open the database and therefore cannot use, view, or change any data.

Database administrators cannot customize this access level.

All database ACLs must have a default entry and at least one manager. Notes doesn't let you delete the -Default- entry or delete or change the last person with manager access.

In addition to the -Default- entry, there is one other special entry, Anonymous, which can be included in an ACL. Use Anonymous to set the access level for unauthenticated users. If you give anonymous users anything other than reader access, their unauthenticated names can appear in the documents that they create. The actual name used by an unauthenticated user would be placed in the document, not the word *anonymous*.

Users are listed in ACLs to give them specific privileges. Servers are listed in ACLs to determine which data will be replicated. This often overlooked point is the root of several common replication problems. For example, if a server is given only reader access, it could receive updates, but not send any updates.

Tip

Servers that aren't listed in a database ACL can't replicate the database (assuming a default of no access). Servers without manager access cannot replicate ACL changes. The default access for servers within a domain should be manager level for all databases, to ensure that ACL changes are propagated to all replicas.

One of the steps of designing your Notes network is to plan your default ACLs. A default ACL is the ACL given to a database when it is first implemented. Notes automatically creates a default ACL when a database is created. Chapter 5 shows you how to create default ACLs for your organization. Proper default ACLs are an important part of minimizing security problems.

Groups and wild cards are two techniques you can use to ease the administrative burden. *Groups* are simply collections of names. User names, server names, and other groups can all be included in a group. You create groups using the Public Address Book, but use them in ACLs (and mail addressing). Always use groups rather than individual names in ACLs.

If you have set up your certificate hierarchy so that members of a department or geographic region are certified by a common certifier, it may be easier to use wild cards than to set up a group. For example, if you wish to restrict access to all members of the legal department, enter */Legal/Acme in the ACL. Wild cards are even easier to use than groups because you don't have to manage any entries in the Name and Address Book. But wild cards require you to plan ahead. If you don't have a consistent naming scheme across the entire organization, wild cards aren't effective.

When you use groups and wild cards in ACLs, the possibility arises that a person may appear more than one time. Notes resolves any conflicts by giving a user or server the highest level of access of any of its entries. The only exception is when the name is explicitly listed in the ACL and isn't just part of a group. In this case, Notes gives the access listed for the name and ignores the group entries.

ROLES

Roles protect access to specific forms, subforms, views, or fields. For example, a purchase order application may have specific individuals who are authorized to approve purchase orders. Database designers can create an Authorizers role in the ACL and protect a signature field so that only Authorizers can sign the field.

Historically, roles aren't used often. You can accomplish the same goals by using groups, often with less administrative overhead. In the purchase order example, you could just as easily create a group called Authorizers and use the group to protect the field. Roles also require the database designer and database manager to work together to define and manage the roles.

The disadvantage to groups (as opposed to roles) is that you can end up creating thousands of groups that are specific to individual databases. This can clutter up the Name and Address book and make it hard to manage. In addition, database managers need the ability to edit group documents in the Name and Address Book that are used in their databases. This can create security problems when too many people have access to the Name and Address Book. This is less of a problem for small organizations where a single person is the server administrator and database administrator. In large organization with many different database administrators, giving database managers access to the Name and Address Book will be a problem.

Using roles is better than listing specific names inside forms, views, and fields properties. Changing an individual's name is easier when that name appears in fewer places. By including an individual's name inside documents and fields, you are increasing the workload necessary to maintain the system.

The other advantage offered by roles is that roles clearly point out something very important about a database: the existence of special roles. Because very few databases have protected forms, views, or fields, it is natural to overlook the few databases that do use them. Because roles are unusual, using them can lead to problems when applications are updated. If the designer isn't clearly reminded of the roles present within an application, he may accidentally unprotect a form, view, or field. Roles are listed in the database ACL and can serve as a reminder to designers.

HIDING DATABASE DESIGNS

You can protect your database designs from being changed. This feature is necessary to support third-party Notes applications, but any organization can take advantage of this feature. You have the option to hide the design of any database. Hiding the design prevents anybody, including those with manager access, from viewing or changing the design of that database. You can set a password on the design of the database so that any user who knows the password can update the design of the database. By protecting the design of all your databases with a password, you can prevent unauthorized or unintended updates to your database design.

Database designers can limit access to specific design elements without hiding the entire design. The options available are

- ◆ Using view or folder properties to restrict who can access a view
- ◆ Using form properties to restrict who can create documents using a form
- ◆ Using form properties to restrict who can see documents created with a form
- ◆ Protecting parts of a document by using sections

Hiding access to views doesn't prevent a user from viewing documents that appear in that view (see Figure 3.8). A user could always view those documents in a different view. To absolutely prevent users from accessing a document, you need to use document-level security.

Figure 3.8.
You can limit access to
a view by using view
properties.

You also can hide the view, not just the documents within a view. This doesn't prevent a user from copying the database, gaining manager access, and unhiding the view.

Form-create access lists are only meant to provide a cleaner interface. Forms with a create-access list aren't listed in the Create menu for users who don't have the ability to create that form. However, the user can use another program to create a document with the restricted form name.

Sections aren't a true security feature. Data appearing in protected sections can still be changed, using a different form. If you need to protect specific fields, you must use encryption.

DOCUMENT-LEVEL SECURITY

You can control on a document-by-document basis who has the right to update, delete, or view each document. In addition, you can control, for each type of document in the database, who has the right to create a document of that type. There are two ways you control access to individual documents: with ReaderNames fields and with AuthorNames fields.

READERNAMES FIELDS

ReaderNames fields are a special category of field provided by Notes specifically to control who can read a document. ReaderNames fields contain lists of user IDs or group names. Only people who are listed in the ReaderNames field or in a group in the ReaderNames field can read that document. If a document has a ReaderNames field and a user isn't listed in that ReaderNames field, that document doesn't appear in any view or folder. Keep in mind that ReaderNames fields should be used only as a security feature.

Tip

Of course, if a document contains a ReaderNames field, and a user isn't listed in that ReaderNames field, he or she can't replicate that document. This fact tempts many people into using ReaderNames fields as a method of minimizing their replication costs. Don't do it! Only use ReaderNames fields when you actually want to secure access to that document. Using ReaderNames fields as a means of minimizing replication costs is inefficient and puts a great burden on your administrators. If you want to minimize replication costs, use selective replication, not ReaderNames fields.

AUTHORNAMES FIELDS

AuthorNames fields are checked only for users who have author access to the database. If a user has editor access to a database, he can edit any document that he can view, regardless of whether that document has an AuthorNames field. If a person has only reader access to a database, he cannot edit any documents, even if he is listed in the AuthorNames field. A person with author access to a database who is listed in an AuthorNames field in a document can edit that document. AuthorNames fields are a method of providing people who have only author access the ability to edit their own documents.

AuthorNames fields are used primarily in workflow applications. For example, Charlie creates a document that gets placed in a centralized workflow database. Several other people in Charlie's department are also submitting documents into the workflow database. You want to give Charlie the ability to edit only the documents that he creates. The way to accomplish this is to give author access to the workflow database and list him in an AuthorNames field in every document that he creates. Although he can view work done by other people, he can't change it.

VIEW ACCESS LISTS

Views can have both an edit-access list and a read-access list. You can restrict who can edit documents in a view by using view-edit-access lists. Only names that appear in the view-edit-access list can edit the documents that appear in the view. Read-access lists restrict who can read documents that appear in a view. In reality, these features don't protect documents, because a user can create a private view that lists a document and edit or read it from the private view.

FIELD-LEVEL SECURITY

There are three ways to control access to field-level information in Notes: encryption, field hiding, and protected sections. Only encryption truly protects data. Field hiding and protected sections are useful in creating a good interface and in preventing users from making mistakes. If you want to encrypt fields, you need to plan some way of distributing encryption keys only to the people who should have access to the data.

LOCAL SECURITY

Release 4.0 of Notes introduces the concept of local security. Local security isn't a security feature, but rather a user-interface feature. In the past, people who made replicas of the database on their own machines were given manager access to that database, regardless of any entries in the access control list. They could delete any document and update documents at will. However, because they weren't listed as managers on the server copy of the database, those changes wouldn't replicate, causing a great deal of confusion. With Notes Release 4.0, if a person is listed as having only author access to a database—even if he creates a replica of that database on a laptop—the user interface will behave as if he has only author access. This helps prevent user confusion.

Release 4.0

Even with local security, there is no way to protect data once someone has a copy of the database. Although security is enforced at the user interface, a determined person could easily gain access to the data in a local replica. The only way to protect a database that someone has copied onto his own hard drive is to encrypt that database. If you are very concerned about the security of data on your laptops, the only way to protect that data is to encrypt that database on the hard drive. This method is still a long way from crack-proof, but very few people or organizations have the time or the skill to break through the Notes encryption.

ENCRYPTION

Encryption is the only effective way to protect confidential information. All other ways of limiting read access to data can be compromised if someone manages to get a copy of the database. Even encryption can be broken by someone with enough experience.

Encryption, like roles, is a seldom used feature in Notes. Many administrators will never have to deal with encrypted databases, documents, or fields.

Notes enables you to encrypt fields within a document by using an encryption key. All fields within a document must be encrypted using the same key. Unencrypted fields in a document that contains encrypted fields are still readable by anyone.

You can force Notes to encrypt all documents created with a specific form. Designers can do this in two ways:

◆ Placing an encryption key in the form

◆ Using keywords that refer to encryption keys

You should place encryption keys in a form when you know exactly which key should be used to encrypt the form. Keywords let you create a form that can be encrypted with any one of several keys. When a form is set to automatically encrypt a document, all encryptable fields in the form are encrypted when the document is saved. A user must have access to the encryption keys in order to create and save a document containing encrypted fields. If you take an existing form and add automatic encryption to it, however, existing documents created with that form remain unencrypted.

Notes also provides an easy way to encrypt the body of mail messages. Encrypt mail when you want to maintain privacy. Only the recipient of an encrypted message can read the message, if you encrypt the body of the message using the recipient's public key. Because only the recipient has a copy of the matching private key, only the recipient can decrypt and read the message.

PRINTING, FORWARDING, AND COPYING

No way exists to prevent a user who can read data from physically copying the data by hand and distributing it. Although you can't prevent someone from copying data to paper by hand, Notes does allow administrators to prevent computerized copying. Often all you want is to *discourage* users from copying data. Using form properties, you can prevent anyone from printing, forwarding, or copying (or cutting-and-pasting) data from a document created with that form.

NON-SECURITY FEATURES

Several Notes features are commonly used as security features, when they are in fact only user-interface features, providing no real security. These features include

◆ Hiding views by using view properties

◆ Restricting access to documents in views by using view properties

◆ Hiding forms by using form properties

◆ Restricting access to documents created with a form

- Limiting who can create a document by using a form
- Protecting fields by using protected sections
- Hiding fields

The only way to limit access to documents is to use document-level access lists or to encrypt the document. Likewise, fields truly can be protected only when they are encrypted.

SUMMARY

Authentication and access control are the basic theoretical foundations for all modern network security. Notes uses an advanced form of authentication, based on possession of a specific file. The elements of Notes security are

- Public key encryption

  A method of encrypting data that uses both a private key and a public key.

- Certificates

  Certificates bind public keys to a name. Notes can use flat or hierarchical certificates. All hierarchical certificates are either organizational certificates or organizational unit certificates. Hierarchical certificates that are exchanged between organizations are called cross certificates.

- Access control lists

  When a user or server is authenticated, Notes uses access control lists to determine which databases and documents that user or server can access.

- Roles

  Roles are special groups used to protect specific views, forms, subforms, and fields within a database.

Most administrators will spend a considerable amount of time managing all the various ACLs in Notes. Proper planning is required to minimize administrative overhead and security problems. Chapter 5 and Chapter 18 show you how to plan an effective security system that minimizes administrative effort.

Notes security is a major step forward for most organizations. Most organization's policies and procedures are set up to handle security based on something the user knows, such as a password. Notes security is based on something the user has: an ID file. Chapter 4 covers the implications of this kind of security system for your organization, along with some advanced Notes security features.

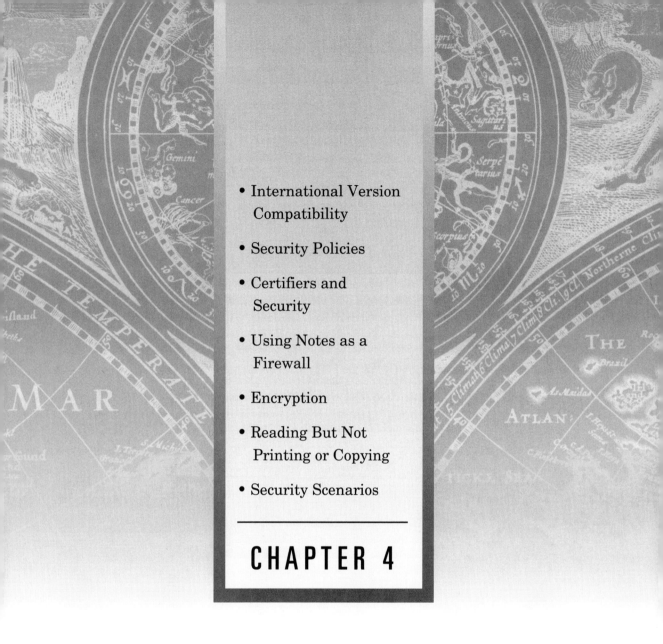

- International Version Compatibility

- Security Policies

- Certifiers and Security

- Using Notes as a Firewall

- Encryption

- Reading But Not Printing or Copying

- Security Scenarios

CHAPTER 4

Advanced Security Issues

For many organizations, Notes security represents a fundamental change in the protection of network data. Changing the policies and procedures designed for a security system based on something you know—for example, a password—to a security system based on something you have—for example, an ID file—is difficult for many organizations. Changes affect users, administrators, and management. Policies and procedures must be rewritten.

This chapter discusses some advanced security features of Notes and the impact that Notes security will have on your organization. Several common scenarios illustrate the issues administrators face when planning a Notes installation. The chapter also discusses new administrator responsibilities, such as creating and backing up ID files. This chapter, along with Chapter 3, provides a basic understanding of the issues involved with security. Chapter 18, "Administering Notes Security," provides a detailed guide to help administrators in their day-to-day responsibilities.

INTERNATIONAL VERSION COMPATIBILITY

Until the release of Lotus Notes Release 4.0, one issue faced by administrators or anyone planning a Notes installation was whether to buy the North American version of Notes or the international version. Notes 3.x users with international licenses can't decrypt messages encrypted using a North American license. Because of this problem, most large corporations used the less-secure international version even in North America, although this meant that some messages were less secure than was possible. The good news is that all Notes 4.0 licenses, both international and North American, are completely interoperable.

Note

Notes uses 64-bit keys to encrypt messages. For comparison, Pretty Good Privacy (PGP), a freeware e-mail program available on the Internet (commercial versions also are available), uses 1024-bit keys. Many cryptoanalysts are taking the position that anything less than 2048 bits isn't secure. In fact, it is unlikely that any system today that relies on software generation of encryption keys is secure.

Unlike most software publishers, Lotus has decided to publish two versions of Lotus Notes, one for the North American market and one for the international market. This is necessitated by U.S. government laws restricting the export of the security software Notes incorporates. Lotus has licensed the public key encryption system from the RSA Corporation. The RSA public key encryption software is classified as munitions under U.S. government law. The U.S. government restricts to 40 bits the key length used in any public key encryption software that is going to be exported. The government restricts the key length to make encrypted messages easy to break. This requirement means that 3.x international versions of Lotus Notes have a weaker encryption scheme than North American versions. The 4.0 international version and the North American version both use 64-bit keys to encrypt messages. Lotus has negotiated an agreement with the U.S. government that gives the government access to 24 bits of an international key, reducing the effective protection to that of a 40-bit key. 40-bit keys are trivial to break. Anyone with access to a college computer lab has the computing resources needed to decode a message encrypted using a 40-bit key.

Technically, it is illegal to install the North American version of Notes on a laptop and carry that laptop out of the United States. As of this writing, several changes in the law were being considered, including a personal exemption law to cover just this scenario. To date, no one has been prosecuted for carrying software out on a laptop, but it never hurts to know the law. You can easily receive different recommendations concerning this area of the law from different people. Most companies doing business internationally decide to buy the international version for all users to avoid any problems.

The biggest security risks you face don't involve someone decrypting messages you send back and forth, but that someone will get a copy of your ID file and gain access to your servers. The increase in security that you get by buying the North American version doesn't affect this risk at all. For this reason, even with Notes 4.0, large organizations should buy the international version. This is just one more example of balancing the need for security versus the costs involved in providing that security.

SECURITY POLICIES

You can't rely on technology alone to protect your Notes data. All effective security systems integrate well-planned policies and procedures. Policies and procedures are the only way to deal with the largest threat you face—the possibility that someone within the organization will gain access to confidential information.

SERVER PASSWORDS

When you install a Lotus Notes server, you can set up a password that is required to boot the software. If you don't want to constantly walk from your office to the site housing your Notes servers, you will want your Notes server to boot without human intervention. The only way to accomplish this objective is to install the Notes server without any password. This system is a potential security leak. Anyone with access to the server has manager access to all databases stored on the server. Without password protection on startup, your data is completely open to anyone with physical access to the server. This system causes people to rely on physical security and security provided by your operating system to protect your Notes servers.

Windows NT users of Lotus Notes can start Notes automatically without having to enter a password at the Notes console—and not compromise security. Instead of requiring a password at the Notes console, protect Notes using NT's security. Windows NT users can start Notes in a session and require a password in order to access programs running in that session. This strategy allows NT users of Notes to set up Notes servers without any Notes password, but still protects the server from unauthorized access.

OS/2's password setup isn't reliable. OS/2 comes with the capacity to set a keyboard password, and the password can be in effect at startup. In theory, this technique would protect all programs running on the machine from anyone who doesn't know the keyboard password. However, because bypassing OS/2's startup password is relatively easy, if you are using the OS/2 version of Notes I recommend that you provide physical security for all servers. You should provide physical security for all your Notes servers in any case. It's a good idea.

PROTECTING IMPORTANT DATABASES

This section uses several databases shipped with Notes to demonstrate effective use of Notes security. The key databases that you need to protect are the Name and Address Book, MAIL.BOX, and a personal mailbox.

NAME AND ADDRESS BOOK

When setting up security for any database, you need to keep in mind the purpose that that database serves. Included in that purpose are your methods of managing that particular database. For example, the Name and Address Book is set up to allow distributed management, meaning that multiple administrators at different geographic sites should have the ability to add, change, and delete documents in the Name and Address Book. This system allows you to have a single Name and Address Book for use in a large organization, without requiring a single administrator to be the sole point of contact for administration.

With Notes, you can have multiple administrators with access to the Name and Address Book. In addition, users should have access to their person records. Users can assume part of the responsibility for maintaining their personal information, such as their address, phone number, and fax number. This technique is certainly less burdensome than some other e-mail programs that force users to manage complete address books, and can significantly reduce the amount of administrative effort required to maintain a working Notes network.

The default settings for the Name and Address Book accomplish all these goals. The default access is set at author access, without giving users the ability to create personal agents and personal folders. The administrator has manager access and can create and delete documents. Other servers that need to replicate your Name and Address Book also have manager access.

The Name and Address Book also has roles, which provide the capability to create and edit groups, networks, servers, and users. These roles enable you to give administrators limited access, based on their specific job responsibilities. This enables administrators to specialize and allows organizations to further distribute the responsibility for maintaining the Address Book.

Your procedures for changing the Name and Address Book should detail who has access to the Name and Address Book and their responsibilities. You should log all attempts to make changes to the Name and Address Book.

MAIL.BOX

MAIL.BOX is a special database used by the mail router in the delivery of e-mail, and is scanned by the mail router on a regular basis. Any document placed in MAIL.BOX which has a "send to" field is processed by the mail router. MAIL.BOX holds

- ◆ Mail in transit
- ◆ Mail that can't be delivered to a personal mailbox

Your goal for MAIL.BOX should be to prevent unauthorized access to e-mail. Administrators need to be able to review dead mail but shouldn't be viewing mail in transit. Users should have only the capability to add mail that they want delivered. Therefore, the default access for a MAIL.BOX file is depositor. Remember that a person with depositor access can create documents but can't view or update any document in the database, including those he creates. The administrators need at least editor access to view, change, and delete dead mail.

PERSONAL MAILBOXES

Each user has his own or her own personal mailbox. The mail router places all mail for that person in his personal mailbox. Personal mailboxes are generally stored on a server, although a mobile user might create a replica of his personal mailbox on his laptop (see Chapter 19, "Supporting Dial-Up Users," for details). A user should be able to access, view, and change any *data* in his personal mailbox. Most organizations don't want users to change the *design* of the personal mailbox, however; therefore, editor access should be provided to users. Editor access gives full rights to the data stored in the database, while preventing any changes to the design or access control list. The administrators need to be able to change the design and access control list for personal mailboxes and therefore need manager access to the personal mailboxes. This may be a touchy situation, especially concerning mailboxes for executives. Administrators with manager access have the capability to read and change mail as they see fit. If this is a concern, you may want to provide a special trusted group of administrators with the ability to have access to personal mailboxes. If you create a special group of administrators with access to personal mailboxes, make sure that only members of this group have access to MAIL.BOX.

DISTRIBUTING ID FILES

Notes security is based on ID files. ID files hold a user's name, his public and private keys, and any certificates that he may have (and some other information—see Chapter 18 for details). The ID file is encrypted and requires a password in order to access it.

ID files are created by the administrator, certified by certifiers, and distributed to users. You have two methods of distributing ID files:

◆ Using the Notes Name and Address Book
◆ Using a floppy disk

The whole process of creating and distributing ID files is fundamentally different from creating and distributing passwords. Passwords used to log on to systems are easy to re-create. Nothing is lost if someone forgets a password; a quick phone call to the help desk creates a new password. Administrators never need to have access to the password; this isn't true for an ID file.

Take care when planning the creation and distribution of ID files. There is no central collection point for ID files; in most organizations, ID files are distributed throughout the organization, on each user's workstation. Some organizations collect ID files on a file server, with each user's ID file placed in a protected directory accessible only by that user. Using a file server can help minimize problems associated with widely distributed ID files, but even then mobile users will have to carry copies of their ID files on their laptops.

Your first step in designing your ID file creation and distribution procedures is to decide whether you are going to store ID files centrally on a file server or distribute them to users. Most organizations distribute ID files to users, although the author doesn't recommend this method. Most users simply aren't capable of securing their ID files against theft, and wouldn't know if their ID files had been stolen. This situation represents a real threat to the security of your Notes network. If you elect to store ID files on individual workstations, make sure that your user education is clear on the need to keep these files secure. Storing ID files on a file server has two advantages:

◆ Users' ID files are easier to distribute securely

◆ Users can log on from any point in the network, not just their workstations

If you elect to distribute ID files, the next decision that you need to make in designing your distribution policy is whether to distribute the ID files using Notes' Name and Address Book or on a floppy disk. The advantage of using the Name and Address Book is that Notes provides automated support. The ID file is deleted from the Name and Address Book the first time the user accesses his person record. Of course, the user would be forced to use his person record before proceeding with any other usage of Notes. Distributing ID files on floppy disk provides a ready-made backup copy of the ID file that the user can store and have available should he lose his hard disk.

BACKING UP ID FILES

When a user forgets a password, providing the user with a new password is a relatively easy task. There is no permanent loss of data involved with forgetting a password. A user who loses an ID file faces far more serious consequences. Any data encrypted using that user's public key is lost forever, because that user's private key is needed in order to decrypt anything that was encrypted with his public key. In addition, replacing a lost ID file entails more administrative burden than replacing a lost or forgotten password. For this reason, keeping a backup copy of an ID file is a good idea.

There is no way to re-create an ID file once it has been lost. You can have a policy that users keep backup copies of their ID files, but quite often users will forget to update backups when their ID files are updated. It often falls to the administrator to keep a backup of all ID files that have been issued. Of course, keeping the administrator's copy of ID files updated is also a large task. A compromise used by many organizations is to have administrators keep a backup of the user's original ID file. This means that the administrator can replace a lost ID file with a backup. The user still must be recertified with any additional certificates that he held in the lost ID file, and get new copies of any encryption keys, but no data is lost. The one exception to this rule is when the user was storing the only copy of an encryption key. If the only copy of an encryption key is lost, any data encrypted with that key is lost. You may be able to find someone capable of breaking the encryption even in cases when no key is available, but you certainly can't rely on this scenario.

No perfect solution exists to the problem of replacing a lost ID file. Having users create and keep backups is unreliable, and many users will not understand this requirement. Most users need to perform this task less than once a year, and their unfamiliarity with backing up an ID file can lead to confusion, or simply choosing not to do the backup. If you choose to have your administrators keep a backup of all ID files, you are forced to provide your administrators with a level of trust that many organizations may not be willing to do. Administrators with access to backups of the ID files have the ability to use an ID file to read any encrypted mail and to assume the identity of any person. Because identities are based on ID files, access to the ID file is synonymous with being able to steal the person's identity. Administrator access to backup ID files is a moot point if your administrator is also your certifier, as a certifier can create IDs and assume an identity simply by creating the identity.

There are some steps you can take to secure backup copies of ID files:

◆ Store backup copies of ID files in a secure, locked safe

◆ Require multiple passwords for backup copies of ID files

Backup copies of ID files should be kept in a secure, locked safe—not in the administrator's desk, where anyone has casual access. Because ID files are the basis of Notes security, access to ID files must be carefully controlled. ID files are encrypted and protected with a password, but backup copies of ID files often share a common password. Because you don't want to rely on a single administrator knowing the password to your ID files, this password can become fairly well known throughout the organization, at least among the administrative staff. Thus, the backup copies of your ID files can become an easy target for hackers wishing to penetrate your security system.

Requiring multiple passwords can minimize the chance that an administrator will use a backup copy of an ID file to impersonate another user. To replace a lost ID file using a copy with multiple passwords, you first make a copy of the backup ID. Two administrators together can then remove one of the passwords on the ID file and deliver it to the user.

If someone has lost an ID file, and you fear that it may have been stolen, don't just redistribute a backup copy of the ID file. If an ID file is stolen, you need to issue a new ID and prevent anyone from using the old ID file. Before destroying the backup copy of the ID file, you need to use it to decrypt any data encrypted with the original ID file. Your procedure for decrypting documents using a backup copy of an ID file after someone has lost their ID file should specify that this should take place only in the presence of the person owning the file. You should be prepared to immediately re-encrypt the files with the new ID file.

FORCING A PASSWORD CHANGE

Notes ID files are protected by passwords. This strategy leads many organizations to attempt to extend their policies and procedures regarding passwords to the passwords protecting Notes ID files—a waste of company resources. Passwords used to log on to a system and passwords used to protect an ID file are protecting fundamentally different things. Passwords used to log on to a system are part of an authentication system. A person is identified by presenting the correct user ID/ password combination. A password protecting an ID file is an access control mechanism that attempts to restrict access to the ID file. A password on an ID file isn't involved in authentication at all.

Common policies regarding passwords include the life span of a password, the minimum length of a password, and requirements for both numeric and alpha characters in a password. Policies surrounding passwords are generally designed to make passwords hard to guess. In traditional password-protected systems, knowledge of a password is all that is needed to gain access to a system. But knowing the password to a person's ID file is useless without having a copy of the ID file. The password alone provides no access to the Notes system. Only the Notes ID file can provide access to the Notes system.

If someone has a copy of the ID file, but doesn't know the password, he can try to guess the password protecting the ID file. If the hacker has a copy of the ID file, changing the password on an ID file held by one of your users does nothing to the copy of the ID file held by the hacker. In addition, the hacker is free to attempt to guess as many passwords as he cares to in an attempt to break into the ID file. Because this process takes place on a system disconnected from your service, you have no way of knowing if someone is attempting to guess a password associated with an ID file. This problem is why Lotus hasn't incorporated a method of forcing users to change the passwords on their ID files. It's simply pointless.

Even though changing passwords on ID files is pointless, in some organizations it is easier to go along than to change policies. Explaining the difference between a logon password and a Notes ID password may be a difficult process in some organizations. Satisfying your auditors may mean having a policy asking users to change their passwords on their ID files. Even with a policy, Notes provides no way to enforce this policy.

The only recourse you have if an ID file has fallen into unauthorized hands is to create a new public and private key for the user and to issue a new ID file for that user. Before deleting the old ID file, make sure that you decrypt all information that was encrypted using the old ID file, and then re-encrypt this information, using the new ID file.

SECURITY AUDITS AND NOTES

Security audits are concerned with ensuring that a company can track all changes to its databases and has the capability of detecting a security violation when one occurs. When designing your policies and procedures, ask yourself, "How would I know if a security violation occurred?" To restrict a security audit, you need to know the answer to this question for all databases in your Notes network. You need written procedures for

◆ Updating the design of your Notes applications

◆ Monitoring access to your Notes resources

◆ Knowing who makes changes and when changes are made to your Notes designs

◆ Changing the Name and Address Book

◆ Replacing a lost ID file

◆ Decrypting documents after someone loses an ID file

If you are working in a financial institution, you probably have lived through a few security audits and have experience meeting audit requirements. You probably have already written procedures for controlling updates to your applications and databases. Similar policies need to be developed to control updates to your Notes application designs and databases. Keep in mind that a Notes database is data and application in one package and that data, application, and access control are tightly integrated. Keeping track of all changes to a Notes design and access control list is even more important than tracking code changes for many other applications.

LOGGING AND AUDIT TRAILS

Although authentication and access control form the basis of all security systems, you should record activity so that you can reconstruct any security violations. There are two levels of recording you need to consider:

◆ Logging

◆ Audit trails

Logging is simply collecting information about any security-related event, such as logging into a system. Most systems today, including Notes, routinely log this type of information. The second level of monitoring, audit trails, is based on logging. A log becomes a useful *audit trail* when it contains context information, such as the time and the specific actions (such as documents accessed) that occurred. For example, knowing that a person attempted to access a server is fine, but logging the fact that a user attempted to access the system at 10:23, typed in three wrong passwords, along with logging those three wrong passwords, is far more useful. The second thing that must happen for a log to become a useful audit trail is that the log must be protected. It must be impossible for the log to be deleted or modified. This includes all users, including administrators.

The Notes log meets the first essential characteristic of an audit trail. It logs essential access-control events and it records much of the context surrounding each event. However, in Notes there is no way to prevent an administrator from changing the log, so the Notes log in and of itself isn't a foolproof audit trail. There are two reasons why you would want to keep an audit trail:

◆ To analyze an incident after the fact, you need to be able to analyze an audit trail.

◆ A true audit trail provides a higher confidence level that the log is accurate.

Notes provides built-in ways for administrators to monitor changes to ACLs. You can configure databases to e-mail all changes to your personal mailbox, or you can set up a central database to record all changes. This feature helps track changes to ACLs, but isn't a true audit trail.

UPDATING DESIGNS

Typical procedures for updating a Notes design include having servers specifically designated as production servers and not allowing application designers to make changes directly to the production server. By requiring administrators to approve and then roll out changes, you can track the source and time of all design changes. Figure 4.1 shows the recommended process for updating Notes applications.

Figure 4.1.
You can avoid problems
by enforcing a two-step
design-update process.

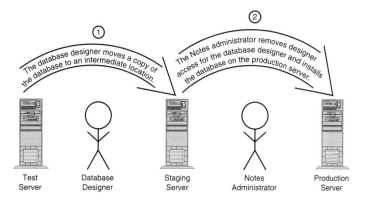

① The database designer moves a copy of the database to an intermediate location.

② The Notes administrator removes designer access for the database designer and installs the database on the production server.

| Test Server | Database Designer | Staging Server | Notes Administrator | Production Server |

You should provide designer access to production databases only to the administrators with responsibility for the server, not the entire application development staff.

PASSWORDS AND ID FILES

Discovering that a security violation has occurred is more difficult in Notes than in a password-protected system. The primary method used by many organizations to detect attempted break-ins on password-protected systems is to track the number of logon attempts for a single user ID. Repeated failed attempts to log on are a sign of hackers attempting to break into your system. However, with Notes you have no way of tracking hackers' attempts to guess passwords for ID files. Anyone with a copy of an ID file can run a guessing program on his or her local machine until finding the password. The Notes server isn't involved in the process of protecting ID files, and therefore can't track attempts to break into a Notes ID file.

Once a hacker gains access to an ID file and has guessed the password for that ID file, he can gain instant access to your Notes system. His access won't appear any different initially than an ordinary access by the real user. Notes authentication succeeds because the hacker has the correct certificates. You need to know the typical usage patterns of your users for clues that a hacker is accessing the system. Perhaps the access is being made at an unusual hour for that user, or the hacker may be attempting to access databases not normally used by that account. Currently, automated tools to detect these user patterns don't exist, making detection difficult in large Notes networks. You should focus your efforts on the critical portions of the Notes system: the Name and Address Book, mailboxes, and any highly sensitive databases within your organization. Monitoring is a critical part of any security system. For now, Notes relies on administrators randomly scanning log records to notice any particular potential violations.

TRACKING ACCESS TO NOTES RESOURCES

Tracking changes to your system requires that all users have and use personal ID files. There is little point in tracking changes if you can't tell exactly who is making the changes. Many organizations try to ease their administrative burden by using a common ID file for all administrators. This makes changing/creating access control lists easier. Don't do it!!! If you are serious about security, avoid issuing a common ID file to all administrators. Because administrators will make most of the changes to your database design and access control lists, they represent the most serious security threat. Tracking the person actually making the changes is important for your security audits.

CERTIFIERS AND SECURITY

Certifiers are extremely powerful. They can masquerade as any user in your organization. Through the ability to create ID files, certifiers have complete access to your Notes resources. Both Notes servers and Notes clients rely on certificates to authenticate identities. Authentication succeeds because both the server and client trust a common third party—the certifier who issued the certificate they have in common. Note the word "trust." If the certifier who issued the certificates isn't trustworthy, your Notes network isn't secure. Choose your certifiers carefully.

If a certifier should leave your corporation under less than ideal circumstances (no post office jokes here, please), you will be faced with the large task of recertifying all users certified by that certifier. You must discard any certificates for which this certifier had access, and create new certificates for each user. Because you can't know in advance whether you will face this situation, proper planning is required. Luckily, planning can reduce the effort required to recover from a disgruntled certifier.

One thing your certifiers should never do is certify people by using the organizational certificate. If your organizational certificate is used to certify ID files, you would need to recertify every user in the organization when a certifier left the company. You should only use the organizational certificate to create organizational unit certificates. ID files should only be certified using organizational unit certificates. This reduces the number of users that must be recertified when a certifier leaves. Figure 4.2 shows the users who would need to be recertified if the Marketing/L3Comm certifier leaves the company. By using an organizational unit certifier to certify ID files, L3Comm reduces the number of users who need to be recertified. In this case, only the Marketing department needs to be recertified.

Figure 4.2.
Users must be
recertified when their
certificates no longer
can be trusted.

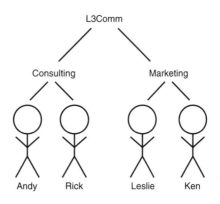

Only Leslie and Ken need to be recertified if the Marketing certifier is lost.

Chapter 3, "Understanding Security," gives the complete background on organizational and organizational unit certificates. Chapter 18, "Administering Notes Security," shows you how to create and use organizational and organizational unit certificates.

One other way to reduce the threat posed by certifiers is to require at least two passwords on all certifier ID files. Access to certifier ID files is what gives certifiers the ability to issue certificates. By requiring two certifiers to be present to use a certifier ID file, you lower the odds that a certifier will create fraudulent ID files for his personal use. You should require two passwords on all organizational unit certifier ID files and three passwords on the organizational certifier ID file.

Using Notes as a Firewall

Firewalls protect your company's computers from external threats. This issue generally arises when a company is trying to connect to the Internet, but Internet protection need not be the only use of firewalls within your company. Firewalls can be set up between divisions of your company. For example, you may want to place a firewall between North American and international divisions.

Firewalls attempt to isolate two networks from each other. Figure 4.3 illustrates a typical firewall. A firewall attempts to prevent unauthorized network packets from passing through to your protected networks. Firewalls are a relatively expensive security feature, ranging in price from a few thousand to several hundred thousand dollars. Complex firewalls can easily run tens of thousands of dollars in hardware costs alone.

Figure 4.3.
A typical firewall
configuration.

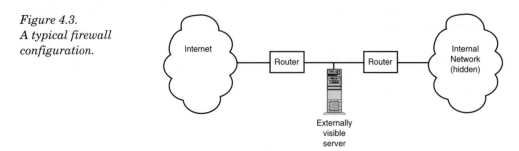

If you're looking for a low-cost way to provide moderate protection from Internet attacks, you can use two Notes servers as a firewall. A Notes-based firewall is different in nature from typical firewalls. Typical firewalls rely on rules specified by administrators to filter TCP/IP packets that can enter or exit the network. Notes-based firewalls rely on Notes security features to block attacks. If you decide to use Notes as a firewall, you need to purchase additional software to provide access to FTP, Usenet newsgroups, the World Wide Web, and e-mail.

Firewalls are designed primarily to prevent TCP/IP network packets from passing through the firewall. An extremely good technique of isolating your internal network from unauthorized TCP/IP packets is not to use TCP/IP on your internal network. Notes firewalls are based on this technique. The connection between the external server and the internal server shouldn't be a TCP/IP connection. This system forces all traffic from the Internet to be translated into a different protocol. In Figure 4.4, the two Notes servers are connected with a null modem cable. Notes does all protocol conversions to allow Notes users to access the Internet.

Figure 4.4.
A Notes-based firewall.

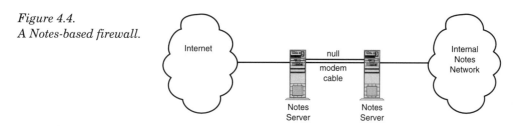

You could also set up each server with two network interface cards (NICs). In each server, one NIC runs IPX and one runs TCP/IP. All communications between these two servers is done using IPX. This prevents any TCP/IP packets coming from the Internet to travel through your server to your internal network. Notes traffic is automatically handled by the Notes server. The Notes server will transfer the data coming in from the Internet to the correct protocol when passing it on to the internal server. Authorized Notes traffic can pass through, but no TCP/IP packets are allowed into your internal network. In this case, you can use all the security features of Notes to filter the Notes traffic that is allowed into your internal network.

The real benefit to using Notes as a firewall is that it enables you to tightly control access from within the corporation to the Internet. You can use Notes add-on products such as newsreaders and Web page readers to translate Internet data into Notes format and provide this data to your employees. Because these add-ons are controlled by your Notes administrator, users who want to access a new portion of the Internet must have your administrator first set up the add-on product to read that portion of the Internet. This technique enables you to provide unlimited access for business uses, while limiting or eliminating personal access to the Internet. For example, you can limit access to specific Usenet groups by configuring your Notes server to monitor only the desired groups. In Figure 4.5, the administrator has selected a subset of all possible Usenet groups. Employees can access only the groups stored as a Notes database on the local server.

Notes firewalls enable you to filter the traffic going from your internal employees to the Internet. Because all Internet data is translated to/from documents in Notes databases, you can use all of your Notes administrative tools to restrict or monitor the information being sent and type of access being allowed.

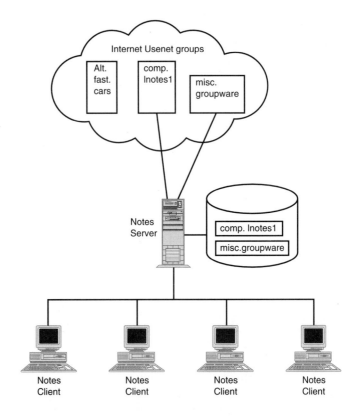

Figure 4.5.
Notes enables a
company to limit access
to legitimate Internet
resources.

It also makes sense to integrate Internet data into your Notes network. Users will appreciate having the power of Notes to view and search Internet data. By providing a common tool for accessing internal and external data, you eliminate the need to configure special tools just to access Internet data. Users also appreciate—or at least tend to be less dissatisfied with—an administrator who does a good job of identifying useful Internet resources and making them available through Notes.

Life isn't full of just good news, though. You do lose some capabilities when you place Notes between your employees and the Internet. You can expect to lose access to some of the latest, greatest Web features. You will have access only to the features supported by the products that connect Notes to the Internet. Also, Notes isn't designed to be a firewall, and only provides a moderate amount of protection. A complete discussion of firewalls and all the desirable features is beyond the scope of this book.

For a Notes firewall to be effective at limiting access to the Internet, it must be the only connection from your company to the Internet. Otherwise, employees can use the alternate path to access Internet resources.

As with all Notes servers, Notes firewalls shouldn't be used as file servers, FTP servers, or distributed file system (NFS) servers.

Chapter 20, "Connecting Notes to the Internet with InterNotes," provides additional detail on ways to integrate Notes and the Internet.

ENCRYPTION

Many organizations will never need to worry about encryption. However, data security goes beyond controlling access to data. What if you need to verify that a memo sent two months ago came from the person listed in the "from" field? What if you need to encrypt your data while it is being sent from the server to the client? You can accomplish these things with Notes.

ENCRYPTING MAIL

If you need to send a "For Eyes Only" memo that you want only one person to be able to read, you can encrypt that memo, using your intended recipient's public key. Because you have used the recipient's public key to encrypt a message, only that recipient's private key can decrypt that message.

DIGITAL SIGNATURES

When you need to guarantee that a memo came from the person listed in the "from" field, you should use digital signatures. Digital signatures use the user's private key to attach an encrypted field to the memo. If the memo is altered or changed in any way after the memo has been digitally signed, you can tell. Therefore, you can guarantee months after the memo has been sent that it actually came from the person listed in the "from" field.

Figure 4.6 depicts the process of digitally signing a document. The first step is to apply a mathematical function (known as a *hash function*) to the document to create a fixed-length fingerprint. This is done in a way that makes it impossible to know anything about the original document from just the fingerprint. The next step is to use the signer's private key to encrypt the fingerprint. The encrypted fingerprint is the digital signature.

Digital signatures are verified using the public key of the signer. The signature is decrypted to give the original fingerprint. The verifier then generates a new fingerprint based on the current state of the document. Figure 4.7 shows the process of verifying a signature.

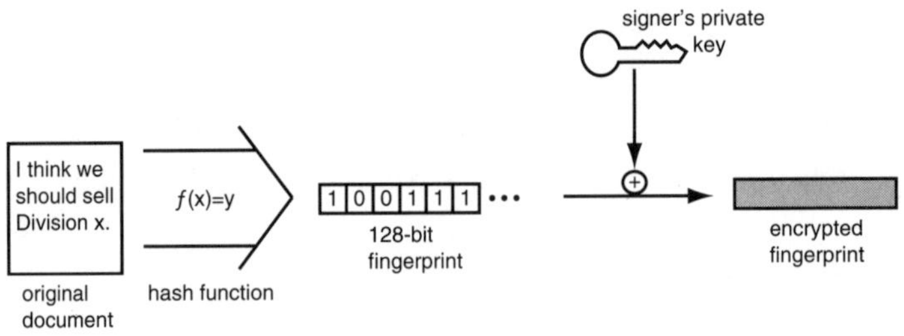

Figure 4.6.
A digital signature is
an encrypted finger-
print of the document
being signed.

Figure 4.7.
Verifying a digital
signature ensures that
the document hasn't
been changed.

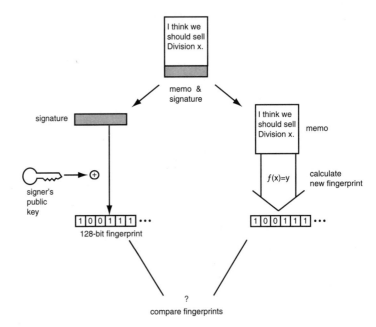

If the document hasn't been changed, and the correct public key is used to decrypt the signature, you know that the document hasn't been changed since the document was signed and you know the identity of the person signing the document.

PORT ENCRYPTION

Notes doesn't by default encrypt data being transmitted over a network. Notes makes the reasonable assumption that either

◆ You have a secure network

  or

◆ You don't care if data is intercepted while being transmitted

This is the way most corporations have been operating for many years and is therefore a reasonable assumption for Lotus to make. If these aren't valid assumptions for your network, you can configure Notes to provide its own secure communications channel.

PUBLIC KEY DISTRIBUTION

In order to use digital signatures or privacy-enhanced memos, both users need to have access to a common Name and Address Book. The Name and Address Book is where public keys are stored. Of course, private keys are stored in the ID file, which should be in a secure place accessible only by the actual owner of that ID file. For example, you digitally sign a memo using your own private key, but someone needs access to your public key stored in the Name and Address Book before they can verify the signature. The same is true for privacy-enhanced mail. You need access to someone's public key, stored in the Name and Address Book, in order to send that person private mail. This level of coordination, having each person have access to a common Name and Address Book, is a major drawback to using Notes as a basis for private communications across separate enterprises.

Users can mail copies of encryption keys to other users, but only regular users of encryption are likely to do this.

READING BUT NOT PRINTING OR COPYING

One question that many organizations have is, "How can we allow users read-access to data while preventing them from printing or copying this data?" Of course, there is no way to absolutely prevent users from copying data that they can read, because they can always get out a pencil and paper and write down all the information. However, Notes Release 4.0 databases can be set to disable copying via cutting-and-pasting, forwarding, or printing of documents in the database.

SECURITY SCENARIOS

Let's wrap up the discussion of the security basics by using the Notes security elements to accomplish some specific goals. These scenarios are meant as illustrations to help you understand the intent behind each of the Notes security features.

SCENARIO 1—ALLOW EDITOR ACCESS TO PART OF A DOCUMENT

You can protect parts of a document by using protective sections. When creating the form, divide the form into sections. For the section that you want to protect, assign a group name that will hold all users with rights to edit that section. The default access to the database should be author access. Users with author access can create documents and read documents, but not edit documents. Only those sections of your documents specifically granting editor access can be edited—and then only by those users specifically listed in the group name for that protected section.

SCENARIO 2—CREATE DOCUMENTS BUT NOT MODIFY THEM

This ability is often useful in workflow applications. For example, a user may have the right to generate a purchase order document, but shouldn't be allowed to change the document. This technique would prevent someone from changing a purchase order after it has been authorized. Give author access to the database, but don't create any AuthorNames fields in documents. Users can create documents but, because they aren't listed in an AuthorNames field, they don't have the ability to edit any documents.

SCENARIO 3—READ ONLY DOCUMENTS I CREATE

When you are collecting sensitive information, you want to make sure that users can't read information submitted from other users. In this case, you want to protect documents from everyone except the person who created it. You do this using reader fields. When the document is created, a reader field that lists the user should be created automatically (using a macro). Don't forget to include any administrative groups and servers that will need access to the document.

SCENARIO 4—PREVENT CHANGES TO FIELD VALUES

If your application uses fields that should be modified only by your programs and macros, you want to protect that field from accidental alteration by users. You can accomplish this by setting the field as Calculated and entering the name of that field in its formula.

SUMMARY

As a Notes administrator, you need to be particularly concerned with the security setup for each database on your server. Security is the primary source of problems in many Notes installations. Notes uses a combination of certificates, public and private keys, and access control lists to provide a finely granulated level of security. The primary weakness in Notes security (in any security system, actually) is the security policies that your organization chooses to implement. The most likely route for an attack on your Notes system is to gain access ID files containing the private keys and certificates from your organization. You will need to carefully design and plan out your policies and procedures for managing your ID files. Each organization will have to balance the costs versus the benefits.

Notes has tightly integrated encryption capabilities based on public key cryptography technology licensed from RSA. Public key encryption is the basis for mail encryption, digital signatures, and secure communications channels. Public key encryption is useful only when there is a convenient way to exchange public keys. Other Internet software, such as PGP, has already spawned a small industry to support the exchange of public keys. Let's hope that, in the near future, public key management in inter-enterprise and extra-enterprise applications becomes easier for Notes. Until that time, privacy-enhanced mail and digital signatures are primarily useful within a single domain. If you need to transmit data between two servers and you don't have a trusted connection between the two servers, you can use port encryption. The data is decrypted by the receiving server. This eliminates the possibility of anyone eavesdropping on your conversation.

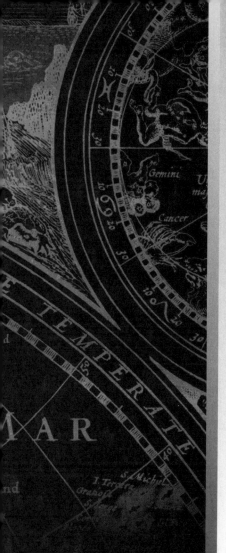

- Building a
  Deployment Plan

- Customizing Your
  Deployment Plan

- Determining
  Hardware and
  Software Needs

- Preparing Your
  Organization

- Designing Your Notes
  Network

PART II

Planning Your Notes Installation

- Ways to Fail

- Developing a
  Deployment Plan

CHAPTER 5

Building a
Deployment Plan

This chapter covers the fundamentals of planning for a Notes installation. The text gives you the ammunition to take to your manager or executive to get the time up front for the necessary planning. This chapter shows you what is involved in a typical deployment plan; the next chapter shows you how to customize each of the steps in this typical deployment plan.

To a project manager responsible for installing Notes, a deployment plan should be like a soldier and his rifle; you should never be without one. A deployment plan is your overall plan for designing/installing/configuring Notes.

Why build a deployment plan? You're busy. Your users are busy. Maybe you've never done a Notes installation and don't know what to plan for anyway (and consultants are expensive)...

Wrong. Planning saves money. Planning saves time. You will save time and money by planning ahead, even if it means bringing in a consultant. All Notes installations, large or small, should go through the steps outlined here and in Chapter 6, "Customizing Your Deployment Plan."

You build a deployment plan because there is no other way to build an accurate budget and schedule. If you happen to work in an organization that has the luxury of working without budgets and schedules, then you should consider the headaches that you can avoid for yourself and others by doing a little planning. Every organization should plan its Notes installation, regardless of the current workload, urgency, or corporate culture. In short, develop a deployment plan before installing Notes in a production environment. This chapter shows you the basic steps you should follow when deploying Notes. Each deployment will have some unique needs. Chapter 6 shows you how to customize a deployment plan for your organization.

Notes is a client/server product. A deployment plan for Notes resembles a deployment plan for any other client/server system. As with any client/server system, you install the servers before installing the clients, you assign user IDs and passwords, and you need to have a help desk available to answer questions. If your organization has already been through a major client/server deployment, the lessons learned there will apply to a Notes deployment. The major difference involves the impact Notes has on the working relationships within an organization.

Most organizations that have difficulty deploying Notes have not properly prepared. Behavioral and cultural barriers can block the successful adoption of Notes. For Notes to be successful, people must share information with each other and with other departments. In organizations that reward individual performance, this cooperation can be a difficult goal to achieve. In many organizations, information is power; sharing information can mean a loss of power. People will simply refuse to use Notes if it means losing power. Simply providing training is not enough; many organizations will need to change policies regarding performance appraisals and pay. We cannot stress this enough: Pay attention to the people within your organization. The people who will use Notes will determine the success or failure of Notes.

Studies clearly show that your chance for success increases for projects that are well connected. Make sure your Notes project team

◆ Is well-connected politically.

For an enterprise-wide product such as Notes, support from the very top is crucial. The CEO should personally use and support Notes. Executives should make a point of attending at least some formal training with front line staff.

◆ Is connected to many information sources.

There is no excuse for a Notes project being information-poor. Information on Notes is widely available. Consultants, Lotus support, Internet Usenet groups, and CompuServe forums are all rich sources of information and tips. Be sure to subscribe to the magazines specializing in Notes, such as *Lotus Notes Advisor* (619-483-6400) or *The View* (Wellesley Information Services, 800-810-1800). If your team is new to Notes, hire consultants and get some training. In addition to Notes-specific information, the project team should know about operating systems, rapid-application-development techniques, and networking.

◆ Is internally cohesive.

Allowing the project manager to select her own staff will help. Travel, long hours, and technical headaches are part of many Notes deployments. Make sure that people know what they are getting into when they join the team. Allow members to back out if necessary.

Just to emphasize the importance of planning, we start out with some common nightmare scenarios.

Ways to Fail

Don't say you've never been warned. Planning saves time. Planning saves money. You are NOT too busy to plan. Nonetheless, it's an easy step for many people to skip, because the pain comes later. What can you expect if you fail to plan your Lotus Notes deployment or if you do a poor job of it? We will discuss a few of the common scenarios that will lead you down the path to disaster with Lotus Notes.

FAILURE 1: MULTIPLE ISOLATED PILOTS

In large organizations, controlling (or even influencing) the actions of independent business units or departments is extremely difficult. The press is full of articles about Lotus Notes, and it is quite natural for more than one department within an organization to be researching Lotus Notes. As these research projects become pilots and get rolled out into production usage, you end up with multiple, isolated islands of Lotus Notes within an organization. You are then faced with the difficult task of reconciling all the different domains, naming conventions, network selections, and operating systems utilized in the various pilots. More than likely, the domains never will be completely reconciled, leading to permanently higher administration costs associated with administering multiple domains.

Having multiple isolated pilots also tends to waste dollars on Notes licenses. You lose the ability to buy in bulk and get your volume discount.

To avoid the isolated pilots syndrome, you need to widely publicize the "officially blessed" Notes pilot. Communicate the advantages of rolling up other pilots into the officially blessed one, as well as the advantages of waiting for the rollout of the blessed pilot. Corporate newsletters, department meetings, and e-mail are typical ways of publicizing your official Notes pilot. You should try to reach anyone with the power and budget to set up an independent Notes pilot. This usually includes all departmental managers throughout the organization. Usually, communicating the bottom line (saving on administration costs and Notes licenses) is enough. If you need to get into the more esoteric advantages of integrating efforts with the rest of the organization, then you probably have already lost the battle.

You can lower resistance to the official pilot if you make it easy for other unofficial pilots to join up. One way to do this is to establish a corporate owner to serve as a clearinghouse for naming standards, certificates, and the Public Address Book. The corporate owner does not control these independent pilots, but does make it easy for the official pilot to control those aspects of Notes (naming, security, standards) that can get out of hand. Over time, many unofficial Notes pilots will find it easier to combine forces with the official pilot rather than continue to manage an independent Notes network.

FAILURE 2: LACK OF TRAINING

Parts of Notes resemble other products that are already on the market. If you do a poor job of training—or no training at all—people will interpret Notes based on products with which they are already familiar. It is extremely common for end users to look at Notes as a very large—but not particularly fancy—e-mail package.

You need to plan training for administrators and application developers. Don't rely solely on on-the-job training. Notes is not just an extension of traditional IS systems.

Notes represents a new kind of application, which can lead to a long learning curve for untrained personnel. If you don't properly train administrators and application developers, they will have poor productivity during an extended learning curve. You also risk permanently higher costs supporting poor applications developed during the learning phase. The largest cost associated with skipping training is lost opportunities. Properly trained users, administrators, and application developers generate fresh, creative ways to use Notes. Untrained personnel will be frustrated, wondering what the big deal is.

Users require training in Notes and possibly in a new operating system. Deploying Notes is not the same as deploying a spreadsheet or word processing program. Notes is a systems product, not a finished application. It is more complex and requires more training than a word processor or spreadsheet.

FAILURE 3: GROWING TOO FAST

The most common way that Notes projects fail is that they grow faster than the IS organization can support them. Initial successes generate a huge demand for new applications. After Notes is installed, ideas for new applications are generated every day. Business units waiting for Notes wonder why IS cannot just install Notes everywhere. Why should they wait? The pressure on IS to step up the number of installations can result in some poor decisions. Don't install more Notes clients than your support organization is ready to handle! Unsupported users can quickly lose enthusiasm. Once that enthusiasm is lost, it's difficult to regain it.

Avoid growing pains by designing your Notes network to support the entire organization. This strategy lays the base for installing Notes quickly when business demand kicks in. Plan big when deploying Notes. Underestimating the work to be done can cause you to have an overloaded staff.

FAILURE 4: THE IS ORGANIZATION FAILS TO RESPOND ADEQUATELY

The IS organization within many corporations is threatened by Lotus Notes or doesn't understand Lotus Notes very well. When there is a lack of leadership from the IS organization, business units step in and develop their own solutions. One of the bugaboos of Notes is that almost any organization can set up a small network with a few simple applications. A common result of these "roll-your-own" mini-Notes networks is poorly implemented applications that don't scale to large numbers of users. Little thought is given to the underlying network, meaning that fewer users and applications can be supported. Even if these independent business units manage to develop a popular application, it fails when an attempt is made to let large numbers of people use it. For example, an application that makes heavy use of agents can be great when only a few users access a database. When hundreds or thousands of people create their own agents, the database cannot carry the load. You could end up with a set of daily agents that take more than a day to run.

These applications also tend to be difficult to change. The application often needs to be rewritten when incorporating simple changes. This costs money and leads to frustrated users. Once the precedent is set of allowing these applications to be developed, it will be difficult to stop. We'll let you explain to these cowboy developers (ever so politely) that their applications are no good.

You also lose the opportunity of buying Notes licenses in volume in this scenario.

FAILURE 5: NEGLECTING TO SET STANDARDS

Control is a fundamental cultural issue within many corporations. Power means having a clearly defined turf. This leads to problems with Lotus Notes. Managers are reluctant to give up control over information and control over application development. With Notes, users and IS staff both have the ability to develop applications (except for desktop licenses). IS, the traditional home of application development, may view letting users develop applications as a loss of power. IS staffs should develop guidelines for Notes application development. The two ends of the spectrum are complete control (everything must pass strict standards) and complete chaos (anything goes). Most companies end up somewhere in the middle. Users can develop their own applications but are subject to some simple standards, while the IS staff controls the Notes servers and charges business units a small fee to house their applications. Address this issue early on—before you actually roll out any production applications.

You must have standards in place for screen design and for field naming, and you need to set some guidelines for which applications will be subject to these standards. Mission-critical applications should be tightly controlled, while departmental applications require less control (for example, less testing required, no enforced color scheme). Discussion databases for small projects may only need to be based on a common template.

One way to approach the standards issue is to divide applications into three categories:

◆ Enterprise/Strategic

◆ Departmental/Tactical

◆ Personal/Single task

Obviously, more control is required for Enterprise/Strategic applications than for Departmental or Personal applications. Only you can decide which applications fall into which category.

Once Notes applications have been rolled out without using any standards, you can't go back. You cannot enforce standards after the fact, and you will have a very difficult time getting people who have been used to total freedom to follow new standards. If you don't enforce standards early on, you will have applications that don't cross platforms, that have crazy selections for colors and fonts, and that don't integrate with IS systems. You will end up with many slight variations on common themes, causing confusion among your users, and you will lose the ability to generate a common look and feel for your key corporate applications.

FAILURE 6: ASSUMING THAT APPLICATION DEVELOPMENT IS EASY

Forget the myth that developing Notes applications is trivial. It is true that an intelligent person who has had exposure to simple application-development tools for about half an hour can build his first simple discussion database. It is also true that Notes is a true rapid-application-development environment. Notes has integrated user interface development, networking, and database-development capabilities, enabling anyone to quickly "throw together" functioning applications. The ease and speed of developing a Notes pilot leads to the expectation that all Notes application development is trivial. But *quick* does not equal *easy*!

There are several minefields along the way that will become evident only when you try to scale these applications and roll them out to multiple business units. Notes is most useful when coordinating the activities of multiple groups. A good Notes application reconciles the needs of many groups; integrating functionality from multiple groups into a functioning application requires experience. Your application developers should at least have experience in client/server and end-user interface development.

Developing client/server applications that can scale from hundreds to thousands of users requires special knowledge. Building applications that minimize administration costs requires planning. You should dispel the myth that Notes development can be done by anyone. Reasonable guidelines controlling Notes application development can help educate users about the steps involved in developing and maintaining complex applications.

Now that you know the consequences of poor planning, you should be able to convince your management to build in some time and money for planning. If you follow the deployment plan outlined here, you will maximize your chances of avoiding these problems.

DEVELOPING A DEPLOYMENT PLAN

This section gives an overview of the typical steps in a Notes deployment. Remember, there is no single right way to deploy Notes. You still have work to do in planning out your Notes deployment. Even small organizations should follow every step here.

Deploying Notes is similar to deploying other client/server systems products. The same level of detailed planning is required, and the progression of the deployment plan is similar. You start by setting some goals, then do some design work, staff a support center, train users, pilot some applications, and repeat. A Notes deployment cycles through a series of planning/doing loops. Start by forming a project team. They plan a set of applications. The applications are built and deployed. Feedback is gathered and used to plan the next phase. Every cycle should be no more than six months.

Your plan will be greatly influenced by the size of your ultimate planned installation. If your goal is an enterprise-wide installation, you don't necessarily take the same approach as if you are only planning a departmental installation. For example, Notes e-mail becomes critical when planning an enterprise-wide installation. You need to be far more concerned about user naming and e-mail reliability with an enterprise installation than with a departmental installation. In a departmental installation, the chance of having duplicate names is low, and there are easy-to-use backups (phone, sneakernet), should e-mail go down for an afternoon.

Be sure that you plan for the number of users to grow to 200% of the initial pilot over the first year. You will pilot the application to a small number of users—typically a work group. You will use everything you learn during the pilot to change and update all of your processes, training, etc., for the initial rollout. The pilot step is extremely important! Therefore, choose that first application very carefully.

Following are the steps involved in a Notes deployment:

1. Form a project team.
2. Assess the enterprise.
3. Define the scope of your deployment.
4. Design your Notes network.
5. Create a Notes support organization.
6. Develop your standard operating procedures.
7. Build the pilot application.
8. Implementation and training.

This chapter lays out the concepts common to most installations. Chapters 6-9 provide more detail on carrying out the steps discussed here.

STEP 1: FORM A PROJECT TEAM

You need to involve everyone who will be affected by the Notes deployment as early as possible. We recommend forming a project team to lead the efforts. You should have

- A project manager
- A Notes server administrator
- A Notes database manager
- A member of the operations staff
- At least one user
- An application developer
- A trainer
- A member from the help desk

Chapter 8, "Preparing Your Organization," covers the responsibilities assigned to each role. Some people may fill multiple roles. For example, in many small organizations one person plays the role of administrator, database manager, and application developer (we're not recommending this, but it is somewhat common). If you cannot identify all team members at the beginning of the project, add them to the group as soon as possible. For a small organization, the project team may be three or four people, with only one or two full time. For a large corporate rollout, we recommend a team of ten people essentially full time over the course of the initial deployment (6 to 18 months).

Exit criteria: When each role has been assigned to a person, step 1 is done. It is possible to advance to step 2 while some support roles have not been assigned. Make sure that you have a project manager and an experienced application developer before advancing to step 2.

STEP 2: ASSESS THE ENTERPRISE

You need to assess both the organizational and physical readiness of your organization. You need to assess the culture, skills, and policies throughout your organization to identify future roadblocks. You need an accurate inventory of the current network and workstations installed to plan the upgrades needed.

CULTURAL READINESS

The first action your project team needs to take is to review your organization's decision to use Notes. Ask yourself these questions (and more!):

- Was the decision to use Notes based on real business needs?
- Is there a commitment that can overcome some initial missteps?

◆ Are you just experimenting with new technology?

◆ Are there competitive pressures you are trying to address?

When you know your general goals, draw up a chart showing potential applications by department. For each department, assess the department's readiness for the applications. We recommend having several half-day sessions with groups of five to eight people that will be affected by the Notes rollout. Include people from different departments in a single session. These sessions should include at least one experienced Notes application developer to give some feedback on what is attainable in what time frame.

You may recognize this technique as a variation of the joint application design (JAD) technique pioneered many years ago inside IBM for use on key application-development projects. JAD is a proven technique for discovering requirements and solutions quickly. Use JAD sessions to lay out the issues and get preliminary decisions made. There are whole weeklong trainings on JAD sessions, so we won't be able to provide a complete description here. Following are some key points regarding JAD sessions:

◆ JAD sessions are highly structured meetings with people playing specific roles.

◆ All JAD sessions should have a moderator.

◆ All JAD sessions should have a scribe.

◆ Keep the number of participants to twelve or less.

Be sure to get an experienced moderator for your JAD sessions. The moderator must keep the meeting on track. A good moderator knows when to cut a conversation short and can get everyone to contribute. The scribe is responsible for taking all notes. If possible, the scribe should be taking notes on a blackboard or overhead so that everyone can see the notes. This enables a person to see that his ideas are being accurately reported. The moderator and scribe should not be adding content to the meeting. A good moderator can make the difference between a successful and wasted session. There are several consulting groups, possibly within your organization, where you can get experienced moderators for these design sessions.

Holding these preliminary sessions is an extremely important step in the Notes deployment plan. Notes has the potential to change the culture within organizations, affecting the whole enterprise. You need to get at the underlying issues, fears, and considerations as early as possible. Before holding your JAD sessions, pass out a report/questionnaire containing an overview of the Notes project, the applications being considered, and the possible impact on the company. You should consider highlighting how Notes is being used in other companies. A short testimonial from your CEO couldn't hurt. Explain the goals for the meeting specifically. Your Notes deployment will not be successful without "buy-in" by all participating members.

Addressing all concerns helps to build the momentum necessary for enthusiastic cooperation.

After getting everyone's issues and comments on the table, the project team should choose an application and a department for the initial pilot. Before building large-scale production applications, build a small but useful application. This pilot application should be important to the business and not time-critical.

The pilot application is a critical choice. Success or failure with the pilot can set the tone of your Notes deployment. Many organizations begin with a few discussion databases. We don't recommend choosing a discussion database as the pilot application. There just isn't enough depth to a discussion database to provide a learning experience for the project team. Develop some discussion databases for use by the team during the rollout, but don't choose a discussion database as the pilot application.

After choosing a pilot application, the team should decide on some success criteria. How will you measure a successful pilot? A successful deployment? Common answers to these questions involve reducing cycle times and lowering costs. If you want to make some before/after comparisons, the team will need some baseline measurements before rolling out Notes. Many organizations don't define specific success criteria. These organizations rely on anecdotal success stories related to the Notes deployment as the measure of success. Either method, before/after measurements or anecdotal stories, can work, depending on the culture within an organization.

PHYSICAL READINESS

You have two goals. You need a detailed plan for the pilot and a long-range plan for the entire organization.

You should have an accurate inventory of all servers and workstations that will be involved with the pilot, to plan the specific hardware/software upgrades needed.

You also need to start a dialogue with any group within your organization involved with planning and supporting the network. You need to evaluate any current plans to support remote and mobile users. You may need to provide estimates for the amount of network traffic generated by Notes. Notes itself places an insignificant load on a network. The amount of data transferred is dependent on your application's design. The best way to develop estimates for your applications is to build some small demos and run some tests.

Chapter 7, "Determining Hardware and Software Needs," has more information on planning for your hardware and software needs (including forms you can use to gather information).

Exit criteria: This step is complete when you have identified cultural issues that will be affected by Notes, identified a Notes pilot application, and completed an evaluation of the current network.

STEP 3: DEFINE THE SCOPE OF YOUR DEPLOYMENT

This step directly addresses failure 3, growing too fast. "Fast" is a relative term. Quick growth isn't bad if you've planned for it. Unplanned growth can lead to failure. You need to plan for growth in several areas:

◆ The number and types (local, remote, mobile) of users

◆ The number of applications

◆ The number of servers

◆ The number of geographic locations with Notes

Develop estimates for each of these categories. Chapter 6 shows you how to turn these estimates into the number of administrators you need to train and the budget you should plan. Plan for success. You won't be disappointed.

Exit criteria: This step is complete when you have developed estimates for the number and types of users, applications, servers, and geographic locations that will use Notes.

STEP 4: DESIGN YOUR NOTES NETWORK

This is the step where you start to use the information gathered in steps 1 through 3. This is also the first step where detailed technical knowledge of Notes is needed. Make sure that your application developers and administrators have completed (or will soon complete) their training before starting this step. Remember to plan big, but implement in small chunks. Learn from your mistakes and revise your standards and plans accordingly. I don't mean for the following list to imply that you can completely design your Notes network before you have any real-world experience. Your Notes network will evolve over time. Use this list as a guideline for designing and revising your plans.

These are the steps you should follow when designing a Notes network (in order):

1. Identify supported desktop platforms.
2. Identify supported server platforms.
3. Identify supported network protocols.
4. Develop a WAN strategy for remote access.
5. Decide the location of servers.

6. Identify your replication architecture (network topology).

7. Size the hardware for desktop and servers.

8. Identify current IS systems that must integrate with Notes.

9. Identify current desktop applications that must integrate with Notes.

10. Decide which application development tools to support.

11. Create naming guidelines for people, servers, and groups.

12. Name your Notes domains.

13. Name your Notes networks.

14. Name your Notes servers.

15. Choose gateways for mail, fax, Internet, etc.

16. Assign users to home servers.

Chapter 7, "Determining Hardware and Software Needs," and Chapter 9, "Designing Your Notes Network," cover all the details you need to carry out these steps.

Exit criteria: This step is complete when you have initial plans showing where servers will be placed, standards showing how the decision to place a server will be made, estimates for how many users and applications each server must support, the name of each item in the Notes network (servers, domains, networks), and the systems that must integrate with the Notes network.

STEP 5: CREATE A NOTES SUPPORT ORGANIZATION

You can start this step as soon as you have formed a project team. You should complete this step before proceeding to step 6. We recommend having the new support organization involved with developing the standard operating procedures.

Chapter 8 discusses this step in more detail.

Exit criteria: This step is complete when you have selected the personnel for the support team.

STEP 6: DEVELOP STANDARD OPERATING PROCEDURES

Notes integrates application development and administrative functions in a single interface. It is remarkably easy for application developers to place unnecessary burdens on administrators and vice versa. Although a set of standard operating procedures can help, nothing beats a close working relationship between your application developers and administrators.

You may not want to develop policies for all the issues outlined here. Large organizations need more structure than small ones. The project team should at least discuss each issue listed here to decide if a formal policy is required.

You should develop a standard operating procedure or policy for each of the following items.

Security
> Default server ACLs
> Default database ACLs
> Remote access security policies
> Passthru restrictions
> Internet access via Notes
> Connections to external Notes domains
> Certification

Mail
> Maximum size of personal mailboxes

Change policies
> Step-by-step guide to get an application from testing to production
> Testing and review requirements for each class of application

This level of security will be new to anyone new to Notes. Release 4 has added several new security features; even an organization with experience using Release 3 should revise its security policies. For these reasons, security will be given special consideration here.

SECURITY POLICIES AND PROCEDURES

Notes is probably your first encounter with a client/server system with integrated military-level security. Much of an administrator's time is spent maintaining various elements of Notes security (user IDs, certificates, access control lists). Planning can save considerable expense later by reducing the amount of administrative effort required for your Notes installation. In addition, the security of your network and data depends on correctly designing your security policies and procedures. Follow these steps to set up your security system:

1. Assign people to roles.
2. Create your organizational certificate.
3. Create your organizational unit certificates.
4. Create special administrator groups.
5. Define default access control lists for databases.
6. Define access control lists for special databases.

7. Define default access control lists for servers.

8. For each server, create a group of common users.

9. Provide physical security for all servers.

Each of these items is discussed in detail in the following sections.

BUILD THE SECURITY TEAM

Even though Notes includes some of the best security technology available, you must pay special attention to the way you divide roles and responsibilities. Giving too much responsibility to a single individual opens security loopholes. Involving too many people in Notes security produces an unworkable system. The following roles play a part in maintaining Notes security:

- ◆ Database managers
- ◆ Notes administrators
- ◆ Certifiers

During the initial rollout, you should assign at least one person to each of these roles. Each database will need a database manager (at this stage, one database manager should be able to handle all databases). Each server should have an administrator (one administrator can cover multiple servers). The number of certifiers you need will depend on the security policies and naming standards you implement. You should try to centralize management of certifiers as much as possible to minimize security leaks. Chapter 17, "Administering Notes Databases," contains detailed information for database managers; Chapter 18, "Administering Notes Security," outlines the responsibilities of an administrator. In summary, the security responsibilities of a database manager include

- ◆ Maintaining the database access control list
- ◆ Updating ReaderNames and AuthorNames fields as necessary

The security responsibilities of an administrator include

- ◆ Maintaining server access control lists
- ◆ Monitoring server logs for possible security violations

The security responsibilities of a certifier include

- ◆ Certifying user IDs

The most important role is that of the certifier. The certifier is the person who essentially serves as a notary public, guaranteeing the identity of the user IDs within your organization. The certifier, through the ability to create user IDs, has complete access to your entire Notes system. Therefore, you need to choose your certifier carefully. Should one of your certifiers leave the company, to be absolutely certain of your security you need to create a new certificate and recertify all people certified with a certificate to which the certifier had access. Unfortunately, recertifying hundreds or thousands of users is impractical, which means that you must find other ways to help increase your security level.

One way to minimize the security problems associated with certifiers is to require three or more passwords for each certifier ID created. This method forces two people to be involved in the creation of each user ID, preventing a single certifier from creating fake user IDs.

Another way to maintain security after a certifier leaves is to limit access to servers to people listed in the Public Address Book. When this feature is enabled, Notes checks the public key contained in the Public Address Book against the one from the user attempting to access the server. Because a certifier cannot re-create the public key of users, just the users' names, this prevents a certifier who has left the company from gaining access to servers with fake user IDs. This feature hurts performance, however, because the server needs to check every access against the Public Address Book. This method is also impractical if you need to allow access to your servers from several domains.

SECURITY POLICY OVERVIEW

There are a few guiding principles you should follow when designing your security scheme. Despite the number of new concepts involved, Notes security is really very straightforward :

- ◆ Physical server security is limited to a select subset of administrators and/or operators.
- ◆ All databases have a default access level of no access.
- ◆ Database managers, LocalDomainServers, and Notes administrators have manager access to non-administrative databases.
- ◆ Database managers decide who gets what access level below designer.
- ◆ LocalDomainServers and Notes administrators have manager access to all administrative databases.
- ◆ Designer access is severely limited (but not eliminated) in production databases.
- ◆ Certification and user ID administration is kept as centralized as possible, considering the logical, organizational, political, and physical topology of your organization.
- ◆ You trust your administrators (within the flexibility of the new R4 administration roles model).
- ◆ Use administration agents intelligently to help a human keep an eye on things.

Before setting out to design a Notes security scheme, you need to ensure that your servers are physically secure. They should be kept under lock and key at all times. If your servers are not physically secure, your Notes data is not secure.

You won't always be able to follow these guidelines. In particular, you may need to customize your ACLs to help avoid mistakes.

DEFINE DEFAULT ACCESS CONTROL LISTS

Your default access control lists should be set up to ensure smooth operation of your Notes network. This includes replication between servers, mail routing, and proper administrator access, in addition to denying access to external servers and unauthorized personnel. These recommendations are for internal applications. Access control lists for externally available databases need to be determined on a case-by-case basis. See Chapter 6 for recommendations on creating access control lists for extra-enterprise applications. Chapter 18 contains step-by-step instructions for adding and deleting items in an ACL.

Your first step in creating your access control lists is to answer these questions:

- ◆ How much access should administrators have to sensitive data?
- ◆ Who should have manager access to your databases?
- ◆ Who should have access to your servers?
- ◆ Who should have designer access to your databases?

The answers to these questions determine the default ACLs for your databases and servers.

The default ACL contains the name of the person who created the database. You should remove this name. Avoid putting any user names in ACLs. Each person who needs access to a database should be part of a group. This can save time when you need to change a user's name or the user leaves the company. It also enables an administrator to enforce correct change procedures. If application developers had their names listed explicitly in the ACL as managers, there would be no way to stop them from making changes directly to a production database. You should delete the name of the database creator from the production copy of the database.

There are exceptions to this rule of not allowing user names in ACLs. A user who doesn't belong in any current group may have a legitimate need to access a database. In this case, you would be forced to create a group for a single user, or put that user's name directly into the ACL. Realistically, it's just not worth the trouble of creating many groups with one or two names just to avoid putting those names in ACLs. This is an area that requires judgment on the part of the administrator.

There are several groups of people who should be accounted for in your Notes ACLs. Add the following groups to your default ACLs:

◆ Terminated group

The Terminated group should be set at no access. In this group, list the IDs of all people who have left the company.

◆ Administrators

This group is meant for use by administrators and database managers. The Administrators group only provides designer access. This prevents accidental alteration of an ACL, one of the trickiest problems to resolve and a potential security leak. Both administrators and database managers should be listed in the Administrators group. Administrators each need two IDs— one for when they want to change ACLs, and one for all other work. List the administrator ID for everyday work in the Administrators group. Use the Administrators group for all non-ACL work. Having two IDs doesn't enhance security; it merely helps to avoid problems with ACLs.

◆ Managers

Each administrator and database manager should have a second ID listed in the Managers group. The Managers group provides manager access. Only use this ID when you want to make changes to the ACL of a database. Give each administrator and database manager a unique ID for use with this group. You will not be able maintain an audit trail if you provide an ID for use by more than one person.

This default ACL doesn't apply to the Notes Name and Address Book, MAIL.BOX, or the Notes log. Each of these databases is a special case.

DEFINE ACCESS CONTROL LISTS FOR SPECIAL DATABASES

The Notes log, MAIL.BOX, and Name and Address Book are special administrative databases that deserve special consideration. Most organizations will use the default settings for these databases. Make sure that you understand the reasoning behind the default settings.

The Name and Address Book security settings should be set up to ease the administrative burden by enabling distributed management of the NAB. Large organizations can divide the task of managing the Name and Address Book by department or geographic location. For example, each department can have a certifier responsible for adding and deleting users in that department. The administrative burden is eased by allowing more than one administrator to create and manage persons and groups and by allowing individuals to fill in miscellaneous information in their person documents.

Users also have a role in maintaining the Name and Address Book. The Name and Address Book is designed to have individuals edit certain portions of their own person records (phone number, address, etc.). Most users will need training before they edit their own person record in the Name and Address Book. You can provide even more help by having a macro fill in fields, such as Address, which are the same for large numbers of users.

The Name and Address Book is the directory for all users and servers, and the repository for server connection documents, groups, and network entries (and more!). The Name and Address Book is also used for scheduling tasks and for mail routing. Because access to the Name and Address Book is used for so many key functions within Notes, you should limit access to the Name and Address Book while still allowing for distributed management. In particular you need to limit manager and editor access to those administrators who will be responsible for mail routing and certifying users. Chapter 13, "Administrative Tools," covers the Name and Address Book in complete detail.

The default settings for MAIL.BOX should be left unchanged. The default access is depositor, which prevents anyone from reading mail while it is being routed, and enables users to add new mail. Only administrators need to be able to read entries in MAIL.BOX. Administrators need to be able to access dead mail, which is also stored in MAIL.BOX.

The Notes log contains information that should never be changed. The log contains information about activity on your Notes servers and isn't of much interest to normal users. If you have any hesitation about users seeing how often John Doe is accessing database XYZ, limit access to the log to administrators. Otherwise, the default reader access is acceptable.

ADMINISTRATORS AND SECURITY

Many organizations want to restrict manager access to data so that administrators do not have complete access to databases. Unfortunately, Notes does not yet have the access levels needed to accomplish this goal. At the present time, Notes administrators need manager access to databases to change access control lists, a task most administrators must be able to perform. The author recommends giving manager access to administrators who are responsible for servers for these reasons:

◆ If an administrator has access to the local console of a server, he has manager access to all databases on that server. Therefore, you are not actually increasing your level of security by denying manager access.

◆ Administrators with access to the Name and Address Book can create groups and put themselves in that group. Any group within an access control list with manager access is a potential security leak.

So it's actually impossible to prevent your administrators from gaining manager access to data. There simply is no way to close off all possibilities to someone who has high-level access to system resources. To even attempt to do so will simply add to his administrative burden while not actually increasing the security of your data. If you need to protect your data from access by administrators, you need to encrypt it with a key that administrators don't have. In this case, administrators still have manager access to the database, but wouldn't be able to read the data. Because encrypting data isn't practical for the vast majority of applications, however (the point of Notes is to share information), you must allow administrators to have access to data.

USE DEDICATED NOTES SERVERS

Notes servers should not be file servers. This is fundamental to Notes security. The only access people should have to a Notes server is through a Notes client. If you provide access through a file server or through Telnet or FTP, none of the security provided by the Notes server prevents users from copying database files to their local hard drives. Once a database file is on the local hard drive, the user can gain access to all the data in the database. There are many ways to breach the security of a Notes server that also functions as a file server. If you care about security, deploy only dedicated Notes servers.

CREATE YOUR ORGANIZATIONAL CERTIFICATE

You need to create a single organizational certificate. The only use for this certificate is to create the organizational unit certificates. Do not certify users with the organizational certificate. Certifying users with the organizational certificate makes it difficult to set up default ACLs that use wild cards.

Tip

Choose people for the role of certifier carefully. Restrict access to your organizational certificate to one or a few people. Store the certificate in a safe place.

You need to store the organizational certificate in a safe place. Restrict access to the certificate. For organizations serious about security, require at least three passwords to access an organizational certificate.

Chapter 18 contains step-by-step instructions for creating an organizational certificate.

CREATE YOUR ORGANIZATIONAL UNIT CERTIFICATES

You need to create one certificate for each of your organizational units. You should require two passwords to access an organizational unit certificate.

Chapter 18 contains step-by-step instructions for creating organizational unit certificates.

CREATE SPECIAL ADMINISTRATIVE IDS

You must create two IDs for each administrator if you want to use the default ACL recommended above: one for use in everyday administrative duties, and one for use when changing access control lists. The normal administrative ID is the one used for mail routing and making changes and updates to databases, except for those changes that affect the access control lists. When she has to update an access control list for a database, the administrator would change to her manager access ID, change the access control list, and then log off. This scheme protects you from inadvertent changes to the access control lists—one of the main sources of problems in many Notes networks. It also allows you to restrict access to ACLs to a small group of administrators. Don't give a special manager ID to those administrators who should not be changing the access control lists.

PHYSICAL SECURITY

None of these security steps has any meaning if people have physical access to the server machines; anyone with access to the server console has manager access to all databases on that server, including the Name and Address Book. For a medium-to-large corporation, set up servers in the computer room. For a small organization, or if you are setting up servers at remote sites, you may need to put the servers in a locked closet.

APPLICATION DEVELOPMENT METHODOLOGY

All organizations with more than a single application developer should set some application development guidelines. These guidelines can be suggestions or requirements, depending on the type of application being built. All applications that will be used by people outside of your company (extra-enterprise applications) should have a common look and feel. Applications developed to support a specific project should have fewer restrictions—but are you sure that the application won't be used elsewhere? You need to specify this look and feel before you begin developing applications. You are not likely to go back and change your applications after the fact.

Guidelines should specify acceptable fonts, colors, and point sizes. Common forms or sections of forms can be built for all application developers to use. Your application development guidelines should also specify an overall approach for your application development. Most applications should use a prototyping approach, with the one exception being extra-enterprise applications (see Chapter 6 for details).

STEP 7: BUILD A PILOT APPLICATION

You should have chosen a pilot application back in step 2 of the planning process. Now it's time to make it a reality. You should complete a pilot application within six months of the beginning of your Notes project (three months isn't an unreasonable goal, either). This is an aggressive schedule for some organizations that are used to longer development schedules. You must strive to deliver useful functionality to the business within six months. This will enable you to gain some experience first-hand that you can use to refine your procedures and application designs. The authors have yet to encounter a situation where it was not practical to deliver valuable functionality within six months. If six months sounds too aggressive for your application, rethink your application.

Pilot users should be very involved in the development of the pilot application. Set the expectation level of your pilot users. They should know that they are being used as guinea pigs. A pilot application should deliver value to the business, but its primary purpose is to teach your organization how to build and maintain Notes applications.

Whole books have been written on the topic of Notes application development, so this book cannot do justice to this topic. Chapter 17 covers some tips for developing administrator-friendly applications.

But far more important than any set of tips and tricks is your overall approach. The author feels that using the correct development methodology (or even just *having* a development methodology) is crucial. You are more likely to end up with the correct functionality by following the correct approach. Notes applications are best developed using a prototyping methodology. You should spend a few days (up to two weeks maximum) developing some functionality, show it to users, get feedback, and repeat. You should then be able to zero in on a useful design. When you have a design that you want to put into production, spend a few weeks making the application production-quality. Test the application and roll it out.

Always deliver functionality in small chunks. You should avoid at all costs the "big bang" method of developing applications. Smaller chunks represent a smaller resource commitment. By controlling the resource investment in each deliverable, you give yourself greater freedom to make midcourse corrections. It's much easier to throw out six weeks of work than it is to throw out six months of work. This strategy allows you to remain responsive to end users in the face of constant change. One of the things that makes Notes great is the ease with which you can develop powerful applications. Notes frees you from the need to chart multi-year application development projects with all the associated risk and heartache. There isn't a better platform for developing non-transaction-oriented applications.

STEP 8: IMPLEMENTATION AND TRAINING

We have grouped implementation and training because you should strive to schedule end-user training and installation together. Users should receive training within 48 hours of having Notes installed on their workstations (either before or after). Several steps must be carried out for each user.

This phase takes longer than the other phases combined. All the planning is meant to save you time during the actual rollout of Notes. Implementation should be divided into at least two phases: a pilot phase and a production phase. Large organizations will have even more phases (see Chapter 6). A team of five people should be capable of adding 50-100 users a week, assuming that the team will also provide support for current Notes users. When planning your initial timeline, plan to add 50 users a week starting at the end of the pilot phase. This is a conservative estimate. Most organizations can add more than 50 Notes users per week once the team has some experience.

CREATE USER IDs

You will create one user ID file for each Notes user. You need to plan and set up a standard operating procedure for the creation, distribution, and backup of user ID files. Some organizations create all user ID files with a default password. When the user first accesses the user ID file, she changes the password to her own personal preference. To protect against lost user ID files, the administrator should back up all user ID files created. While keeping these backups up to date is a burden, it's worthwhile for organizations that use encrypted data. Keeping backup copies of ID files makes it possible to decrypt data that was encrypted using an ID file.

SUMMARY

There are good reasons to plan your Notes installation. You can save money, time, and heartache while increasing your chances of success if you follow the eight-step plan outlined in this chapter. Starting from scratch and taking you through to full production, this plan outlines the steps you must accomplish when installing Notes.

The key concepts to remember for any situation are these: phase your implementation, gather feedback, and use that feedback in the next phase. No matter what situation you're in, you should be able to deliver meaningful functionality to your end users within three to six months. If your schedule doesn't call for a production deployment within the first three to six months, you need to reexamine the functionality or choice of application. Always remember to choose an application for your pilot that is important for your business so that there is enough business demand, but one that is not time-critical. Deploying a time-critical application with brand new technology is a high-risk strategy. While it may pay off, you will often end up with an extreme case of frustration. However, deploying Notes need not be an exercise in frustration. With a little foresight in the form of a proper deployment plan, deploying Notes should be a relatively straightforward process.

This Notes installation blueprint is the starting point for all Notes installation projects. You will need to customize the plan for your circumstances. Chapter 6 shows you how to customize this eight-step plan for your organization.

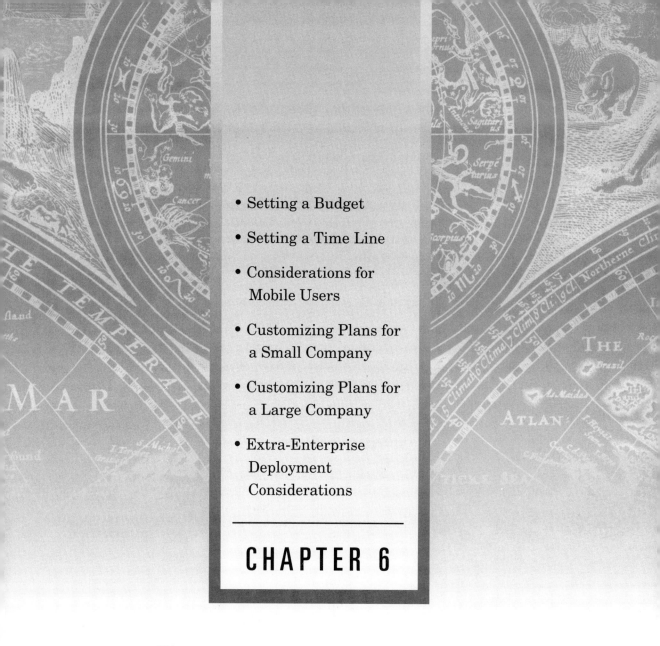

- Setting a Budget

- Setting a Time Line

- Considerations for Mobile Users

- Customizing Plans for a Small Company

- Customizing Plans for a Large Company

- Extra-Enterprise Deployment Considerations

CHAPTER 6

Customizing Your Deployment Plan

Chapter 5, "Building a Deployment Plan," presents the concepts and steps of a typical Notes deployment plan. Because every Notes installation is unique, you should expect to customize your deployment plan. You need to customize your deployment plan if your organization is rolling out more than one type of application or serving more than one type of user. For example, you may be supporting both headquarters users and mobile users, and you may be developing applications for IBM's Notes network or CompuServe Enterprise Connect for Notes. Consult each of the relevant sections of this chapter and modify the deployment plan for each class of application and user that you are going to support.

In this chapter, you learn how to customize a deployment plan for your particular situation. You learn how to

- Generate initial estimates for a schedule and budget
- Plan for mobile users
- Customize a deployment for small organizations
- Customize a deployment for large organizations
- Extend Notes beyond your organization, using services such as CompuServe Enterprise Connect for Notes or the IBM Notes network

SETTING A BUDGET

First, a disclaimer. These are guidelines only; your mileage may vary. The hardest question to answer (impossible, actually) without some information about your particular organization is, "How much will Notes cost?" The real costs aren't in software licenses but in support, training, and application development. How do you plan and budget ahead of time for a product as complex as Notes? Start with an initial guess and refine it constantly.

DETERMINING HARDWARE AND SOFTWARE COSTS

The first step in determining your budget is to add up your hardware and software costs. These should be fairly straightforward to determine (see Chapter 7, "Determining Hardware and Software Needs," for details). Determining your personnel costs is a bit more difficult.

DETERMINING PERSONNEL COSTS

Every organization with which this author works wants to know, "How many people will we need?" This question is particularly difficult to answer with Notes, because Notes isn't an application that you just install and start using. Each organization will develop its own applications that run on top of Notes. The number of support people needed is determined by the type of applications being developed, the quality of your development, and the amount of planning you put into your Notes network (see Chapter 5 for details). Organizations do need to have some initial personnel estimates to work with, and this section is meant to help you generate those estimates. If your first guess is within 25 percent, feel lucky.

DETERMINING THE NUMBER OF ADMINISTRATORS

The numbers that we present in this section are based on experience with Notes Release 3.x. Notes Release 4.0 contains features that reduce the cost associated with administering Notes. Also, as NotesView and its companion products become widespread, administrators should be able to handle more users. Therefore, consider the numbers in this section a minimum base for the number of users per administrator. Unless you have a very special situation, the estimates in this section should result in you overestimating the number of administrators you need. If you use these numbers in your budgeting, you should have a safe budget for your overall deployment.

There is a wide variety across organizations in the number of users that a Notes administrator supports. The numbers range from one administrator per two hundred users up to one administrator per one thousand users. In a few cases, organizations have only one administrator per two or three thousand users (in these organizations, Notes isn't being used effectively, or most of the work is being offloaded onto other departments). There is more than a 10 to 1 variance from the lowest to the highest number of users that an administrator can support. Why would that be? First, an administrator's job definition varies from one organization to the next. "Administrator" doesn't mean the same thing from one corporation to another. In some corporations, a single administrator handles everything (help desk, installation, troubleshooting, application development, etc.); in other organizations, administrators are specialized. Some administrators work 80 hours a week, throwing off the numbers somewhat. Consider the number of variables involved in estimating the number of users that your administrators can support:

- ◆ The number of people at your main headquarters
- ◆ The number of large (greater than 35 people) remote offices
- ◆ The number of small remote offices
- ◆ The number of foreign offices
- ◆ The number of traveling or mobile users that you need to support
- ◆ The complexity of the applications that you are going to develop
- ◆ The number of add-on products and gateways that you need to support
- ◆ The skill level of your administrators

Given the number of variables involved, how do you arrive at an estimate for your organization? To arrive at a rough estimate, just calculate the number of users you need to support in each of the following categories, estimate the number of administrators needed to support each category, and add up the total number of administrators. You should have a fair estimate of the numbers of administrators and support personnel that you will need.

◆ Main campus: One administrator per 500 users.

◆ Small remote offices (fewer than 35 people): One administrator per 200 users.

◆ Large remote offices: One administrator per 300 users.

◆ Mobile users: One administrator per 200 users.

Foreign offices should be handled as a main campus or remote office, depending on the size of the international office.

Add one remote-site coordinator for each remote office. A remote-site coordinator must be capable of rebooting the server, but doesn't need to be a fully trained administrator.

Complex applications and additional add-on products require more administrators. Estimating the additional effort required to administer complex applications and additional add-on products isn't possible in the general case. During the pilot, you need to measure how many hours are going into administering your applications and add-on products, and revise your cost estimates accordingly.

Poorly trained administrators not only make maintaining your Notes network more expensive, they also increase the number of user complaints. In the extreme, they can give your entire Notes project a bad reputation before you even get to the first production installation.

Add up the number of administrators for each category and use that as your initial estimate. Don't forget to refine this estimate based on your experience during the initial rollout and pilot application. Note also that these numbers assume that you have properly trained administrators and that you are rolling out Notes on tested, stable hardware and software configurations for both your server and desktop.

DETERMINING THE NUMBER OF APPLICATION DEVELOPERS

The next estimate to tackle is the number of application developers you will need. The number of application developers varies even more than the number of administrators. The factors that affect the number of developers are

◆ The number of applications being developed by users.

There are two extremes an organization can adopt when developing Notes applications: the IS staff develops and controls all applications; or users are free to develop and use their own applications with no restrictions. Most organizations end up somewhere in the middle. Your corporate culture will have a significant impact on your approach. The author recommends having the IS staff control all mission-critical applications and review all other non-discussion-database applications. You should also consider supplying application templates for use by various departments. If IS will develop most applications, plan for three to five Notes developers. If users will develop most applications, plan for $\frac{1}{2}$ to two application developers.

◆ The number of applications you will develop.

The number of application developers is also dependent on the number and complexity of the applications that you plan to roll out. If your applications will have custom links to other systems, the number of developers needed will rise dramatically. If your applications require the use of non-Notes development tools, the number of developers needed will rise.

◆ The skill level of your support staff.

Notes application developers can easily get drawn into ongoing support. A skilled support staff that has a good relationship with the development staff can play an important role in minimizing the number of developers needed.

◆ The skill level of your developers.

Empirical studies have shown that the productivity of application developers can vary by more than an order of magnitude from a poor application developer to an excellent application developer. Hiring well is extremely important, but training always helps. Proper training is essential in holding down the number of application developers that you need.

The number of developers varies widely from one organization to the next, with no real rhyme or reason. The number of users per application developer varies from 100 to over 2,000, with the factors enumerated above being the key variables.

SETTING A TIME LINE

One of the first activities your deployment team should complete is to develop an initial time line for the project. Your key deliverables on the time line should revolve around something of value to the corporation, such as a usable mini-application or even e-mail. Be sure to set deadlines for the choice for your first deliverable, the pilot phase for your first application, and your first production use of an application. Your time line should also include other events that lead up to these deadlines. For example, you should include the expected arrival date for all your hardware and software. Chapter 7 recommends buying name-brand hardware. Because there is often a backlog for servers and popular desktops, determining your hardware and software needs early and placing orders helps eliminate the small disasters that can kill a Notes deployment. You also should include your training schedule in your time line. Publishing a time line that includes a training schedule helps to involve the rest of the corporation. It's a way to get other departments involved in planning before you need to commit to signing contract trainers.

CONSIDERATIONS FOR MOBILE USERS

Mobile users are primarily laptop users who connect to your headquarters offices via dial-up. Special considerations for mobile users include training, the timing of your installation, distributing and updating large databases, security, and Name and Address Book management.

Training is particularly important for mobile users. Mobile users must perform some tasks that are normally performed by an administrator. These tasks include creating replica databases and managing a Personal Address Book. Developing a training schedule for your mobile users is complicated by the fact that they aren't often at headquarters. Even when they are at headquarters, it's difficult to know in advance what their schedule is going to be. It may not be possible to have all mobile users attend sit-down training sessions. When developing training for mobile users, consider computer-based training and customized screen cams (video recordings). Try to provide some personal introduction to Notes for all mobile users, even if they are unable to attend a regularly scheduled Notes training.

Note

One way to train remote users is to distribute custom screen cams. ScreenCam is a Lotus product that you can use to create movies (including voiceover) to explain a computer product. Use this technology to create introductory training for your organization's applications.

Timing the Notes installation for a mobile user is also difficult. You need to pick a time when you know he is going to be at headquarters. The user must be able to do without his computer for an hour so that you can install and test Notes. You should coordinate the installation of Notes with end user training. If the mobile user can't attend a training session, schedule the installation while he is at lunch or in a long meeting.

Mobile users also have the highest rate of support problems due to the use of modems, a particularly troubling spot in many organizations. You should spend extra time testing the hardware and software combinations used by your mobile users. You should have access during platform testing to each type of laptop and modem used by your mobile users.

Mobile users often need off-hours support. Make sure that someone from the support team is available 24 hours a day to handle emergencies. You should involve the support staff in planning for this type of support.

The application developers and administrators must pay particular attention to the applications used by mobile users. Of particular concern are large databases or databases requiring data to be updated more than twice a day. Because your mobile users are dialing in, the cost of distributing large amounts of data is greater than it is for headquarters users. Not only do you have the connection charge, which is the predominant cost, but you also have the cost of maintaining the extra disk space for each user. There may be additional costs involved with upgrading laptops to support very large databases. Notes Release 4 comes with several features to simplify developing applications for mobile users. These features include field-level replication and passthru. *Field-level replication* reduces the cost of updating large documents by replicating only the individual fields that have changed. Notes *passthru* lets you use Notes as the entry point into your Notes network, eliminating the need to set up special servers for mobile users or have modems and phone connections for each server. Figure 6.1 shows a mobile user using passthru.

Figure 6.1.
Notes passthru enables
mobile users to connect
to Notes servers on an
internal network. Non-
Notes servers can't be
accessed by using
passthru.

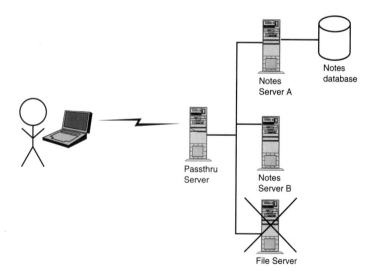

Dial-in users can dial in to a Notes server and access some or all of the Notes servers on the LAN. Each passthru server can be configured to allow or deny passthru connections to any other server on the network. In addition, each server can be configured to accept or reject passthru connections.

Mobile users must be concerned about the security of data on their laptops. There has been more than one case when laptops have been stolen by competitors. You can't stop theft, but Notes does allow you to prevent anyone from reading the data in your Notes databases. Notes enables you to encrypt all the databases on a laptop. Notes encryption is strong enough to force thieves to spend several days breaking the code. There is one drawback to this approach. If the laptop user ever loses his user ID file, which was used to encrypt all the data on his laptop, you may have to rebuild all the databases on the laptop. Keeping a backup copy of ID files will prevent this situation only if you make sure to keep those backups up to date.

The real support problems for most mobile users concern the Name and Address Book. Mobile users should have access to the person documents contained in the Public Address Book. One straightforward way to accomplish this objective is to have mobile users replicate the corporate Name and Address Book. Another (not exclusive) method is to have mobile users manage person documents in their own Personal Address Books. Replicating the corporate Name and Address Book often isn't practical because of the file size and cost involved. I don't recommend having mobile users replicate the Public Address Book. Excluding this option means that the mobile user needs to type the full name and address into the To: field, or maintain person documents in his or her Personal Address Book.

Actually, a third option is available to handle the problem of mail addressing for mobile users, but this method requires some planning. You can create a new database that includes only person documents. Have mobile users replicate this database and specify it as a secondary address book. Make sure that the database inherits its design from the Public Address Book template, but isn't a replica of the Public Address Book. You need to have some way of automatically updating this database with changes to person documents in the Public Address Book. The DB/Utilities package from DSSI (818-991-0200) contains utilities that can accomplish this task.

If any of your applications use ReaderNames fields to control replication, mobile users need to create server group documents in the Personal Address Book. The most common group documents are LocalDomainServers and OtherDomainServers. When sending mail, Notes uses connection and location documents in the Personal Address Book to determine the proper routing path. Even if you use user profiles to generate the initial connection and location documents in Personal Address Books, you should plan on helping mobile users to modify or add connection and location documents as they travel to new locations.

You also need to develop special installation scripts to handle the specialized Name and Address Book needs of mobile users. Some mobile users will want a local replica of the corporate Name and Address Book. This requires you to set up two Name and Address Books on the laptop. This goal is accomplished by setting the NOTES.INI Names parameter. The Names entry should be as follows:

```
Names=userid,names,corpname.nsf
```

where *corpname.nsf* is the name of the database containing person documents from the corporate Public Address Book.

The Personal Address Book should be used as the primary address book. The primary address book is the first one listed in the Names parameter. Using the Personal Address Book as the primary address book saves memory.

When configuring passthru servers for mobile users, plan for peak usage. It won't take very many busy signals to drive your mobile users to some other solution. Having users encounter a few busy signals may not sound so bad to an administrator, and it does save a bit on modem costs, but the lost productivity outweighs any savings. Because reliable access to headquarters information is very important, be sure to buy enough modems to handle more than your peak number of planned dial-in users. The bottom line is that you need to have enough phone lines to handle your peak volume. Volume depends on the number of mobile users, the average length of the calls, the frequency of calls (once a day, once an hour, and so on), and the reliability of the connections (some international calls have very poor reliability). Some organizations need only two modems, but most should consider an 8- or 16-multi-port card such as the one built by Digiboard. For complete details on supporting mobile users, see Chapter 19, "Supporting Dial-Up Users." Here we have only pointed out those issues that you need to take into consideration when developing your deployment plan.

Customizing Plans for a Small Company

Any company with 20 to 500 Notes licenses is considered a small Notes installation. While 500 licenses may seem to be a rather large cutoff, the tasks and the number of people involved don't vary much between 20 and 500 users. We refer to installations with fewer than 20 licenses as *micro installations*. Micro installations are usually handled by a single person over one or two weeks.

Small companies often choose Notes because it can fill many application slots and has the ability to grow with the business. For example, Notes can be used as a message center, as a fax server, for e-mail, and so on. Small companies operate under constraints that large organizations don't have. Primarily, small companies have a concern about the availability of skilled personnel to support Notes. The Notes administrator in a small company must be a true jack-of-all-trades.

Small companies can't justify the expense of a full-time administrator. Notes is a rather large product encompassing replication, database design, application development, network protocols, remote-site management, mobile-user support, and military-level security. Packing all the information needed to support all aspects of Notes into one or two heads is a daunting task and requires some special planning.

Steps must be taken to minimize the amount of information that the support staff must master. Large organizations are concerned about this, but small companies must make this priority number one.

When deploying Notes in a small organization, the project staff is faced with constant temptation. There is always considerable pressure to take the easy route, the quick route. The administrator in a small organization may not have enough information to lobby effectively for some planning time. In this section, we show you where it is okay to take the easy route and where you need to bite the bullet, do the planning, and take a little extra time up front to avoid problems later.

So let's go through our standard deployment plan step by step and discuss the ways a small enterprise will customize this deployment plan.

STEP 1: FORM A PROJECT TEAM

Whereas in a large organization you have a support team of eight to ten people, a small company's project team may consist of a single administrator. It isn't uncommon (although not recommended) to have a single person as your system administrator, application developer, and support engineer. People deploying Notes within a small organization have to wear more hats than people deploying Notes in a large organization.

STEP 2: ASSESS THE ENTERPRISE

Assessing the enterprise within a small organization may sound less daunting than assessing the enterprise within a large organization. However, the lack of time and resources constrains the amount of detailed work that a small company is able to do. Hopefully, your small organization has only one operating system installed (if any). This minimizes the number of variables that you need to deal with. It is still cost-effective to have a temporary worker go to each desktop and confirm the hardware and software installed.

Follow the guidelines in Chapter 5 when assessing the cultural readiness and physical readiness of your small organization.

STEP 3: DEFINE THE SCOPE OF YOUR DEPLOYMENT

Small organizations often plan from the start to deploy Notes across the entire enterprise. Even if this case isn't true for you, determining the geographic and organizational scope of your Notes deployment should be straightforward. In addition, it's fairly easy to estimate the number of users you are likely to have six months, one year, and two years into the future. You should plan to place everyone in your company on Notes in a matter of months. The only difficult estimate for a small company is the number of applications to be developed over the first year.

Step 4: Design Your Notes Network

The design stage is where a small company will make or break their Notes deployment. If you do a good job of designing your Notes network, your support costs stay affordable. If you do a poor job, your support costs blossom out of control.

Your primary consideration should be to minimize the number of network protocols and operating systems. One is ideal; two should be the absolute maximum for a small organization. Attempting to force all the knowledge needed to adequately support more than one protocol or more than one desktop operating system into the head of a single person is a recipe for disaster. When you add responsibilities for support and application development, this is also a recipe for burnout. Your Notes administrator is an expensive asset to replace midway through a Notes deployment. If your small organization is deploying its first client/server applications, you have a wonderful opportunity to standardize on a single operating system and network protocol, typically TCP/IP. If you already have more than one network installed, you should make a case for standardizing the hardware and software throughout your organization, if at all possible. If you must support multiple protocols or operating systems, spend time testing the configurations you will support and developing standard operating procedures for each platform. As a minimum, develop standard procedures for installation and updates.

One area where it is tempting for a small company to cut corners is in developing naming schemes. Because you are likely to have only a few servers and one network, the effort required to recover from mistakes is small. On the other hand, because you only have a few servers and one network, it shouldn't take very long to write down some naming guidelines. Even if you can get away with not planning your network names, you should still plan the names of each of your servers, especially if you are using TCP/IP (administration is easier if the TCP/IP server name and the Notes server name are identical).

When devising a naming scheme for a small company, you may be tempted to skip the hassle of coming up with a hierarchical naming scheme. The reasons for a small company to use hierarchical naming are less compelling than for a large company. One of the main advantages of hierarchical naming—resolving ambiguity in mail routing—isn't a problem for small organizations. Nevertheless, you should use hierarchical naming. After all, if your organization grows, mail routing will become a problem. More importantly, if you want to extend Notes beyond your organization, odds are that you will have to use hierarchical naming to do so. Starting from scratch with hierarchical naming avoids a costly and expensive conversion later. In the end, the primary reason you should use hierarchical naming is that Notes is a system designed to use hierarchical naming. If you use flat naming, over time your administration costs will rise and the number of features available to you will decrease.

STEP 5: CREATE A NOTES SUPPORT ORGANIZATION

Creating a Notes support organization typically isn't a very difficult task within a small organization. The key decision is whether to train or hire Notes skill. If you decide to train in-house personnel, having a consultant help out part-time during the initial deployment can be cost-effective even for small businesses.

STEP 6: DEVELOP STANDARD OPERATING PROCEDURES

Small organizations can manage with few standard operating procedures (SOPs). When a single person is responsible for developing and supporting all Notes applications, communication among the support staff becomes a moot point. If you are going to involve your users in the development of Notes applications, write a one- or two-page "cheat sheet" specifying colors, fonts, and common field names. The primary benefit of SOPs to small organizations is to minimize the impact of losing key personnel. If your administrator leaves, you can continue to operate by using the SOPs. However, in terms of having a successful rollout, defining your standard operating procedures before the deployment of your first production application is less critical in a small organization than in a large organization.

STEP 7: BUILD A PILOT APPLICATION

The criteria for selecting a pilot application and first production applications are no different for a small organization than for a large organization. You still need to choose an application that's important to the business, but not time-critical to the business. You still need to meet any internal return-on-investment guidelines. You need to push hard to get your application deployed within the first three to six months of your Notes project.

Not all companies should start with custom-developed applications. Some organizations can use off-the-shelf applications; others can implement e-mail as the first piece of functionality. Your organization may not need to start with a full-fledged application.

STEP 8: IMPLEMENTATION AND TRAINING

Don't skimp on the training. Lack of training simply extends the learning curve for Notes. If you have goals for your Notes deployment, you need to train your end users and your administrators so that they can be productive as soon as possible.

Consultants can be cost-effective during the learning phase. Although Notes consultants are typically some of the highest-paid consultants, having one work closely with your IS staff during the initial planning stages and then again during the initial development of your applications can be a cost-effective way to train your own staff and teach them a few of the tips and tricks.

CUSTOMIZING PLANS FOR A LARGE COMPANY

The biggest issue facing a large organization is the culture within that organization. Will Notes be accepted? Will users try to control information rather than share information? Running a distant second is the difficulty of coordinating the Notes rollout. Let's examine each step in a deployment plan and see how these issues affect your planning.

STEP 1: FORM A PROJECT TEAM

Your primary Notes team should have eight to twelve members, with each of the following key roles assigned to a member:

- Notes evangelist
- Project manager
- Notes administrator
- Support engineer
- Network administrator
- End user representative
- Operations representative
- Database manager (preferably the manager for the pilot database)
- Application developer
- Trainer
- Help desk representative
- Remote-site coordinator (at least one should be involved)

Chapter 8, "Preparing Your Organization," discusses each of these roles in detail.

The Notes evangelist plays a critical role in a large organization rollout. The technical issues won't kill your Notes rollout; cultural and organizational issues are far more likely to derail Notes. Notes changes the working relationships and information flow within an organization. Resistance both before and after a Notes installation should be expected. Enthusiasm, information, and close contact with the project team will help overcome this resistance.

The primary job of the Notes evangelist is communicating the advantages of Notes, generating enthusiasm for Notes, and generating some demand for Notes. The Notes evangelist adds a sense of urgency within the organization. The Notes evangelist helps deal with the cultural and people issues that arise during a Notes deployment.

A large organization will have more specialization among team members. While a small organization may have one person covering both the administrator and support engineer roles, a large organization will have multiple support engineers.

The administrative and support members selected for your core project team are likely to become team leaders in the later phases of your Notes deployment. They will be the ones in your organization with the most expertise in implementing and supporting Notes. During the rollout phases of your deployment, they will have to take on the role of training and leading the teams tasked with installing Notes throughout your organization. Ideally, the administrators and support personnel should have a combination of technical and supervisory experience. Choose these roles carefully. Your core project team should be the team that will continue to provide ongoing support after your initial rollout phases.

The project team for a large organization can grow quite large when all decision makers and implementers are included. When your project team grows beyond ten people, consider splitting into multiple teams during the deployment of Notes. Split the team into a management team and a technical team. The following sections discuss each of these teams individually.

MANAGEMENT TEAM

The management team is formed by key personnel from participating business units and the IS staff. The management team is responsible for

◆ All budgetary decisions regarding the Notes deployment

◆ Determining the initial application to develop

◆ The internal "marketing" of Notes

◆ Coordinating all your Notes license purchases to take advantage of volume discounts

You should also have someone with some visibility within your organization on the Notes management team to sponsor an internal Notes newsletter. A dedicated newsletter is a great way to distribute information about the progress of the Notes deployment. In addition, a member of the management team should be assigned as a sponsor or Notes "coach" to each business unit participating in the initial deployment of Notes.

TECHNICAL TEAM

The technical team is responsible for providing input and making recommendations to the management team. The technical team's primary responsibility is setting up the architecture and designing the Notes network. The technical team also recommends all hardware and software platforms.

Step 2: Assess the Enterprise

Assessing the readiness of a large organization requires careful planning and timing. The hardware and network(s) in most large organizations are in a state of constant change. You need to coordinate your assessment of the installed hardware and software with the planned upgrade and installation of Notes in each business unit. Don't attempt to assess the complete installation for your entire organization and then install Notes one business unit at a time. By the time you want to install Notes, the installed network and workstations will have changed, requiring you to repeat the physical assessment step. Assess the network and workstations one business unit at a time (assuming that you are installing one business unit at a time).

When assessing the cultural readiness of a large organization to receive Notes, you need to plan for the expected changes that Notes typically brings to an organization. Installing Notes will result in the development of new sources of information within your corporation and make information more accessible in general.

You need to conduct interviews to determine the flow of information within your organization. You need to answer questions such as these:

- Is information tightly controlled?
- Is information used as a weapon?
- Where is information generated?
- What external information sources does your organization use?

Keep in mind that behavioral changes certainly won't occur overnight. If your pilot application requires a high degree of cooperation among users to succeed, make sure that the pilot group has a history of teamwork.

Step 3: Define the Scope of Your Deployment

While Notes often is purchased initially by a single business unit, its true value is when it is adopted by an entire enterprise. Although you probably won't have a commitment for an enterprise-wide deployment at the very beginning of your Notes deployment, you need to plan for radical growth in both the number of users and the number of applications that you need to support. One of the primary difficulties large organizations face is rolling out Notes fast enough to satisfy business demand, while still providing adequate support to continue to generate successes and enthusiasm. When charting the geographic and organizational scope of your Notes deployment, plan big. If your organization is international, plan to support international organizations and contact them early in your planning to see if there is any initial interest. Contact other divisions and departments early.

STEP 4: DESIGN YOUR NOTES NETWORK

What is true for a small organization in this case is also true for a large organization. That is, the fewer the network protocols and the fewer the operating systems, the better. A large organization is more likely to be constrained by an installed base or intransigent business units than is a small organization. A reasonable goal for most large organizations is two network protocols, two desktop operating systems, and two server platforms. Of course, you need to staff your support organization from the beginning with the expectation in mind that you will have multiple protocols and multiple operating systems running in multiple geographic locations.

You should at least gain some control over the configurations you will support by specifying a minimum configuration for each of your operating systems for desktops and servers. For example, if on the desktop you are supporting Macintosh and Windows, you should specify the minimum CPU, memory, and disk space required for both Mac and Windows. You should enforce your configuration restrictions by simply not installing Notes on deficient workstations.

When designing naming conventions for users and servers, a large organization should use hierarchical naming.

Release
4.0

Tip

If you are upgrading from Notes Release 3.x to 4.x, now is a good time to switch your organization from flat to hierarchical naming. Lotus ships an application designed to ease the transition. Detailed steps on switching to hierarchical naming are in Chapter 18, "Administering Notes Security."

When creating domains, a large organization should create one domain for production use, at least one domain for developers to use, at least one domain for testing, and one domain for external communications—a minimum of four domains. You should create a developer domain only if you have a central development staff and the applications that you develop require changes to the Public Address Book. In this case, providing a developer domain enables the developers to play with the Public Address Book without endangering the production network. Some organizations can use the development domain as the test domain also. You can leave this decision up to the application developers. You should add more domains only if forced by limitations of the Notes Name and Address Book, or by test applications running on a service provider, such as CompuServe Enterprise Connect for Lotus Notes or IBM's Notes network.

The maximum size of a Name and Address Book is around 10,000 users. If you expect a domain to grow beyond 50,000 users, plan from the outset to have two domains. This scheme avoids changing the domain of thousands of users who have been certified already and are using Notes. Don't create multiple domains simply to have distributed management of the Name and Address Book.

Don't add extra domains simply to accommodate international users. Because one of the main goals of Notes is to break down the barriers of time and space, creating separate domains for your geographically dispersed users violates one of the main reasons to install Notes in the first place.

Large organizations need to pay particular attention to the strategy for remote access. You should weigh WAN (wide area network) costs against the costs of calling in over regular phone lines. WAN alternatives to consider include leased lines (T1, T3, fractional T1) and switched ISDN. You should

◆ Calculate the number of hours of connect time your users will need, and compare it to the cost of placing an extra server at a remote site

◆ Consider the performance remote users will get by dialing into a central site

For additional information, see Chapter 19.

One key element of the Notes deployment plan for a large organization is e-mail gateways. Nearly every large organization today has installed some e-mail program. When installing Notes, you need to choose an e-mail system. Even if you don't want to use Notes e-mail, you need to integrate Notes e-mail with whatever e-mail systems you currently use. This fact requires you to implement a gateway that supports directory synchronization (*directory synchronization* is the process of updating address books). You must integrate the e-mail system in use at your company with Notes to take advantage of any messaging capabilities in your Notes applications. Without messaging capability, you may as well not implement Notes at all.

Lobby hard to reconcile users to one mail system. Supporting multiple e-mail packages requires increased administrative effort. Migrating to one e-mail system lowers costs and eliminates compatability problems for things like graphics, colors, and fonts. You should never move to a system where users have more than one "in box," although you can survive (with headaches) with different users having different e-mail systems.

STEP 5: CREATE A NOTES SUPPORT ORGANIZATION

As discussed under step 1, your core Notes team should become your core Notes support organization. However, when you are staffing up for your support group within a large organization, you need to take into account the need to support a large number of new users during the rollout phases. You may need to assign extra personnel to the support team during the rollout. When the rollout begins to wind down, these people can return to their regular jobs (the rollout can take as long as a year).

STEP 6: DEVELOP STANDARD OPERATING PROCEDURES

Although it is tempting within many large organizations to develop very large guidelines and booklets, you should avoid overcontrol of the Notes environment. But you definitely need to develop standard operating procedures (SOPs) for these phases:

- ◆ The rollout
- ◆ The installation of Notes
- ◆ Application development
- ◆ Changing applications
- ◆ Changing server configurations
- ◆ Escalating problems

Keep your SOPs brief and to the point. Your deliverables should be detailed, step-by-step guides for each procedure, no more than five to ten pages in length. You should have a "Getting Started" guide for users that answers, within the context of your own organization, common questions such as, "Who do I contact if I need a new user ID?" The "Getting Started" guide should be published as a Notes database. You should have a guide for administrators describing the tasks required for each administrator's job, along with standard operating procedures for each of the tasks outlined in Part IV of this book, "Administering Notes." These tasks include maintaining a Notes server, maintaining Notes security, and maintaining Notes databases.

STEP 7: BUILD YOUR APPLICATIONS

If your large organization has familiarity with client/server development, you are well-suited to begin development of Notes applications. Your IS staff can probably be trained quickly, using a combination of formal and on-the-job training. If not, consider bringing in consultants to help your IS staff. Consultants can show you the tricks not available in any training and help you avoid costly mistakes. There are good books available on developing Notes applications, but make sure that your developers have at least one morning of formal training before developing the pilot application.

STEP 8: IMPLEMENTATION AND TRAINING

Here is where the sheer number of users in a large organization begins to affect the scale of activities of the deployment plan. You should plan for multiple rollout stages, the first being a pilot implementation of your first application. Seek to have your pilot application up and running within six months from the formation of your project team. If you're dealing with an application consultant who can't commit to having the first application up in six months, you are probably dealing with someone who isn't comfortable with rapid-application-development methodologies.

Following the pilot, you go into phase one production, where you attempt to add approximately 100 users per week. Of course, you should only roll out Notes to users who have something to do with Notes. If you don't have applications for users, scale back the pace of activity. If you are implementing Notes e-mail across your organization, plan on installing Notes on every desktop even if no other applications are needed for that user. The purpose of your phase one production should be to test your Notes infrastructure, so choose applications that have a broad audience. You need to generate enough load on your servers and enough questions for your support staff that you can truly shake out the last few bugs that may have made it through your pilot implementation.

Phases two and three are when you roll out Notes to the entire organization. We split the remaining rollout into two phases to emphasize the importance of continually gathering feedback and updating your procedures. In phase two production, you attempt to add up to 150 users per week. In this stage, you definitely need multiple implementation teams, multiple training rooms, and multiple project managers coordinating their activities. In phase three production, you add several hundred users per week across wide geographic zones, including international users, mobile users, small remote offices, and the like.

Remember that the point of a phased implementation is to get feedback as quickly as possible. Don't forget at the end of each phase to pause and analyze what went well and what went wrong, and incorporate this feedback into the planning of your next phase. In addition to reviewing the experiences of the implementation team, you should seek feedback from new users during that phase, as well as from users who have been using Notes for some time. You should use a variety of techniques, including interviews, questionnaires, and Notes discussion databases, to gather feedback.

Notes success stories can have a way of spreading through the organization on their own. You can get a tremendous amount of enthusiasm going within business units before they even have Notes installed. At this point, demand can often outstrip your IS ability to respond. In order to keep business units in line and retain the advantages of a coordinated rollout, you should communicate to all business units the advantages of waiting for the "officially blessed" Notes rollout. Most will be satisfied when they understand the dollars that they will save just on Notes licenses by going with volume purchases. However, you can offer other goodies as entice-ments for Notes business units to wait their turn, including getting a personal Notes helper to help them plan their Notes applications. The fact that your feedback will help them avoid costly mistakes may be enough to help them wait. And, as a last resort, you can consider moving them up on the implementation schedule. Of course, you will be constrained by the fact that every time you move someone up, someone else has to fall back. Rescheduling may become commonplace. In some organiza-tions, it won't cause any problems; in others, it can lead to fighting. So take into consideration your own culture and plan accordingly.

EXTRA-ENTERPRISE DEPLOYMENT CONSIDERATIONS

Extra-enterprise applications include all applications to be used by many compa-nies, not just your company or a few partner companies. You may be deploying your extra-enterprise applications over the Internet, or use one of the services such as CompuServe Enterprise Connect, IBM's Notes network, or WorldCom.

At the time of this writing, CompuServe Enterprise Connect and WorldCom had been in business for two years, and IBM was launching a service. These companies are offering services, not products. The recent surge of Lotus Notes and the World Wide Web have brought back the old idea of *timesharing*—renting time on a computer, CompuServe's original business more than 15 years ago. These new services also handle facilities management and security, major concerns for extra-enterprise applications. CompuServe can bill users of your database for the time they spend online. The use of these services is driven by cost and security concerns.

The bulk of extra-enterprise applications fall into one of four categories:

- ◆ Multi-enterprise collaboration.

  Notes technology helps you rapidly form teams consisting of people from multiple organizations. Notes is the glue that holds these teams together.
- ◆ Disseminate information to suppliers, distributors, and customers.

  Notes is a good vehicle for circulating a variety of types of information, including product information, videos, and brochures.
- ◆ Publishing news and magazines.

  Notes' built-in search engines make it particularly useful for scanning, searching, and clipping news. More and more news organizations are offering their information in Notes format, typically selling it through one or more of the services.

◆ Electronic commerce.

With its digital signatures and authentication technologies, Notes is a good platform for electronic commerce. Make sure that your service provider can handle a variety of billing arrangements to provide you with the flexibility to experiment.

You can follow a modified version of the standard deployment plan when implementing extra-enterprise solutions. The following sections describe each step in detail.

Step 1: Form a Project Team

Several key issues arise when staffing for extra-enterprise applications. Customers using your applications form impressions of your company based on those applications. Any application aimed at customers should be considered part of the marketing message your company sends, even if customers aren't paying to access your Notes application. All your extra-enterprise applications should be consistent with the marketing message and materials that your company distributes through other channels. Consider whether you really even want your IS staff to develop marketing materials. On the other hand, having your marketers develop software isn't necessarily a good solution.

When staffing a project team for extra-enterprise applications, include members from your marketing and PR staffs. The team for an extra-enterprise application should be considerably more interdisciplinary than for other Notes rollouts. Content and presentation become much more important.

Just as most firms hire an agency to handle their advertising, companies are now farming out the development of extra-enterprise applications. Most advertising firms have already added the ability to develop Web sites. Consulting companies specializing in extra-enterprise applications also are popping up. If you need help developing extra-enterprise applications, look for a firm that combines marketing and Notes experience when developing an application aimed at customers. For inter-business applications aimed at distributors and suppliers, look for a company combining business-to-business communication skill and Notes experience.

Step 2: Define the Scope of Your Deployment

You must determine a target audience or market. Only then can you determine the likely number of users and their location.

Step 3: Assess the Enterprise

You need to have a target audience and goal in mind before you can identify the "enterprise" to assess. You need to assess the willingness and capability of the

Release
4.0

application's target users (customers, partners, suppliers, etc.) to use Notes. A few organizations are in the position of being able to mandate the use of Notes for all external organizations that want access to data. You probably will need to survey potential users to determine whether Notes is the correct platform. The World Wide Web is an alternative for many extra-enterprise applications. You don't need to choose either Notes or the Web; you can develop a Notes application and link it to the Web for minimal cost, using off-the-shelf software from the Lotus InterNotes suite of products. The InterNotes Web Publisher from Lotus now ships free with every Notes server and can be used to publish Notes databases to the Web.

STEP 4: DESIGN YOUR NOTES NETWORK

Consider hosting all extra-enterprise applications on a service provider's computer. A service provider can buffer your network from direct contact with external networks. Service provider personnel will be more skilled than your staff at handling security because they work with extra-enterprise applications daily. Service providers also can provide generic Notes support to organizations using your application, thus reducing the load on your support staff.

Be careful in naming groups and roles in your access control list in your extra-enterprise applications. Names that you choose must not conflict with names in your customer's Name and Address Book. To prevent conflict, you should prepend the name of your company or application to any name in the ACL. However, avoid names, such as "New England Marketing," that can give away your internal organizational chart.

STEP 5: CREATE A NOTES SUPPORT ORGANIZATION

The quality of support that you provide for your extra-enterprise application will affect your customers' impressions of your company. Even if you release a reliable, consistent application, you still have to provide excellent support for an extra-enterprise application. Even though all of your customers (presumably) have installed and are using Notes, you can't assume that they have any Notes expertise. Your support requirements will go well beyond supporting your application. You should be ready to field general Notes support questions. Questions such as "It's not replicating; what's wrong?" are common. The problem may have nothing to do with your application. Your application may just be the first place where the symptom appeared. Supporting Notes remotely can be an unexpected expense associated with extra-enterprise applications. Check with your service provider or consultant on the possibility of getting help with general Notes support. We don't recommend building an elaborate support structure to rival the Lotus support structure. Just make sure that your support staff will handle these questions with grace and forward the questions to the proper support channel.

Your extra-enterprise application should include a way to submit questions regarding usage and bugs. We recommend having a general-purpose Help! form that customers can use to compose questions and comments. The form should be routed automatically to your support staff. You should provide an immediate follow-up to all submitted questions. If you don't have an answer, give an expected time for getting back to the customer with an answer. Return a "thank you" for all comments.

In addition to requiring a higher level of support than may be needed in-house, there are additional challenges in administering an extra-enterprise application. Consider the case of undeliverable mail. Your Name and Address Book may have been corrupted. The customer's Name and Address Book may be wrong. One of the intermediate servers may not be functioning properly. It's often quite difficult to resolve this type of problem and requires cooperation over the phone between your administrator and your customer's administrator (not easy for international clients). Because your customer's administrators are at varying levels of skill and experience, the administrator that you select to support your extra-enterprise applications should be able to debug a Name and Address Book problem over the phone. The administrator you choose to support your extra-enterprise applications must be a good people person with an infinite amount of patience and, if applicable to your application, an ability to understand virtually every spoken language in the world.

Since you'll be using hierarchical naming in your application, you'll have to become familiar with cross-certifying servers. For details on cross-certifying servers, see Chapter 18.

You'll also want to provide a single external contact from your support organization to support all of the extra-enterprise applications that you deploy. You should require each of your end users to provide a single point of contact for dealing with usage and support problems.

STEP 6: DEVELOP STANDARD OPERATING PROCEDURES

Even if you don't enforce any restrictions on internal applications, you should develop and enforce standards for your extra-enterprise applications. You need to ensure consistency between your various extra-enterprise applications. Consistency includes the look and feel, button naming, colors, fonts, and so on.

Document and enforce a change procedure for making design updates to the application. You should clearly identify all sources of information for the application.

STEP 7: BUILD YOUR APPLICATIONS

Extra-enterprise applications differ technically from ordinary in-house applications. Your application development methodology, testing procedures, application design, security precautions, and performance goals are all affected.

RAPID-APPLICATION-DEVELOPMENT METHODOLOGY MAY NOT APPLY

The overriding key issue that you must consider when developing, deploying, and supporting an extra-enterprise application is that your users are external to your application. Most Notes application development follows a rapid-application-development methodology, where you work intensely with the targeted end users. This methodology may not be possible for an extra-enterprise application. In this case, a marketing vision will replace user feedback. The phased delivery recommended in Chapter 5 may not be applicable for your extra-enterprise application. Releasing a constant stream of upgrades to the public may cause confusion among your end users. Less frequent, major upgrades are more manageable in this environment. The fact that your users are customers can have a dramatic impact on the methodology you use to develop your applications.

HIGH RELIABILITY IS REQUIRED

Extra-enterprise applications require extra testing resources. Your applications must be highly reliable. Releasing buggy applications on a service like WorldCom or CompuServe Enterprise Connect can have a detrimental effect on your company's image. This is true whether the audience is customers, suppliers, distributors, or joint venture partners.

MULTIPLE DOMAINS

The primary technical difference between an in-house application and an extra-enterprise application is the proliferation of domains. Figure 6.2 shows the domains involved with a typical extra-enterprise application.

The service provider has a domain, the customer has external and internal domains, and you have internal and external domains, for a total of five domains. The number of domains affects the role of replication and mail routing, and requires a special test configuration. Create at least a three-domain test environment to do basic testing of your extra-enterprise applications. You can save yourself time by performing this testing before even placing an application on your service provider's host computer.

Figure 6.2.
Typical domains in
an extra-enterprise
application.

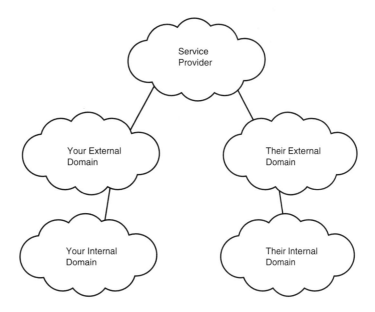

There are two strategies for tracking the full e-mail address of anyone submitting information to your database. You can have each user fill out a form the first time he submits information, include this information in the submission, and replicate submissions; or you can have all submissions mailed to a central database. Because many users won't know the complete mail address, we recommend mailing submissions to a central database. The Notes router automatically maintains the full e-mail address as the submission is routed through the network.

An extra-enterprise application typically includes five domains. Thus, replication goes through four hops to get from your input server to the customer server, introducing a delay that may not be acceptable for your application. Even if you dial up your service host on a regular basis, you don't have any control over how often your end users dial in. Therefore, you need to plan on handling cases with a two-day turnaround from the time you put data out on your system to the time it actually reaches an end user. This situation can happen when a user who dials in once a day connects to the service provider just before your data reaches that host. His server won't get that data until the next day when it dials in again. Then, at some point during that second day, the end user will check the data currently on his server. In the worst case, this can be a two-day turnaround.

If you have particularly urgent data, you'll have to use high-priority e-mail. This only works if your service provider will dial out to end users to deliver mail. In order to dial out, you need a phone number for each end user domain. This is problematic for publishing and electronic commerce applications, where you may not even know the identity of your customers. E-mail notifications work best for extra-enterprise collaborations. To avoid cluttering personal mailboxes, provide each end user domain with a mail-in database to receive e-mail notifications concerning your application.

MULTIPLE CLIENT PLATFORMS

You can't assume any restriction on the type of platforms that will be used to view your application. You must assume that every available Notes client will be used, and that users will have a variety of monitors, resolutions, and colors. At a minimum, you should test your application in each of the standard resolutions (VGA, SVGA, and 1280×1024) to ensure that the screens are at least intelligible. You'll have to stick to standard color choices if you want to have them supported across a wide range of platforms.

UNDERPOWERED SERVERS AND CLIENTS

Your application must perform acceptably on a minimally configured server and client. You can't assume that every end user domain will be using a high-powered server. If views take several minutes to open, users will stop using your application.

SLOW CONNECT SPEEDS

As of this writing, you can expect end users of your extra-enterprise applications to be using modems to access your service provider's host. Even at 28.8 kbps with field-level replication, you need to consider the amount of data that you change on a regular basis. You also should put in place special procedures to avoid massive updates to a database. Update fields instead of whole documents. If any of your users are still using Notes Release 3, you'll need to organize your application to use many small documents rather than one large one. This makes it easier to distribute changes to your data without having to replicate extremely large documents. Because of the slow connect speed, most users will access your data by replicating it to a server of their own rather than sitting online, running up access charges. Therefore, your applications should assume that users will be accessing replicated databases in a different domain.

NO DEFAULT ACL ENTRIES

When designing your access control list, don't assume any default entries in the Name and Address Book. You need to set up the default access to enable end users to access all features of your application. At the same time, you must prevent information from accidentally replicating between customers.

It's best to avoid relying on any particular groups when building extra-enterprise applications. Other organizations may not be happy about the need to maintain groups in their Public Address Book just for your application. Keep your extra-enterprise applications simple. Because you can't rely on any specific group being present in the Public Address Book, you can't rely on any entries in the default ACL. This situation forces you to change the default access from the typical no access to whatever is needed to run the application.

CUSTOMERS MAY REPLICATE WITH EACH OTHER

When your database is replicated around the world to many organizations, you run the risk that two companies will replicate directly with each other. When two companies, both with replicas of your database, replicate with each other, confidential information can leak from one customer to another, and they may not be aware of this problem until it's too late. This situation will reflect badly on your company, and could result in liability. If each company creates a replica of your database, when their servers call each other your database will be updated. This behavior may not be proper for your database. In fact, if this results in the sharing of confidential information between potential competitors, you may be getting a phone call that you definitely won't enjoy! Your database ACL should explicitly list the domains that can replicate the database. List your internal and external domains and the service provider domain. Your customers will want to replicate from their external domain to their internal domain. As you can't predict the names of these domains, you should provide details in the About and Using documents on adding entries to the ACL. Your default access should be set so that no information created at a customer site will replicate with any server other than your domains and the service provider's domain.

You need to use ReaderNames and AuthorNames fields to control access to documents. All documents composed and submitted by users should have a ReaderNames field. The ReaderNames field should include the person composing the document, the server name of the service provider's server, your external and internal servers, and your default extra-enterprise administrator group.

HIERARCHICAL NAMING

Your service provider almost certainly will require you to use hierarchical naming for all servers and administrators that will access the service provider's host. This requirement doesn't mean that you have to convert all your internal users to hierarchical naming; it simply means that you need to set up a hierarchically named external server for use with your service provider's host. You also may need to set up hierarchically named administrator accounts to directly access a service provider's host.

RESTRICTIONS ON THE USE OF AGENTS

A service provider may impose some restrictions on your Notes applications. You may not be allowed to use all the design features that Notes provides. For example, you may not be allowed to run agents, or doing so may incur an additional charge. Your end users may not be allowed to create agents. Any restrictions need to be described in the About document for your application.

USE THE NOTES INTERFACE ONLY

You should design your user interface using only the capabilities of the native Notes application builder. Building additional interfaces on top of your Notes database using Visual Basic, PowerBuilder, etc., while possible, is an additional administrative burden that isn't justifiable for most extra-enterprise applications. Some method of distributing and installing your application would need to be worked out. If you are going to develop an application using Visual Basic, PowerBuilder, or C, and you want to reach as wide an audience as possible, you'll have to provide that application under Mac, Windows, OS/2, and UNIX. Providing a consistent look and feel across all these platforms is something with which most corporate IS staffs are unfamiliar, and which they're ill-equipped to handle. The application developers developing your extra-enterprise applications need to be more creative in their use of the Notes interface elements. You should strive for a distinctive look and feel that separates your applications from the rest of the pack while still providing a consistent look and feel with your other marketing materials.

STEP 8: IMPLEMENTATION AND TRAINING

Your only training concern is that users know how to use your application. You can write very detailed help screens, but users probably won't read them. You need to spend some time when developing the application, making sure that everything in the interface is clear. No amount of help screens can make up for a poorly designed application. If you deploy a poorly designed extra-enterprise application, your support costs will escalate quickly.

A key part of implementing an extra-enterprise application is getting the word out. If you are providing customer support through Notes, mention this fact in your product literature. If you are selling information online, advertise. You should contact your public relations (PR) department for more ideas. If your company has a Web site, contact the team responsible for maintaining the site and have links to your Notes application added.

SUMMARY

In this chapter we have highlighted the key issues that you need to consider for each of several possible situations. Always follow the basic guidelines outlined in Chapter 5 when developing a deployment plan. However, you need to customize your deployment for each type of application and class of users for which you are developing. The customization can affect not only the deployment plan, but your application development methodologies, your standards and practices, the size of your rollout team, and the roles for the rollout project.

The remaining chapters in this part of the book provide the detail you need to execute the deployment plan. Chapter 7 provides more detail on determining your hardware and software needs. Chapter 8 shows you how to prepare your organization for Notes. Chapter 9 shows you how to design a reliable Notes network that minimizes support costs.

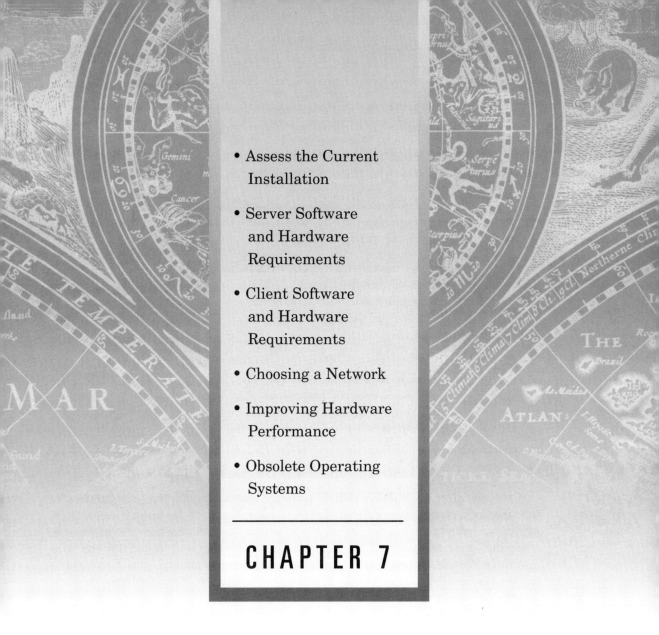

CHAPTER 7

Determining Hardware and Software Needs

You probably will need to upgrade your hardware and software before installing Notes in your organization. Determining your hardware and software needs can be a simple process. You need to assess your installed base, determine your requirements, and compute the difference. From there, you need to test your hardware/software choices (including the operating system and network software) and schedule the installation. This chapter helps you through this process by recommending minimum configurations for your desktop clients and servers and providing you with some rough formulas for determining the needs of your organization. In putting together your hardware and software configurations, keep in mind the following key ideas:

◆ Buy as much as you can afford.

◆ Under no circumstances should you skimp on the amount of memory.

◆ Buy a brand name. (The weird, crazy bugs that result from the purchase of cheaper hardware will drive your support staff crazy and will cost you money in the long run.)

Hardware and software costs can be daunting. They are easier to identify than the administrative and support costs associated with underpowered systems. You should follow the guidelines outlined here when developing your cost estimates and avoid trying to cut corners.

ASSESS THE CURRENT INSTALLATION

Before you can put together a list of hardware upgrade requirements, you need to know what has already been installed. The upgrade list is the difference between what you have and what you need. If you are in the enviable position of already knowing your current installation's hardware and software, congratulations! You are the exception rather than the rule. If you don't, you aren't alone. You need to develop a detailed list of all of your current hardware. That includes desktop machines, server machines, and network hardware.

For each desktop machine, you need to determine:

◆ Processor and speed

◆ Current operating system level

◆ Total disk space

◆ Free disk space

◆ Network card

◆ Type and revision level for any networking software

◆ Amount of memory

◆ Monitor type (VGA, SVGA, 14 inches, 15 inches)

- ◆ Word processor used
- ◆ Spreadsheet used
- ◆ Electronic mail program used
- ◆ Any graphics package used
- ◆ Modem speed
- ◆ Mouse

One easy way to collect this information is to develop a checklist that you can fill out for each desktop machine. See Figure 7.1 for a simple information sheet. This information sheet is available on the CD-ROM in the back of this book as SITEPREP.DOC (Word for Windows 6.0 format). I have found that it is relatively easy to train a temporary worker to go around to the machines and fill out the information sheets. This is a low-cost way of getting the most accurate data on your current installation.

Figure 7.1.
Fill in an information sheet for each worksta-tion that will get Notes.

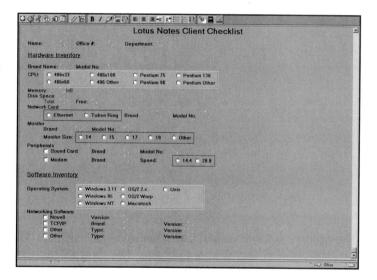

You also should fill in an information sheet for each file and print server. You'll need to have your administrators determine the software and hardware configuration of any routers and hubs on your network. You also should make sure that you have an up-to-date diagram of your network, including all LANS, bridges between these LANS, remote offices, and any leased lines or dial-in servers. For each workgroup to receive Notes, fill out a network information sheet. An example network information worksheet is available in ADMFORMS.NSF, which is on the CD-ROM included with this book.

Before you can determine the upgrade requirements for your organization, you need to determine the recommended configuration for Notes clients, Notes servers, and the network.

SERVER SOFTWARE AND HARDWARE REQUIREMENTS

Your server configurations largely determine the stability of your Notes network. Notes servers that are underpowered also seem to be plagued with strange errors. Because Notes networks have the potential to grow quickly, I recommend buying quality hardware for servers. You won't be wasting money; you'll be making an investment.

THE CHEAPEST NOTES SERVER

For companies that want the cheapest first step down the Notes path, I recommend the following minimum configuration for a Notes server. Normally, I recommend choosing an operating system and network protocol before sizing the hardware. For those on a severely limited budget, nothing beats a single OS/2 server. You retain maximum flexibility of third-party products and benefit from the competitive pricing of Intel-based hardware while retaining an easy growth path for future expansion. If you are going to install only a single server, don't install anything less than this configuration:

◆ Install OS/2 2.11 or OS/2 Warp.

◆ Install IBM TCP/IP.

◆ Use a quality network adapter—Ethernet or token ring.

◆ Install a minimum of 32 megabytes of memory.

◆ You should have two SCSI-2 drives totaling one gigabyte or more total disk space.

◆ You definitely should have a CD-ROM (any type will work).

◆ Make sure that you have a tape backup unit.

◆ Your system processor should be a 100 MHz 486 or better.

◆ Although you can get by without a mouse (or other pointing device), having one can save you some frustration.

An additional consideration is based on whether you need to support mobile users or remote offices. If so, you should definitely budget at least four 28.8 modems and get the SIO COM port drivers for OS/2. SIO replaces OS/2's standard COM port drivers, which do not support high-speed modems. SIO is a set of specialized OS/2 asynchronous drivers available on CompuServe in the OS/2 support forum. If more than a dozen remote users will be dialing in, get a multiport modem. For large quantities of dial-in users, consider installing large multiport async boards. The multiport modem most commonly used in an OS/2 environment at this time is the Digiboard 16-port board. For more detail on configuring a dial-up server see Chapter 19, "Supporting Dial-Up Users."

Tip

If you're using OS/2, get Ray Gwinn's SIO COM port drivers. They are available from CompuServe in the OS/2 support forum.

CHOOSING A SERVER OPERATING SYSTEM (OS)

Before determining the hardware and software requirements for your servers, you need to first determine what operating system you will use for your servers. I recommend standardizing on a single Notes server platform for production databases. Use alternate OS platforms only for special purpose servers. It is perfectly reasonable to set up your production database servers as one operating system, and a gateway server under a different operating system. Large organizations should strive to support only two Notes server platforms. Support costs escalate as the number of server operating systems increases. The server OS decision is influenced by the following considerations (in order of importance):

1. Administrative and support skills in your organization
2. Administrative and support skills available in the marketplace
3. Current operating systems in your organization
4. Availability of third-party software to extend and enhance your Notes servers
5. Availability of consultants to help plan, install, and troubleshoot your installation
6. Performance and capacity of Notes on each platform
7. Popularity of Notes on different platforms

Notice what is missing from this list: hardware and software costs. The cost of the hardware and software is a very small part of the overall budget. If you are considering the cost of the hardware and software when choosing an OS, you probably haven't thought enough about the important issues.

The primary consideration when choosing an OS is the availability of administrators, application developers, and support personnel within your organization. The reliability of your Notes network is largely determined by the skill of the people who plan and design it. For most organizations, this should be the first and last consideration. The benefits of staying with a standard operating system include reduced support costs, reduced training costs, less investment in new software, and easier planning and installation. If your organization supports every OS ever invented, consider the availability (and cost) of outside help.

OS/2 has been the server of choice for Notes over the last few years. Even if organizations did not have any other OS/2 server, OS/2 was used for Notes. Most consultants in the Notes arena are skilled in OS/2. NT is gaining in popularity as a Notes server because of the ability to run *big* Notes servers on DEC Alpha machines.

Sometimes you just have no choice. A software add-on package you want to run comes only in OS/2. This situation is the cause for most multiple-platform Notes server installations. The organization selects NT or UNIX and then installs a single OS/2 box to run a particular software package. Most firms selling software for Notes release the OS/2 version first and then follow with NT and UNIX. This is the opposite of the normal relationship between Windows and OS/2.

Note

As NT slowly gains in popularity, the NT software toolkit will become available, along with more NT-based third-party products. At that point, the number of Notes installations running on NT should increase as well.

For Notes 4.0, the situation is changing so that OS/2 and NT have virtually identical support, but you need to understand the gateways that you want as well as their capabilities for each of the platforms that you are considering. Historically, the need to support and run gateways has caused many people to install a single OS/2 server as their gateway Notes server. The Internet gateway, gateways to other mail systems, and the gateway to other corporate information systems are prime culprits.

Now that IBM owns Lotus, the possibility exists that Notes upgrades will be released first on OS/2 and then on other platforms. I would discount stories to this effect. In the last few years, IBM products have been extremely standards-oriented. The pressure within IBM to use and support products from other divisions is considerably less than a few years back.

If you absolutely must have very large, multiple-processor machines, you are virtually forced at this point in time into using Windows NT or the UNIX version of

Notes. In this case, many organizations will end up with a single NT server being their large production server for Notes.

Your choice of server OS influences the network and clients you will support. I would discount any benchmarks between platforms run using Release 3 Notes software. The OS/2 Notes Release 3 server was an old 16-bit implementation. New benchmarks should be available soon after the release of the production version of Notes 4.0.

There are minor differences between the operating systems. They differ in their capacity to be remotely managed, capability of participating in remote Notes management, networking software, and ease of installation. These considerations pale beside the availability of trained consultants, the availability of trained support personnel, and the requirement to run certain add-on third-party applications.

Starting from a clean slate, I would recommend choosing OS/2 or Windows NT as your server platform (depending on whether your particular organization leans East or West). I would like to point out that any of the platforms Notes supports—with the exception of Windows—make a viable server platform. I have included special notes on OS/2 throughout this book because it is our expectation that many people will be installing OS/2 specifically for Notes, and that this will be a new experience for them. It is not a default recommendation that everyone use OS/2 for their Notes server. There are organizations today successfully running Notes on NLM, OS/2, NT, and Solaris. Your choice of server platform is not irrevocable and will not doom your Notes installation. One of the great features of Notes is its capacity to provide a consistent interface across so many platforms.

MINIMUM SERVER CONFIGURATIONS

No one should even consider rolling out a Notes server on a box smaller than that described earlier, in the section "The Cheapest Notes Server." Configurations for other platforms (NLM, NT, UNIX) are even larger. Table 7.1 summarizes the recommended hardware configurations for all server platforms. I don't list the Windows server because you shouldn't use the Windows server for production applications. Too many limitations are associated with the Windows server.

TABLE 7.1. RECOMMENDED HARDWARE CONFIGURATIONS BY PLATFORM.

CPU	OS/2 Pentium	Windows NT Pentium	UNIX Platform-Dependent
Memory (megabytes)	32	48	48
Disk (gigabytes)	1	1	1

7

HARDWARE AND SOFTWARE NEEDS

MULTI-PROCESSOR PLATFORMS

OS/2, Windows NT, and UNIX all are available in Symmetric Multi-Processing (SMP) versions. One of the major reasons for choosing the NT platform is the availability of a well-designed SMP configuration that runs on Intel processors (Compaq builds a popular one). The DEC Alpha is currently the SMP of choice for Windows NT. OS/2's SMP versions have been less than impressive. Some installations even experienced slower Notes performance with the multi-processor version of OS/2. If you want to minimize the number of servers, the best choice today is Windows NT running on a DEC Alpha SMP machine. A new version of SMP OS/2 is due out in 1996, and this will certainly be cause for reconsidering this recommendation.

SPECIALIZED SERVERS

Break Notes servers out by the functions that they will perform. Reducing the number of separate tasks that a server must perform can increase performance. You should not run a Notes server on a file server. This can cause performance and security problems.

Having specialized servers doesn't mean that there is any difference in the hardware operating system used for the server, only that there is a difference between the type of functions for which the server is used. For example, a server could be set up as a hub server, a mail server, a database server, a dial-up server, or a gateway server. Setting up servers dedicated to a particular function eases administration and can improve the overall performance of the Notes system. Mail servers, for example, store all users' mailboxes, and all mail routed across the network goes through the mail server.

You definitely will want to set up a dedicated mail server when you need to reduce network traffic, as mail routed between users on a machine discourages network traffic. Also, mail is one of the highest-priority applications in any organization. The mail system is also used in Notes applications as an alert system. Therefore, you want to be able to reliably predict the performance that your Notes mail users are going to get, and the only way to do that is to dedicate a server to mail. Because mail databases often contain particularly sensitive information, including personal information, security is also increased when you set up a dedicated mail server and keep access to that server to only those administrators who require access to that particular server. When you set up a mail server, by default the other servers will be dedicated to non-mail applications. Non-mail Notes applications include discussion databases, workflow applications, documentation databases, and so on.

Under the category of database server, you also can subdivide server types by the amount of data that they need to replicate, the amount of security needed for the data on that server, and the usage patterns that that server will experience. You should install more than one non-mail production database server only when you find that your users are not obtaining adequate performance on a single server.

Overall, in determining the server hardware requirements, bigger is better, everything matters, and memory is king.

CONSIDERATIONS FOR HUB SERVERS

Hub servers replicate all day. Hub servers must have enough disk space to hold all databases on all spoke servers, and so should have at least 9 gigabytes of hard drive space. If you need less than that, you probably don't need a hub server.

Because users are not accessing the hub server directly, performance is less critical. Replication under Notes Release 4.0 uses fewer resources than under previous releases, so an old CPU hooked to a large disk drive is an ideal hub server.

CONSIDERATIONS FOR DATABASE SERVERS

Users access database servers directly. You need to evaluate the load that each server is likely to experience. Plan enough capacity to handle peak usage gracefully; when Notes servers exceed their capacity, performance can degrade quickly.

CONSIDERATIONS FOR BACKUP SERVERS

Use backup servers to avoid the need to shut down other servers. Backup servers have the same requirements as hub servers. In addition, backup servers need tape drives.

CONSIDERATIONS FOR DIAL-UP/PASSTHRU SERVERS

Dial-up servers need to have a copy of each database used by mobile users. Passthru servers avoid this problem by allowing users to connect directly to other servers. Connection speed is the most important aspect of a passthru server. It is unlikely that the CPU will be heavily burdened or that disk space will be much of a concern.

CONSIDERATIONS FOR MAIL SERVERS

Mail servers are the most important part of your Notes network. E-mail delivery is the foundation of communications within many organizations. Users count on reliable delivery of mail.

Mail servers are ideal candidates for mirrored disk drives. Mirrored drives make it unlikely that you will ever lose mail due to hardware failure. This is especially important for mail servers because the transient nature of mail makes it difficult to back up mailboxes often enough to satisfy your users.

One thing that can cause more headaches than it is worth is running out of disk space on a mail server. Make sure that you have enough disk space to hold each user's personal mailbox. (Enforce limits on mailbox sizes to further guarantee that you will not run out of disk space.)

The mail server generally will have the highest number of simultaneous users. Each user requires some system memory. Configure your mail servers to accept a high number of connections and install extra memory.

See Chapter 16, "Administering Notes Servers," for details on configuring a server.

ESTIMATING THE NUMBER OF SERVERS TO BUY

In addition to the various components that should be included, I also recommend that your servers be one of the name brands such as IBM, Compaq, or Dell (or a DEC Alpha if you're going to run NT). This may be difficult in some companies that have already standardized on another hardware server platform. I expect that most people in this situation will choose to roll out Notes on their standard hardware platforms. However, don't call me when you get unusual errors in the middle of the night.

A harder number to estimate is the number of servers needed. Strive to minimize the number of servers and the number of geographic locations that have servers. This strategy will lower your support costs and keep your administrators much happier. Therefore they'll likely stay longer.

Everyone wants a rough guess, some guidelines to follow, but experience at your site is the only true indicator. Use the pilot installation to measure performance, and revise your estimate on the number of servers needed (one more reason your pilot application needs to be a serious application, not just a discussion database). There are simply too many variables to arrive at a completely accurate estimate before you have started to roll out applications. For example, if you are going to have a mail server, which I definitely recommend, how many users can use that mail server? It will vary dramatically between companies and even within business units. Think about a group of application developers who are exchanging mostly textual e-mail. Compare that with publishers who may be mailing around whole chapters with graphics. Of course, the number of users that a mail server can support will differ dramatically in these two cases.

The ideal Notes domain is a one-server domain that handles all the users in that domain. A single-server domain is not a realistic alternative at this time for all but the smallest installations. Depending on your usage patterns, a single server will suffice for 50 users. If your eventual installation is more than 50 users, plan from the start to have at least a mail server and a database server. For database servers, typical capacity ranges from 50 to 500 users per server. The lower part of this range is for complex applications that have lookups into other databases, that process large numbers of documents in a day (more than 1,000), or that contain large numbers of documents (more than 30,000). You can expect to get upwards of 500 users or more on mail servers.

Plan for peak usage when determining the capacity of your servers. Notes server performance falls quickly when the number of concurrent users exceeds server capacity. The Notes server begins to thrash, constantly forcing users off the system to make way for new users (who were just forced off the system themselves). Notes forces inactive users off the server when the number of concurrent users reaches a threshold. For example, if the maximum number of concurrent sessions for a server is 70, when the 71st user attempts to access the server, the least active person is forced off the system. Notes users are unaware of the fact that they have been forced off the system. The only indication is that, when they next access the server, the client and server re-authenticate each other and the user's access rights are checked again. In effect, the user is being re-logged onto the Notes server. Attaching to a Notes server is a CPU-intensive operation, an activity to be avoided as much as possible. When there are 90 people trying to access a server with a threshold of 70, very little productive work gets done before a user is forced off the system. More time is spent reattaching users than fulfilling user requests. Although Notes gives the impression that it is serving 90 people simultaneously, the amount of actual work being accomplished falls. To avoid thrashing, monitor the peak number of users and plan to add servers when the peak usage exceeds the configured threshold on a regular basis. Please keep in mind that these numbers are based on experience with Notes 3.x and that experience with Notes 4.x may change these numbers.

When determining the number of servers needed, don't forget to count specialized servers (mail servers, backup servers, and hub servers). I always recommend separating mailboxes onto their own server and dedicating one server as the mail server for any installation over 50 users.

If you are going to have applications that exist on more than one server, you'll have to set up replication between the multiple servers. If you have more than three production database servers, I recommend moving to a hub-and-spoke arrangement for replication, with one server dedicated to replicating data among the other servers. Many organizations claim high availability is an absolutely critical factor; however, high availability with Notes means that you have to find some tricky way to back up the server. Installing a separate server that replicates all databases is one method of keeping your other production servers up 7 days a week, 24 hours a day.

Once you've determined the number of servers that you will need for the first year, you are ready to lay actual configurations for each of these servers. To estimate the number of servers, first calculate the number of production database servers, mail servers, hub servers, backup servers, dial-up servers, and external servers for each site to receive a server. If there are less than 50 users at a site, a single server suffices. The number of production databases at a site is the total number of users to receive Notes divided by the number of users per server. The total number of mail servers is the number of users divided by the number of mail users per server (estimate 250). If there are more than four production and mail servers, add a hub server and a backup server. If this site will connect to the Internet or other companies, add an external server. If more than a dozen mobile or remote users will be dialing in, add a dial-up server. The dial-up server isn't needed strictly on performance/capacity grounds. I recommend a dial-up server to help isolate problems.

CHOOSING DISK DRIVES

Pay particular attention to your disk drives in setting up a Notes server. You will definitely (okay, almost definitely) see a performance improvement if you buy faster hard drives. I recommend buying SCSI-2 disks. Installations concerned with providing maximum reliability should buy a RAID disk array or a mirrored disk array. Having a faster hard drive is a lower priority than having sufficient memory, but given that you've already installed sufficient memory for the platform that you're installing, consider installing SCSI-2 disks.

Another common disk system consideration is whether to install arrayed disks or mirroring disks. *Arrayed disks* are a way of maintaining the operation of the server even in the face of a hard disk error—the setup duplicates data across multiple disks. Figure 7.2 illustrates the arrayed disk concept.

Figure 7.2.
A disk array writes
data to multiple disks
simultaneously. If one
disk is lost, its contents
can be reconstructed
from the contents of the
other disks.

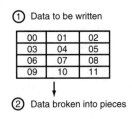

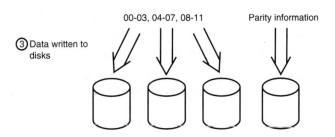

For example, if you have a disk array with three disks, and a disk is destroyed or goes bad, it can be re-created from data stored on the other two disks. In the process, though, arrayed disks cause you to lose some disk space, because part of each disk is used to hold information needed to reconstruct data on other disk drives. There are many kinds of arrayed disks, with each type specified as a level. Here I have discussed array level 5 or arrayed level 5+, the only type of disk arrays that you should consider for Notes servers.

Mirroring is duplicating your entire disk setup so that you have two identical disks or disk arrays set up. With mirroring, you can have complete duplication of your disk subsystem—including the disk controller and the disk. If a disk should go bad, it can be reconstructed from its partner disk. The advantage of mirroring is that reads can be extremely fast, because you can read the data from either one of the mirrored disks. Writes, while being slower than a write to a single disk, are not as bad as writing to an arrayed array. Mirroring is the most expensive disk system because you end up buying duplicate hardware. Most mirroring and arrayed products allow hot swapping of disks so that you can remove and install hard disks without turning off the machine.

You should also consider bus mastering your network cards and disks. *Bus mastering* is a technology that allows data to be transferred from a network card or your network to the disk system (or vice versa) or into the system memory, without requiring the intervention of the CPU. This leaves the CPU free to continue doing other chores. Bus mastering is available on EISA systems and Microchannel systems.

Calculating Disk and Memory Requirements

Most organizations are very interested in being able to calculate the disk and memory requirement beforehand. But there really is no way to calculate the disk requirements for Notes databases ahead of time. You would need an accurate estimate of the amount of information to be automated, the type of information, and the application designs you will use. A minimum configuration is 1GB, but most people should consider starting with a 2GB drive for a small server. I recommend considering a 9GB drive if the money permits.

When you are determining your memory requirements for OS/2, you should start with a minimum of 32M. See Table 7.1, earlier in this chapter, for the minimum recommended amount of memory per platform. These standards apply to both mail servers and production servers. One way to determine whether you have enough memory is to see whether the swap file is larger than its default size. If the swap file is larger than 2M (the default size), your server is swapping. To check the swap file size under OS/2, go to the partition where your operating system is installed. Check in \os2\system for the swapper.dat file. The size of that file, if you haven't changed the default setting, should be 2M. If your `swapper.dat` has increased in size from its default, you need to install more memory. This is counter to the recommendation that you'll find in most OS/2 books, which point out that it's generally okay to have some swapping going on during the initial startup of your OS/2 machine. However, I'm talking about using OS/2 as an application server, not as a desktop workstation. There is a difference. While a user may not notice some minor swapping, an application server that is swapping is overloaded.

You definitely need to have adequate memory in all of your servers, and not just for performance. This is a key point. Having adequate memory seems to be extremely important in having stable servers. If you cut back on money for memory, you'll end up spending that money on support costs. You might as well spend money up front on memory, save yourself the support headaches, and get the performance benefits of having adequate memory.

CLIENT SOFTWARE AND HARDWARE REQUIREMENTS

The choice of client platform should be guided by your current installation and the direction your organization has chosen. If you have an installed base, your client hardware platform is chosen. Don't change your client platform just for Notes. If you already have another reason to change your client platform, the Notes deployment is a good time to perform the change.

I recommend the use of Windows 3.1 or Windows 95 for most users. This platform offers the tightest integration with other applications and the easiest availability of support tools and personnel. If DOS is installed on your client machines, either OS/2 or Windows is suitable, depending on other goals your organization may have.

MINIMUM CLIENT HARDWARE REQUIREMENTS

The following sections detail the recommended minimal configurations for the Windows, OS/2, and Mac clients. The Windows client runs fine under OS/2, Windows 3.1, Windows 95, or NT.

WINDOWS MINIMUM CLIENT CONFIGURATION

Although Notes will run on a smaller platform than the one recommended here, your users will not enjoy the experience:

- ◆ 80486 or better processor
- ◆ Windows 3.1 or Windows 95

- ◆ 8M RAM and 8M virtual memory for Windows 3.1, 16M RAM for Windows 95
- ◆ 300M hard disk
- ◆ Mouse

OS/2 Minimum Client Configuration

The minimum OS/2 client configuration is as follows:

- ◆ OS/2 3.0 or 2.1
- ◆ 80486DX2 or better
- ◆ 12M RAM memory
- ◆ 300M hard disk
- ◆ Mouse

Mac Client Configuration

The minimum Mac client configuration is described in the following list:

- ◆ System 7.5 or higher
- ◆ Mac II-based Performa, Quadra, or PowerBook (except model 100) with a 68030 or better processor
- ◆ 12M RAM
- ◆ 40M virtual memory available
- ◆ Apple Shared Library Manager

These are the minimum configurations. If your users run multiple applications in addition to Notes, add 4M to 8M of RAM to each recommendation.

Calculating the Number of Workstations to Buy

To determine the number of new client machines to buy, you need to know the number of people getting Notes. Any person getting Notes should have at least a 486DX2 machine (or equivalent Mac or UNIX workstation). I recommend one desktop machine per user. It is possible to share a Notes desktop between users, but this is an atypical installation.

CHOOSING A NETWORK

The server and client must share a common network protocol in order to communicate. The most common protocols used with Notes are TCP/IP and Novell NetWare SPX. Your choice of protocol should be guided by the availability of skill within your organization. Most Notes problems are really network problems in disguise. Having a trained support staff for the protocol you choose is vital.

SELECTING A NETWORK PROTOCOL

The following network operating systems are compatible with Notes:

◆ AppleTalk
◆ Banyan VINES
◆ DEC PATHWORKS
◆ FTP Software PC/TCP for OS/2
◆ IBM OS/2 EE LAN Requester for Ethernet
◆ IBM TCP/IP for OS/2
◆ Microsoft LAN Manager
◆ Novell NetWare NetBIOS emulator
◆ Novell NetWare Requester with SPX

Protocols are not all alike. Ease of management, speed, ease of use, and reliability differ between protocols. Considerations when selecting the protocol for a Notes network include the following issues:

◆ NetBIOS, AppleTalk, and Banyan VINES are easy to install and use.
◆ NetWare SPX is a highly secure network operating system.
◆ NetWare and Notes have had a buggy relationship through Release 3.x.
◆ TCP/IP gives better performance (in the Notes environment), but has potential security leaks.

You can use different protocols for different situations. For example, you may use NetBIOS for your LAN, NetWare SPX for inter-LAN replication and mail routing, and TCP/IP for Internet access.

Use NetWare SPX if your organization already has installed a Novell network. For anyone with a choice, I recommend TCP/IP for use with Notes.

Tables 7.2 and 7.3 show which networks you can use with each platform.

TABLE 7.2. NETWORK PROTOCOLS SUPPORTED BY THE SERVER OPERATING SYSTEM.

Notes Server Operating System	LAN Protocols Supported
OS/2 Release 3.0 and 2.11	AppleTalk
	Banyan VINES
	NetBIOS, NetBEUI
	Novell NetWare SPX
	TCP/IP
Windows 3.1 and Windows for Workgroups 3.11	NetBIOS, NetBEUI
	TCP/IP
	Novell NetWare SPX
	Banyan VINES
Windows NT v. 3.5 and higher	AppleTalk
	Banyan VINES
	NetBIOS, NetBEUI
	Novell NetWare and Microsoft SPX, Microsoft SPX II
	TCP/IP
UNIX Solaris 2.x	SPX
	TCP/IP
UNIX HP-UX	SPX
	TCP/IP

TABLE 7.3. NETWORK PROTOCOLS SUPPORTED BY THE CLIENT OPERATING SYSTEM.

Notes Workstation Operating System	LAN Protocols Supported
OS/2 Release 3.0 and 2.11	Banyan VINES
	NetBIOS, NetBEUI
	Novell NetWare SPX
	TCP/IP
	Lotus Notes Connect for SNA v3.0a

continues

TABLE 7.3. CONTINUED

Notes Workstation Operating System	LAN Protocols Supported
Windows 3.1 and Windows for Workgroups 3.11	Banyan VINES
	NetBIOS, NetBEUI
	Novell NetWare SPX
	TCP/IP
Windows 95, Windows NT	AppleTalk
	Banyan VINES
	NetBIOS, NetBEUI
	Novell NetWare SPX, Microsoft SPX, Microsoft SPX II
	TCP/IP
Macintosh System 7.5 and higher	AppleTalk
	TCP/IP (MacTCP)
UNIX HP-UX	SPX
	TCP/IP
UNIX Solaris 2.X	SPX
	TCP/IP

You can configure your Notes servers and workstations to use more than one network protocol. Installing an additional protocol can involve installing additional software, editing system files, and possibly adding NICs to your Notes server.

Using multiple network protocols increases the complexity of your network. This causes your administrative costs to increase. Multiple protocols also hurt the performance of your network. Each protocol puts an additional overhead load in the network, hurting overall performance. Installing multiple protocols on a single server or workstation is the largest hurdle to using multiple network protocols. Each combination of protocols has its own unique set of problems (which change with each revision level). Installing a single network protocol is difficult the first time you try it. Installing two network protocols is *always* difficult, with the exception of common combinations such as NetWare SPX and TCP/IP. Installing three or more network protocols on a single server (you wouldn't do this to a workstation, would you?) is a jungle adventure. You're on your own. The exact sequence of steps during machine startup can be critical. Timing problems can cause connections to drop. I would avoid environments with more than two network protocols.

SUPPORTED NETWORK PROTOCOL STANDARDS

I hope it comes as no surprise that network protocols have their own set of standards. NDIS (network driver interface specification) and ODI (open data link interface) enable network drivers to communicate with NICs. Notes supports both NDIS and ODI.

NDIS BASICS

You can use Notes with any Ethernet and token ring NICs that use network drivers compliant with NDIS. NDIS is designed to allow up to four NDIS-compliant network protocols on one NIC. Figure 7.3 shows the basic NDIS architecture.

Figure 7.3.
The NDIS Architecture.

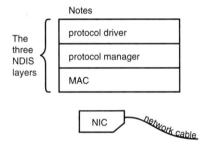

The NDIS standard details three software layers. Each layer translates between the two adjoining layers. The goal is take requests from Notes and translate them into the language of the actual networking hardware. The protocol driver is shipped with your networking software (SPX, TCP/IP, etc.) and communicates directly with Notes. The protocol manager, also shipped with your networking software, enables the protocol driver and MAC (media access control) driver to communicate with each other. The MAC driver directly controls the actual hardware NIC. MAC drivers are unique to each NIC and are shipped with the NIC.

ODI BASICS

ODI allows multiple ODI-compliant protocols to coexist simultaneously on a single card. Novell ships a set of drivers called ODI NDIS Support (ODINSUP) that enable multiple protocol drivers that comply with NDIS or ODI to share a single card. ODI saves money by eliminating the need to install multiple NIC cards in multiple protocol environments. I recommend using ODI-compliant network software even

7

HARDWARE AND SOFTWARE NEEDS

if you are not planning a multi-protocol environment. Future expansion is not limited by your networking software when you choose ODI-compliant protocols.

MULTIPLE NETBIOS PROTOCOLS

A Notes server or workstation can use only one NetBIOS-based protocol at a time. The only exception is networks based on Microsoft LAN Manager. LAN Manager is a NetBIOS-based network operating system that can run multiple NetBIOS protocols concurrently. You can configure one Notes port for each LAN Manager protocol. For example, if you are running NetBIOS and NetBEUI concurrently on a LAN Manager network, you can configure two Notes ports—one for NetBIOS and one for NetBEUI.

The following sections detail which protocol drivers are NetBIOS-based. All NetBIOS-based protocols have the word NetBIOS in parentheses. You must install one NIC card in each server or workstation for each NetBIOS-based protocol supported by that server or workstation.

NDIS STANDARD PROTOCOLS

The following protocols comply with the NDIS protocol:

- ◆ AppleTalk
- ◆ Banyan VINES with NDIS drivers
- ◆ DEC PATHWORKS (NetBIOS)
- ◆ FTP Software PC/TCP (TCP/IP)
- ◆ IBM OS/2 EE LAN Requester for Ethernet (NetBIOS)
- ◆ IBM OS/2 LAN Server (IBM NetBIOS)
- ◆ IBM TCP/IP
- ◆ Microsoft LAN Manager (NetBIOS)

ODI STANDARD PROTOCOLS

The following network protocols comply with the ODI standard:

- ◆ Novell NetBIOS
- ◆ Novell NetWare SPX

Selecting a Notes Network Interface Card (NIC)

You need a network interface card (NIC) to connect your Notes server or workstation to a LAN or WAN network. NICs, unlike modems, are installed inside the computer case. NICs usually support one of two basic data transfer schemes: Ethernet or token ring. The NIC you buy determines whether your network will be Ethernet or token ring. Buy only one type of card for any single LAN. All servers and workstations on a LAN must agree on Ethernet or token ring. In a large organization, the choice of Ethernet or token ring involves more variables than I can discuss here. For small or medium organizations, consider the following issues when choosing a NIC type:

◆ Ethernet and token ring give equivalent performance on lightly loaded networks.

◆ Token ring performs better in heavily loaded networks.

◆ The Ethernet market is very competitive.

SPX, TCP/IP, AppleTalk, NetBIOS, and all the other protocols mentioned earlier in this chapter will work with either Ethernet or token ring.

The most popular network cards in use with Notes today are the 3Com 3C509 network card series. I recommend this card for client workstations. Stick with brand name network cards when configuring your Notes network. Notes can be finicky when it comes to network cards.

Improving Hardware Performance

Throughout this chapter, I have recommended fast disks and plenty of memory. You should use your actual experience with the pilot application to refine these recommendations. You should determine the subsystem (CPU, disk, network) causing performance problems and upgrade that subsystem first. Here are some other tips that should help you increase performance:

◆ Use many small disks rather than one large disk.

◆ Choose a hardware platform that can grow with your needs, without the need for a totally new configuration. Generally, this means buying servers that can be upgraded to multi-processing speedsters.

◆ Put your swap file in the most-used directory on the least-used drive on your system.

◆ OS/2 systems should use HPFS instead of FAT. HPFS is well-suited for drives containing thousands of small files. HPFS drives resist fragmentation, a problem with FAT drives.

For more information on performance tuning, see Chapter 16, "Administering Notes Servers."

OBSOLETE OPERATING SYSTEMS

I know that no one considering Notes would still be running any of these platforms (sarcasm), but forewarned is forearmed. The following operating systems are not supported by Notes:

◆ Windows 3.0 or earlier

◆ OS/2 2.0 or earlier

◆ Macintosh 6.0 or earlier

◆ Standard mode Windows

In addition, Notes no longer supports EGA screens.

SUMMARY

Pay attention to detail when designing the hardware and software configurations for your Notes network. Notes is particularly sensitive to revision levels. Don't assume that Notes has been tested with the latest revision of any particular piece of software. Check your documentation or call Lotus for the revision levels of your OS and network that Notes supports. You should plan to keep your software updated. Many organizations let their software get years out of date before upgrading. This is not a good strategy with Notes.

For offices requiring more than a single server, I recommend configuring specialized servers for backup, passthru, hub/spokes, and mail. If you are going to run exactly two servers, they should be a mail server and "other."

Be sure to test each client and server configuration before installing them in a production environment. After installing, track problems by configuration. Testing and tracking are eased when you use a standard configuration for all servers.

The hardware to run a Notes network can be expensive. I encourage you to learn from others' misery. Don't skimp on memory. Notes caches a great deal of information in memory. Lack of memory can lead to some troubling problems. Try to think of your hardware purchases as an investment—an investment in stability and sanity.

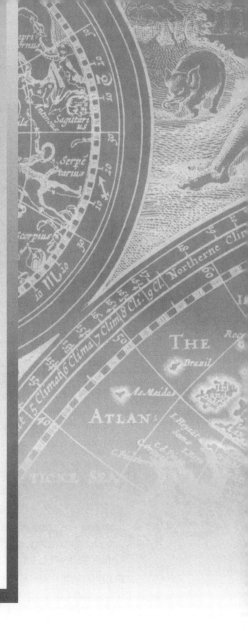

CHAPTER 8

Preparing Your Organization

Organizational issues should always be foremost in your mind when deploying a Notes application. The issues that will cause the failure of your Notes project are overwhelmingly likely to be organizational and political issues, not technical issues. There is no way to overemphasize the importance of putting together a strong project team and actively involving the entire organization. For Notes to be successful, most organizations have to change both the way they work and the prevailing attitude about sharing information. You need to communicate the benefits that each person will see as well as the benefits to the whole organization, and do it in a way that people will accept and understand.

This chapter explores the issues involved in preparing organizations, both large and small, for Notes. The human side of a Notes deployment is discussed. Specifically, this chapter discusses

◆ Forming a project team

◆ Skills requirements

◆ Training strategies for end users and support staff

◆ Policies and procedures

This chapter is an extension of Chapter 5, "Building a Deployment Plan." Chapter 5 presents the overall approach, and this chapter discusses a few points in more detail.

FORMING A PROJECT TEAM

Each company will follow its own path getting from that first kernel of an idea when someone in your organization decides, "We should use Notes," to the point where you are ready to form a project team to explore ways of actually using Notes. Somewhere along the way, early in the process of evaluating Notes, each company will form a project team that will become the core group responsible for the overall success of the Notes implementation in your organization. Your primary Notes team should have one member assigned to each of the key roles described in the following sections.

You may notice that similar but slightly different lists appear in Chapters 6 and 7. The list in this chapter is the most detailed and represents a compilation and extension of those lists.

NOTES EVANGELIST

The role of the Notes evangelist can be critical to the success of Notes in a medium-to-large organization. The evangelist has the responsibility to spread the word, generate enthusiasm, gather feedback, and generate interest. Most organizations can't start with an enterprise-wide commitment to Notes. You will have to generate that development through successes and by talking about those successes.

The evangelist can generate enthusiasm about Notes in several ways. After a few people are using Notes databases, Notes provides one natural way to spread the word. Other ways include

◆ Newsletters dedicated to the Notes project

◆ Open houses where you demonstrate potential applications of particular interest to different business units

◆ Traveling demos that demonstrate real applications to executives and users

◆ The use of JAD sessions (discussed in Chapter 5, where you gather issues and make decisions in a group atmosphere)

The evangelist needs to recruit key people in each of your business units and geographic locations, using this expanded team to communicate to the entire organization.

No matter what methods you use to communicate information about your Notes project, you should be utterly relentless in publicizing Notes and the advantages it brings, the coming organizational changes, the organization's reasons for adopting Notes, and the benefits/challenges each person faces.

The evangelist should be someone, usually an executive, with visibility throughout the entire organization. This visibility can be critical in gaining acceptance from various operating divisions.

PROJECT MANAGER

The key job of the project manager is to develop a time line and budget, track progress against the budget, and communicate that progress to the executive steering committee. A Notes rollout project manager faces the following issues:

◆ The choice of the first application.

The first application should be a high-profile, innovative solution for your business, but not time-critical. Time-critical applications are ones that must be completed by a certain date. Changes mandated by regulations are one example of a time-critical application. Avoid starting with several discussion databases if you are trying to show Notes' viability as a strategic system.

◆ Resistance to change.

Organizational inertia can be quite severe when new systems are introduced. Active resistance, lack of knowledge, and conflicting priorities are common causes of inertia.

◆ Avoiding function creep.

Function creep is the never-ending dance of revisions and updates between users and application developers in quest for utter perfection. A good manager knows when to cut off enhancements, install what's done, gather actual production experience, and then move ahead.

Notes project managers should have experience with client/server projects. A mix of applications development and operations experience is especially helpful.

NOTES SERVER ADMINISTRATOR

The Notes server administrator will be responsible for maintaining the Notes servers after they are installed. The Notes server administrator should be the person who will eventually head up the support staff on an ongoing basis. The server administrator is responsible for the following tasks:

◆ Monitoring server performance

◆ Troubleshooting server problems

◆ Scheduling all server tasks, including routine maintenance

◆ Monitoring mail routing

◆ Backing up files

◆ Creating replicas

◆ Helping the help desk answer tough questions

Notes system administrators should have experience with desktop operating systems (Windows, OS/2, or UNIX, depending on which ones you are using), experience with client/server applications, and, most importantly, experience administering network operating systems. Experience administering network operating systems is a must because most problems with Notes involve the network in some manner. Individuals with all these skills are in high demand and many organizations will have to accept someone with only some of this experience and provide training to round out his skills.

DATABASE MANAGER

Responsibilities of a database manager (preferably the manager for the pilot database) involve approving changes to the access control list and to the design of the database. Each organization has many database managers, each responsible for a different set of databases. Database managers often are business unit executives or managers responsible for the people who primarily use an application, or for the department that "owns" the data in a particular database. The database manager doesn't have to be the person who physically updates the database, although she should be the person who approves all updates. If the database manager isn't the person who actually performs the updates to the access control lists and design elements, you should create some kind of Notes workflow application that automatically documents all the database manager's approvals.

DATABASE ADMINISTRATOR

The database administrator is responsible for monitoring the database logs to ensure that replication is working, and for checking the performance of the database. The database administrator role often is performed by the Notes server administrator. The database administrator should work closely with the database manager who "owns" the data stored in the database.

A Notes database administrator needs to understand Notes security and replication. A background administering other client/server databases is desirable, but not necessary.

SUPPORT ENGINEER

The support engineer is the primary person responsible for installing and troubleshooting Notes. The support engineer should be capable of installing the operating systems, network, Notes software, and hardware. In a large organization, the support engineer on the rollout team will become responsible for managing whole teams during the latter stages of the rollout. These teams will install (or upgrade) the hardware and software required for your Notes network. As with the Notes administrator, the support engineer on the rollout team should be the one responsible for Notes support in an ongoing manner. The experience gained through the rollout is critical in the long-term success of Notes. A typical Notes support staff person should have several years' experience with network hardware and software, especially the type of network with which you intend to run Notes, and including telecommunications if you intend to use modem dial-up.

NETWORK ADMINISTRATOR

You should have a network administrator on the Notes deployment team. The network administrator will be responsible for participating in designing the Notes network and bringing to the team the knowledge gained through rollout and support of current client/server applications.

END USER REPRESENTATIVE

The rollout team also must have a representative of the users of the pilot applications. Normally, this is a first-line manager responsible for supervising the people who will be using the application, but it also can be a key user. The user representative often isn't a full-time member of the team. You don't need to limit this representation to one person. You can involve whole groups of users, at various points and at various levels of time commitment. This method is definitely encouraged, although there needs to be someone actively involved in the rollout plan who represents and can bring to the table the interests of the people who actually have to use the application.

OPERATIONS REPRESENTATIVE

It is also important to have an operations representative. With client/server applications development in the past, you probably have not had to involve operations staff from the very beginning. With Notes, the operations staff will need to work very closely with the application development staff. There have been cases where the operations staff has caused huge headaches for the applications and support staff. It's also easy for the application developers to cause distress for the operations staff. It's important to bring both of these representatives together early in the rollout.

The operations person will be responsible for helping to develop the standard operating procedures for Notes, and for making plans for rolling out the Notes servers into the environment that is currently supported. He must make sure that the standard operating procedures integrate well (to the extent possible) with the current operating procedures. It's also important for the operations staff person to have knowledge of the current operating procedures within the organization, as well as the skill level of the operations staff.

APPLICATION DEVELOPER

The application developer is responsible for designing and implementing the pilot application. The application developer should be familiar with rapid-application-development methodologies, have some understanding of an operations staff job, and have experience in client/server application development. Experience gathering requirements from multiple groups and reconciling those into a single application is desirable. Obviously, the application developer for your Notes rollout should have experienced the rollout of a major client/server application in the past.

TRAINER

The trainer is responsible for developing the training strategy for the deployment team, end users, and support staff. The trainer may run trainings and/or evaluate training companies. The trainer will be responsible for developing a skills assessment for the user base and coordinating their training with the Notes rollout.

Involve a trainer early in the Notes project. Training is a key element in any Notes deployment, not an incidental requirement.

HELP DESK REPRESENTATIVE

It's a good idea to include someone from your help desk on the Notes rollout team so that he or she can gain experience with the Notes platform in your organization. This experience cannot be gained in training sessions and after-the-fact discussions with the rollout team. Ideally, the help desk person assigned to the rollout team will be responsible for designing and implementing a strategy for staffing and training the help desk.

REMOTE-SITE COORDINATOR

Each remote site will need at least one remote-site coordinator. Responsibilities of the remote-site coordinator include rebooting servers and helping the support staff. The ability to answer usage questions would be a plus. If your pilot application involves any remote sites, select and train a remote-site coordinator early. This position is not a full-time position.

CERTIFIER

The certifier is responsible for verifying the identity of Notes users, safeguarding the certifier ID files for the organization, issuing certificates, and issuing cross certificates. The certifier must ensure that the person receiving a certificate is actually the person whose name is listed in the ID file. Certifiers shouldn't routinely certify ID files without checking with the person requesting the certificate to verify that the request is valid.

ISSUES TO CONSIDER WHEN STAFFING A ROLLOUT TEAM

Carefully select the project manager and evangelist. They should have the confidence of your CEO.

The executive team should be involved with any Notes deployment, and the managers of the deployment should be comfortable dealing with executives.

The first step in preparing your organization is to staff your rollout team. As they start to develop and execute the deployment plan, they will begin to involve other parts of the organization.

Not every one of these people will be full-time immediately, depending upon the size of your organization and the speed with which you roll out Notes. You may start with a project manager, an application developer, and a systems administrator. Even if everyone will not be actively involved full-time at the beginning, you should identify the members of the team.

Some roles may not be filled immediately, but add them as soon as you possibly can. You will have a core team of IS staff responsible for installing Notes, developing applications, and supporting end users, along with managers and executives to provide support and direction. Without this combination, your Notes installation could be in trouble.

The tasks that the rollout team has to accomplish are listed in Chapter 5. They need to assess the current status of the enterprise. They should generate an accurate inventory of computer and networking equipment currently installed. The team should also evaluate the political readiness of the organization. They need to gather input from key parties throughout the organization and define the scope of the Notes deployment, design the Notes network, begin to staff the ongoing support organization, define the standard operating procedures, choose and build the pilot application, train users, install hardware and software, and organize and implement the rollout of the pilot and the first production applications. Then the team must make sure that all lessons learned are passed on to the ongoing support team.

PROJECT TEAM TRANSITIONS

The project team will not necessarily have the same set of players for the entire Notes deployment. In addition to the natural attrition any team faces, a Notes deployment has several phases that require a different mix of skills. As with any client/server systems rollout, there is a difference in the skill set needed to initially develop Notes applications and the skills needed to maintain Notes applications.

The key difference between the rollout team and the ongoing support team is that the project manager responsible for planning and implementing the rollout project may not be the same project manager responsible for long-term support of Notes. Several of the issues, such as dealing with change and generating enthusiasm, go away to some degree with an ongoing support role. However, in many organizations, the project manager will stay the same. The ongoing support team will be more heavily loaded with support engineers and administrators than the initial rollout team, and probably will not have a permanent representative from the users staff.

Another key difference is that the rollout team, due to the heavy workload involved with upgrading and installing hardware and software and the extra troubleshooting and testing involved during the initial rollout, will probably be larger than the ongoing support staff. You should plan to start filling the ongoing support staff positions as soon as possible. Whenever possible, the people on the rollout team should be the people chosen to be the ongoing support staff.

PUTTING THE TEAM INTO ACTION

After staffing the rollout team, the next step is to assess the readiness of your organization. We recommend holding joint-application-design sessions—very specialized meetings designed to quickly get all the issues and concerns on the table. One key side benefit of holding JAD sessions is visibility across the enterprise as you start to involve different business units in the Notes rollout project. The rollout team will start to design and implement the deployment plan.

PLANNING FOR ONGOING SUPPORT

As your Notes rollout project proceeds, you need to begin filling the permanent support staff positions. As you begin to lay out the issues, define the scope of the deployment, and design your Notes network, you will have a better approximation of the number of people you will need to support Notes on an ongoing basis. Typical tasks for which you need to plan in an ongoing Notes support include troubleshooting your installed Notes applications, testing new Notes applications, administering Notes, handling problems with end users, training new users, developing new Notes applications, and managing the continued rollout of Notes past the first production implementation. Specifically, ongoing support includes

- Hardware maintenance and installation
- Monitoring replication and mail routing
- Operating system support and installation
- Network support and troubleshooting
- Notes server administration, including monitoring disk space, monitoring performance, and backing up servers
- Certifying users
- Handling terminations
- Training new users, new support staff, and new application developers
- Database/application development and deployment
- Administering mail, including gateways to other mail systems
- Modem setup and support

A key task is assigning someone to terminate access to Notes users who leave the organization. There must be a person assigned to removing access. Terminating access involves removing the user's ID from the Name and Address Book and adding the name to the deny-access lists for all servers.

A typical support staff will number around ten people for a large organization. This number includes just the centralized support staff. You also need one person at each remote site who can, at a minimum, reboot the server. Chapter 5 suggests a way to estimate the size of the support staff for your organization's size and characteristics.

TRAINING STRATEGIES

You need to develop a training strategy for your rollout team, the ongoing support staff, and end users . Some of the questions people often have include, "Is on-the-job training enough?" and "Can Notes be self-taught?" The answer to both these questions is yes. Notes can be self-taught. Most people using Notes on the job eventually catch on. However, a price must be paid. Depending on the person, the price of skipping formal training varies from a longer learning curve to permanently lower productivity.

You must keep in mind that Notes isn't a finished application. Notes, as shipped, is virtually useless for anything other than e-mail. It differs quite markedly from other desktop personal productivity applications like Word, Excel, 1-2-3, etc. Notes is a tool for developing applications. It integrates several features, such as e-mail, an application builder, and security, into a single package. Notes has a considerably larger scope than a personal productivity application. When people teach themselves Notes, there is a real tendency to view Notes as an extension of something they already know, whether the user is an application developer, network administrator, or someone familiar with e-mail. People that skip formal training may never quite grasp the power of the integrated feature set that Notes provides. One result of allowing self-teaching is that Notes often ends up being used only as an e-mail package. You can install Notes, but you cannot force people to use it. Proper training can empower users, allowing them to use Notes confidently with a very short learning curve.

Training your end users empowers your end users. Training them in the various applications for which Notes can be used allows them to contribute ideas more readily than if they don't go through training. The ideas contributed by properly trained end users will easily make up the cost of training. Don't skip training. Take the time to evaluate the training requirements and develop a training plan for each class of users and each geographic location.

NEEDS ASSESSMENT

The first step in developing your training strategy is to assess the current skill level in your organization. Not all corporations need the same training. You need to know who needs training. Develop a list of end users, administrators, and application developers. You need to determine the current level of expertise for each person. Are your end users already familiar with a graphical desktop? How long have users been using a graphical environment? Have your users ever been involved in or contributed to an application design in the past? You must determine who needs to be trained, what they need, where they are located, and when they need their training. The needs assessment for each person should include a list of skills to be learned and a time frame for learning each skill. The needs for administrators will differ from those for end users.

Don't overlook training in non-Notes material. For end users, for example, you may need to offer training in desktop operating systems and applications that you integrate with Notes, such as word processors and spreadsheets. For your support staff, consider updating training in the network protocols that you are using. Your application developers may need training in rapid-application-development methodologies, object-oriented databases, and client/server development.

At a minimum, after completing training end users should

- ◆ Be familiar with a graphical operating system
- ◆ Understand e-mail and Notes e-mail options
- ◆ Understand the first applications that will be installed
- ◆ Have a clear understanding of why Notes is being installed

Mobile users also will need to know how to

- ◆ Create replicas on their laptops and replicate changes
- ◆ Create and use different locations
- ◆ Encrypt databases
- ◆ Manage their Personal Address Book

After users have some experience with Notes, you can consider an advanced class that teaches

- ◆ Creating personal agents
- ◆ Creating personal views
- ◆ Searching databases

8

Administrators need to know everything end users know, plus

- Basic networking concepts
- How to control server tasks
- Replication
- Mail routing
- Indexing
- How to install clients and servers
- Notes security
- How to create personal views and agents
- Everything else in this book!

Application developers should have a basic understanding of everything an administrator knows, plus

- A prototyping application development methodology
- LotusScript
- Notes API, if you will be developing applications in C/C++
- Agents
- Database searching
- Notes design elements such as navigators, folders, views, documents, sections, subforms, and forms
- Workflow concepts

Application developers must have a sense for the load their applications will place on a Notes server. Most applications can be built in many different ways, with most being CPU/memory/disk hogs. It's also useful when application developers have knowledge of mainframe relational databases such as SQL Server so that they can properly judge whether Notes is the correct database platform for the problem at hand.

Develop a detailed list of who is to be trained from among all your end users, application developers, network administrators, and support engineers. To determine what each administrator or application developer needs to learn, compare the current skill level to the job description for that position. For end users, the goal is to be able to use the specific applications that your rollout team will develop.

TRAINING REMOTE USERS

The location of your users is another critical aspect in planning your training. Remote users require a different training strategy than headquarters users.

Whether you decide it's worth the expense of flying them in for a day or two of training at a central site, or use some kind of automated training, training of remote users is likely to be more expensive and require more planning than training for your central headquarters staff.

TRAINING OPTIONS

After you have an assessment of your training needs, you must determine which of the available training options you will use.

For your administrators and application developers, you can rely on the standard training materials published by Lotus. Self-paced training throughout the deployment process often is appropriate, using computer-based training combined with hands-on experience. We do recommend that application developers who have a background in relational database design go through the training before they start to experiment with developing Notes applications. Notes is definitely not a relational database, and developers will be very frustrated if they think about it as if it were.

For remote training, you have the option of using standard computer-based training from Notes or from another training organization. You also can develop screen cams (recordings of someone using Notes) of your applications and distribute those to remote locations. ScreenCam is a product that allows you to record your desktop and add voice annotations.

Lastly, don't forget to consider using Notes itself to support your training efforts. You can use Notes to schedule your training efforts, track equipment and rooms available for training, track successful completion of training, distribute post-training reviews and comments, and for follow-up in the weeks after the initial installation and training.

Check the Lotus Partners catalog for a nearly complete listing of all the Notes training centers in your area. Authorized education centers are required to keep certified Notes trainers on staff. These centers should be very enthusiastic and willing to customize their training for your end users.

EXECUTIVE TRAINING

Training for executives often takes the form of customized hand-holding. Each executive is assigned a person from the rollout team or ongoing support staff. The executive calls that person directly whenever he has a question. That person is responsible for going to the executive's office, demonstrating applications, and answering any questions for the executive. Even with an executive's busy schedule, there are definite advantages to having them attend some regular training meetings, even if only for half a day. As Notes has the potential to dramatically change the way people do their jobs, one of the largest problems is resistance to change. Seeing executives participating in the training is one way of emphasizing the importance of making Notes work throughout the organization. Seeing executives take time from a busy schedule to sit in training is a particularly effective way of emphasizing the importance that the organization is placing on Notes.

Executives in particular should get some background in using groupware to change collaborative processes. Redesigning collaborative processes goes beyond normal process reengineering. Make sure that your executive training includes some coverage of this topic.

SCHEDULING TRAINING

For end users, the most important thing is to coordinate the training and installation of Notes on their desktops. You want to minimize the amount of time end users spend in the classroom. One way to do that is to make sure that the end user training is customized to the applications that the end user is actually going to be using. One half day to one full day should be adequate for most end users.

Users should receive training within 48 hours of having Notes installed on their desktops. You should develop a complete schedule for each person, showing when you expect Notes to be installed on his desktop, and plan to train him within 48 hours either before or after installation. This scheme keeps users productive and increases the value of your training dollar.

Proper scheduling is important enough that you should have some kind of carrot/stick approach to get users to attend training. Take attendance at your training sessions and require people to attend the full training. Don't distribute their user IDs until they have completed their training. This is one way to emphasize the importance of completing the Notes training and making sure that each person completes the training.

Of course, the support staff, administrators, and application developers should receive training as early as possible in the rollout of Notes.

TRAINING FOR CURRENT NOTES USERS

Notes Release 4.0 has more than enough new features to justify a half-day session for end users. Administrators and application developers should get updated copies of CBT courses. Lotus has included a special help database for current Notes users. If you are looking for a menu selection and can't find it, use the Release 3 Menu Finder (available under the Help menu).

SUPPORT STRATEGIES

At the beginning of Chapter 5 we noted that one of the key elements of any successful project is being well-connected to information sources. What that means with Notes is putting together a proper support plan. You should plan where you will get information on an ongoing basis. Possibilities are CompuServe with the Lotus Communication forum (Go LotusC), the World Wide Web sites for Lotus and Iris (http://www.lotus.com and http://www.iris.com), and the Lotus knowledge base. The *Lotus knowledge base* is a collection of questions and answers from the Notes support staff that is available on CD for an annual fee. Check with Lotus for their current offerings for their support programs. There are several levels of automated support from which you can choose, including a fax-back service, phone support where you can call in and report bugs, and going through consultants or outsourcing your support. Going through consultants or outsourcing is a good strategy for many organizations in dealing with difficult network problems and modem problems, and can be a cost-effective alternative with mission-critical applications.

As a final note in developing your support strategy, think about automated support. Automated support is any support delivered without intervention by or direct contact with another human being. This includes the fax-back service offered by Lotus, CompuServe forums, and so on. Automated support is cost effective for dealing with common problems, but you should not rely on this type of support to solve all your problems; even if you have a problem that someone else has had, it is often difficult to determine if that is actually the case.

PHONE SUPPORT

The next level of support is phone support provided by Lotus. This is a paid source of support, and Lotus offers several levels of support for application developers and administrators where they work with a technician at Lotus to solve their particular problem. There are several phone support programs. Telephone support is appropriate for questions on simple installations and usage of Notes, including basic LotusScript programming questions.

The highest level of support—one that you should consider for mission-critical applications or large, complex enterprise-wide applications—is retaining consultants or outsourcing your support altogether. Even if you are not outsourcing support for your complete client/server network, you can outsource complete support for your Notes installation, including the administrative and support roles. Or you can simply retain a consultant for when you have problems that your in-house support staff can't handle.

DEVELOP AN IN-HOUSE KNOWLEDGE BASE

Before rolling out the first pilot application, you should develop and have available an in-house knowledge base accessible to all users. This is essentially a discussion database that holds common questions and answers that you have encountered while developing the first Notes applications. Notes is shipped with a database template (discuss4.ntf) that you can use to create this database. The content of this database will be different for each organization.

APPLICATION DEVELOPMENT STRATEGIES

There are two approaches to Notes application development that can be adopted by organizations. One extreme is that anyone is allowed to create a database, and the other is that only application developers from the IS staff can create databases. It's certainly possible to take an approach between these extremes.

Your choice of application development strategy will be determined in large part by the culture in your organization. However, when considering what level of control you should have over application development, you should take into account these facts:

◆ It is virtually impossible to add more control after allowing users to develop a few of their own applications.

◆ Some applications are more important than others.

You should start out with the following set of guidelines and decide after the initial pilot is in production whether to allow greater flexibility:

◆ Applications that have implications across more than one business unit or that are critical to the success of a particular business unit should be developed by a trained IS application developer.

◆ You should require less important applications, such as in-house discussion databases or simple workflow applications, to meet or surpass a set of standards.

◆ Miscellaneous or non-business-related databases (if you even allow these) can be developed by anyone without regard to standards or protocol.

Another aspect of your application development strategy is which tools you need to support. You certainly have a very large number of application development tools from which to choose, including the Notes Interface builder with LotusScript, the old Lotus Notes Release 3.x macro language, the Notes C++ API, and Visual Basic—to name just a few leading contenders. There are certainly more tools available than any one support staff can reliably support.

Choosing the tool set that you want to support is a matter of deciding what types of applications you need to build and matching up the tools to those applications. For example, the great majority of applications can be built using the application builder that comes integrated with Notes. You can develop quite complex applications using the forms and view builder and LotusScript. For some details on using this method, see Chapter 16, "Administering Notes Servers." The primary use for the Notes C API interface is to build custom links to other systems, including your corporate database systems. There are already products available that link Notes to Oracle, SQL Server, and other relational database systems. If you can't find a product that links Notes directly to your corporate database system, you should investigate exporting Notes data to a common format such as ASCII text, and then importing these files into your corporate systems. There are tools such as Zmerge from Granite Software (508-634-3200) that can automate the import and export of ASCII text and a variety of other formats into and out of Notes.

The last key element of your application-development strategy is the standard operating procedure for rolling out new applications. In order to enforce any standards, you need an authorized method for getting an application from development through testing and into production. You also need to set up guidelines for how an application already in production gets updated. We recommend that application developers not directly alter production applications. Administrators must be responsible for installing all new databases, whether they are developed by the IS staff or end users. Having an administrator be responsible for installing all Notes databases on a production domain ensures that

◆ The proper steps will be taken to see that those databases will be backed up properly.

◆ Applications are placed on servers that can handle the load.

◆ There is sufficient disk space for that application.

◆ Access control is properly set before the application is made available to users.

◆ Placing that database on a particular server doesn't cause problems with other scheduled hardware upgrades or application installations.

We recommend that your rollout strategy for new applications involve at least several days' testing in a test domain before having those changes rolled out to a production domain, and that your administrators be responsible for updating all existing applications. Although administrators are responsible for installing applications, application developers will inevitably be involved in installing large or important applications.

PREPARING THE IS ORGANIZATION

If you have read between the lines in the previous sections on developing a support strategy, developing a training strategy, and developing an application development strategy, you can tell that Notes has a requirement for close cooperation between the various groups within your IS organization. In particular, there is a need for a good working relationship between your application developers and your support engineers and administrative staff. Without a good working relationship, it will be far more difficult to develop and maintain Notes at a reasonable cost.

Tip

Notes is meant to support quick, easy communication between people. A great place to start is with the IS organization that is supporting Notes!

A close working relationship starts with the managers of the organizations and requires that the application developers and administrators have at least some understanding of the other person's job. It doesn't mean that an application developer needs to know all the standard steps involved in certifying a new user; however, an application developer should have some feel for the amount of work he is going to generate for support staff if he structures an access control list a certain way. An application developer should also develop some empathy for the workload caused by upgrading an application. Likewise, an administrator should have some understanding of what goes into designing and implementing a Notes application for use across multiple organizational units. A Notes administrator should have some basic abilities to build specialized views for his own use.

PLANNING FOR CHANGE

It certainly is true that nature hates a vacuum. What's true for nature and air is also true for companies and information. Any gap in information will be filled with rumors. If you are doing a large deployment of Notes, people will talk about it, whether they have any actual knowledge or not, so you might as well provide them with accurate information on your Notes deployment. Your information should include the current status of the project, as well as document the successes in an optimistic manner and communicate the benefits that the organization is seeing from Notes. Accurate information is far more likely to generate enthusiasm and overcome resistance than are rumors.

The preceding paragraph goes to the heart of most resistance to Notes. Information is power. In some organizations, sharing information means losing power. If the preceding paragraph seems more like a good joke than a possibility in your company, then your Notes deployment will not succeed unless you tackle people's resistance head-on. The best way to start is by setting a good example yourself.

Of course, you need to plan for and expect change. Why would you install Notes if you didn't intend to change the organization in some manner? However, the changes that Notes brings often go far beyond reengineering your business processes. When you reengineer a business process, you need to design explicit steps to accomplish a task. The changes for which you must plan can be identified. You should know the people affected and what their new tasks are. Notes planning involves a far more difficult task: identifying the flow of information within a company. You need to identify sources of information, common paths of information flow, and information users. This information can be critical in identifying probable sources of resistance (information generators) and support (information users). Because of the informal nature of much information within a company, you may never be able to fully identify the information sources and users.

After installing Notes, you can expect that

- More information will be generated at lower levels in the organization.
- Information will flow across department boundaries.
- New information users will emerge as new applications are developed.
- Managers and executives will become more accessible through the use of e-mail.

You should expect that, after installing Notes, information will tend to flow more horizontally, as workflow applications are implemented that automatically route data between departmental units rather than up and down departmental reporting structures. As users from multiple business units participate in joint-application-design sessions, there might be for the first time an active working partnership formed between units that have been in conflict in the past. Expect information to be created at more spots within your organization. Expect users to begin contributing ideas and making suggestions to the IS organization more than they may have in the past. Expect your IS organization to need to become far more responsive and creative in their responses than they might have had to be in the past. Expect your executives, through e-mail and shared data, to become more visible and accessible to the people throughout your organization. You need to communicate these changes as you see them coming and discuss them openly in your organization.

If information within your organization currently tends to flow from the top down and/or is rigidly controlled, you should plan on two to five years before Notes is fully implemented (for medium and large organizations). This time will be required to overcome resistance within the organization.

SUMMARY

Preparing your organization for the changes that Notes will bring is the key element in successfully deploying Notes. These are the key steps in preparing your organization:

- ◆ Staffing and training the rollout team
- ◆ Staffing and training the ongoing support team
- ◆ Involving the entire organization early and often
- ◆ Communicating the advantages and benefits of Notes throughout the deployment cycle
- ◆ Developing cost-effective training strategies, support strategies, and application development strategies for each type of application and each geographic location that needs to be supported

But most of all, plan for and expect resistance to change. Notes will change the relative power of people within your organization, as well as the way information is generated and used. Overcoming resistance caused by these factors will take visible commitment from executives and a strong role model. The key morals for this chapter are: everyone gets trained, and everyone gets involved.

- Identify Supported Platforms and Protocols

- Design Your WAN Strategy

- Size the Hardware

- Identify Current Systems and Applications

- Decide Which Tools to Support

- Develop Naming Guidelines

- Choose Gateways

- Assign Users to Home Servers

CHAPTER 9

Designing Your Notes Network

Designing your Notes network involves making all the decisions necessary to configure your Notes servers and clients and to design and implement your pilot application. Of particular importance is the creation of a naming scheme for your users and servers that balances the competing requirements of administrative overhead, user convenience, and security. The other key goal is to design network topologies that are easy to administer while providing a scalable, extendable architecture.

This chapter covers the advantages and disadvantages of hierarchical naming. Naming schemes for your servers, users, domains, and networks are recommended. The chapter also discusses configuring mail routing and Notes network topologies. Before designing your Notes network, you should review Chapter 5, "Building a Deployment Plan." It's okay to install a few Notes clients and servers for use by the project team before you begin to design your production network. Just make sure that everyone realizes that the network built for the project team isn't the production network. You shouldn't design your production network before you have taken an assessment of your enterprise and defined the scope of your Notes deployment. These are critical factors in deciding the naming schemes and network topologies that will best suit your organization.

In Chapter 5, sixteen steps common to designing any Notes network are listed. Of those sixteen, several have already been covered in Chapter 7, "Determining Hardware and Software Needs." This chapter covers the remaining steps. These are the steps to designing a Notes network:

1. Identify supported desktop platforms.
2. Identify supported server platforms.
3. Identify supported network protocols.
4. Develop a WAN strategy for remote access.
5. Decide the location of servers.
6. Identify your replication architecture (network topology).
7. Size the hardware for desktop and servers.
8. Identify current IS systems that must integrate with Notes.
9. Identify current desktop applications that must integrate with Notes.
10. Decide which application development tools to support.
11. Create naming guidelines for people, servers, and groups.

12. Name your Notes domains.

13. Name your Notes networks.

14. Name your Notes servers.

15. Choose gateways for mail, fax, Internet, etc.

16. Assign users to home servers.

Chapter 7 covers steps 1, 2, 3, and 6. The rest of this chapter is organized around the remaining steps in designing your Notes network. When you complete the design of your network, you should have decided everything you need to begin installing Notes servers and clients. Before releasing a pilot application, you should also complete the development of your standard operating procedures as outined in Chapter 5.

Throughout this chapter, exit criteria appear for each step. Remember that, as discussed in Chapter 5, "Building a Deployment Plan," and Chapter 6, "Customizing Your Deployment Plan," the goal isn't to try to plan out your entire installation before taking any action. You repeat (or at least review) every step in this chapter after the pilot, so don't be afraid to make a decision and move ahead. For example, you may severely limit the desktop platforms you support during the pilot, but then decide to support more platforms after the pilot. The only exception to this plan is your naming guidelines. Due to the administrative effort required to change names, you should try to draw up guidelines that can survive as long as Notes survives (because they will survive, whether or not you want them to do so).

STEP 1: IDENTIFY SUPPORTED DESKTOP PLATFORMS

This step is covered in Chapter 7. In summary, your main considerations when choosing a desktop platform are

◆ Consider the in-house availability of support skill.

◆ Small organizations standardize on one platform.

◆ Large organizations should have no more than two platforms.

◆ Don't change platforms just to use Notes.

This step is complete when you can specify every client platform that you will need to support over the next year of your Notes deployment.

STEP 2: IDENTIFY SUPPORTED SERVER PLATFORMS

This step is also covered in Chapter 7. In summary, these are the key points to remember:

◆ Consider the in-house availability of support skill.

◆ Small organizations standardize on one platform.

◆ Large organizations should have no more than two platforms.

◆ Don't change platforms just to use Notes.

This step is complete when you can specify every server platform that you will need to support over the next year of your Notes deployment.

STEP 3: IDENTIFY SUPPORTED NETWORK PROTOCOLS

This step is covered in Chapter 7. In summary, the key points to remember are (all together now)

◆ Consider the in-house availability of support skill.

◆ Small organizations standardize on one platform.

◆ Large organizations should have no more than two platforms.

◆ Don't change platforms just to use Notes.

This step is complete when you can specify every network protocol that you will need to support over the next year of your Notes deployment.

STEP 4: DEVELOP A WAN STRATEGY FOR REMOTE ACCESS

Those enterprises that have mobile users and remote offices need to develop guidelines for when remote users should have a locally available replica of a database and when they should dial directly into your headquarters servers. Your primary considerations are cost and performance. Economics is the primary determinant, although other advantages favor replication of data to a remote server over online access. You should evaluate these types of connections:

◆ WAN connected workstations—the same connectivity as a LAN but often slower and more expensive (this option and the next provide direct access to Notes applications with no replication involved).

◆ WAN connected Notes servers—allows local, fast, cheap access to users local to the server and allows control over the usage of WAN bandwidth through routing and replication schedules.

◆ Dial-up connected Notes servers—same as WAN connected Notes servers, but uses phone lines or other "on demand" connectivity for scheduled routing and replication.

◆ Dial-up connected workstations—each individual connects to a remote Notes server to route and receive mail and to replicate any local replica databases.

The last three options require that data be replicated to a remote server to provide local access to infrequently connected servers and/or workstations, and can't be used in every instance.

You need to perform this analysis for each remote site you plan to support. For each site, ask the following questions:

◆ Which databases does this site need to access? How many hours per day/ week are the databases going to be accessed? What is the total throughput required for all users at the remote site?

◆ Is there a high-speed connection in place? If so, is there enough bandwidth to support your Notes applications? Notes itself places very little overhead on a network, so you simply need to evaluate the load placed by your applications.

◆ What connection speed do you need to support a remote site? A remote site with two or three users will have different bandwidth requirements than a remote site with 25 to 30 users. Your connection options include (but aren't limited to)

   ◆ *Leased T1 lines.* T1 lines offer enough throughput to support nearly any remote site. Fractional T1s are also available.

   ◆ *ISDN lines.* ISDN lines aren't much more expensive than an ordinary phone line and offer 56Kb throughput. Multiple people can share an ISDN line. With ISDN, users will experience a delay of a few seconds while a call is placed, but performance after that should be acceptable for any text-based application.

   ◆ *Modem.* Get at least a 28.8 modem for each user.

   ◆ *Internet.* Remote sites that must place a long-distance call can consider replicating over the Internet, using ISDN lines or ordinary phone lines.

◆ *Private networks.* Network companies such as CompuServe can connect your headquarters and remote sites at a very competitive rate. Dial-up and frame-relay connections (just to name two popular options) are available.

You can mix and match local access to a replica and dialing into headquarters. Use local replica copies for commonly used databases and direct dialing for infrequently used databases. Always bias your selections toward online access (except for dial-up users, who should favor local replicas). Online access minimizes support costs and is getting cheaper all the time. By the time you actually get a working application installed, the cost of supporting online access will be less than your estimate because telecommunication costs are constantly falling.

These are the advantages of having your users dial directly into your headquarters servers:

◆ Timeliness of data. The user gets the latest data without having to wait for a scheduled replication to her remote server.

◆ You save the expense of placing a remote server. This expense includes the cost of the hardware and the extra administrative burden.

These are the advantages of placing a server in a remote office and replicating databases:

◆ Users accessing replica copies generally get better performance.

◆ Users can continue to work when the network is down.

◆ You keep control over replication. If you don't place a server in a remote office, one thing that can happen is that people in the remote office create their own replicas. If you have five people in a remote office, you can end up with three or four of them each having their own replica of a headquarters database. Each worker can end up with a slightly different version of the database, and phone costs skyrocket as each user replicates the entire database. You may not save on hardware or support costs by not placing a remote server. Your overall goal should be to minimize the number of servers, but you must consider carefully the needs of your users.

The following list shows the disadvantages of having your users dial directly into headquarters:

◆ The cost of the phone lines and the connection charges users incur when calling headquarters can add up quickly.

◆ Modems are some of the most troublesome components of a Notes network, requiring a higher percentage of administrative time than users connected locally to their own servers. Setting up a remote server with a single multi-port modem may save time troubleshooting modem problems.

◆ Performance over a 28.8 modem can leave something to be desired. Make sure that the performance of online access is within acceptable limits. You may need to price out higher bandwidth connections or place a remote server if performance is unacceptable.

◆ A remote-site coordinator is needed for each site with a Notes server. The availability of trained personnel can limit your ability to place remote servers.

There are two ways to support online users: have them dial directly into the network with some network package, such as TCP/IP with a SLIP connection; or have them use Notes passthru. These options are available no matter what form of remote connection you choose (dial-up, Internet, private network). Network packages will allow remote users to access every server on the network, not just Notes servers. Notes passthru allows access only to Notes servers, but has some nice security features. For many people, configuring passthru will be easier and more natural than setting up a SLIP connection (or any functionally similar connection). SLIP connections can be a potential security leak on your network. Use remote network connections when your mobile users need to access non-Notes servers, or if you already support remote connections to your network. Use Notes passthru when only Notes resources are needed or security is a concern.

Before completing the design of a remote-access strategy, you should have a written set of guidelines for use by your administrators on when they should place a remote server and when they should have users connect through dial-up. The cost of online access versus replicating a database should be the primary determinant. Figure 9.1 shows the basic calculations used to compare the cost of placing a remote server and the cost of users dialing into a central server. You should perform these calculations for a variety of database sizes and connection costs and distribute the results to anyone responsible for placing remote servers.

Sites that already have a remote server usually prefer to create replicas of any new databases. Once you have placed a remote server, the cost of replicating an extra database is small. Each application still should be analyzed before automatically creating a new replica. If users need access to the latest data, if the database is infrequently used, or if the remote server is operating at capacity, don't create a new replica.

Don't forget to update the grid often. Telecommunications costs are falling rapidly, making online access more attractive over time. Review the placement of remote servers every six months.

Figure 9.1.
Compare the costs of
online access versus
replicating databases
when deciding to place
a remote server.

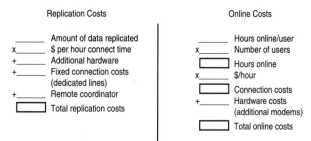

This step is complete when you can detail the communications costs associated with each remote site. You must be able to specify the type of connection and whether a remote server will be placed. You should have a general idea of the performance remote users can expect.

STEP 5: DECIDE THE LOCATION OF SERVERS

Once you have set up your guidelines for remote placement of servers, you are ready to decide the location of your servers. Place database servers and mail servers first, and then decide on dial-up servers. Hub servers will depend on the replication architecture you choose.

Servers at the headquarters location should be stored in a secure environment, not randomly placed around the various floors. Remote locations should consider using secure closets to house the Notes server. Decide the number of servers that you need, taking into account the specialized roles that each server should play. I recommend dedicating servers to mail, dial-up, and hubs. Most installations will start with a single hub server, if they have one at all.

This step is complete when each site has a list of the servers that will be installed at that site.

STEP 6: DESIGN YOUR NETWORK TOPOLOGY

Before deciding your Notes network topology, you should have an up-to-date diagram of your telecommunications network, including all current printers, servers, bridges, and routers. The diagram should clearly identify any remote servers. There are two basic topologies for a Notes network: the hub-and-spoke topology and the serial-connection topology; Figure 9.2 shows an example of each network topology. The connections between servers are determined by the Notes connection documents in the Notes Name and Address Book.

Figure 9.2.
The two basic Notes
network topologies.

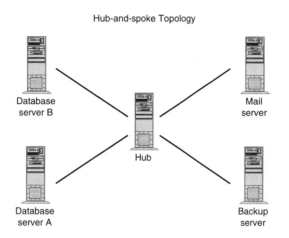

Hub-and-spoke Topology

Database
server B

Mail
server

Hub

Database
server A

Backup
server

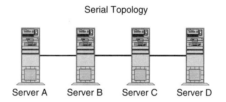

Serial Topology

Server A   Server B   Server C   Server D

HUB-AND-SPOKE TOPOLOGY

I recommend that anyone with more than five servers use a hub-and-spoke network topology with specialized servers for mail, hubs, and backup. The Notes hub server is completely dedicated to replicating data between the various spokes. The spoke servers don't connect directly to each other, so for a change on Spoke A to get replicated to Spoke B, it first has to replicate through the hub. The hub initiates all replications in a "round robin" manner, going around the spokes. The number of spokes that you can connect to a particular hub is completely dependent on the types of applications that you roll out, the frequency of your replications, the amount of data transferred, and the hardware configurations you are using. Typically, 5 to 20 servers can replicate with a single hub. If you need multiple hubs, consider forming a tree configuration with your production database servers forming the leaves of the tree. Figure 9.3 shows a tree configuration.

The hub machine can also serve as a natural link between multiple networks. Having a gateway hub saves money by eliminating the need to install dual-protocol stacks or multiple network cards in all your spoke machines. The hub machine is also a natural server to function as a bridge between various Notes domains.

Figure 9.3.
*A tree topology allows
multiple hubs to
communicate in an
orderly manner.*

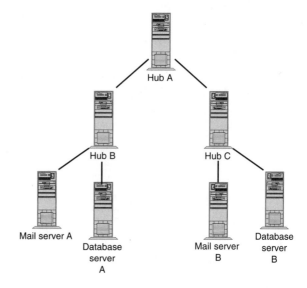

There are several advantages to using a hub-and-spoke topology:

◆ Your connection documents are easier to manage.

Connection documents on your spoke will be small variations on a theme. Thus, your procedures for adding a new spoke server are almost error-free.

◆ Server schedules are easier to develop and maintain.

A server schedule based on a hub-and-spoke architecture is easier to maintain than a schedule based on an architecture in which all machines are connecting to all other machines. Because the hub encapsulates your total replication schedule, you can more easily chart and manage your total server schedule.

◆ It's easier to track the performance of your servers when you use hub-and-spoke architecture.

Replication is a hog. If you replicate between servers frequently, your online users will definitely notice when a replication is in progress. Having all the spokes constantly dialing each other can lead to a large replication load and unnecessary replication on your network.

◆ A hub-and-spoke architecture is more reliable.

Not only are the connection documents easier to set up, but replication problems are reduced. If you have many servers trying to replicate with a particular spoke server, it is possible that Notes will lose a replication request, causing data not to be replicated between those two particular servers.

Note

> Even when using a hub-and-spoke network topology, you can set up a few direct connections between servers for replicating high-priority data or for replicating large amounts of data between two servers. Be careful. You should have clear guidelines on when you will or won't set up a direct connection between two servers. Specify in the connection document the exact databases that these two servers should replicate. Otherwise, if you set up a direct connection between two servers to service a single application, those two servers will replicate all databases that they have in common. Default replication is between servers, not between databases.

See Chapter 10, "Installing and Configuring Notes Servers," for details on setting up a hub-and-spoke architecture.

RING TOPOLOGY

For smaller organizations with only a few Notes servers, the cost of an additional hub server isn't justified. In this case, you should set up connection documents so that all servers contact all other servers. Figure 9.4 shows a diagram of this topology.

Figure 9.4.
When you have fewer
than five Notes servers,
set them up in a ring.

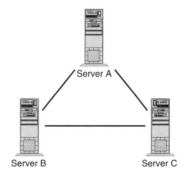

Server A

Server B   Server C

Note that the number of connection documents grows quickly as the number of servers increases. Plan ahead. If there is any possibility that you will install more than five servers over the first year or two, begin planning immediately for a hub-and-spoke topology. Designate spokes and let one server function as a hub. During the initial phases, it makes sense for small organizations to have all servers connect directly to each other.

See Chapter 10 for details on setting up a ring network.

In addition to deciding the replication architecture for your Notes network, you should dedicate servers to particular roles. The following servers should be set up:

◆ At least one dedicated mail server (can handle 75 to 500 users)

◆ At least one dedicated hub server (hub-and-spoke networks only, can handle 5 to 20 spokes)

◆ At least one production database server

◆ A server for external domains

◆ A backup server

Enterprises that require 24 hours per day/7 days per week operation need to set up a backup server. The backup server connects to your hub server.

Mail servers, backup servers, and external servers connect directly to your hub just like any other spoke server.

This step is complete when you can draw a network diagram that shows the logical connections between Notes servers. All servers planned for the first year should be listed.

Step 7: Size the Hardware for Desktop and Servers

When you know the geographic location of each database server, you can estimate the hardware configurations needed for each site. This step is covered in Chapter 7. In summary, the key points to consider are these:

◆ Don't install underpowered configurations.

◆ Install enough memory.

This step is complete when you have a minimum supported configuration for each client and server platform in your organization. Specialized configurations for backup servers, dial-up servers, and hub servers should be slight variations on a central theme. You should be able to generate purchase orders for hardware at this point.

Step 8: Identify Current IS Systems That Must Integrate with Notes

The planning that you have done before attempting to design your Notes network is useful here. In your assessment of the enterprise, you held joint design sessions with key stakeholders throughout the enterprise. You have identified the types of applications that you are likely to develop for each of your business units, and you have identified the information feeds available for each of these applications. Now is the time to decide how you will actually get that data into Notes. If the data is already stored in a current IS system, you need to decide whether you can rely on a third-party product to provide the link, or whether you need custom development.

Notes system integration is perhaps one of the most challenging parts of a Notes rollout, often requiring custom application development using the Notes C API. Before diving into custom programming, closely investigate the products available. More and more third-party products are capable of connecting Notes servers to an ever-increasing range of legacy IS systems, eliminating the need to develop your own (expensive) bridges.

The first step in deciding whether to buy or build connections to your back-end systems is identifying which ones have to integrate directly with Notes. For example, you may have an order-entry system already implemented and working fine. You may want to feed orders into Notes and then use Notes' workflow capabilities to process those orders, routing them through your internal departments. If your order-entry system is built on a mainframe system using an old hierarchical database, you need to develop custom code that pulls data on a regular basis and feeds it into a Notes database.

When you have identified the IS systems that must be integrated with Notes, enter them onto your Notes network diagram. Your diagram should indicate which servers will connect to your other systems.

This step is complete when you have an updated diagram of your Notes network, showing all systems that will provide data or get data from Notes (at least for the pilot application).

STEP 9: IDENTIFY CURRENT DESKTOP APPLICATIONS THAT MUST INTEGRATE WITH NOTES

You probably have already rolled out some desktop applications for your users. In some applications, it makes sense to integrate the data into Notes. You need to identify the applications that people are currently using (which you should have accomplished when you assessed the enterprise) and decide which ones need to integrate with Notes. The desktop integration issues are different for each of the supported platforms—Mac, Windows, OS/2, and UNIX. Your application developers will have to decide the best way to link Notes and personal productivity applications. Linking them is really an application development issue. Check with any of the books on Notes application development.

This step is complete when you have a list of the applications that must integrate with Notes (at least for the pilot). You don't need to decide exactly how each application will be integrated. This is accomplished in the next step.

Step 10: Decide Which Application Development Tools to Support

When you have a list of systems that will connect to Notes, and a general idea (from the enterprise assessment) of the types of applications you need to develop, you are ready to decide which application development tools to support. Remember, fewer tools is better and one tool is best. If you can build your applications using only the Notes interface, I recommend doing so.

The Notes interface, while more powerful in Release 4 than in previous versions, is still limited. To have complete freedom at the user-interface level, you will have to move to a tool such as Visual Basic or PowerBuilder. There are specialized products that link Visual Basic, PowerBuilder, and others to Notes. In fact, virtually every application development tool developer is building a package that allows the program to work with Notes databases. Carefully evaluate the power of these links. Some of them may not allow direct access to all Notes features, including access to views, navigators, and the creation of agents. Be sure to run a few quick tests with all tools to quickly exercise their abilities before making a final decision.

This step is complete when you have a complete list of the application development tools that will be used to build Notes applications. You should specify a tool or product for each type of application you will build and for each system or product that must integrate with Notes. This list will be used to develop a training shedule for developers and administrators.

Step 11: Develop Naming Guidelines for Users, Servers, and Groups

Naming is one of the most important and least understood parts of Notes. The names you choose will affect the amount of effort needed to support your Notes network. When developing naming guidelines for your users and servers, you need to

◆ Decide whether you have a compelling reason not to use hierarchical names. If not, use them!

◆ Develop a list of organizational unit certificates (for use with hierarchical names only).

- ◆ Develop guidelines for naming users.
- ◆ Develop guidelines for naming groups.
- ◆ Develop guidlines for naming servers.

You have two fundamental ways to name servers and users: flat names and hierarchical names. Flat names are simple names—for example, John Doe or Mary Smith. Hierarchical names are a combination of a person's name along with some other distinguishing characteristic, such as the name of the company he works for and perhaps the name of the organizational unit that he works in. Hierarchical names are designed to solve the problem of uniquely identifying people on large networks. The use of flat names often leads to mail IDs such as ADAHL3. If you want to send mail to Andrew Dahl, should you send it to ADAHL, ADAHL2, or ADAHL3? It's not clear. The hierarchical names for these three people make this clear:

Andrew Dahl/Publishing/L3Comm

Alan Dahl/Marketing/Acme

Alexa Dahl/Drivers/Jeep

I recommend hierarchical names for all organizations, large and small. The world is moving to hierarchical names; if you ever expect to tap into a network beyond your own company limits, you should be using hierarchical names.

Let's take a look at how hierarchical names—also known as *distinguished names*— are put together. A hierarchical name in Notes is modeled after the X.500 specification. A distinguished name is a combination of a common name, an organizational unit, the organization, and an optional country name.

- ◆ *Common name.* Your common name is your first name, last name, and perhaps a middle initial.
- ◆ *Organizational unit.* Organizational units quickly identify the department or geographic location of the person. A hierarchical name may use more than one organizational unit within a single name. Examples of organizational units are North America, Europe, Marketing, Sales, New York, or perhaps a combination like Sales/New York.
- ◆ *Organization.* The organization name is typically the name of your business. For example, Acme, IBM, or L3Comm.
- ◆ *Country name.* Country names are an optional part of hierarchical names and aren't used very often. A country name is a two-letter abbreviation for a country. Before you use a country name, you should register your organizational name with the clearinghouse of other X.500 names within your country. You can view current X.500 names and register yours by using the World Wide Web at http://gopher.gsfc.nasa.gov/services/email/x.500.html. Use country names only when you are very concerned about the complete

uniqueness of your names on a worldwide basis, both within and outside your organization. Two examples of country names are US for the United States and CA for Canada.

You combine these units in each component of a distinguished name with slashes. Examples of valid distinguished names:

Scott Comeon/Columbus/Publishing/QuickCon

Mike Crashwell/Development/HAL

ADVANTAGES OF HIERARCHICAL NAMES

Hierarchical naming is quickly becoming the preferred method of naming users and servers. Hierarchical naming takes some planning, but offers several benefits:

◆ Each user and server can have a unique name.

◆ Hierarchical names provide a clue as to the role of a person or server within your organization.

For example, John Doe by itself gives no clue as to whether John delivers mail or is the CEO for the organization, but John Doe/Marketing/Acme clearly identifies John as a member of the Marketing staff. The same is true for servers that have hierarchical names. For example, Mail/Marketing/Acme is clearly the mail server for the Marketing department at Acme.

◆ Hierarchical names allow the use of wild cards in your access control lists.

For example, if a database has the name John Doe/*/* in the access control list, or in a group listed in the access control list, both John Doe/Ohio/Acme and John Doe/California/Acme have the same level of access to that database. However, the use of distinguished names within an access control list, for example John Doe/Ohio, means that John Doe/California would have no access to that data. If you have a database that should only be accessed by the Marketing department, you can put */Marketing/Acme in the access control list, and only people who are in your Marketing department will have access to that database (assuming that the default access is no access).

◆ Using hierarchical names allows you to use hierarchical certificates, which have several advantages over the use of flat certificates:

  ◆ Hierarchical certificates enable decentralized management of your Name and Address Book. (You can still centrally manage your NAB if you want.)

  To use hierarchical names within your organization, you need to create a certificate for each organizational unit. You start with an organizational certificate, Acme, and then add several organizational unit certificates: Marketing/Acme, Product Development/Acme, Research/Acme. The organizational certificate is kept in a secure place, and the organizational unit certificates (stored in certifier ID files) are handed out to certifiers within the various departments. Thus, hierarchical certificates, by allowing you to create certificates for each department, enable you to have multiple people involved in the management of your Name and Address Book.

Contrast this with flat names, where there is only one certificate in the entire enterprise—the organizational certificate. In this case, anyone with access to the organizational certificate can create any name he wants, and give himself complete access to any data within your organization. People with access to organizational unit certificates can create only names that match the name of the organizational unit certificate. For example, using the certificate Marketing/Acme, a certifier could create the user ID Jerome/Marketing/Acme but not the user ID Jerome/Sales/Acme. User IDs certified with an organizational unit certificate will inherit the organizational name that is part of that certificate.

◆ Hierarchical certificates allow you to react quickly in case of a compromised certificate.

Because your users are all certified with a particular organizational certificate, and different users are certified with different organizational unit certificates, fewer people will have to be recertified when a certificate is lost or stolen. If an organizational unit certificate is compromised—that is, falls into the hands of an untrusted party— only those users who have been certified with that particular organizational unit certificate need to be recertified. Don't forget that you also need to recertify servers that have been certified with that particular organizational unit certificate. Step-by-step instructions to recertify users and servers are included in Chapter 16, "Administering Notes Servers."

◆ With hierarchical certificates, you can create a deny-access entry in your server document to prevent any user IDs certified by a compromised certificate from accessing the server.

Contrast this with a flat naming scheme when an organizational certificate is compromised. In this situation, all users and all servers throughout the entire organization must be recertified. This is a much larger job.

◆ Hierarchical certificates allow users within an organization to verify each other's identities.

Using hierarchical certificates or organizational certificates that all descend from a common organizational certificate means that all users within an enterprise share a common certificate, namely the organizational certificate. Because they share a certificate, they can authenticate each other's identities with no further administrative overhead.

Contrast this with having multiple flat certificates within an organization. This case could arise in a large enterprise where you have multiple pilots that have grown into multiple production spheres. When you have multiple flat certificates in an organization, in order for a user from one to authenticate a user on another, one or the other user would have to be certified with the other person's flat certifier certificate.

◆ Hierarchical names give you tight control over external access to your databases.

If the Sales department certifies a customer server, allowing that customer server to access the Sales department's server, the customer doesn't automatically gain access to any other server in your organization. The customer can access only servers certified by the Sales certificate or by a descendant of the Sales certificate. A server certified by Product Development couldn't be accessed by this customer.

Figure 9.5 shows the servers that could be accessed by an external server certified with a hierarchical certificate.

Figure 9.5.
External servers can access servers certified by descendants of the external server's cross certificate.

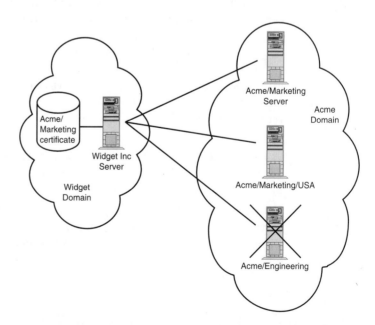

When using flat certificates, an external server certified by your organizational certificate can access any of your internal servers.

DISADVANTAGES OF HIERARCHICAL NAMES

I recommend that all Notes installations use hierarchical naming. Whether yours is a large organization or a very small organization, the advantages outweigh the disadvantages. In the spirit of full disclosure, however, I hereby list the disadvantages that are associated with using hierarchical names:

◆ Hierarchical naming requires planning. Perhaps the largest disadvantage to using hierarchical names is the up-front planning that must go into creating the organizational unit certificates. The quality of this up-front planning greatly determines the amount of downstream administrative burden required to maintain your Notes installation. Careful planning is a must, but you must balance the time spent on planning with the need to get your first pilot applications done as quickly as possible.

◆ Hierarchical naming results in having to recertify users when they transfer. See the next section, "Creating Organizational Unit Certificates," for a discussion of ways to minimize this burden.

◆ When you deal with many distinguished names, the screen can get cluttered. Applications that you design that display names should parse the hierarchical name to display only the common name for that particular user. Application design and construction may take slightly longer when using hierarchical certificates.

I hope you're not surprised that the list of disadvantages is shorter than the list of advantages. For a complete discussion of certificates and how they are used to create distinguished names, see Chapter 3, "Understanding Security."

CREATING ORGANIZATIONAL UNIT CERTIFICATES

One issue common to naming both people and servers is whether your organizational unit certificates' names should be based on departments or on geographic locations. Creating organizational unit certificates based on departments will more easily provide a tight level of security to your data through the use of wild cards (assuming that access to your data will be based on departments more often than geography). I recommend the use of departmental naming schemes. In large organizations, you may need to use more than one level of organizational unit certificate (for example, John Doe/Legal/Marketing/Acme). If your organization is highly decentralized, with each geographic entity acting as an independent business, use a combination of departments and geographic names (for example, John Doe/Legal/Columbus/Acme).

Departmental naming schemes can result in increased administrative burden due to reorganizations and transfers. When your corporation reorganizes, whole departments go away and the people in them are assigned to other departments. To maintain a consistent naming scheme, you will have to recertify all users affected, as well as update any access control lists or groups in which they appeared. Transfers between departments result in a steady stream of recertifications when names are based on departments. When Bertie (Bertie/Fittings/Acme) transfers to Accounting, her name must be changed to Bertie/Accounting/Acme. Whenever a person's user ID changes, the user ID must be recertified.

The use of geographic names minimizes this problem because it is less common, although still possible, that people transfer between geographic locations or that geographic locations disappear. When names are based on geographic locations, you don't have to change a person's user ID when he transfers between departments but stays at the same site.

Both departmental and geographic naming are equivalent in providing unique names within your organization. Department names and geographic names also are equivalent in their capacity to provide security, although departmental naming is likely to reduce the administrative burden of maintaining tight control through the use of wild cards. Geographically based organizational units can work better in providing decentralized management of your certificates, allowing you to have a certifier at each of your major geographic locations. This strategy avoids having a remote certifier certify users he's never met. Departmental and geographic certificates are equivalent in providing the capability to segregate users into groups, so that you only need to recertify a small portion of your organization should a certificate become compromised. Departmental and geographic certificates that all inherit a common organizational unit are equivalent in allowing users to authenticate each other's identity.

Whether you go with departmental or geographic names, the actual names that you use should be cleared with the people who are going to have those names. Names are, in some corporate cultures, a particularly sensitive area.

NAMING PEOPLE

Keep in mind the purposes for which a person's name will be used. A person's name is used in mail routing and in access control lists. For both of these uses, the uniqueness of a person's name is the *key* requirement.

When addressing mail, people don't like to type long names. You may think that this would be a major disadvantage of hierarchical names (they can get quite long). This isn't the case. When addressing mail, just type the common name of your recipient. Notes will search the Name and Address Book for matches. When there are multiple matches, a list is presented. Simply choose the correct name from the list. The use of hierarchical names occasionally results in a few extra mouse clicks. These extra mouse clicks can be avoided for commonly used recipients by creating an entry in your Personal Address Book. Use a memorable but unique alias for the recipient when creating the entry. When addressing mail, simply enter the alias. Notes will take care of the rest.

Of far more concern is Notes' capability to deliver mail. To deliver mail, Notes requires unique names within a domain. Hierarchical names are designed to provide unique names. Flat names result in strange abbreviations in an effort to provide uniqueness. Flat names can end up making mail addressing more difficult.

Even hierarchical names can be further clarified through the use of middle initials. I recommend the use of middle initials. Even in small organizations, you should plan ahead and use middle initials to help distinguish names from one another. The middle initial should appear only as part of a person's fully qualified name (Robert E. Lee/Columbus/Reps). The person's simple name shouldn't contain the middle initial (Robert Lee). This system keeps mail addressing simple while making name conflicts even more unlikely.

Here I'm talking about the actual name entered in the Name and Address Book for each person. Whether to use aliases is a more difficult decision. You need to decide whether allowing aliases will create more confusion in your organization (with users wondering, "What is that person's name?" and "Who belongs to this name?") than it removes.

Another scenario to consider is when people are commonly known around the office by a nickname, and people want to send mail to that nickname. If you require a person's Notes name to be their full legal name, you will have some confusion and cause your support staff to spend time explaining why mail isn't being delivered to this person. I have no recommendations on the use of aliases. In most organizations, they aren't a problem. If you allow aliases or nicknames, you need to decide whether that nickname will be that person's only name in Notes, or whether that person should have multiple documents in the Name and Address Book, one with the real name and one with the nickname. If you allow nicknames, I recommend creating a second entry in the Name and Address Book for that person.

Avoid using names with underscores, because Internet gateways will translate an underscore into a space. This will prevent your internal staff from sending or receiving mail from the Internet.

NAMING SERVERS

Server names are visible to the user and should provide some clue as to the data stored on that particular server. Server naming is an easy-to-overlook aspect of designing your Notes network. It's an extremely important step in your Notes network design. Notes server names will be visible to users as part of the names of the databases on their desktops as well as in the list of servers from which they are allowed to choose. Server names are also difficult to change. They appear in many places, so it's important to choose names that can help guide your users to a proper selection when they are searching for a database. Choose server names that will retain their meaning as you shift servers around and as your Notes deployment grows. When naming your servers, take into account the following possible issues:

◆ Use names that meet the requirements of your network.

   If you are using TCP/IP, your server name should be identical to your TCP/IP host name. In this case, you are forced to take into account all the needs of your Notes topology when creating your TCP/IP server names.

◆ Avoid spaces and underscores in server names.

   As a practical matter, it's easier for an administrator (who will be typing the name of a server quite often) to avoid typing spaces. It's also good to avoid having any names in your system that use underscores, as underscores are translated by gateways into other characters.

◆ Use simple names.

   If yours is an international enterprise, your server names aren't translated when they are transmitted to international sites. Keeping your names simple will help your international users to understand the purpose of those servers.

◆ Use separate names for different types of servers.

   When designing your Notes network, you will be assigning servers to particular tasks. For example, all but the smallest installations will have a separate server set up to hold mailboxes. In addition, you likely will be setting up hub servers for replication purposes and dial-up servers to help support remote users. You may be dividing your production data servers into different categories, based on department or type of application supported. The names of each of these servers should imply the type of server. For example, a mail server may be called Mail 1/Acme. A dial-up server could be called Passthru/Acme. Pay particular importance to server names that will be visible outside your organization. This includes all servers in your external domain. Use a name that reflects well on your corporation.

Avoid cutesy names, such as those named after people's dogs, places of birth, or favorite artists, unless the whole organization is willing to use one scheme (for example, cartoon characters).

There is one disadvantage to naming your servers based on the type of server. Changing the function of a server is difficult. This doesn't in any way inhibit the growth of your Notes deployment. It's far more common that you will simply add a new server to your network rather than change the function of an existing server.

◆ Avoid using names with underscores, because Internet gateways translate an underscore into a space.

Naming Groups

Groups are simply lists of people and servers. Groups are used, as are people's names, for mail routing and access control. The primary benefit of using a group is that users save keystrokes when sending broadcast messages. For example, if you have twelve people in your Marketing department, you can create a group called Marketing and list all twelve people in it. To send a message to all twelve people, you simply need to type `Marketing` for the address and the message is sent to all twelve people.

Groups also simplify access control lists. Groups of servers are common in access control lists. Because access control lists are duplicated to many databases, the administrator saves significant time by using groups. For example, without the use of groups, when a new server is added to a domain, every database in that domain might have to have the new server's name added to the access control list. With groups, the new server is added once to the group of servers comprising the domain (this group is generally called LocalDomainServers).

Group names should be relatively short and easy to guess. Group names should also be fairly descriptive of the purpose of the group. There are two situations to consider: permanent groups within your organization, and temporary teams. You may create groups for particular projects, or you may create group names based on geographic or departmental boundaries within an organization. You don't need to choose a single way of naming groups. You can easily create and delete groups as you need them. Some group names are created to ease the administrative burden, such as the default groups listed in Notes databases (LocalDomainServers and OtherDomainServers). Early in the Notes deployment, the only issues you need to resolve about groups are the standard groups that you are going to support for administrative purposes. These groups will be included in every database's access control list. It's best to create your default administrator groups before you have too many databases.

Another important step in your deployment, creating standard groups, is covered in Chapter 5 in the section "Step 6: Develop Standard Operating Procedures."

This step is complete when you have developed guidelines for naming people, servers, and groups. These guidelines should be available to all people responsible for creating or certifying ID files.

STEP 12: NAME YOUR NOTES DOMAINS

One of the most confusing concepts in Notes for many people is that of a domain. A *domain* is a logical collection of servers. The servers can be running on multiple networks, at multiple sites, including international sites. Users within a domain can be using different certificates, operating systems, and naming schemes.

Domains are often confused with certificates. The confusion arises because most organizations use their company name for their domain and the company name also appears in their certificates. Certificates and domains are two entirely separate concepts. Certificates are used in authentication and are a security measure. Domains have nothing to do with security. It is entirely possible to protect servers within a single domain from each other. You can change a domain name without recertifying users and servers, or recertify users and servers without changing the domain name.

Each domain has a single Name and Address Book that contains all the entries for all people and servers within that domain. This makes sending mail to people within the same domain more convenient than sending mail to a different domain. To address mail to someone within the same domain, you need only specify his or her distinguished name. To route mail to users in other domains, you have to specify not only the distinguished name, but the domain as well. For example, any user within the Cat Stuff domain wishing to send mail to Les Linko, a user in the Cat Stuff domain, would type

Les Linko/Toys/Cat Stuff

in the Recipient field. Someone from the Dog Stuff domain would have to type

Les Linko/Toys/Cat Stuff @ Cat Stuff

Having multiple domains implies that you will be managing multiple Name and Address Books. There is only one advantage to having multiple Name and Address Books: you can manage more than 50,000 users. If you are going to have more than 50,000 users within a single domain, however, you should consider creating more than one domain.

I recommend creating one domain for your production data servers, one domain for your application developers, at least one test domain (three if you're building extra-enterprise applications), and an external domain. Some people will also choose to have an international domain, although that isn't necessary. When naming each of your domains, you should provide short, meaningful names. The names that you use for your test domain and application development domain aren't as important. For example, it is easy to use AcmeTest or AcmeDev.

This step is complete when you have a list of named domains for your organization.

Step 13: Name Your Notes Networks

As with servers, naming your networks is an easy-to-overlook aspect of your Notes design. However, the names that you give your various networks have implications for other aspects of Notes. The key decision that you will face in creating the names of your Notes networks is when to have one network and when to use multiple networks.

You should pay particular attention to the naming of your networks. First, you need to understand how Notes uses your network names. All servers listed on a particular network have to be able to talk to each other using a single protocol. All servers grouped into a single network should be physically available either on the same LAN or through a bridge. Servers available only through dial-up or that require a second protocol to communicate can't be part of the same network. For example, three servers on a LAN all set up to connect with TCP/IP can be within the same network, although they need not be. See Figure 9.6 for servers on a single network.

Figure 9.6.
A Notes server on a
single network must be
able to communicate
using a single protocol.

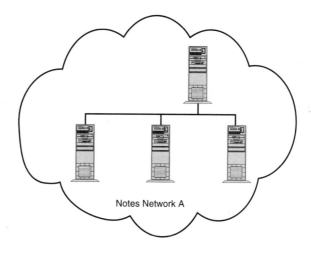

Notes Network A

Servers within a network instantaneously route mail to other servers on the same network. Servers on separate networks must have connection documents set up in the Name and Address Book. The connection documents list the times and criteria that determine when a connection will be made to route mail. Servers within the same network are visible to users in the server lists in the Open Database list box. If you have a large number of servers, even if they are all on the same LAN, you should consider creating separate networks. List the production database servers on one network and other types of servers on a separate network. For example, if you have a large number of servers at your headquarters location—some backup servers, some passthru servers, some hub servers—it can be confusing to users to see all these servers listed in the Open Database list box. Users shouldn't be accessing databases directly from these servers. Any server that shouldn't be directly accessed by users should be set up on a separate network. For networks that share a LAN, set the connection documents to route mail when a single piece of mail arrives.

Use a combination of your geographic location and network type when naming networks; for example, BostonNetBios or ColumbusNetware.

Using One Network Name

In today's world of wide area networks, bridges and routers are extremely common. This gives you the option of having servers in remote locations being physically available over a common protocol. So, for example, you may have a server farm in Columbus, Ohio, and another server farm in Milwaukee. The LAN in both of these locations could be connected via a bridge, giving you an option when naming your Notes network to include servers at both of these sites on the same Notes network.

Advantages of using one network name:

◆ Your mail is routed instantaneously between these servers.

◆ The location of the servers becomes transparent to the end users. The end users are presented with a list of server names without regard to their geographic location.

Disadvantages of using one network name for your entire Notes network:

◆ The location of servers is transparent to your end users. This can cause frustration when users select servers at a remote location when they could be selecting servers at a headquarters site. This can increase traffic over your bridge or router.

◆ Traffic across your bridge or router increases, especially when you have users browsing remote servers. Of course, you can always design your bridge or router so that only your servers can use it to communicate. This restriction may actually cause problems, as administrators often will need to manage remote servers from their desktops.

USING MORE THAN ONE NETWORK NAME

If you need to have more than one network name, I recommend choosing a different network name for each geographic location, even when those geographic locations are connected via a bridge or router. Using multiple Notes networks, the users see only those servers in the Open Database list box where the vast majority of their data should be located. Because users don't see servers on the other side of the bridge or router, you can manage traffic through your bridge or router. Figure 9.7 shows multiple LANs divided into multiple Notes networks.

Figure 9.7.
Using multiple Notes
networks to reduce
traffic over a bridge.

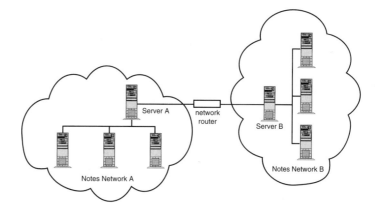

Probably the most significant advantage to having multiple network names in a WAN environment is that you can manage the messaging traffic that Notes generates. In most cases, the traffic isn't significant, but, if you are saddled with numerous slow links that are heavily used, you can schedule message routing periodically, allowing you to control what I call the "spill" level (that is, the number of waiting messages that will cause the server to route regardless of the schedule).

One disadvantage to this approach is that the mail router doesn't know about servers on other LANs until you add a connection document. You need to set up a connection between at least one computer on each LAN. In Figure 9.7, one connection document is used to link Server A to Server B. All mail traffic between these two Notes networks goes through A and B. You don't need to set up a connection document between every pair of servers.

Also, you will be limiting the databases that users can access. Because users can't directly access servers in other Notes networks, you will need to create replicas of common databases at each site. The exception to this rule is servers in a single-protocol WAN environment. In this environment, users can access any server directly by choosing File | Database | Open and typing the name of the desired database in the dialog box.

This step is complete when you have divided your Notes servers into Notes networks. Each network should have a name and protocol specified.

STEP 14: NAME YOUR NOTES SERVERS

At this point you should know how many servers you need and where they are being placed. Use the guidelines developed in step 11 to assign names to each server.

You have completed this step when every server has a name, a network, and a domain. You should be able to register the actual servers (create ID files, server documents, and so on) at this point.

STEP 15: CHOOSE GATEWAYS FOR MAIL, FAX, INTERNET, ETC.

These gateways are common to most installations. The products you choose depend completely on your requirements.

If you have more than one e-mail package, you know that keeping the directories of multiple mail products synchronized is a fair challenge that doubles the amount of administrative overhead. Routing mail reliably between two different mail products has also been a challenge. You will need to decide whether you are going to try to standardize on one mail package or support two mail packages. You don't need to use Notes Mail. Notes can directly use any mail system that supports the VIM or MAPI protocols.

For many people, supporting multiple mail packages is unavoidable. If you are one of the unlucky ones, you will have to install gateways between the two mail systems. There are already off-the-shelf gateways connecting Notes to virtually every other mail system. Notes is now the closest thing to a global mail hub that exists in the marketplace. You can route mail into or out of Notes from virtually any other product or destination, including the Internet, Microsoft Mail, IBM Profs, and MHS. You will need to get copies of competing gateways and evaluate them according to their ability to minimize your administrative time, keep directories synchronized, and support MIME and other mail standards.

In addition to mail gateways, you may want to consider setting up fax and Internet gateways. If you have a particularly large volume of mail going to and from the Internet, you may need to use special configurations to support the load. The key strategy is to split your inbound and outbound gateways.

When this step is complete, you should be able to draw a complete diagram of your Notes network. The diagram should include each server, printer, and bridge. Each server should have a hierarchical name, a network name, and a domain name assigned. Links to other systems should be shown.

STEP 16: ASSIGN USERS TO HOME SERVERS

In Notes, each user must have a home server. I recommend assigning a secondary home server as well. The secondary home server is used when the primary home server is down. A mail server can handle, depending upon usage, anywhere from 100 to 500 users. The maximum load that you can place on a mail server is completely dependent upon the peak simultaneous usage. Chapter 7 provides detailed information on sizing mail servers. Chapter 14, "Administering Notes Mail," contains more details on administering Notes Mail.

The home server is the user's mail server. Using a dedicated mail server (discussed in Chapters 7 and 9) makes this step trivial. Simply assign users to the closest mail server, remembering to balance the load in locations that have more than one mail server. This step must be completed before installing the pilot application.

This step is complete when you have assigned every pilot user to a home server. This is just a planning step. You will use this information when you create ID files for users. You don't need to create the actual user IDs until you are ready to roll out an application.

SUMMARY

Designing your Notes network correctly is a key step in minimizing your administrative overhead over the long haul. Designing your Notes network isn't the first step in your deployment plan. Before designing your Notes network, make sure that you have done an accurate assessment of your enterprise, and have some basic idea of the types of applications that you will likely develop. Once you have done your assessment, designing your Notes network can be fairly straightforward.

When you are done designing your Notes network, you should have

- ◆ Decided on platforms for clients and servers
- ◆ Chosen a network protocol
- ◆ Planned out and created all of your organizational unit certificates
- ◆ Created your server documents
- ◆ Created guidelines for naming people, servers, and groups
- ◆ Configured your replication topology

◆ Completely updated your telecommunications network diagram with your planned Notes servers and planned Notes connections

◆ Formed a clear plan for assigning users to individual servers, giving you some feel for the number of users that you plan on supporting with each server

The next step after designing your Notes network is to develop your standard operating procedures. From there you move on to building your applications. When you are ready to build your applications, plan to exercise your Notes network early on and gather feedback on the quality of the network. Set up your Notes network with growth in mind, but use feedback from your actual experiences early on to tune or change your Notes design.

- Installing and
  Configuring
  Notes Servers

- Installing Notes
  Clients

- Migrating from
  Notes 3.x

P A R T III

Installing Notes

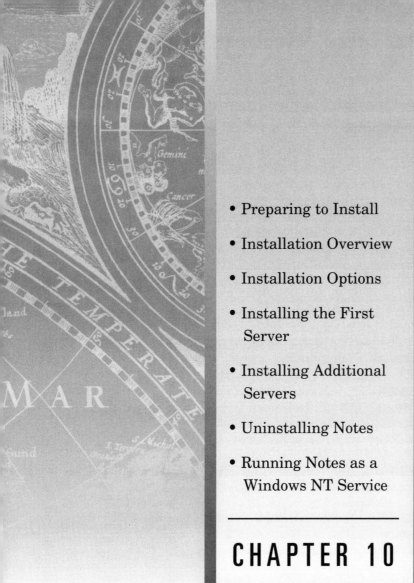

CHAPTER 10

Installing and Configuring Notes Servers

PREPARING TO INSTALL

To deploy Notes for the first time or to upgrade an existing Notes installation to Lotus Notes Release 4, you must get an idea about how Notes actually works. Even then, planning your Notes setup is vital, especially for large Notes networks. The better you develop your Notes deployment plan, the less time you will find yourself spending performing administrative maintenance on your network. After you have the preliminaries completed, it is time to deploy and install Notes. This chapter takes a step-by-step look at installing Notes servers. Specifically, it walks you through the Notes installation process on OS/2 and Windows NT servers.

Before you install Lotus Notes, you have to ensure that the computer meets the minimum hardware requirements, the operating system is properly configured, and the necessary operating system network drivers are in place. The importance of planning your Notes network before installation cannot be exaggerated. Planning your Notes network involves architecting and naming your domain(s), organization(s), and Notes named network(s); designing a server topology; planning a naming scheme; and deciding names for the servers and users. Changing the design of the Notes network is often a nontrivial task. Notes network design is covered in detail in Chapter 9, "Designing Your Notes Network."

PRE-INSTALLATION PLANNING

Before you install your first Notes production server, be sure to review the following chapters:

- ◆ Chapter 5, "Building a Deployment Plan"
- ◆ Chapter 6, "Customizing Your Deployment Plan"
- ◆ Chapter 7, "Determining Hardware and Software Needs"
- ◆ Chapter 8, "Preparing Your Organization"
- ◆ Chapter 9, "Designing Your Notes Network"

It's especially important that you review Chapter 9. If you are migrating from Notes Release 3.x, you also should review Chapter 12, "Migrating from Notes 3.x."

The following sections describe the items that you must plan before installation.

NETWORK DRIVERS

Lotus Notes is a client/server application that permits groups of people to collaborate by using networks. Server-to-server and client-to-server communication can take place over local area networks (LANs) or wide area networks (WANs). Notes communication also can take place over remote connections, using protocols such as

X.25 or X.PC. In order to set up Notes communication on a LAN, the communicating entities (servers and/or workstations) must "speak" the same LAN protocol.

Naming Conventions for Notes Networks

Before setting up the first server in the organization, you should make decisions about the names that you are going to use for the domain, organization, Notes named network, and server. The following sections provide some guidelines for naming conventions and requirements.

Domain Names

A domain name can be up to 31 bytes in length, with no spaces. You shouldn't use periods within the name; reserve periods for compatibility with other mail systems. The author doesn't recommend the use of commas in the domain name, to avoid problems with mail routing. For example, you should use Acme instead of Acme Inc. to avoid using a space and period.

Organization Names

Typically, the organization name is the same as the domain name because, in most cases, a one-to-one correspondence between the domain and the organization is recommended. The organization name becomes the name of the organizational certificate, and it can be up to 64 bytes long. The author also recommends a minimum length of 3 characters.

Notes Named Network Names

A Notes named network is a group of servers that are physically connected in the same location (on the same LAN or routed/bridged internetwork), and share the same network protocol. The Notes named network name should be 31 bytes or less. For the purpose of clarity, the name should be chosen to identify

◆ The physical location of the servers within the Notes named network

◆ The network protocol, for example TCP/IP

The servers within a Notes named network appear in the Open Database dialog box of a Notes client on the same Notes named network. The name also is used for automatic mail routing and server grouping in the Server view of the Public Address Book.

Server Names

Server names should have their first 15 characters unique within the organization, and otherwise can be up to 79 characters in length. Strive to limit server names to

10 characters, however, because short server names are easier to read in the various dialog boxes.

Choose server names carefully; changing the server name later on is an involved procedure, requiring recertification of the ID and changing the name in the server document, group documents, ACLs, and connection documents. Assigning a generic name like that of the department is useful, versus assigning the name of the server location, which is likely to change. See Chapter 16, "Administering Notes Servers," for details on changing the name of a server.

Although spaces are permitted in a server name, avoiding spaces eases administration; some network protocols have problems identifying the server on the network if the server name contains spaces. You should also avoid underscores in server names to avoid problems using DNS (domain name serving) in TCP/IP networks.

INSTALLATION OVERVIEW

Typically, Notes server installation requires the following steps:

1. The install program copies the Notes program files to the hard disk and creates Notes Server and Notes Workstation icons on the desktop.
2. After the program files have been copied, double-clicking the Workstation icon brings you to a dialog box from which Notes setup begins.

You must run server setup before you can run the server. Setup actually creates many of the databases and files needed to run a Notes server. The first server setup does the following:

1. Creates a new domain and Notes named network.
2. Creates the certifier ID, server ID, and administrator's user ID.
3. Creates a new Public Address Book, using the PUBNAMES.NTF template. The Notes administrator and the server are listed as manager by default in the access control list of the database.
4. Creates a person document in the Public Address Book for the administrator and attaches the user ID to it.
5. Creates a server document in the Public Address Book for the server.
6. Enables the network and/or serial ports.
7. Creates a certificate document for the organizational certificate in the Public Address Book.
8. Creates LocalDomainServers and OtherDomainServers groups and adds the server name to the LocalDomainServers group.
9. Creates the Notes log database in the data directory.

10. Creates the mail file for the administrator in the mail directory (under the main Notes directory).

11. Certifies the user ID and server ID with the organizational certificate.

Note

The certifier ID, in the hands of any malicious intruder, can seriously breach the security of your Notes network. Store the certifier ID on a floppy disk in a place safe from others, except authorized administrators.

INSTALLATION OPTIONS

Three options exist for Lotus Notes server installation:

◆ CD-ROM

◆ 3½-inch floppy disks

◆ Installing from a network distribution on the file server

INSTALLING FROM CD-ROM

Because Lotus Notes ships only on CD-ROM, that's the easiest media from which to install. If you don't have a CD-ROM in all of the servers you want to install, follow the directions for creating floppy disks, or set up an installation server.

INSTALLING FROM FLOPPY DISKS

If the computer on which you want to install Notes doesn't have access to a CD-ROM drive, you can create a 3½-inch floppy disk installation set from the Lotus Notes CD-ROM.

CREATING A SET OF INSTALL DISKS FOR OS/2

Before you begin creating a set of install disks for OS/2, you need 16 high-density floppy disks. Make sure that they are blank and formatted. To create the install disks, perform the following steps:

1. Insert the Lotus Notes CD-ROM into the CD-ROM drive.

2. From the OS/2 command prompt, open the OS/2 directory on the CD-ROM (at the time of this writing it was \OS2) and go to the DISK_KIT directory. The DISK_KIT directory has the following subdirectories:

   ◆ INSTAL1 (contains installation files)

   ◆ P32SRV1 (contains Notes server files)

◆ P32WRK1 to P32WRK7 (contains Notes workstation files)

◆ DATA1 to DATA6 (contains Notes data files)

3. Insert one of the floppy disks into the floppy drive.

4. Copy the files from one of the directories listed in step 2 to the floppy disk.

5. Use the LABEL command to label the disk with the name of the directory. The syntax of the command is

```
LABEL [<drive>:][<label>]
```

where *<drive>* is the drive letter and *<label>* is the directory name.

6. Remove the disk from the drive and label the disk.

7. Repeat steps 4 through 6 for all the directories.

CREATING A SET OF INSTALL DISKS FOR WINDOWS NT

Before you begin creating a set of install disks for Windows NT, you need 17 high-density floppy disks. Make sure that they are blank and formatted. To create the install disks, perform the following steps:

1. Insert the Lotus Notes CD-ROM into the CD-ROM drive.

2. Insert one of the floppy disks into the floppy drive.

3. From the Main program group in Program Manager, double-click the File Manager icon.

4. Open up a window for the CD-ROM drive by clicking its icon. Double-click the Win32 directory and open the DISK_KIT subdirectory.

5. The DISK_KIT directory has 17 subdirectories labeled DISK1 through DISK17. Copy the files from one of these directories to the floppy disk by clicking and dragging the icon of the subdirectory to the icon of the floppy drive.

6. Remove the disk from the drive and label the disk with the name of the directory.

7. Repeat steps 5 and 6 for all the subdirectories.

INSTALLING FROM A NETWORK DISTRIBUTION FILE SERVER

Notes can be installed on a file server so that the actual installation can be done on Notes workstations or servers over the network. By using a file server, you can install on clients without a CD-ROM. You also don't need to hand out copies of the Notes installation media (CD-ROM, floppy disks).

To set up a network distribution server, Notes copies the Notes installation files in compressed form to a file server. Users can access the file server and install a copy of the application on their hard disks. Everything proceeds just as in a regular install from CD-ROM, except that the source of the files is a file server. To install Notes to a network distribution file server, do the following:

1. Insert the CD-ROM (or floppy disk, for a disk install) into the drive.

2. (Windows NT) Choose File | Run from the Program Manager menu, and in the Command Line box enter the following command:

   `<drive>:\<Install_Path>\Install`

   where *<drive>* is the drive letter, and *<Install_Path>* is the path for the install files.

   or

   (OS/2) Type `<drive>:\<Install_Path>\InstPM` in the OS/2 window, where *<drive>* is the drive letter, and *<Install_Path>* is the path for the install files.

3. In the dialog box that appears, enter the person's name and company name under which the software has been registered. (Note that the names you supply are for software registration purposes only and aren't used in the actual Notes setup.)

4. Check the Install on a File Server check box.

5. Click Next.

   The install program asks whether you want to install the files to a file server or create a network distribution.

6. Click the Network Distribution radio button.

7. Click Next.

   The Specify Distribution Directory dialog box opens.

8. Specify the drive and the installation folder for the Notes network distribution directory.

9. Click Next.

   The install program asks whether you want to copy the files to the hard disk.

10. Click Yes.

The Notes program files are copied to the file server in compressed form. Any user who can access the network drive can run the Notes install program to install Notes on his local machine.

To install from a file server, follow these steps:

1. Open the directory under which the network distribution files are stored on the file server.
2. Type **Install** at the command prompt.
3. Press Enter.

The install program runs just like the CD-ROM installation (see the later sections on installing the first server, divided by operating system type).

INSTALLING THE FIRST SERVER—OS/2

Lotus Notes for the OS/2 operating system requires OS/2 Warp version 3 or OS/2 Warp Connect Version 3. Installation of a Notes server takes two steps:

1. Running the installation program.
2. Running server setup.

Before running the installation program, make sure that you have reviewed the installation options outlined earlier in this chapter.

RUNNING THE INSTALLATION PROGRAM

To run the Notes server software installation for OS/2, follow these steps:

1. Disable any screen savers and turn off any virus-detection software.
2. If you are upgrading from an existing version of Notes, back up any of the following files that you have:
   - ◆ Organizational certifier ID (usually cert.id)
   - ◆ Organizational unit certifier IDs (if any)
   - ◆ Server ID(s)
   - ◆ User IDs (if they aren't already stored as attachments to person documents in the Public Address Book)
   - ◆ names.nsf, the Public Address Book
   - ◆ catalog.nsf, the database catalog
   - ◆ notes.ini, the Notes configuration file
   - ◆ log.nsf, the Notes log database
   - ◆ desktop.dsk, the desktop settings file
   - ◆ Any customized template (.NTF), modem (.MDM), script (.SCR), SmartIcons (.SMI or .TBL), or bitmap (.BMP) files
3. Insert the CD-ROM (or floppy disk for a disk install) into the drive.

4. Open an OS/2 window and type the following command

   `<drive>:\<Install_Path>\InstPM`

   where *<drive>* is the drive letter, and *<Install_Path>* is the path for the install files. Press Enter.

   The initial Notes installation dialog box is displayed.

5. Enter the name and company name under which the software has been registered.

   The names you supply are for software registration purposes only and aren't used in the actual Notes setup.

6. If you are installing from CD-ROM or floppy disks, make sure that the Install on a File Server check box is unchecked.

7. Click Next.

8. (optional) Customize your installation. Select Customized Features—Manual Install to choose the components you want to install. (The author recommends that all the available components be installed.) At the minimum, for a server install, select the Notes Server, Notes Client, and Personal Data components.

9. Notes offers two install options: Standard Installation and Server Installation. Select Server Install—Notes Server.

10. Enter the name of the directory and drive where you want your Notes program files and your Notes data files to reside. If the directories you specify don't already exist, Notes creates them for you.

11. Click Next.

    Notes gives you a choice of having the CONFIG.SYS file updated with the Notes server path information, or doing it yourself after the installation. If you choose to make the changes manually, Notes stores the additions that are to be made into a file named CONFIG.ADD and saves it in the same directory as CONFIG.SYS. Notes also presents an option to overwrite any program files that might be present from a previous installation in the same directory.

12. If you have backed up your CONFIG.SYS file, select Update Config.SYS. Otherwise, make sure that this option isn't selected.

13. Choose OK.

14. Click Install to begin installation.

    Notes begins to copy the program files to the directories you specified.

15. After all the files are copied, click OK to complete the installation.

OS/2 requires the computer to be restarted after installation so that the changes that Notes made in the CONFIG.SYS file can take effect.

10

INSTALLING/CONFIGURING NOTES SERVERS

If you chose not to have Notes update the CONFIG.SYS automatically, the contents of the CONFIG.ADD file should be added to CONFIG.SYS before rebooting.

RUNNING FIRST SERVER SETUP

After the program files have been installed and the computer rebooted for the changes in the NOTES.INI file to take effect, the computer is ready for first server setup. First server software setup involves running the Notes Workstation software. For Notes to be set up successfully, the server setup program has to be completed. If you try to run the Notes server before completing server setup, the server exits with a message:

```
You must type "Notes" to set up your system.
```

Follow these steps to complete server setup:

1. Double-click the Lotus Notes Workstation icon.

   The Notes Server Setup dialog box appears.

2. Because you are installing Notes for the first time, select The First Lotus Notes Server in Your Organization.

3. Click OK.

   The First Server setup box appears.

Note

In this dialog box, *organization* refers to your company. It doesn't necessarily mean the same thing as the specific term *Organization* used with respect to Notes naming conventions.

4. Enter a name for the Notes server in the Server Name box.

5. Enter the name of your company in the Organization box.

6. Enter the first name, middle initial, and last name for the Notes administrator in the administrator boxes.

7. Enter a password in the Administration Password box. Because this password is echoed on the screen as you type, you might want to ensure that nobody is looking over your shoulder. The password is case-sensitive.

8. Select the type of network in the Network Type drop-down list box.

9. If the administrator plans to use the server as his personal workstation, check the option Server Is Also Administrator's Personal Workstation. This causes Notes to use the administrator's ID when a workstation session is open on the server. If this option isn't selected, the server ID is used on workstation sessions.

10. If there is a modem on a serial port on the server, select a COM port in the Serial Port box, the type of dialing (tone or pulse), and the type of modem in the Modem Type box.

11. Click the Advanced button to bring up the Advanced Options dialog box. It contains the following settings:

    ◆ *Domain Name.* Notes automatically assigns the Organization name to the domain (remember that one organization per domain is recommended).

    ◆ *Network Name.* Notes uses Network1 as the default.

    ◆ *Country Code.* When companies communicate on a global scale using Notes, it is essential that each company have a unique (domain) name. Using a country code minimizes the chance that any other company has the same (fully distinguished) name. The country code is appended to the end of the fully distinguished name, hence reducing the chances of duplication in names. The International Standards Organization (ISO) has defined a set of two-letter country codes in ISO 3166. See Appendix A, "Country Codes," for a complete list.

    ◆ *Log Modem I/O.* Selecting Log Modem I/O sets up modem event logging in the Notes log. You can use this option for troubleshooting modem issues.

    ◆ *Log All Replication Events.* Select this option to set up logging of all replication events to the Notes log.

    ◆ *Log All Client Session Events.* Select this option if you want Notes to make an entry in the Notes log whenever a user accesses a server.

    ◆ *Create Organization Certifier ID and Create Server ID.* Select these options when setting up the first server. If you already have an organization and server ID from a previous installation, make sure that this option isn't selected.

    ◆ *Create Administrator ID.* Use this option if you are creating a new ID for the administrator.

    ◆ *Minimum Admin and Certifier Password Length.* Enter the minimum length for the administrator and certifier password (these are the same). The default is eight characters.

12. After selecting the desired Advanced options, click OK.

    Notes displays the Time Zone Setup dialog box.

13. Select the time zone for the server's location and check Observe Daylight Savings Time April-October if the server's time zone observes Daylight Savings time.

Because disparate pieces of a Notes network can be global, the time zones for different servers on the network most likely will be different. This fact can be important when communicating on a worldwide scale. For example, replication schedules, especially when they don't all originate from a hub server, have to be designed to take into account the fact that the servers on the schedule are on different time zones.

14. Click OK.

INSTALLING ADDITIONAL OS/2 SERVERS

The process of installing additional servers on a network involves three steps. They have to be registered, installed, and set up. You can install the new server before or after registering the new server, but you must complete installation and registration before running Setup.

You install additional servers using any of the three installation methods outlined earlier in this chapter, in the section "Installation Options."

REGISTERING ADDITIONAL SERVERS

The process of registration performs two main tasks:

1. Creation of a server document in the Public Address Book.
2. Creation of a server ID for the new server.

To perform additional server registration, you must make a decision about which certifier ID to use for registration. For additional information about hierarchical certification and naming, see Chapter 9.

You can perform additional server registration from a workstation session on the server, or from a Notes client that has network access or remote access to the registration server. Also, you need to have physical access to the certifier ID and its associated password. If you are performing additional server registration from a personal workstation, the registration server must be up and running. If you are registering the additional server from a workstation session on the registration server, the server may or may not be running. In any case, the person performing the registration should have at least author access to the Public Address Book.

The choice of registration server decides which replica of the Public Address Book will receive the changes made by the new server registration process. It is recommended that after the new server is registered, you manually replicate the Public Address Book at the registration server to servers throughout the network. You can perform manual replication by issuing the following command from the server console:

```
replicate <target_server> <public_name_and_address_book>
```

where *<target_server>* is the name of the server to receive the updates and *<public_name_and_address_book>* is the file name of the Public Address Book.

For more information about replication, and for other ways in which you can perform this replication, see Chapter 15, "Administering Replication."

Notes performs these steps during additional server registration:

1. Notes creates a server ID for the new server and certifies it with the certificate specified by the administrator.

2. Notes creates a new server document in the Public Address Book of the registration server.

3. The name of the Notes administrator is added to the Administrators field of the server document. The server ID is encrypted and appended (attached) to the server document, or saved in a file as specified by the administrator.

4. The server name is added to the LocalDomainServers group in the Public Address Book.

5. An entry for a new server is created in the certification log (if it exists) on the registration server. The certification log is a database that keeps a log of all certified servers and users in a Notes domain. For more information about the certification log, see Chapter 18, "Administering Notes Security."

Follow these steps to register an additional server:

1. Start the Notes Workstation program.

2. Choose File | Tools | Server Administration.

3. Select the server that is to be the registration server.

   The registration server must be currently available to complete registration.

4. Click the Servers icon and select Register Server.

   Notes reminds you that a separate software license is required for each server registered, and asks if you purchased a license.

5. Click Yes if you purchased a server software license.

   Notes prompts you for the Certifier ID password. Notes always defaults to the last certifier used for registration. If you want to choose another certifier for registration, choose Cancel when you are prompted for the certifier ID password, and Notes displays a dialog box prompting you for the certifier ID to use.

6. Enter this certifier's password.

7. Click OK.

Notes displays the Register Servers dialog box. If you want to choose a different registration server, click the Registration Server button and select the server you will use as the registration server.

8. Click OK.

9. Choose North American or International in the Security field.

   Notes relies on RSA public key encryption technology, which the National Security Agency classes as munitions subject to U.S. export controls. You should have decided which license type to use when you designed your Notes network. See Chapters 9 and 18 for more information on international licenses.

10. Enter a certificate expiration date in the Certificate Expiration Date box. The format for the date is mm-dd-yyyy.

    Notes suggests a certificate expiration date one hundred years from the time of registration.

11. Click Continue.

12. Enter a name for the server in the Server Name box. For guidelines for naming servers, refer to Chapter 9.

13. Enter a password for the server ID in the password box. The length of this password has to be at least that specified in the Minimum Password Length box. All passwords are case-sensitive.

14. Enter a domain name in the Domain box. Notes suggests a default name, which is usually the name of the organizational certificate.

15. In the Administrator field, enter the name of the administrator for the new server. Notes defaults to the name of the person performing the server registration.

16. Click on the Other tab at the left side of the dialog box to bring up miscellaneous settings for the new server.

17. In the Server Title box, enter a title for the new server. This title will be used in the Server Title field of the server document in the Public Address Book.

18. In the Network field, enter the Notes named network to which this server will belong.

19. Notes can store the server ID of the server as a file or as an attachment to the server document in the Public Address Book. Click the In Address Book check box if you want to store it in the Public Address Book, or the In File check box if you want to store it in a file. You can specify the location of the file by clicking the Set ID File button. This way, you can also store the ID on a network drive.

20. Click Next to register additional servers and repeat steps 8 through 19 for each additional server.

21. Click Register to register all the servers you specified.

SETTING UP ADDITIONAL SERVERS

After you register a server and install Notes program files, you must complete the process of server setup before the server becomes operational.

Notes performs the following steps when additional servers are set up:

1. The setup process on the new server looks for the Public Address Book on a target server specified by the administrator.

2. Notes searches the Public Address Book for the server document created during additional server registration.

3. Notes uses a server ID stored on a floppy disk (or a hard disk or network drive, for that matter), or retrieves the server ID from the server document in the Public Address Book.

4. Notes creates a replica copy of the Public Address Book in the data directory of the new server.

5. Other administrative databases, such as the Notes log, are created on the new server.

6. Notes sets up the selected network and serial ports on the new server.

Follow these steps to set up additional servers:

1. Make sure that Notes installed the program files on the new server and that it has been registered.

2. Double-click the Notes Workstation icon.

3. Notes asks if this is the first server in your organization or an additional server in your organization. Because this is an additional server, select the latter and click OK.

4. Notes brings up the Additional Server Setup dialog box. Enter the name of the server in the New Server Name box as you entered it during additional server registration.

5. Enter the name of the registration server (or one that contains a replica copy of the Public Address Book containing the server document of the new server) in the Get Domain Address Book from Server Name box.

6. Enter the fully distinguished name if there is more than one server with the same name (perhaps you have two Marketing servers in two different organizations) in the domain.

10

INSTALLING/CONFIGURING NOTES SERVERS

7. If the server will connect over the network, select the Via Network radio button.

8. If the connection will be over a serial port, select the Via Serial Port radio button. Enter the telephone number of the dial-up server.

9. In the Network Type drop-down list box, select the network protocol to use if connecting over a network, or choose the serial port on which the modem resides if using a dial-up connection. Select a modem type from the Modem Type drop-down list box. Select Tone Dial or Pulse Dial.

10. If the server's ID resides in a physical file (not attached to the server document in the Public Address Book), select the New Server's ID Supplied in a File check box.

11. If the administrator plans to use the server as his personal workstation, select the Server Is Also Administrator's Personal Workstation check box.

12. Click the Advanced button to open the Advanced Server Setup Options dialog box. Check any of the following options as appropriate:

   ◆ *Log Modem I/O.* To log all the modem events, check Log Modem I/O.

   ◆ *Log All Replication Events.* Select this option to log the beginning and end events for replication.

   ◆ *Log All Client Session Events.* Use this option to log access to the server by clients.

13. Click OK to close the Advanced Server Setup Options dialog box.

14. Click OK again to accept the Additional Server Setup options.

   The new server attempts to connect to the registration server and creates a replica copy of the Public Address Book in its own data directory.

   After the connection is established and the replica copy of the Public Address Book is created, Notes asks you to select a time zone for the server. The significance of the time zone is that, because disparate pieces of a Notes network can be global, the time zones for different servers on the network most likely will differ. This can be important when communicating internationally. For example, replication schedules, especially when they don't all originate from a hub server, must be designed to take into account the fact that the servers on the schedule are in different time zones.

15. Select Observe Daylight Savings Time April-October if the server's time zone observes Daylight Savings time.

16. Choose OK.

   Notes creates the Notes log database (log.nsf) and adds it to the workspace.

REPEATING SERVER SETUP

If you decide to redo the server setup process after the server has been set up, or have made errors during server setup, perform the following steps. This process is called *breaking down* the server:

1. Close the Notes Workstation program at the server by choosing File | Exit.

2. Shut down the server by entering the EXIT command at the server console.

3. Go to the OS/2 command prompt, and change the current directory to the Notes data directory.

4. Type **e notes.ini** and press Enter to edit the NOTES.INI file.

5. Delete all but the first three lines in the file.

   The resulting NOTES.INI file is

   ```
   [Notes]
   Directory=<drive>:\<data_path>
   KitType=2
   ```

   where *<drive>* is the drive where Notes resides and *<data_path>* is the path of the Notes data directory.

6. Save the file by choosing File | Save.

7. Choose File | Exit to exit the editor.

8. Delete the following files from the Notes data directory:

   - names.nsf
   - log.nsf
   - catalog.nsf
   - server.id
   - cert.id
   - user.id
   - desktop.dsk (unless you want to preserve your current Notes workspace settings)
   - Any mail files that you might have in the MAIL subdirectory under the Notes data directory
   - Any data files that you don't want to keep

9. Start the Notes Workstation software on the server by double-clicking its icon. This will bring up the Notes Server Setup dialog box and begin the server setup process. Follow the steps in the preceding section.

INSTALLING THE FIRST SERVER— WINDOWS NT

Lotus Notes for the Windows NT operating system requires at least Windows NT Server version 3.51. You have the same three options when installing Notes as you do for OS/2. You can install from CD, floppy disks, or a network directory. See the section "Installation Options," earlier in this chapter, for directions on preparing to install Notes using one of these three techniques.

RUNNING THE INSTALLATION PROGRAM

To run the Notes server software installation for Windows NT, follow these steps:

1. Disable any screen savers and turn off any virus-detection software.

2. If you are upgrading from an existing version of Notes, back up any of the following files that you have:

   ◆ Organizational certifier ID (usually cert.id)

   ◆ Organizational unit certifier IDs (if any)

   ◆ Server ID(s)

   ◆ User IDs (if they aren't already stored as attachments to person documents in the Public Address Book)

   ◆ names.nsf, the Public Address Book

   ◆ catalog.nsf, the database catalog

   ◆ notes.ini, the Notes configuration file

   ◆ log.nsf, the Notes log database

   ◆ desktop.dsk, the desktop settings file

   ◆ Any customized template (.NTF), modem (.MDM), script (.SCR), SmartIcons (.SMI or .TBL), or bitmap (.BMP) files

3. Insert the CD-ROM (or floppy disk for a disk install) into the drive.

4. Choose File | Run from the Program Manager menu and enter the following command in the Command Line box:

   `n:\<Install_Path>\InstPM`

   where *n* is the drive letter, and *<Install_Path>* is the path for the install files.

5. In the dialog box that appears, enter the name and company name under which the software has been registered. The names you supply are for software registration purposes only and aren't used in the actual Notes setup.

6. Make sure that the Install on a File Server check box is unchecked.

7. Click Next.

   Notes offers two install options: Standard Installation and Server Installation.

8. (optional) Select Customized Features—Manual Install to choose the components you want installed. It is recommended that all the available components be installed. At the minimum, for a server install, select the Notes Server, Notes Client, and Personal Data components.

9. Select Server Install—Notes Server.

10. Enter the name of the directory and drive where you want your Notes program files and your Notes data files to reside. If the directories you specify don't already exist, Notes creates them for you.

11. If you chose to do manual installation, select the components you want installed, and click OK. Otherwise just click Install.

    Notes begins to copy the program files to the directories you specified.

12. After all the files are copied, click OK to complete the installation. Lotus Notes for Windows NT doesn't require the computer to be restarted after installation.

RUNNING FIRST SERVER SETUP

After the program files have been installed, the computer is ready for first server setup. First server software setup involves running the Notes Workstation software. Specifically, you must perform the following steps:

1. Double-click the Lotus Notes Workstation icon.

   The Notes Server Setup dialog box appears.

2. Because Notes is being installed for the first time, select The First Lotus Notes Server in Your Organization.

3. Click OK.

   The First Server Setup dialog box opens.

4. Enter a name for the first server.

5. Enter the name of your company in the Organization box.

Note

In this dialog box, *organization* refers to your company. It doesn't mean the same thing as the specific term *Organization* used with respect to Notes naming conventions.

6. Enter the first name, middle initial, and last name for the Notes administrator in the administrator boxes.

7. Enter a password in the Administration Password box. Because this password is echoed on the screen as you type, make sure that nobody is looking over your shoulder. The password is case-sensitive.

8. Select the type of network in the Network Type drop-down list box.

9. If the administrator plans to use the server as his personal workstation, select the option Server Is Also Administrator's Personal Workstation. This action causes Notes to use the administrator's ID when a workstation session is open on the server. If this option isn't selected, Notes uses the server ID on workstation sessions.

10. If a modem is connected to the server, select a COM port in the Serial Port box, the type of dialing (tone or pulse), and the type of modem in the Modem Type box.

11. Click the Advanced button to bring up the Advanced Options dialog box. It contains the following settings:

   ◆ *Domain Name.* Notes automatically assigns the organization name to the domain (remember that one organization per domain is recommended).

   ◆ *Network Name.* Notes uses Network1 as the default.

   ◆ *Country Code.* When companies communicate on a global scale using Notes, it is essential that the company have a unique (domain) name. Using a country code minimizes the chance that any other company has the same (fully distinguished) name. The country code is appended to the end of the fully distinguished name, hence reducing the chances of duplication in names. The International Standards Organization (ISO) has defined a set of two-letter country codes in ISO 3166. See Appendix A, "Country Codes," for a complete list.

   ◆ *Log Modem I/O.* Selecting Log Modem I/O sets up modem event logging in the Notes log. You can use this for troubleshooting modem issues.

   ◆ *Log All Replication Events.* Select this option to set up logging of all replication events to the Notes log.

   ◆ *Log All Client Session Events.* Use this option if you want Notes to make an entry in the Notes log whenever a user accesses a server.

   ◆ *Create Organization Certifier ID and Create Server ID.* Select these options because you are setting up the first server. If you already have an organization and server ID from a previous installation, make sure that this option isn't selected.

◆ *Create Administrator ID*. Choose this option if you are creating a new ID for the administrator.

◆ *Minimum Admin and Certifier Password Length*. Enter the minimum length for the administrator and certifier password (these are the same). The default is eight characters.

12. Select the time zone for the server and check Observe Daylight Savings Time April-October if the server's time zone observes Daylight Savings time. Because disparate pieces of a Notes network can be global, the time zones for different servers on the network most likely will be different. This fact can be important when communicating on a worldwide scale. For example, replication schedules, especially when they don't all originate from a hub server, must be designed to take into account the fact that the servers on the schedule are on different time zones.

13. Click OK.

When Notes completes server setup, you can start the Notes server.

INSTALLING ADDITIONAL WINDOWS NT SERVERS

The process of adding additional servers to a network involves three steps. They have to be registered, installed, and set up. You can install the new server before or after registering the new server, but you must complete installation and registration before running Setup.

You install additional servers using any of the three methods outlined in the earlier section "Installation Options."

REGISTERING ADDITIONAL SERVERS

The process of registration performs two main tasks:

1. Creation of a server document in the Public Address Book.
2. Creation of a server ID for the new server.

To perform additional server registration, you must make a decision about which certifier ID to use for registration. Knowing your company's hierarchical naming scheme is useful for this purpose. For additional information about hierarchical certification and naming, see Chapter 9.

You can register additional servers from a workstation session on the server, or from a Notes client that has network access or remote access to the registration server. Also, you need to have physical access to the certifier ID and its associated password.

If you are performing additional server registration from a personal workstation, the registration server must be up and running. If you are registering from a workstation session on the registration server, the server may or may not be running. In any case, the person performing the registration should have at least author access to the Public Address Book.

The choice of registration server decides which replica of the Public Address Book will receive the changes made by the new server registration process. It is recommended that, after the new server is registered, you manually replicate the Public Address Book at the registration server to servers throughout the network. You can perform manual replication by issuing the following command from the server console:

```
replicate <target_server> <public_name_and_address_book>
```

where *<target_server>* is the name of the server that will receive the updates and *<public_name_and_address_book>* is the file name of the Public Address Book.

For more information about replication, and for other ways in which you can perform this replication, see Chapter 15.

Notes takes these actions during additional server registration:

1. Notes creates a server ID for the new server and certifies it with the certifier specified by the administrator.
2. Notes creates a new server document in the Public Address Book of the registration server.
3. The name of the Notes administrator is added to the Administrators field of the server document. The server ID is encrypted and appended (attached) to the server document or saved in a file as specified by the administrator.
4. Notes adds the server name to the LocalDomainServers group in the Public Address Book.
5. Notes creates an entry for a new server in the certification log (if it exists) on the registration server. The certification log is a database that keeps a log of all certified servers and users in a Notes domain. For more information about the certification log, see Chapter 18.

Follow these steps to register an additional server:

1. Start the Notes workstation program.
2. Choose File | Tools | Server Administration.
3. Select the server that is to be the registration server.
4. Click the Server icon and select Register Server.

Notes reminds you that you need to purchase a separate software license for each server registered and asks if you purchased a license.

5. Click Yes if you purchased a server software license.

   Notes prompts you for the certifier ID password. Notes always defaults to the last certifier used for registration.

6. If you want to choose another certifier for registration, choose Cancel when you are prompted for the certifier ID password. Notes displays a dialog box prompting you for the certifier ID to use.

7. Enter the certifier's password.

8. Click OK.

   Notes displays the Register Servers dialog box.

9. If you want to choose a different registration server, click on the Registration Server button and select the server that you will use as the registration server. The registration server must be available on the network to complete registration.

10. Click OK.

11. At this point, you can change the certifier ID to be used for registration. To use a different certifier ID, click the Certifier ID button and select the certifier ID file you want to use. Click OK, enter the password for the certifier ID, and click OK again.

12. Choose North American or International in the Security field. Notes relies on RSA public key encryption technology, which the National Security Agency classes as munitions subject to U.S. export controls. For more information on international licenses, see Chapters 9 and 18.

13. Enter an expiration date for the certificate. Notes suggests an expiration date a hundred years from the time of registration. You can change this setting in the Certificate Expiration Date box. The format for the date is mm-dd-yyyy.

14. Click Continue.

15. Enter a name for the server in the Server Name box. For guidelines for naming servers, see Chapter 9.

16. Enter a case-sensitive password for the server ID in the Password box. The length of this password has to be at least that specified in the Minimum Password Length box.

17. Enter a domain name in the Domain box (Notes suggests a default name, which is usually the name of the organizational certificate).

10

INSTALLING/CONFIGURING NOTES SERVERS

18. In the Administrator field, enter the name of the administrator for the new server. Notes defaults to the name of the person performing the server registration.

19. Click on the Other tab on the left side of the dialog box to display miscellaneous settings for the new server.

20. Enter a title for the new server in the Server Title field. This title will be used in the Server Title field of the server document in the Public Address Book.

21. In the Network field, enter the Notes named network to which this server will belong.

22. Notes can store the server ID of the server as a file or as an attachment to the server document in the Public Address Book. Click the In Address Book check box to store it in the Public Address Book, or click the In File check box to store it in a file. You can specify the location of the file by clicking the Set ID File button. This way, the ID can also be stored on a network drive.

23. Click Next to register additional servers, and repeat steps 12 through 22 for each additional server.

24. Click Register to register all the servers you specified.

Setting Up Additional Servers

After registering and installing Notes program files on the new server, the process of server setup has to be completed before the new server becomes operational.

Notes performs the following steps when additional servers are set up:

1. The setup process on the new server looks for the Public Address Book on a target server specified by the Administrator.

2. Notes searches the Public Address Book for the server document that was created during additional server setup.

3. Notes uses the server ID stored on a floppy disk (or a hard disk or network drive, for that matter), or retrieves it from the server document in the Public Address Book.

4. Notes creates a replica copy of the Public Address Book in the data directory of the new server.

5. Other administrative databases are created on the new server.

6. The selected network and serial ports are set up on the new server.

Follow these steps to set up additional servers:

1. Make sure that the program files have been installed on the new server and that it has been registered.

2. Double-click the Workstation icon.

3. Notes asks if this is the first server in your organization or an additional server in your organization. As this is an additional server, select the latter.

4. Click OK.

5. Notes brings up the Additional Server Setup dialog box. Enter the name of the server in the New Server Name box as you entered it during additional server registration.

6. Enter the name of the registration server (or one that contains a replica copy of the Public Address Book containing the server document of the new server) in the Get Domain Address Book from Server Name box. Enter the fully distinguished name if more than one server has the same name in the domain.

7. Select a network connection type. If the server will connect over the network, select the Via Network radio button. If the connection will be over a serial port, select the Via Serial Port radio button and enter the telephone number of the dial-up server.

8. Select the protocol to use. If connecting over a network, select the protocol from the Network Type drop-down list box. For a dial-up connection, select a modem type from the Modem Type drop-down list box. Select Tone Dial or Pulse Dial.

9. If the server's ID resides in a physical file (not attached to the server document in the Public Address Book), select the New Server's ID Supplied in a File check box.

10. If the administrator plans to use the server as his personal workstation, select the Server Is Also Administrator's Personal Workstation check box.

11. Click the Advanced button to open the Advanced Server Setup Options dialog box. Check any of the following options:

    ◆ To log all the modem events, check Log Modem I/O.

    ◆ To log the beginning and end events for replication, select Log All Replication Events.

    ◆ To log access to the server by clients, select Log All Client Session Events.

    ◆ If your (the server administrator's) ID is stored in a file on a floppy disk, check Administrator's ID Is Supplied in a File. If the box is left unchecked, Notes looks at the administrator's person document in the Public Address Book.

12. Click OK to close the Advanced Server Setup Options dialog box.

13. Click OK again to accept the Additional Server Setup options.

    The new server attempts to connect to the registration server and creates a replica copy of the Public Address Book in its own data directory.

    After the connection is established and the replica copy of the Public Address Book is created, Notes asks you to select a time zone for the server. The significance of the time zone is that, because disparate pieces of a Notes network can be global, the time zones for different servers on the network most likely will be different. This fact can be important when communicating internationally. For example, replication schedules, especially when they don't all originate from a hub server, must be designed to take into account the fact that the servers on the schedule are in different time zones.

14. Check Observe Daylight Savings Time April-October if the server's time zone observes Daylight Savings time.

15. Click OK.

    Notes creates the Notes log database (log.nsf) and adds it to the workspace. At this point, additional server setup is complete.

REPEATING SERVER SETUP

If you decide to redo the server setup process after the server has been set up, or you have made errors during server setup, follow these steps (this process is called *breaking down* the server):

1. Close the Notes Workstation program at the server by choosing File | Exit.

2. Shut down the server by entering the EXIT command at the server console.

3. Go to the command prompt and change the current directory to the Notes data directory.

4. Open the NOTES.INI file for editing.

5. Delete all but the first three lines in the file.

    The resulting NOTES.INI file is

    ```
    [Notes]
    Directory=<drive>:\<data_path>
    KitType=2
    ```

    where *<drive>* is the drive where Notes resides and *<data_path>* is the path of the Notes data directory.

6. Save the file.

7. Exit the editor.

8. Delete the following files from the Notes data directory:

   ◆ names.nsf

   ◆ log.nsf

   ◆ catalog.nsf

   ◆ server.id

   ◆ cert.id

   ◆ user.id

   ◆ desktop.dsk (unless you want to preserve your current Notes workspace settings)

   ◆ Any mail files that you might have in the MAIL subdirectory under the Notes data directory

   ◆ Any data files that you don't want to keep

9. Start the Notes Workstation software on the server by double-clicking its icon. This action brings up the Notes Server Setup dialog box and begins the server setup process. Follow the steps in the preceding section.

UNINSTALLING NOTES

Lotus Notes Release 4 comes with an uninstall utility that uninstalls the Notes program files if you don't want Notes on the workstation anymore. This isn't the same as breaking down the server, because breaking down the server doesn't delete Notes program files—only the key files created during server setup.

To uninstall Notes, follow these steps:

1. Double-click the Notes Uninstall icon in the program group in which the Lotus Notes icons were installed.

2. When asked to confirm that you want to uninstall Notes, click Yes.

3. The Uninstall program begins removing Notes program files from the computer. If any files were modified after Notes was originally installed, the Uninstall program asks you to confirm that you want to delete them. Uninstall removes all files in the Notes directory; it doesn't remove the NOTES.INI file, which is stored in the Windows directory.

RUNNING NOTES AS A WINDOWS NT SERVICE

Notes can be installed and run under Windows NT as a service. The main advantage of this technique is that if Notes is set up to run as an automatic service, then it will run whether or not anyone is logged in at the computer. Also, this option permits the server to be started from a remote location, using Windows NT's administra-tion capabilities. Further, in case of a power outage, the Notes server starts automatically when the NT server comes up again. If you are running Notes under Windows NT, I recommend that you start/stop Notes using the Services panel only. This method enables you to monitor Notes remotely, using NT administration features.

To run a Notes server as a Windows NT service, follow these steps:

1. From the Windows NT Program Manager, choose File | Run.

2. In the Command Line box, enter this command:

   ```
   <drive>:\<notes_dir>\ntsvinst -c
   ```

   where *<drive>* is the drive where the Notes files reside, and *<notes_dir>* is the Notes program directory. Click OK.

3. Open the Main program group in Program Manager. Double-click the Control Panel icon. Opening the Services icon shows a list of the installed Windows NT services. Notes Server should now be one of the installed services.

4. Click Close to close the Services dialog box.

CONFIGURING NOTES AS A MANUAL SERVICE

When Notes is configured as a manual Windows NT service, it must be started manually from the Services icon in Control Panel. To run a Notes server as a manual service, follow these steps:

1. Double-click the Main program group from Program Manager.

2. Open Control Panel by double-clicking the Control Panel icon.

3. Double-click the Services icon in Control Panel.

4. From the list of services installed in Windows NT, select the Lotus Notes Server—Manual service.

5. Click Start to start the Notes server. To shut down the server, click Stop.

6. Click Close to close the Services dialog box.

CONFIGURING NOTES AS AN AUTOMATIC SERVICE

When Notes is configured as an automatic service, it starts whenever the NT server reboots. To run Notes as an automatic Windows NT service, follow these steps:

1. Double-click the Main program group from the Windows NT Program Manager.

2. Open Control Panel by double-clicking the Control Panel icon.

3. Double-click the Services icon in Control Panel.

4. From the list of services installed in Windows NT, select the Lotus Notes Server—Manual service.

5. Click the Startup button to select the appropriate startup option.

6. Select Automatic to enable automatic starting of the Notes Server. Click System Account in the Log On As box.

7. Select Allow Service to Interact with Desktop. This setting causes the Notes server console to appear when the administrator logs in. Leaving this option deselected causes the server console not to appear.

8. Click OK.

9. The automatic startup option will take effect the next time the system is started up. If you want the Notes server service to be started immediately, click Start.

10. Click Close to close the Services dialog box.

REMOVING NOTES SERVER AS A WINDOWS NT SERVICE

If you want to remove the Notes server program as a Windows NT service, and only run it manually in a login session, perform the following steps:

1. Shut down the Notes server by typing `exit` and pressing Enter at the server console.

2. From Program Manager, choose File | Run.

3. In the Command Line box, enter this command:

   `<drive>:\<notes_dir>\ntsvinst -d`

   where *<drive>* is the drive where the Notes files reside, and *<notes_dir>* is the Notes program directory. Click OK.

4. Open Control Panel in the Main program group in Program Manager. Double-click the Services icon to show a list of Windows NT services. Notes Server should no longer be one of the installed services.

5. Click Close to exit the Services dialog box.

SUMMARY

Lotus Notes server installation demands up-front planning to ensure lower maintenance costs after Notes deployment. Planning usually entails making decisions about naming conventions for the Notes network and the hierarchical naming structure of the organization.

Installing the first Notes server is a two-step process:

1. Copying Notes program files to the hard disk.
2. Server setup.

Installing additional Notes servers entails three steps:

1. Copying Notes program files to the hard disk.
2. Registering the new server.
3. Running server setup.

First server installs differ from additional server installs in that the first server install creates a new certifier ID, whereas additional servers use this certifier ID (or others created after first server install). OS/2 and Windows NT installs proceed along the same lines, except for some minor cosmetic differences.

CHAPTER 11

Installing Notes Clients

One of the most labor-intensive portions of a Notes deployment is installing Notes clients. The sheer number of clients in many networks makes installing Notes clients a big job. The standard Notes client installation requires the physical presence of someone at the client during installation. Administrators should write a set of instructions for installing Notes (you can use the instructions from this chapter) so that they don't have to personally install Notes on every client.

This chapter explains

◆ Notes licensing options

◆ Different installation options for Notes clients

◆ The Notes client installation program

◆ How to set up Notes clients

Some planning is required to minimize problems during a Notes install. Chapter 5, "Building a Deployment Plan," and Chapter 6, "Customizing Your Deployment Plan," present the overall sequence you should follow before installing a Notes network.

UNDERSTANDING NOTES CLIENT LICENSING

Just as in any other major endeavor in life, Notes installation lends itself to some up-front planning. Before installing Notes clients, it's a good idea to understand the licensing options for Notes client software. There are three types of client licenses:

◆ Notes Mail

◆ Notes Desktop

◆ Notes Client (Full)

The different types of Notes licenses give users different levels of access to Notes databases and Notes database templates. In addition, different license types imply different levels of design capabilities for Notes databases, and different levels of Notes administration capabilities.

LOTUS NOTES MAIL LICENSES

Notes Mail license users have access to only the following types of databases:

◆ Databases created with the Lotus Notes Mail database template.

This template is a predefined Lotus Notes template, and Notes automatically creates a mail file for the user from this template when his ID file is generated.

- ◆ Communications and collaboration databases created from communications and collaboration database templates.

    These databases help the user to work with other workgroup users.

- ◆ Documentation databases.

    These databases are provided by Notes for users' reference.

- ◆ Administration databases.

    These databases store information about activity on the Notes network and are useful for maintaining and troubleshooting the system.

If a Notes Mail license user attempts to access a database not listed here, Notes will refuse access. Notes Mail licenses are primarily used by organizations migrating from cc:Mail.

LOTUS NOTES DESKTOP LICENSES

Lotus Notes Desktop licenses provide the next level of access after Notes Mail licenses. A Notes Desktop user has access to all types of Notes databases and database templates, including:

- ◆ Databases created with the Lotus Notes Mail database template.

    This template is a predefined Lotus Notes template, and Notes automatically creates a mail file for the user from this template when his ID file is created.

- ◆ Communications and collaboration databases created from communications and collaboration database templates.

    These databases help the user to work with other workgroup users.

- ◆ Documentation databases.

    These databases are provided by Notes for users' reference.

- ◆ Administration databases.

    These databases store information about activity on the Notes network and are useful for maintaining and troubleshooting the system.

- ◆ Any custom or third-party databases and templates available to the user.

    The Notes Desktop license doesn't permit the user to use any Notes design or administrative features. Lotus Desktop licenses should be used for users who don't need to create personal views or agents. Some organizations will make widespread use of Notes Desktop licenses. Application developers, IS management, and end-user management should all participate in the decision to use a Notes Desktop license instead of a full Notes Client license.

FULL LOTUS NOTES CLIENT LICENSES

Lotus Notes licenses allow the user to access all types of Notes databases and database templates. In addition, unlike the users of the other two license types, Lotus Notes Client license users can also perform design and administration functions such as

◆ Creating a new database from an existing template

◆ Creating their own Notes database templates

◆ Customizing any existing Notes databases or templates

Lotus Notes licenses also allow the user to perform Notes administrative functions like registering new users and servers, certifying files, and so on.

PLANNING FOR INSTALLATION

Just as in the server installation phase of the Notes network, the client installation phase requires a little up-front planning to ensure reduced maintenance after installation. Because a Notes client install will typically include installation of mobile clients that may be available only for short periods of time, planning and scheduling the install helps to coordinate the whole process. In the experience of the author, scheduling the installation phase is a much-neglected aspect that, although seemingly trivial, can save a lot of heartache. A realistic schedule that lists every user to receive Notes can help set expectations for both users and administrators.

Because mobile client users are usually out of the office, and hence unable to connect to the corporate LAN most of the time, they have to be taken care of during the (brief) time that they are in the office. Building the schedule of each person to be installed thus can save a lot of overhead time spent (unproductively) in coordinating the installs. Although client installation could theoretically be done over the telephone line (using remote-access software packages), the large volume of data being transferred would render the process very slow and expensive. Besides, that system would require the user to perform the installation himself, which, in the case of novice computer users, would be difficult.

Installation should always be coordinated with training. Users should receive training within 48 hours of having Notes installed on their desktops. There are few things that waste the Notes administrator's productivity more than inexperienced users asking novice questions, which could well be handled by a simple hour of classroom-style instruction. Distributing documentation helps, but it can never take the place of hands-on interactive instruction, especially since most users don't find the time to read literature if they don't have to do so.

UNDERSTANDING INSTALLATION OPTIONS

There are four options for Lotus Notes client installation:

◆ CD-ROM

◆ 3 ½-inch floppy disks

◆ Installing from a network distribution on the file server

◆ Installing Notes on a shared directory on the file server

The following sections cover each option.

INSTALLING FROM CD-ROM

Lotus Notes ships only on CD-ROM, so that is the easiest medium from which to install. Installing from CD-ROM requires the computer to have access to a local or network CD-ROM drive. Although installing from CD-ROM takes the least pre-installation work, other options may take less effort overall.

INSTALLING FROM FLOPPY DISKS

If the computer on which you want to install Notes doesn't have access to a CD-ROM drive, you can create your own set of install disks on 3 ½-inch floppy disks from the Lotus Notes CD-ROM. Because most computers these days have floppy disks, most computers can take advantage of this installation method, but installing Notes from floppy disks can be much slower, because the installer must wait while the installation program runs so that floppy disks can be fed into the machine.

CREATING A SET OF INSTALL DISKS FOR OS/2

Before you begin creating a set of install disks for OS/2, you need 16 high-density floppy disks. Make sure that they are blank and formatted. To create the install disks, perform the following steps:

1. Insert the Lotus Notes CD-ROM into the CD-ROM drive.

2. From the OS/2 command prompt, open the OS/2 directory on the CD-ROM (at the time of this writing it was \OS2) and go to the DISK_KIT directory. The DISK_KIT directory has the following subdirectories:

   ◆ INSTAL1 (containing installation files)

   ◆ P32WRK1 to P32WRK7 (containing Notes workstation files)

   ◆ DATA1 to DATA6 (containing Notes data files)

3. Insert one of the floppy disks into the floppy drive.

4. Copy the files from one of the directories listed in step 2 to the floppy disk.

5. Use the LABEL command to label the disk with the name of the directory. The syntax of the command is

   ```
   LABEL [<drive>:][<label>]
   ```

   where *<drive>* is the drive letter and *<label>* is the directory name.

6. Remove the disk from the drive and label the disk.

7. Repeat steps 4 through 6 for all the directories.

CREATING A SET OF INSTALL DISKS FOR WINDOWS NT

Before you begin creating a set of install disks for Windows NT, you need 17 high-density floppy disks. Make sure that they are blank and formatted. To create the install disks, perform the following steps:

1. Insert the Lotus Notes CD-ROM into the CD-ROM drive.

2. Insert one of the floppy disks into the floppy drive.

3. From the Main program group in Program Manager, double-click the File Manager icon.

4. Open a window for the CD-ROM drive by clicking its icon. Double-click the Win32 directory and open the DISK_KIT subdirectory.

5. The DISK_KIT directory has 17 subdirectories labeled DISK1 through DISK17. Copy the files from one of these directories to the floppy disk by clicking and dragging the icon of the subdirectory to the icon of the floppy drive.

6. Remove the disk from the drive and label the disk with the name of the directory.

7. Repeat steps 5 and 6 for all the subdirectories.

INSTALLING FROM A NETWORK DISTRIBUTION FILE SERVER

Notes can be installed on a file server so that the actual installation can be done on Notes workstations over the network. By using a file server, you can install on clients without a CD-ROM. You also don't need to hand out copies of the Notes installation media (CD-ROM, floppy disks).

Most organizations should install from a file server. This method enables one person to install several Notes clients at one time. You can start up the install program on several machines because there are no disks to feed to the machine, and you don't need multiple copies of a CD. Installing from a file server also ensures that the network is working at the time of installation.

To set up a network distribution server, Notes copies the Notes installation files in compressed form to a file server. Users can access the file server and install a copy of the application on their hard disks. Everything proceeds just as in a regular install from CD-ROM, except that the source of the files is a file server. To install Notes to a network distribution file server, do the following:

1. Insert the CD-ROM (or floppy disk, for a disk install) into the drive.

2. (Windows NT) Choose File | Run from the Program Manager menu, and in the Command Line box enter the following command:

   `<drive>:\<Install_Path>\Install`

   where *<drive>* is the drive letter, and *<Install_Path>* is the path for the install files.

   or

   (OS/2) Type `<drive>:\<Install_Path>\InstPM` in the OS/2 window, where *<drive>* is the drive letter, and *<Install_Path>* is the path for the install files.

3. In the dialog box that appears, enter the person's name and company name under which the software has been registered. (Note that the names you supply are for software registration purposes only and aren't used in the actual Notes setup.)

4. Check the Install on a File Server check box.

5. Choose Next.

   The install program asks whether you want to install the files to a file server or create a network distribution.

6. Click the Network Distribution radio button.

7. Choose Next.

   The Specify Distribution Directory dialog box opens.

8. Specify the drive and the installation folder for the Notes network distribution directory.

9. Choose Next.

   The install program asks whether you want to copy the files to the hard disk.

10. Choose Yes.

The Notes program files are copied to the file server in compressed form. Any user who can access the network drive can run the Notes install program to install Notes on his local machine.

To install from a file server, follow these steps:

1. Open the directory under which the network distribution files are stored on the file server.

2. Type `Install` at the command prompt. Press Enter.

The install program runs just like the CD-ROM installation (see the later sections on running the install program for details).

INSTALLING NOTES FROM A SHARED PROGRAM DIRECTORY

Suppose that you are installing Notes client software on workstations that are low on disk space, or you don't feel justified in having copies of Notes program files occupying space on multiple computers in your network. You should consider storing the Notes program files in a shared directory on a file server. A user can then perform a client install on his machine over the network, copying only a minimal set of files to the local hard disk. The client runs Notes using the program files on the server.

These are the benefits of installing Notes from a shared program directory:

◆ Only one set of program files needs to be installed on the server, instead of one set on every workstation, thereby conserving disk space.

◆ Workstations with smaller hard disks can be made Notes clients. (Indeed, you could even use diskless workstations.)

◆ Files can be backed up at a central location, instead of having to perform backups of multiple locations.

◆ Software upgrades become easier to perform, as only the software on the server is upgraded instead of every single workstation.

◆ Applications, files, and templates can be distributed quickly and are immediately available to the users.

These are the disadvantages of installing Notes from a shared program directory:

◆ Just as with any other file server application, running Notes over the network can constrict network bandwidth and cause a bottleneck at the server. In addition to increasing network throughput, this system can cause performance problems at the file server.

◆ Running Notes from the file server requires the user to be constantly LAN-connected to the server. This plan may not be suitable for users who want to use the mobile features of Notes.

◆ In the event of a server crash, all Notes activity on the network comes to a halt. Because all the files reside on the server, users can't use Notes in disconnected client-only mode.

An administrator needs to set up the shared program directory before clients can install from the shared program directory. The shared directory setup

◆ Installs the Notes program files in a directory on the file server.

◆ Creates a node install program. This program creates a minimum set of configuration files on the workstation in order to run the Notes client using the files on the file server.

Each client must run the node install program before using Notes.

MAKING A DECISION ABOUT THE LOCATION OF PERSONAL DIRECTORIES

For a user to run an application over the network from a file server, he must have a personal directory. This directory contains the Notes configuration files for that user. A data subdirectory could also be set up to hold personal databases.

When running a node install on a workstation, there is a choice of locating the personal directory on the local hard disk or on the file server. Locating personal directories on a server

◆ Enables administrators to back up personal databases

◆ Increases network traffic from users accessing files in their personal directories

◆ Saves disk space on client machines

Be sure to protect personal directories stored on a file server, using whatever security mechanisms are offered by your file server. Uncontrolled access to user files stored on a server completely destroys any other security you may want to enforce.

PERFORMING A NODE INSTALL ON A NETWORK NODE

To perform a node install on a network node, perform the following steps:

1. From the client machine, open the main directory on the file server where the program files reside. This step requires the network administrator to give at least read privileges to the user for the shared directory that contains Notes.

2. Run the Install program.

3. A dialog box appears, asking the user for the personal directory. A personal directory is one in which important configuration files are stored (see the preceding section). Enter the directory name and choose Next.

The Install program copies files to their destinations.

Note

A node install can be used only for Notes client installs. Notes servers can't run from files stored on a file server. Server installation requires the Notes program files to reside on the hard disk.

Don't use the file server containing users' personal directories and data files as a Notes server or client. If the file server is used as a Notes client, the user at the workstation will have local access to other users' Notes databases. In Lotus Notes Release 3, users with local access to Notes databases could bypass the Access Control List (ACL) of the database. Release 4 of Notes implements security on local databases. Even so, it may compromise database security (see Chapter 18, "Administering Notes Security," for details). Similarly, if the file server is used as a Notes server, users with access to the file server may gain local access to server-based databases if file-system-level security isn't implemented properly.

For users to be able to perform node installs on Notes clients, they must have network access to the directory containing the Notes node install program. This usually involves creating a share for this directory, and assigning (at least read) permissions to the users. In most cases, this task is performed by the network administrator.

When a user performs a Notes node install on a network node, he must use the same drive letter that he will use when running Notes from the file server. Windows 95–based clients can access the server using either of two formats:

`<drive_letter>:\<path>`

where *<drive_letter>* is the drive letter that has been mapped to the share on the file server and *<path>* is the path relative to the share

or

`\\<server_name> \<share_name>\<path>`

where *<server_name>* is the name of the file server, *<share_name>* is the name of the share, and *<path>* is the path relative to the share

In either case, the program directory and the personal directory must use the same absolute path as the node install.

INSTALLING NOTES ON A WORKSTATION

Installation of a Notes client takes three steps:

1. Registering the user.
2. Running the installation program.
3. Running workstation setup.

Before running the installation program, make sure that you have reviewed your installation options, as outlined in earlier sections.

REGISTERING A NEW USER

The first step in client installation is registering the user who will use the Notes workstation in the Public Address Book. This procedure is done by a person who has administrator privileges for the registration server (meaning that he is listed in the Administrators field in the server document of the Public Address Book on the server used for registering the user), or by the server itself (on a workstation session on the server). Registering a new user

◆ Creates a person document for the person in the Public Address Book and populates it with the details supplied by the administrator during the registration process.

◆ Creates a user ID for the person and certifies it with the certifier ID specified by the administrator. The user ID is encrypted and appended (attached) to the user's person document or saved in a file as specified by the administrator.

See Chapter 18 for more details on registering users.

RUNNING THE INSTALLATION PROGRAM—OS/2

Lotus Notes for the OS/2 operating system requires OS/2 Warp version 3 or OS/2 Warp Connect version 3. You have four options when installing Notes for OS/2. You can install from CD, floppy disk, a file server, or a shared directory. See the earlier section "Understanding Installation Options" for directions on preparing to install Notes with one of these four techniques.

To run the Notes client software installation for OS/2, follow these steps:

1. Shut down any screen savers and turn off any virus-detection software.
2. Close any applications that might be running in the background.
3. If you are upgrading from an existing version of Notes, back up any of the following files that you have:

◆ user.id (if it isn't already stored as an attachment to the person document in the Public Address Book)

◆ names.nsf, the personal Name and Address Book

◆ notes.ini, the Notes configuration file

◆ desktop.dsk, the desktop settings file

◆ Any customized template (.NTF), modem (.MDM), script (.SCR), SmartIcons (.SMI or .TBL), or bitmap (.BMP) files

4. Insert the CD-ROM (or floppy disk #1 for a floppy disk install) into the drive. If you are installing from a file server or shared program directory, make sure that you have access to the shared drive.

5. Open an OS/2 window, and type

   `<drive>:\<Install_Path>\InstPM`

   where *<drive>* is the drive letter, and *<Install_Path>* is the path for the install files. Press Enter.

   The initial Notes installation dialog box is displayed.

6. Enter the name and company name under which the software has been registered.

   The names you supply are for software registration purposes only and aren't used in the actual Notes setup.

7. Make sure that the Install on a File Server check box is unchecked.

8. Choose Next.

   Notes offers install options: Standard Installation, Server Installation, and Customized Features—Manual Install. Standard Installation installs the workstation files to your computer, Server Installation installs the server software, and Customized Features—Manual Install enables you to select the components you want to install. Don't select Server Installation when installing just the Notes client.

9. If you chose Customized Features—Manual Install in step 8, select the components you want to install. Make sure that the Notes Server option isn't selected.

10. Enter the name of the directory and drive where you want your Notes program files and your Notes data files to reside. If the directories you specify don't already exist, Notes creates them for you.

11. Choose Next.

12. Choose Next.

    Notes gives you a choice of having the CONFIG.SYS file updated with the Notes server path information, or doing it yourself after the installation. If you choose to make the changes manually, Notes stores the additions that are to be made in a file named CONFIG.ADD and saves it in the same directory as CONFIG.SYS. Notes also presents an option to overwrite any program files that might be present from a previous installation in the same directory.

13. If you have backed up your CONFIG.SYS file, select Update Config.SYS. Otherwise, make sure that this option isn't selected.

14. Choose OK.

15. Choose Install to begin installation.

   Notes begins to copy the program files to the directories you specified.

16. After all the files are copied, choose OK to complete the installation.

OS/2 requires the computer to be restarted after installation so that the changes that Notes made in the CONFIG.SYS file can take effect.

If you chose not to have Notes update the CONFIG.SYS automatically, the contents of the CONFIG.ADD file should be added to CONFIG.SYS before rebooting. Use the OS/2 System Editor to update CONFIG.SYS manually.

RUNNING THE INSTALLATION PROGRAM— WINDOWS NT

Lotus Notes for the Windows NT operating system requires at least Windows NT version 3.51. You have the same four options when installing Notes on Windows NT as you do for OS/2. You can install from CD, floppy disks, a file server, or shared program directory. See the earlier section "Understanding Installation Options" for directions on preparing to install Notes with one of these four techniques.

To run the Notes software installation for Windows NT, follow these steps:

1. Disable any screen savers and turn off any virus-detection software.

2. Close any applications that might be running in the background.

3. If you are upgrading from an existing version of Notes, back up any of the following files that you have:

   ◆ user.id (if it isn't already stored as an attachment to the person document in the Public Address Book)

   ◆ names.nsf, the personal Name and Address Book

   ◆ notes.ini, the Notes configuration file (stored in the Windows directory)

   ◆ desktop.dsk, the desktop settings file

   ◆ Any customized template (.NTF), modem (.MDM), script (.SCR), SmartIcons (.SMI or .TBL), or bitmap (.BMP) files

4. Insert the CD-ROM or floppy disk into the drive.

5. Choose File | Run from the Program Manager menu and enter `n:\<Install_Path>\InstPM` in the Command Line box, where *n* is the drive letter, and *<Install_Path>* is the path for the install files.

6. In the dialog box that appears, enter the name and company name under which the software has been registered. The names you supply are for software registration purposes only and aren't used in the actual Notes setup.

7. Make sure that the Install on a File Server check box is unchecked.

8. Choose Next.

    Notes offers three install options: Standard Installation, Server Installation, and Customized Features—Manual Install. Standard Installation installs the workstation files to your computer, Server Installation installs the server software, and Customized Features—Manual Install enables you to select the components you want to install. Don't select Server Installation when installing just the Notes client.

9. If you chose Customized Features—Manual Install in step 8, select the components you want to install. If you are installing a server, you should include the documentation and examples so that the clients don't need to install them. This plan saves disk space on your Notes clients.

10. To perform just a basic workstation installation, choose Standard Installation.

11. Enter the name of the directory and drive where you want your Notes program files and your Notes data files to reside. If the directories you specify don't already exist, Notes creates them for you.

12. Choose Next.

13. Notes prompts you for the program group in which to install the Notes icon. Choose an existing group, or type the name of a new group. Choose Next.

    After asking for confirmation to copy the Notes program files to your hard disk, Notes begins to copy the program files to the directories you specified.

    After all the files are copied, Notes creates the Lotus Notes icon in Program Manager.

14. When the Notes Installation Complete dialog box appears, choose OK to complete the installation. Lotus Notes for Windows NT doesn't require the computer to be restarted after installation.

RUNNING WORKSTATION SETUP

After you have registered the new user and installed the workstation program files on the computer, the Notes workstation setup procedure must be performed to complete installation. Before beginning workstation setup, you will need the following information:

◆ The user's fully distinguished name as it appears on the user ID, and the password associated with the user ID.

◆ The fully distinguished name of the home server of the user. The *home server* is the Notes server on which the mail file of the user will reside.

◆ Physical access to the user's ID file. This can be either an attachment to the user's person document in the Public Address Book or a file on a floppy disk, local hard disk, or network drive.

◆ The password for the user's ID file.

◆ The type of connection that the user's workstation will have to the server, and the network protocol used to connect to the server. If the user connects to the server over a LAN, you need to know the appropriate LAN protocol. The connection can also be over a phone line, in which case you also need to know the telephone number of the server and the type of modem that the computer uses.

The client setup program should only be performed by a trusted person, as she will have access to the user's ID file and password. Workstation setup for users who will have a high level of access (such as administrators, database managers, and executives) should be performed by a core member of the deployment team.

SETTING UP A LOTUS NOTES WORKSTATION

If you have all the above-mentioned setup parameters handy, the workstation setup procedure is ready to commence. To complete workstation setup, perform the following steps:

1. Double-click the Lotus Notes icon on the desktop.

   The Notes Workstation Setup dialog box appears.

2. Select the type of connection you have to your server. There are four options for server connectivity:

   ◆ If the workstation connects to the server over a LAN, choose Network Connection (via LAN).

   ◆ If the workstation connects to the server over a phone line, choose Remote Connection (via Modem).

◆ If the workstation connects to the server over a LAN and over a phone line, choose Network and Remote Connections.

◆ If the workstation isn't connected to a server, choose No Connection to a Server.

3. If the user's ID file is present as an attachment in the user's person document in the Public Address Book, leave the User ID Supplied in a File check box unchecked. If the user's ID file resides on a disk, select the check box.

4. If the User ID Supplied in a File box was checked in step 3, Notes prompts for the location of the file. Specify the drive, directory, and file name for the ID file, and choose OK.

5. Notes asks if you want the user ID file copied to the data directory. Choose Yes.

6. Notes prompts you for the password associated with the user ID. Enter the password and choose OK.

At this point, the remaining steps in the procedure depend on your choice in the Notes Workstation Setup dialog box in step 2. The following four sections explain what steps to take, depending on your selection. After completing the network connection steps, continue the installation with the steps in the section "Completing the Installation."

NETWORK CONNECTION VIA LAN

If you chose Network Connection (via LAN) in the Notes Workstation Setup dialog box, follow these steps:

1. In the Network Workstation Setup dialog box, enter the fully distinguished name of the user in the Your User Name box. If you are using a hierarchical naming system, and use the common name of the user, Notes assumes that the name was certified by the organizational certifier.

2. Enter the fully distinguished name of the user's home server in the Home Server Name dialog box. Again, if a common name is specified, by default Notes assumes that the server has a "top level" name.

3. In the Network Type drop-down box, specify the type of LAN on which the workstation connects to the server. This action identifies the network protocol that the workstation will use to communicate with the server. The choices are

◆ NetBIOS (NetWare, LAN Manager, and so on)

◆ NetWare SPX

◆ TCP/IP

◆ Banyan VINES

REMOTE CONNECTION VIA MODEM

If you chose Remote Connection (via Modem) in the Notes Workstation Setup dialog box, do the following:

1. Enter the fully distinguished name of the user in the Your User Name box. If you are using a hierarchical naming system, and use the common name of the user, Notes assumes that the name was certified by the organizational certifier.

2. Enter the fully distinguished name of the user's home server in the Home Server Name dialog box. Again, if a common name is specified, by default Notes assumes that the server has a "top level" name.

3. Enter the telephone number of the home server in the Home Server Phone Number box.

4. In the Phone Dialing Prefix box, enter any prefix needed to dial the server's telephone number.

5. Choose the port to which the modem is connected in the Modem Port drop-down list box. Select the appropriate radio button for the dialing method (tone or pulse dialing).

6. Select the type of the dialing modem in the Modem Type drop-down list box.

NETWORK AND REMOTE CONNECTIONS

If you chose Network and Remote Connections in the Notes Workstation Setup dialog box, do the following:

1. Enter the fully distinguished name of the user in the Your User Name box. If you are using a hierarchical naming system, and use the common name of the user, Notes assumes that the name was certified by the organizational certifier.

2. Enter the fully distinguished name of the user's home server in the Home Server Name dialog box. Again, if a common name is specified, by default Notes assumes that the server has a "top level" name.

3. Make the appropriate selection in the Connect to Server Now box. If the LAN connection is going to be used to connect to the server during workstation setup, select the Via Network radio button, or if the connection is going to be made over a phone line, select the Via Modem radio button.

4. Enter the telephone number of the home server in the Home Server Phone Number box. Telephone number information needs to be entered only if the connection to the server during workstation setup is going to be made over the phone line.

11

INSTALLING NOTES CLIENTS

5. Enter any prefix needed to dial the server's telephone number in the Phone Dialing Prefix box.

6. Choose the port to which the modem is connected in the Modem Port drop-down list box. Select the appropriate radio button for the dialing method (tone or pulse dialing).

7. Select the type of the dialing modem in the Modem Type drop-down list box.

8. In the Network Type drop-down list box, specify the type of LAN on which the workstation connects to the server. This step identifies the network protocol that the workstation will use to communicate with the server. The choices are

   ◆ NetBIOS (NetWare, LAN Manager, and so on)
   ◆ NetWare SPX
   ◆ TCP/IP
   ◆ Banyan VINES

No Connection to a Server

If you chose No Connection to a Server in the Notes Workstation Setup dialog box, Notes prompts you for the full name of the user. Enter the fully distinguished name of the user in the Your User Name box. If you specified that the user ID was supplied in a file, Notes doesn't prompt for the full name, but the name present on the user ID is used automatically.

Completing the Installation

If you chose an option that specified a connection with the server, Notes attempts to connect to the server at this point. After attempting to connect (whether or not the connection was successful), the Time Zone Setup dialog box appears. Follow these steps to complete the installation:

1. Select the appropriate time zone, and click the Observe Daylight Savings Time April-October check box if appropriate.

2. Choose OK.

3. Choose OK when Notes informs you that Notes setup is complete.

You should quickly test to make sure that the client can access the Notes servers on the local network. Users also may want to make a backup copy of their ID files at this time. See Chapter 18 for details on the advantages and disadvantages of having users back up ID files.

UNINSTALLING NOTES

Lotus Notes Release 4 comes with a utility that uninstalls the Notes program files if you don't want Notes on the workstation any more. To uninstall Notes, follow these steps:

1. Double-click the Notes R4.0 Uninstall icon in the program group in which the Lotus Notes icons were installed.

2. When asked to confirm whether you want to uninstall Notes, choose Yes.

3. The Uninstall program begins removing Notes program files from the computer. If any files were modified after Notes was originally installed, you are asked to confirm that you want to delete them. Uninstall removes all files in the Notes directory but doesn't remove the NOTES.INI file, which is stored in the Windows directory in the case of Microsoft Windows, or in the Notes data directory in the case of OS/2.

SUMMARY

Installing Notes clients is a time-consuming process due to the large number of workstations involved. Make sure that you publish a realistic installation schedule, showing when each user is to attend training and have Notes installed.

Installing Notes clients is straightforward. Installing the base operating system and network is more work than installing Notes. You have four options when installing Notes:

◆ Install from CD-ROM
◆ Install from floppy disks
◆ Install from a file server
◆ Install from a shared directory

Most organizations should install from a file server. This method enables one person to install several Notes clients at one time. It also ensures that the network is working at the time of install. After you have the file server set up, you don't need to distribute floppy disks or CDs. You can easily add new users to your Notes network at any time.

- Why Migrate?

- Migration Overview

- Upgrading in a Mixed Environment

- Monitoring the Conversion to Hierarchical Naming

- Administering Mixed Environments

CHAPTER 12

Migrating from Notes 3.x

You should approach your migration with the same careful planning that you used with your initial installation. Careful planning for your migration can help prevent critical problems later on. Before starting your migration, you need to familiarize yourself with the new features in Notes Release 4.

This chapter lays out a standard plan for migrating your installation to Notes Release 4. Migrating can be a large job, and before diving in you should consider whether Notes Release 4 is the correct platform for you.

This chapter covers the following topics:

◆ Basics you should consider when deciding whether to migrate to Release 4

◆ Issues that an administrator needs to keep in mind when administering a mixed environment containing both Release 3 and Release 4 servers and clients

◆ Tools designed to help you migrate from Notes Release 3 to Notes Release 4

WHY MIGRATE?

Lotus certainly acts as if it's a foregone conclusion that you will migrate your Notes installation to Release 4, but this isn't necessarily the case. Migrating to Release 4 involves retraining your support staff and end users, in addition to a considerable amount of planning and time to carry out the migration. Before migrating to Release 4, organizations should review their use of Notes to determine whether a migration to Release 4 is the best investment of their support staff's time.

You certainly will want to migrate to Release 4 if:

◆ Notes is being used for mission-critical applications.

If you depend on Notes to run key parts of your business, you should continue to update your Notes software as new releases are issued. This plan is the best way to maintain a stable, supportable Notes installation.

◆ Yours is a large organization.

Large organizations with thousands of users recoup their investment in training in a fairly short period of time, because Notes Release 4 comes with several system management features that save administrative time and effort. Notes Release 4 also contains features that enable you to reduce your hardware expense.

Medium and small organizations need to do some rough cost/benefit calculations before migrating to Release 4. Even if you decide that moving to Release 4 is a smart choice for your organization, the timing of the move can be important. Waiting for an update to Release 4 may make sense for any organization, large or small, that uses Notes to run mission-critical applications.

If you are currently experiencing problems with Notes Release 3, migrating quickly to Release 4 makes sense. Migrating to Release 4 often is easier than upgrading current Release 3 servers. If you plan to upgrade your Release 3 servers to the latest Notes Release 3.x software, consider migrating to Notes Release 4 instead. Notes 4 servers can coexist with Notes 3 servers and clients without problems, and should prove to be a more stable platform over time.

MIGRATION OVERVIEW

A Notes migration follows an eight-point plan similar to the eight-step plan for installing Notes described in Chapter 5, "Building a Deployment Plan," and Chapter 6, "Customizing Your Deployment Plan." The major difference between migrating and an initial install is that, when migrating, you upgrade your applications after installing Notes software, instead of developing applications before installing. Each of the steps that you followed during an initial installation should be redone during a migration. The eight steps in a migration plan are as follows:

1. Create the migration team.

   The same team that you used to administer Notes, plus power users and IS executives, should be involved in a major systems migration such as migrating to Release 4.

2. Assess the current installation.

   You need to reassess all your current plans regarding Notes, as well as take inventory of your current hardware and software installations.

3. Train your support organization.

   Your entire Notes support staff should be trained, including administrators, application developers, and help desk personnel.

4. Design your Notes network.

   Notes Release 4 has several features that can affect the topology of your Notes network. In addition, if you haven't already migrated to hierarchical naming, you should begin planning now.

5. Update the standard operating procedures.

   Many of the procedures administrators carry out will change after you have installed Release 4. You need to update any documented procedures to reflect the new capabilities that Notes 4 delivers.

6. Upgrade your Notes network.

   In this step, you actually install hardware and software on your system.

7. Upgrade your applications.

   After you have converted your Notes network (or at least a few workgroups in a geographical area) to Release 4, you should begin upgrading applications to take advantage of Notes 4 features.

8. Convert to hierarchical naming.

   Hierarchical naming offers many advantages over flat naming, and many of the disadvantages have been minimized with new administrative tools. Therefore, the author strongly recommends that all organizations convert to hierarchical naming after migrating to Release 4.

The following sections discuss each of these steps in detail. You also should review the chapters in Part II of this book, "Planning Your Notes Installation," before carrying out a migration.

CREATING A MIGRATION TEAM

A Notes migration team resembles a Notes installation team in many regards. The political aspects of migrating are far less important than those involved in initial installation, so the choice of project leader isn't quite as important. You also don't need a Notes evangelist as part of the migration team. A migration team should include the following members:

◆ Project manager.

   The key job of the project manager is to develop a time line and budget, track progress against the budget, and communicate that progress to the IS staff and line of business executives.

   Notes migration project managers should have experience with Notes Release 3 or major experience with some other client/server project.

◆ Notes server administrator.

   The server administrator is responsible for upgrading servers and coordinating all the database upgrades on his servers. He is also responsible for reoptimizing Notes servers to take advantage of Release 4 features.

◆ Database managers.

   The database managers are responsible for upgrading access control lists to take advantage of new features, as well as ensuring that critical databases have been tested with Release 4 before the database is upgraded.

◆ Network administrators.

   Network administrators are responsible for maintaining the network during a Notes migration. A network administrator also may be responsible for reconfiguring access for remote offices and mobile users.

◆ End user representatives.

   Power users and line-of-business managers should be involved in a Notes migration. They should understand the features that Notes 4 delivers and how to take advantage of them in their particular areas. Power users are responsible for helping other end users in the department come up to speed during migration.

- ◆ Operations representatives.

   Involving operations staff during any major systems upgrade is a good idea. This fact is true for Notes as well as other client/server products. The operations staff will be involved in rewriting standard operating procedures.

- ◆ Application developers.

   Application developers are needed to help design test plans for critical applications, as well as adding new features as appropriate after installing Release 4.

- ◆ Trainer.

   The trainer is responsible for developing the training strategy for the migration team, end users, and support staff.

- ◆ Help desk representative.

   Include someone from your help desk on the Notes migration team so that she can gain experience with Notes Release 4. She will be responsible for communicating common problems to other help desk members. By participating in the migration planning and implementation, she can gain experience that can't be gained through training. This strategy will help your help desk be up to speed in time to help users as the migration gets under way.

- ◆ Remote-site coordinators.

   Each remote site should have a remote-site coordinator involved in the migration planning. The remote-site coordinator should be the main contact for people at remote sites concerning the migration.

- ◆ Certifiers.

   Certifiers need to be involved with your migration planning if you need to upgrade from flat naming to hierarchical naming. The certifier is responsible for managing the certificates and creating new IDs.

Large organizations may have both a Notes Release 3 administrative team and a separate migration team at one time. Medium or small organizations most likely will need to carry out the migration to Release 4 while maintaining the current Release 3 network. Consider adding some temporary personnel to the administrative team to help handle the load during the migration period. This method can benefit your organization by getting your organization up to speed with Release 4 faster than otherwise possible.

ASSESSING THE CURRENT INSTALLATION

The first thing you need to assess is your current plan regarding any Release 3 installations in progress. Consider whether it's worth the time to continue installing Release 3 software and then migrate it to Release 4 in the near future. In some cases, switching to Release 4 rather than continuing to install Release 3 software makes sense. Testing Release 4 in your environment before installing it may cause an unacceptable delay for some high-priority planned installations. But there is no other reason to continue installing Release 3 software rather than switching to Release 4. Release 4 clients can access Release 3 servers. Release 4 servers can support both Release 3 clients and servers. Replication mail routing works correctly in a mixed environment.

You also need to do a skills assessment as part of your migration planning, in order to develop a proper training plan. This step should be far easier than your initial Notes installation because all your users should be knowledgeable about Release 3 features and know how to operate a mouse in a graphical environment.

You also need to assess your current installed base of hardware and software. Follow the steps outlined in Chapter 7, "Determining Hardware and Software Needs," just as if you were installing Release 4 on brand-new machines.

TRAINING YOUR SUPPORT ORGANIZATION

You need to train your administrators, application developers, and help desk personnel before you attempt to develop a comprehensive migration plan. Computer-based training is sufficient for many of your support staff. You also can contact a training organization if you want on-site training.

DESIGNING YOUR NOTES NETWORK

Notes Release 4 contains enhanced replication and new mail features that can alter your network topology. In particular, if you aren't already using a hub-and-spoke architecture or hierarchical naming, you should plan to convert now. Chapter 9, "Designing Your Notes Network," contains all the details you need to consider when developing your naming schemes and network topologies, but here is a summary:

- ◆ Use a hub-and-spoke replication architecture to simplify your Notes network.
- ◆ Minimize the number of servers that you need to support.
- ◆ Use passthru to eliminate the need to have dedicated dial-up servers.
- ◆ Notes Release 4 enables you to consolidate several smaller mail servers into a single large server.

You also can bundle other tasks into your migration, such as changing your operating system.

UPDATING STANDARD OPERATING PROCEDURES

The procedures that change when you migrate to Release 4 are those concerned with certifying users, changing names, and issuing cross certificates. The Administration Process handles many of the tasks that were done manually in the past. Although you can register users and servers the same way as you did for Release 3, the Administration Process is designed to ease these tasks. You should update your standard operating procedures for handling employee terminations. Use the Administration Process to delete users from database and server access control lists.

Tip

> When handling employee terminations, be sure to check the Administration Requests database to see that the request to terminate the employee has been completed. When you delete a person record from the Name and Address Book, you must use the button Delete Person rather than the Delete key. Pressing the Delete key doesn't generate a request in the Administration Request database.

Cross certificates now can be issued over the phone. This system eliminates the need to exchange any media or even to have your computers connected at the time cross certificates are issued. Other standard operating procedures—such as backing up servers, monitoring the Notes log, and restoring the Public Address Book—don't change.

UPGRADING YOUR NOTES NETWORK

Following are the steps involved in upgrading a server:

1. Upgrade all hardware and software.
2. Do a complete backup of the server.
3. Install the Notes software.
4. Upgrade the Public Address Book.
5. Configure statistics and events monitoring.

The first step in upgrading your Notes network is to complete your planning. Before proceeding, you should have a complete plan showing when all servers and clients will be upgraded. This plan should include all servers and clients that will be upgraded in the first eight weeks of your migration.

Your migration implementation should proceed by upgrading your servers first, followed by your clients. By upgrading your servers first, you minimize impact on end users and decrease the amount of effort required to perform the migration. Notes Release 4 servers have tools available to help you update and migrate client machines. All Release 3 clients can access Release 4 databases on Release 4 servers. Users shouldn't notice that the server has been upgraded to Release 4 or that databases stored on that server have been converted to Release 4 format.

You should develop a complete schedule for your server and client upgrades. Client upgrades should be coordinated with your training schedule so that each end user receives training within 48 hours of his or her machine being upgraded. During the initial install, you had a way of enforcing the requirement that users receive training before receiving Release 4 on their machines; you could refuse to issue IDs until they received their training. You no longer have this option if users already have their IDs, so you have to rely on persuasion to get users into training. Release 4 is sufficiently different that users should receive some training before you begin to upgrade applications to use new Release 4 features.

Performing System Tests

Before installing any hardware or software, you should upgrade your test environment to Release 4. Test out a representative sample of your applications. Do a complete test of all third-party products (such as mail gateways and application-development tools) that you use in your environment. Contact the company from which you purchased your products for Release 4 upgrades. After you have tested all your gateways and a representative sample of your applications, you are ready to proceed with installing hardware and software.

In addition, test a sampling of your other applications, such as noncritical workflow and simple discussion databases. You should accomplish your testing before migrating a single production server to Release 4.

Upgrading the Hardware

You should have a complete list of your hardware and software upgrades required from Chapter 9. Now is the time to upgrade hardware on your server machines. You can begin to upgrade hardware on client machines as the machines become available. Try to upgrade the hardware and software on any laptops as they become available during the migration. After you have upgraded the hardware, update the operating system and network software on your server machines.

UPGRADING THE FIRST SERVER

Before upgrading any server, perform a complete backup. Back up all Notes databases, as well as DESKTOP.DSK; NOTES.INI; all IDs, including server, user, and certifier IDs; the Public Address Book (NAMES.NSF); the Notes log (LOG.NSF); and the server's mailbox (MAIL.BOX). In addition to these databases, back up any Notes-supplied templates that you have customized, and all directory link files and database redirection files.

The first server upgrade differs from other server upgrades in that you need to upgrade the Public Address Book on the first server where you install Release 4. You should upgrade the Public Address Book on only one server, and then replicate these changes to other Release 4 servers.

After upgrading the hardware, operating system, and networking software on a server and completing a backup, install the Notes Release 4 software. Install the software in the same directories as the Release 3 files, following the steps in Chapter 10, "Installing and Configuring Notes Servers."

After you have completed the install and setup for Notes Release 4, manually copy any customized views or forms from your Release 3 template to your Release 4 template. You should never completely replace a Release 4 design element. Instead, modify existing elements, using your Release 3 customizations as a guide. For example, if you modified the People view in the Public Address Book, don't copy the customized Release 3 People view directly into the Release 4 Public Address Book. Instead, take each of your customizations, including a selection formula, and so on, and enter that information into the existing People view in your Release 4 Public Address Book. When updating forms, copy your customized fields directly into Release 4 templates rather than copying the entire Release 3 form. You also may need to edit the NOTES.INI file. You can use any of the methods outlined in Chapter 13, "Administrative Tools," for editing the Release 4 NOTES.INI file.

Caution

Never copy a Release 3 NOTES.INI file directly over a Notes 4 NOTES.INI file.

The one file you shouldn't need to update is your desktop. DESKTOP.DSK isn't changed during the install program.

The first server you upgrade should be a hub server. By upgrading a hub server first, you minimize problems when replicating your new Public Address Book. You also avoid potential problems with end users accessing a Release 4 server before you've tested it in your production environment.

UPGRADING THE PUBLIC ADDRESS BOOK

Upgrade the Public Address Book in each domain. Notes automatically replicates the changes as you install other Release 4 servers. If you are using cascaded address books, upgrade each of these databases on the first Release 4 server.

You upgrade an address book with these tasks:

◆ Adding and applying roles.

◆ Rebuilding views.

◆ Converting to Release 4 format.

◆ Editing connection documents to take advantage of new replication features.

To upgrade the Public Address Book, follow these steps:

1. Start the workstation program on the Release 4 server.

   Notes asks whether you want to upgrade the Public Address Book.

2. Choose Yes.

3. Select the Public Address Book from the workspace.

4. Choose Actions | Add Admin Roles to Access Control List.

   This step copies all roles from the Release 4 Public Address Book template to your current Public Address Book.

5. Select OK.

   You are now ready to apply these roles to individuals in the access control list.

6. For each entry in the access control list for the Public Address Book, specify the roles in which that entry should participate.

   Administrators who currently have editor access to the Public Address Book should be given author access with the ability to create documents. Administrators with editor access have full ability to edit and change all documents in the Public Address Book, regardless of the roles that they are assigned. To take advantage of the roles in the Public Address Book, you need to limit access to the author level. Not all organizations will want to use roles in the Public Address Book. Review Chapter 13 to decide whether you should use roles in the Address Book. For general information on roles, see Chapter 3, "Understanding Security."

   After you have updated the access control list so that members are assigned proper roles, you need to update all documents in the Public Address Book. The design of these documents, and the documents themselves, must have fields added to them so that administrators can carry out their tasks.

7. For each view in the Public Address Book, open the view, select the documents in the view, and choose Actions | Apply Delegation to All Entries.

Tip

> Do these tasks during off-peak hours, as updating all the documents in a large view can take some time. You may need to perform this step over a period of several days or weeks, depending on the size of your Public Address Book.

8. Shut down the workstation software.

9. Make sure that the Notes server is shut down.

   You are now ready to update the views and file format of the Public Address Book. Because both the workstation and the server always have the Public Address Book open, both of them must be shut down. This means that you must update the views and convert the file format from an operating system command prompt.

10. Rebuild the views in the Public Address Book by entering one of the following commands:

    ◆ (OS/2) `IUPDALL NAMES.NSF`

    ◆ (Windows NT) `NUPDALL NAMES.NSF`

    ◆ (UNIX) `UPDALL NAMES.NSF`

11. Enter your Notes ID password.

12. To convert the Public Address Book to Release 4 format, run the Compact program from an operating system command line by entering one of the following commands:

    ◆ (OS/2) `ICOMPACT NAMES.NSF`

    ◆ (Windows NT) `NCOMPACT NAMES.NSF`

    ◆ (UNIX) `COMPACT NAMES.NSF`

13. Enter your Notes ID at the prompt.

Before converting the file format of the Public Address Book, make sure that you have enough disk space to run Compact. In order to run Compact on a database, you need to have at least enough free disk space to hold a duplicate copy of the database being compacted. Because Public Address Books can be quite large, you should double-check before running Compact on your Public Address Book.

You don't need to rebuild view indexes manually, as Notes automatically updates the indexes when it is restarted. After completing the update of your Public Address Book, you can take advantage of new replication features that allow you to replicate databases more often with less system overhead. After you have converted all the servers in a hub-and-spoke topology, update the connection documents of the spoke servers to use the pull-push replication method. For more information on pull-push replication, see Chapter 15, "Administering Replication."

CONFIGURING STATISTICS AND EVENTS MONITORING

Follow the steps outlined in Chapter 13 to set up statistics and events monitoring. You should configure statistics and events monitoring before continuing to upgrade other Notes servers. Statistics and events monitoring enables you to monitor your network more easily as you migrate servers. Because Release 4 statistics and events monitoring is superior to Release 3 in several ways (see Chapter 13 for details), you should upgrade immediately.

In Release 3, statistics and events monitoring documents were stored in the Public Address Book. In Release 4, they are stored in the Statistics & Events Database. As you no longer need them, you can delete the statistics and events monitoring documents from the Public Address Book by following these steps:

1. Open the Statistics & Events Database (EVENTS4.NSF).
2. Open the Servers to Monitor View.
3. Select Remove Monitor Views from NAB.

Make sure that you have upgraded all views in the Public Address Book before deleting the statistics and events documents from the database. In addition, you will need to have configured the Administration Process on the server before you can delete documents.

You don't need to copy your current statistics and events documents manually from the Public Address Book to the Statistics & Events Database. The Event server task does this the first time it is executed.

UPGRADING OTHER SERVERS

Repeat the process described earlier for upgrading servers, with the exception that you don't need to upgrade the Public Address Book the second time. After you have completed upgrading all servers in a hub-and-spoke topology, edit the connection documents to use pull-push replication.

CONVERTING DATABASES TO RELEASE 4 FORMAT

Actually, this step happens automatically the next time the server runs the Compact program. The Compact program runs on a database every one-third of the purge interval in days. For example, if a database has a purge interval of 90 days, Compact runs on that database every 30 days.

Databases that don't have an .NS3 extension will be converted to Release 4 file format. You can prevent your databases from being converted by changing the file name of the database from an .NSF extension to an .NS3 extension. (If you are going to change the file name of your databases, make sure that you give your users an easy way to update their desktops.)

There really is no advantage to keeping a database stored on a Release 4 server in Release 3 format. Because of the hassle of changing a file name that requires users to update their desktops, you should go ahead and convert files to Release 4 format. If you want to convert a database sooner, you can always run Compact from the server console on the database. For more information on Compact, see Chapter 13.

Converting to Release 4 file format isn't a one-way street. You can revert to Release 3 file format by using the Compact routine. If you want to have a database revert to Release 3 format, enter this command on the server console:

```
Load Compact -R database_name
```

UPGRADING NOTES CLIENTS

Make a complete backup of every Notes client before proceeding with an upgrade. Back up NOTES.INI, DESKTOP.DSK, NAMES.NSF, all ID files, all local databases, directory links, and database redirection files, and any customized templates.

To install the Notes Release 4 workstation software, follow the steps outlined in Chapter 11, "Installing Notes Clients." When you have completed the installation, restart the Notes workstation software. You may need to reenter the setup information if you haven't installed Release 4 in the directory previously used by Release 3. Finally, to allow a user access to several Release 4 features, compact the desktop. To compact a user's desktop, follow these steps:

1. Right-click on the workspace.

   The Properties dialog box opens.

2. Click the Information tab.

3. Click Compact.

After you have compacted the user's database, he will be able to add tabs to and delete tabs from the workspace.

The Install program doesn't alter the user's desktop, Personal Address Book, or customizations in the NOTES.INI file. The desktop file isn't touched at all until you manually compact it. Personal Address Books are automatically upgraded to use the new Release 4 design template (PERNAMES.NTF). Laptops with outgoing mailboxes also overwrite the outgoing mailbox design template (MAILBOX.NTF).

Although the design templates of the mailboxes are updated, the mailboxes themselves aren't automatically upgraded by the Install program. You must use the Convert server task to upgrade mailboxes stored on a server. Users can upgrade local copies of address books, using a new agent stored in the design template for Release 4.

Note

Complete your workstation upgrades for all workstations connected to a mail server before upgrading the mailboxes on the server.

The license types for many Release 3 clients will convert when upgrading to Release 4. The license type determines the features available to a user; the person document for each user must reflect the license type. An administrator needs to edit the user's person document and enter the correct type of license in the Client License field. After the person document has replicated throughout the domain, each user should upgrade her license type by following these steps:

1. Choose File | Tools | User ID.

   The User ID dialog box appears.

2. Choose More Options.

3. Choose Upgrade License.

4. Restart the Notes workstation.

CONVERTING MAIL FILES

You should upgrade mailboxes only after all workstations have been upgraded to Release 4. Users who have customized their mailboxes will need to save these customizations and reapply them after conversion. Although preserving customizations for users would be nice, no automated task exists for this purpose. To upgrade all mail databases on a server, you use the Mail Conversion utility provided with Release 4. To use the Convert Utility to upgrade mailboxes, perform the following procedure:

1. Shut down the router to prevent delivery of mail while the Convert Utility is running. From the server console, enter the following command:

   ```
   Tell Router Exit
   ```

2. Run the Convert Utility. You can use the Convert Utility to update a single database, all databases in a directory, all databases in an entire subdirectory tree, or just those databases listed in a file. Choose the appropriate option from the following list:

   ◆ To upgrade a single database, enter the following command:

   ```
   Load Convert Mailbox.NSF STDNOTESMAIL MAIL4.NTF
   ```

   ◆ To upgrade all mail databases in a directory, enter this command:

   ```
   Load Convert Mail/*NSF STDNOTESMAIL MAIL4.NTF
   ```

   ◆ To upgrade all mail databases in a directory tree, use this command:

   ```
   Load Convert -R Mail/*NSF STDNOTESMAIL MAIL4.NTF
   ```

◆ To upgrade all mail databases listed in a text file (here called maillist.txt), enter the following command:

```
Load Convert -F MailList.TXT STDNOTESMAIL MAIL4.NTF
```

The STDNOTESMAIL and MAIL4.NTF parameters tell the Convert Utility to update the design template to MAIL.4 if and only if the current design template for the database is STDNOTESMAIL. If you don't want to update the design, or if the mailbox already had its design updated, you can skip these two parameters. You also can use wild cards for these parameters. For example, instead of entering **STDNOTESMAIL**, you could always just type **STD***.

For each mail database converted, the Convert Utility does the following:

◆ Replaces the design template.

◆ Creates a folder for each category (up to 200).

◆ Creates a subfolder for each subcategory in any mail message.

◆ Adds mail messages that are categorized to the new folder or subfolder.

◆ Places any uncategorized documents in the In Box.

You can tell the Convert Utility to ignore the upper limit of 200 categories by using the -I parameter.

3. Restart the mail router. At the server console, type the following command:

```
Load ROUTER
```

4. Have the users copy their customized views and forms back into their personal mailboxes. Make sure that users don't completely replace entire views or forms. Rather, they should copy individual fields into forms, and cut-and-paste selection formulas into views.

The syntax of the Convert Utility is as follows:

```
Load CONVERT (-F) (-L) (-R) (-I) (-D) (-N) (FULLPATH) database file name
➡(CurrentDesignTemplate) (NewDesignTemplate)
```

where *CurrentDesignTemplate* is the name of the template that a mail file must be using in order for it to be converted, and *NewDesignTemplate* specifies the name of the new template that will be used by the mail file.

All parameters except the file name of the mail database are optional. The following list describes the parameters:

◆ -F

This parameter tells the Convert Utility to read database file names from a file. In this case, the database file name should be the text file containing the file names.

◆ -L

This parameter causes the Convert Utility to copy the mail files out of the person documents in the Public Address Book for all users who have the current server as their home server. This argument works only with Release 4 Public Address Books. The file name should be the text file name that will be created. If a file name already exists, Convert exits with an error.

You can't use both the -F and -L arguments at one time.

Tip

Use the -L argument to create a list of mail files. Delete the users whose mail files shouldn't be converted. Using -L is normally faster than typing entries by hand, and avoids typos.

◆ -R

This parameter tells the Convert Utility to recurse into subdirectories when searching for mail files.

◆ -I

Use this parameter to tell Convert to ignore the maximum number of categories that can be converted to folders. The default is no more than 200 categories and subcategories. Because Release 3 users can't access a mail file with more than 200 folders, make sure that all users have been upgraded to Release 4 before converting their mail files.

◆ -D

This parameter tells Convert to update the design template with the new template specified, but doesn't convert categories into folders and subfolders.

◆ -N

Use this option to generate a list of databases that Convert would upgrade, but not actually perform an upgrade.

Note

If you don't specify a current template and a new template, the Notes Design won't be upgraded to Release 4. You must always specify a current template and a new template when using the Convert Utility on mail files that aren't already using the Release 4 mail design template.

You need to upgrade only the primary mailbox for each user. If they maintain local replicas, all changes will propagate. Don't upgrade both a user's primary mail file (the mail file to which the router delivers mail) and replicas stored on workstations or laptops. Documents may not appear in the correct folders if you convert both a primary mail database and its replica.

A user who has her primary mailbox on her local machine can upgrade to Release 4 by using an agent contained in the Release 4 mail design template. She must replace the design of the current mailbox so that it uses the new design template for mailboxes, run the agent contained in the design, and then copy over any customized forms or views. The user who wants to convert her personal mailbox should follow these steps:

1. Make sure that the workstation has been upgraded to Release 4.
2. Store any customized forms or views in a temporary database.
3. Select the personal mailbox icon from the workspace.
4. Choose File | Database | Replace Design.

    The Replace Database Design dialog box opens, as shown in Figure 12.1.

Figure 12.1.
Use the Replace
Database Design dialog
box to update the
design of your mailbox.

5. From the list of templates, select the Mail (R4) Design Template (MAIL.NTL).
6. Choose Replace.

    Notes prompts you with a warning that you should copy all customized views and forms before proceeding.

7. Choose Yes.
8. Open the Agent view.
9. Double-click the (Convert Categories to Folders) agent.
10. Choose Actions | Run.
11. Copy any customizations back to your personal mailbox. Don't replace any forms or views that exist in your Release 4 database. If you need to modify any of the forms or views that come standard with Release 4, copy individual fields or formulas rather than the whole design element. Because Notes Release 4 contains many additional standard features, you may not even need to use your customizations any longer.

After you convert a user's primary mailbox on a server to use the new Release 4 mailbox template, the user needs to replicate the new design element to any local replicas of her mailbox, and ensure that all design elements will replicate. To ensure that all design elements replicate, follow these steps:

1. Choose File | Replication | Settings.

   The Replication Settings dialog box opens.

2. Click the Advanced icon.

3. Make sure that all check boxes in the Replicate Incoming section are selected.

4. Choose OK.

Alternatively, to maintain a Release 3 design of any local replicas, uncheck the Forms, Views, Etc. check box and the Agents check box.

UPGRADING YOUR APPLICATIONS

After you have converted a server, workstation, department, or workgroup to Release 4, you can start to take advantage of Release 4 features. You can use some features if even a single server has been upgraded, while other features, such as Release 4 Mail, should be used only after you have converted an entire workgroup.

Notes Release 4 contains two key features that enable you to replicate data faster and with less administrative burden than in Release 3. Release 4 databases can have multiple replicators updating them at a single time. Also, field-level replication reduces the amount of data that must be replicated. Replication is faster in a hub-and-spoke architecture, because Notes Release 4 doesn't scan the disk drive for new databases every time a replication starts, instead storing information on all databases in memory.

These features combine to greatly enhance the speed of replication in a hub-and-spoke topology, where a hub may contain several thousand databases. You can configure the spokes to push changes to the hub rather than relying on the hub to pull changes from a spoke. Because all the spokes can be pushing changes to a database at once, the amount of time it takes for a change to propagate is greatly reduced.

To take advantage of pull-push replication, you need to modify the connection documents for all spokes in your topology.

SETTING UP THE ADMINISTRATION PROCESS

Chapter 13 covers the Administration Process in detail. To set up the administrative process on a Notes server, follow these steps:

1. Make sure that the server has been upgraded to Release 4.
2. Add ADMINP to the ServerTasks parameter in the NOTES.INI file.
3. Convert the Public Address Book and modify its ACL, giving administrators at least author access with the ability to delete documents. Assign administrators to the proper roles.
4. Add the Administration Requests database to your workspace and modify its access control list. Add all the groups or individuals who will need the ability to convert user or server names. They must have at least author access with the ability to create documents.
5. Specify an administration server for the Public Address Book.
6. Assign an administration server for other databases.

After you have the Administration Process up and running on a server, you can begin to convert your names.

USING SHARED MAIL

You can potentially regain a considerable amount of disk space on a server by using the shared mail feature of Release 4. Shared mailboxes that have shared mail enabled store their messages in a single common database on the server. Messages addressed to multiple recipients are stored a single time in the database. Several ways exist to configure shared mail; they are all discussed in Chapter 14, "Administering Notes Mail."

CONVERTING TO HIERARCHICAL NAMING

After you have upgraded your servers and clients to Release 4, you should certainly convert to hierarchical naming if you haven't done so already. The Administration Process greatly simplifies the burden of converting users and servers to hierarchical naming. You should carefully design your naming scheme before proceeding. See Chapter 9 for details on developing a naming scheme for your users, servers, domains, and networks.

PRECONVERSION PLANNING

Before changing the name of a server or user, you need to carefully check the access control lists on other servers. This step is required in order to continue to have a functioning Notes network. If you change a server from flat to hierarchical naming, you may no longer be able to replicate changes to or from the server.

The first thing you need to do is to ensure that there is a certified public key in the server document for all servers that will be upgraded to hierarchical naming. You should also ensure that there is a certified public key in the server document for all administration servers. You can accomplish this by migrating the server to Notes Release 4 and letting the Administration Process run to completion. After the Administration Process is idle, reboot the server. This action will cause a certified public key to be copied into a server document.

Tip

If you are having trouble using the Administration Process, make sure that you are starting the administration server *before* the workstation. If not, you need to shut down the workstation, start the server, and then restart the workstation. The Administration Process doesn't work if the server isn't started before the workstation.

Because the Administration Requests database will hold name-change requests for servers in your organization, you should control access to this database carefully. Only administrators who need to be involved in the conversion to hierarchical naming should have access to this database. Carefully control depositor, editor, and author access to this database. Don't forget to give your local domain servers access to this database so that they can replicate requests.

After you have set up the access control list for your Administration Requests database, turn off ACL replication so that a change made at one workstation doesn't replicate to all. To turn off ACL replication, follow these steps:

1. Highlight the Administration Requests database and choose File | Replication | Settings.

   The Replication Settings dialog box appears.

2. Click the Advanced icon.

3. Uncheck the Access Control List check box.

4. Choose OK.

Processing a renamed-server request causes the Administration Process to access several views and documents in the Public Address Book. Make sure that the index updater isn't running while the Administration Process is handling a rename-server request. Your server's performance will be significantly lowered by contention between these two processes. To ensure maximum performance during a Rename Server command, follow these steps:

1. Shut down the updater by entering the following command at the server console:

   ```
   Tell Update Quit
   ```

2. Shut down the mail router with this command:

   ```
   Tell Router Quit
   ```

3. Shut down the replicator with this command:

    `Tell Replica Quit`

4. Start up a copy of the Administration Process by entering this command:

    `Tell ADMINP Process New`

5. When the status of the Administration Process returns to idle, enter this command:

    `Load Update`

6. When the updater has completed and is idle, restart the router with the following command:

    `Load Router`

7. Now restart the Replicator with this command:

    `Load Replica`

8. You should immediately replicate the server name changes to other replicas of the Public Address Book in your domain. Use this command to force an immediate replication of the Public Address Book:

    `Push ServerName Names.nsf`

    where *ServerName* is the name of the server running the Administration Process.

You can't convert a mail server using shared mail from flat to hierarchical naming. Doing so would prevent you from accessing the shared mail database. The shared mail database is encrypted using the flat ID file for the server. Before converting to hierarchical naming, unlink all mail files. See Chapter 14 for directions on unlinking shared mail files. Unlinking mail files takes at least a day to allow all messages to be purged from the shared mail file.

After you have completed the conversion to hierarchical naming, you can relink all mail files on the server.

Tip

Make sure that you have enough disk space to unlink mail files before attempting to convert to hierarchical naming.

Users and servers that have only their common names listed in a database or server access control list are assumed to have used the same organizational certificate as the server on which the database resides. If this isn't the case, users and servers no longer can access the database or server that contains only their common names. When converting a server to hierarchical naming, you need to review all server access lists and database access lists on that server. Any common names should be converted to their full hierarchical names before converting the server to hierarchical naming. Check off each of the following items:

1. Review all server access lists and database access lists on that server.

2. Examine all group documents in the Public Address Book. Each member should have his or her full hierarchical name listed.

3. Examine the server access control lists, and upgrade all common names to the full hierarchical name.

4. Issue the appropriate cross certificates. You need to issue one cross certificate for every other organization that accesses this server. This system allows your server to authenticate these other users after the upgrade to hierarchical naming.

5. Other organizations should issue a cross certificate for the new organizational certificate for the server. This system allows other organizations to authenticate your server.

6. Make sure that other organizations upgrade their server access lists and database access lists so that the full hierarchical name of the server is listed.

7. Manually change the access control list on all MAIL.BOX files in the domain. The Administration Process can't update the access control list in MAIL.BOX files. Make sure that the server's full hierarchical name is listed.

Even when you take care to upgrade all access control lists, there will be a time during which Release 3 servers can't access a Release 4 server that has had its name upgraded to hierarchical naming. The Public Address Book must replicate throughout the domain in order to reestablish this access.

COMPLETING THE CONVERSION

When you are ready to proceed with your conversion to hierarchical naming, follow these steps:

1. Manually convert a single server to hierarchical naming. You must convert servers to hierarchical naming before you convert users, because only a server that uses hierarchical names can upgrade users to hierarchical naming. Don't change the common name of a server at the same time that you are upgrading it to hierarchical naming. If you want to change the company name of a server, do it either before you begin converting or after you have completed converting.

2. Upgrade user IDs to hierarchical naming.

To convert the first server to hierarchical naming, follow these steps:

1. Choose File | Tools | Server Administration.

   The Server Administration panel opens.

2. Select the server's icon.

3. Open the Servers view.

4. Highlight the first server to be converted to hierarchical naming.

5. Choose Actions | Upgrade Server to Hierarchical.

   A file selection dialog box appears.

6. Select the hierarchical certificate to be used with the current server.

7. Enter an expiration date for the server.

8. Choose Upgrade.

   The server ID file is upgraded to hierarchical naming. When the process is complete, a confirmation dialog box appears.

9. Choose OK.

10. Shut down the Notes server.

11. Open the Public Address Book, using the workstation program.

12. Open the server document for the server that was just converted.

13. Put the server document in Edit mode, and delete the contents of the Certified Public Key field.

14. Open the Administration Requests database.

15. Open the Initiate Rename in Address Book document.

16. Copy the contents of the Certified Public Key field to the server document.

17. Copy the Change Request field to the Change Request field of the server document.

18. Save the server document.

19. Restart the Notes server.

After you have converted a single server to hierarchical naming, you can batch process the rest of the servers. All servers that will be certified using the same certificate can be processed at one time. To convert subsequent servers to hierarchical naming, follow these steps:

1. Choose File | Tools | Server Administration.

   The Server Administration panel appears.

2. Choose Servers.

3. Open the Servers view.

4. Select the servers that will be converted to hierarchical naming. Each of the servers you select must use the same certificate.

5. Choose Actions | Upgrade Server to Hierarchical.

   The file selection dialog box opens.

6. Select the hierarchical certificate for the servers.

7. Enter an expiration date for the certificate.

8. Select Upgrade.

   Requests are entered into the Administration Requests database, and server documents are upgraded by the Administration Process. When complete, Notes displays a confirmation dialog box.

9. Choose OK.

Repeat this process for each set of servers that uses a different certificate.

The Administration Process completes all the steps needed to convert your server names, including:

◆ Updating server documents

◆ Upgrading server ID files

◆ Upgrading group documents as well as all other documents in the Public Address Book

◆ Updating database and access control lists

For more detail on how the Administration Process accomplishes its magic, see Chapter 13.

After these requests have been processed by the Administration Process, you can begin the conversion of users to hierarchical naming. Once again, remember that you shouldn't change a user's common name at the same time that you are upgrading to hierarchical naming. Changing a common name at the same time results in the user being unable to access databases for a brief period of time.

You can batch process all user names that will be certified using the same certifier ID file. To upgrade a group of users to hierarchical naming, follow these steps:

1. Choose File | Tools | Server Administration.

   The Server Administration panel appears.

2. Select People.

3. Open the People view.

4. Select each of the users who will be upgraded to hierarchical naming. Each user will use the same certifier ID file.

5. Choose Actions | Rename Person.

6. Select Upgrade to Hierarchical.

   The file selection dialog box appears.

7. Select the certificate that should be used to certify these users.

8. Enter the expiration date for the certificate.

9. Select Upgrade.

   Notes upgrades the person documents and creates the proper request in the Administration Requests database, and then displays a confirmation box.

10. Choose OK.

Repeat this process for each set of users in your organization.

UPGRADING IN A MIXED ENVIRONMENT

You may not be able to wait until you have completed a migration of all users to Release 4 before beginning your conversion to hierarchical naming. Of course, it is highly recommended that you complete your migration to Release 4 before converting to hierarchical naming because of the massive amount of effort saved with the use of the Administration Process. If this is impossible, keep in mind that access control lists for databases that have no replica on a Release 4 server won't be updated. If you use a hub-and-spoke replication topology, you need only upgrade the hub server to Release 4. For every database on the hub server, specify an administration server. This strategy enables you to have all database ACLs updated by the Administration Process. Changes to databases on the hub server will replicate to the Release 3 spokes.

Release 3 servers can't automatically upgrade users that contact them. Release 4 servers automatically upgrade a user's ID file when appropriate. If you want to upgrade user ID files by using the Administration Process, you should upgrade all mail servers to Release 4 format. Because everyone accesses their mail server frequently, this scheme enables you to have their IDs upgraded automatically when they contact the mail server.

MONITORING THE CONVERSION TO HIERARCHICAL NAMING

Check the Administration Request database several times a day while you are upgrading servers and users to hierarchical naming. The Administration Process creates response documents for all requests, indicating the current status of the request. If an error has occurred, a red x appears next to the response document. Be sure to fix any errors in a timely manner to minimize disruption of your Notes network.

You should set up ACL monitor documents in the Statistics and Events database. This plan causes the Events task to mail any errors directly to your mailbox.

In addition to the Administration Requests database, you need to monitor the Certification Log database (CERTLOG.NSF). Additional information on errors is recorded in the Certification Log database.

ADMINISTERING MIXED ENVIRONMENTS

It is inevitable that for a period of time you will have some servers running Release 3 and some servers running Release 4. In addition, many organizations will end up with some users running Release 4 clients while other users are still running Release 3 clients. Lotus has planned ahead for these eventualities; you should have no problems in these environments if you don't break any of the following rules:

◆ Don't use operating system commands to copy database files from one machine to another.

◆ Don't upgrade applications to use Release 4 features until all users of that database have been upgraded.

Even though Release 3 clients will be able to access the database, the lack of features inevitably will cause problems that disrupt your migration schedule. A user denied access to a particular feature will want to have his priority moved up in the migration schedule. With too many users requesting higher priority, the whole migration schedule can become chaotic.

◆ Don't convert any mail files to the Release 4 design template until all clients using the mail server have been upgraded to Release 4.

Three situations will arise during your migration for which Lotus has planned:

◆ Release 4 servers working with Release 4 clients.

Databases on a Release 4 server can be in either Release 3 format or Release 4 format. A Release 4 client can access either format.

◆ Release 4 servers being accessed by Release 3 clients.

A Release 3 client can access either a Release 3 format or a Release 4 format database stored on a Release 4 server. Release 4 features, such as folders, aren't available to Release 3 clients.

◆ Release 4 servers replicating with Release 3 servers.

Field-level replication doesn't work with Release 3 servers. Replication will occur as if two Release 3 databases were replicating. You need to be careful when upgrading the Address Book or changing any database's ACL.

ACL changes replicate to Release 3 databases, but Release 3 databases won't have all the specific capabilities that can be assigned. For example, the administrators of the Public Address Book may have their access downgraded from editor to author (but with the ability to create or modify documents) and may be added to certain roles. These roles won't exist on a Release 3 database. In addition, administrators who have their access downgraded to author may not be able to work with Release 3 Address Books.

All new databases are created using the file format of the server. You can force a Release 4 server to create a Release 3 format database by specifying an .NS3 extension.

You should never have a Release 4 file format database on a Release 3 server. A Release 3 server can't read a database in Release 4 format.

Release 3 workstations can't edit macros containing Release 4 features. Release 4 workstations, on the other hand, can edit either Release 3 or Release 4 macros. Macros in Release 3 format are stored in Release 3 format. If you alter a Release 3 macro to include features from Release 4, the macro will be stored in Release 4 format and will no longer be editable by Release 3 workstations.

Full-text indexes aren't interoperable across releases. A Release 4 workstation can't access a Release 3 full-text index, and a Release 3 workstation can't access a Release 4 full-text index. Notes Release 4 can read but not update a Release 3 index. During the migration, you may have some clients using Release 3 and some using Release 4. During this period of time, all databases should be maintained in Release 3 format. All updates to full-text indexes should be performed from Release 3 workstations.

Some features in Release 4 databases, such as navigators, don't work correctly when accessed from a Release 3 database. In general, a Release 3 database can't use special features from Release 4. In addition, large views or bitmaps stored in Release 4 databases may cause memory allocation problems in Release 3. The largest memory segment Release 3 can handle is 65,000 bytes.

If you are using a workstation that has both Release 3 and Release 4 installed, you may experience delays when opening databases. Each release of Notes needs to rebuild databases in its own format before using the database. In addition, if you are using a workstation with both Release 3 and Release 4 installed, you shouldn't use the Release 4 Workspace Edit feature. Release 4 allows you to create and delete tabs on the workspace, but Release 3 always handles exactly six tabs. If you use the Release 4 feature to edit your desktop and then later try to access it using Release 3, Release 3 will try to rebuild the desktop, thinking that it is corrupted.

12

MIGRATING FROM NOTES 3.x

Clients using Release 4 mail should be careful when sending mail to Release 3 users—yet another reason why you should wait until all users have been upgraded to Release 4 before upgrading mail files. You can avoid these problems:

◆ Special letterheads can't be displayed on Release 3 workstations. Although all the information is displayed in a Release 3 client, the appearance is somewhat ragged.

◆ Release 4 contains several graphical objects (*mood stamps*) that you can include in the body of a message to convey tone and emotion. These graphics won't be displayed on a Release 3 workstation.

◆ Release 4 allows users to specify a different reply address. This technique allows mail recipients to reply to someone other than the sender of a message by using the Reply To pull-down list. This feature isn't available to users of Release 3 mail.

◆ Because Release 3 doesn't have a Task form, task mail messages sent to a Release 3 user aren't visible. Instead, they get an error message, stating that the Task form can't be located. You can add a Task form to Release 3 so that they will at least be able to read the fields in the message.

◆ Bookmarks allow you to send a reference to a document in a mail message. Release 3 users don't have a Book Mark form in the mail design template and can't open bookmark messages. You can modify the Release 3 template and add a form called Book Mark, if you want.

◆ Release 4 allows you to route a message through a predefined set of users. Because the Release 3 mail design doesn't include a Serial Route Memo form, Release 3 users can't read a Serial Route Memo. You can create a Route form in the Release 3 design template, if you want.

Release 4 OLE objects can't be used by a Release 3 user. If you need to share OLE objects, you must create them using Release 3. Release 4 can launch OLE objects created using a Release 3 workstation.

MANAGING TEMPLATE NAMES IN A MIXED ENVIRONMENT

Several system databases received new design template names in Release 4. You must ensure that these design templates are replicated to all databases. You should avoid the situation where, for example, a Public Address Book on one server has the Release 4 template, and another server has a Release 3 template. This situation can cause your Notes 4 servers to be updated using the Notes 3 design. Avoid this situation by eliminating design updating or design replication. To turn off design updating, you simply need to replicate the R4 template name to all R3 Public Address Books, using the following method:

1. On the Release 3 server, check the Replicate Database Title, Categories, and Template Names box.

2. On the Release 4 server, open the Database Properties dialog box, select the Basics tab, and uncheck the option Do Not Send Changes and Database Title and Catalog Info to Other Replicas.

The next time these two databases replicate, the Release 3 database will inherit the STDR4PublicAddressBook template name from the Release 4 Address Book. The Release 3 design will no longer be updated, because the Release 3 server doesn't have a copy of this template. Instead, the design task on the Release 3 server simply generates an error indicating that it can't find the template.

You can also prevent servers from replicating design changes:

1. On the Release 3 server, open the Replication Settings dialog box. Uncheck the option Replicate Database Title, Categories, and Template Names. Also uncheck the Inherit Design from Template option. Then open the Design Template Options dialog box and delete the Based on Template field.

2. On the Release 4 server, open the Database Properties dialog box, select the Basics tab, and select the option Do Not Send Changes and Database Title and Catalog Info to Other Replicas.

By severing the link that updates the design, you prevent the Release 4 design from being overwritten from the Release 3 database. When the Release 3 server is eventually upgraded to Release 4, be sure to go back and re-enable replication of design changes.

RELEASE 4 WORKSTATIONS ACCESSING RELEASE 3 SERVERS

Upgrade your servers before upgrading users. If you have users with a Release 4 workstation with access to a Release 3 server, the users must know exactly which features can and can't be used. The Release 3 server is unable to support all the features accessible to the client when using a Release 4 workstation.

If you migrate users to Release 4 before you have migrated their mail server to Release 4, they can't use these features:

◆ Folders

◆ Several of the new agents

◆ Selective replication

◆ Advanced mail features

◆ Exchange red marks

Don't use Release 4 workstations to edit formulas of databases stored on a Release 3 server. Any Release 4 functions included in the view won't be recognized by the Release 3 server. Generally the Release 3 server can build a view, although the actual documents in the view probably won't match up with the ones that you wanted.

SUMMARY

This chapter has discussed the whys and hows of migrating from Notes Release 3 to Release 4. Notes includes several tools to ease the transition to Release 4, such as

◆ The Administration Process, which is used to upgrade user and server IDs

◆ Shared mail

◆ The mail Convert Utility

◆ An enhanced Public Address Book

◆ A special Help database called the Release 3 Menu Finder, which can help you find Release 3 menu items in the new Release 4 menu structure

You should approach your migration with the same planning steps that you would use for an initial installation. Create a team, involve the entire organization, assess your hardware and software installation and needs, design your new Notes network, and upgrade your servers, clients, and applications to Release 4.

Don't forget to train your administrative staff and end users before migrating to Release 4. There are enough new and changed features to justify the training expense. The Notes training is the one task that Lotus wasn't able to automate.

You also need to do exhaustive testing on your third-party products and mission-critical applications before migrating to Release 4.

With all the new tools included in Notes, migrating to Release 4 should be simpler than migrating from one Release 3 version to another. With a little bit of planning, you should be able to avoid all critical problems. Be sure to review Part II of this book, "Planning Your Notes Installation," for a complete set of details to consider when installing or migrating Notes.

PART IV

Administering Notes

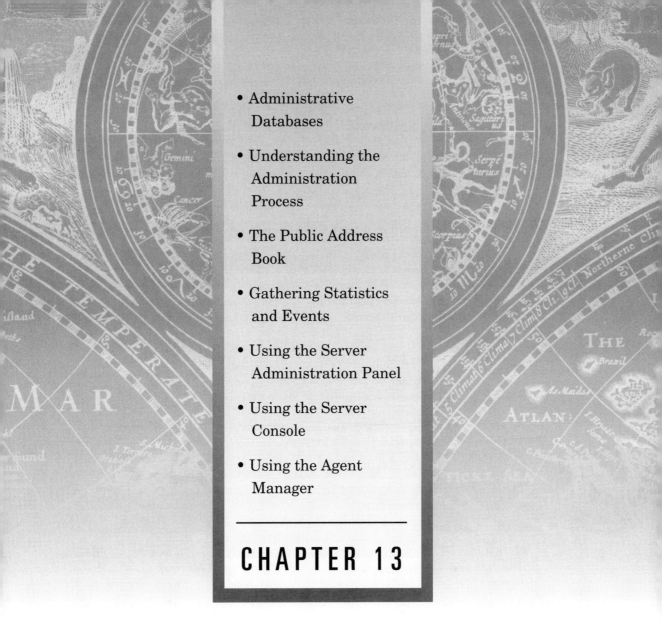

CHAPTER 13

Administrative Tools

Notes administrators must be familiar with the various specialized tools for monitoring and configuring a Notes network. The two biggest challenges a Notes administrator faces are maintaining remote servers and monitoring activity on all Notes databases. Administering local servers and users, while extremely important, has been vastly simplified in Notes 4.0.

This chapter serves as a general introduction to the tasks that an administrator must accomplish. Notes is shipped with a collection of programs and tools to simplify the administrator's job. The primary tools of a Notes administrator are

- ◆ The Public Address Book
- ◆ The server console
- ◆ The remote console
- ◆ The Administration Process
- ◆ A collection of server programs
- ◆ The Agent Manager

In addition to these tools, Notes includes a number of databases that an administrator can use to monitor system activity. The most important of these databases are

- ◆ The Public Address Book
- ◆ The Notes log
- ◆ The Statistics Reporting database
- ◆ The Statistics & Events database
- ◆ The certification log
- ◆ The database catalog

You will quickly notice that the Public Address Book is listed as both an administrative tool and an administrative database. The Public Address Book is the most important database in a Notes network. All Notes administrators should be completely familiar with the Public Address Book.

Notes configuration information is stored in the NOTES.INI file. The NOTES.INI file is a text file stored on each server in the network. Each server has its own copy of NOTES.INI. Notes provides several ways in which you can manage remote NOTES.INI files. In addition to the Public Address Book, Notes administrators should be familiar with each entry in the NOTES.INI file.

ADMINISTRATIVE DATABASES

Notes administrative databases enable you to monitor activity within the Notes network. These databases are

◆ The Notes log.

Every Notes server has a Notes log. The Notes log is a general repository for miscellaneous information about your Notes network. Because the Notes log can become quite large, administrators need to tailor the information that is collected to suit their needs. A Notes log is created automatically the first time you run the Notes server program.

◆ The Statistics Reporting database.

The Statistics Reporting database is used to configure the information and events that you want to monitor. *Events* are one-time happenings, such as an error or a threshold being exceeded. *Statistics* refers to any statistical information such as available disk space and memory in use. The administrator must configure statistics reporting. The default setting is not to report any events or statistics. The Event server program automatically creates the Statistics Reporting database.

◆ The Statistics & Events database.

The Statistics & Events database (EVENTS4.NSF) is used to configure automated responses to alarms and events that you are monitoring with the Statistics Reporting database. You can use the Statistics & Events database to forward alarms to specific administrators. The Event Server program automatically creates the Statistics & Events database.

◆ The certification log.

The certification log (CERTLOG.NSF) contains the names of all users and servers in a domain. You must create a certification log manually if you want to use the Administration Process (highly recommended). The certification log is not created automatically. Use the Certification Log template to create a database specifying the file name CERTLOG.NSF. After creating the first certification log, create replicas of it on all servers running the Administration Process.

◆ The Administration Requests database.

The Administration Requests database is populated by Notes when the administrator makes a request to change the name of a user or server. The Administration Process scans the Administration Requests database for new requests and responds accordingly. The Administration Requests database is created automatically the first time you run the Administration Process on a server. You should maintain a replica of the Administration Requests database on all servers on the network. This system allows change requests entered at one server to replicate to the server running the Administration Process.

USING THE NOTES LOG

The Notes log (LOG.NSF) records information about events and activity on your Notes network, such as replications, database activity, port activity, and mail routing. Check the Notes log on a daily basis to ensure that you are identifying all replications, mail routing, and modem errors.

The Notes log is useful for both server administrators and database managers. Server administrators can track general server statistics, while database managers track detailed activity on their databases.

Because the Notes log serves as a repository for general information about your Notes network, it can grow quite large. To help minimize the size of the log file, you can configure the exact information to be collected in the Notes log. In general, you should collect as much information as possible so that you can analyze problems when they arise, rather than having to reconfigure logging and collect information before being able to solve a problem. The disadvantage of recording all activity on a network is that the Notes log can become unmanageable. In particular, you should consider when to monitor activity on ports. Part of the server administrator's job is to specify what information needs to be monitored on each server in the Notes network.

Even if you carefully tailor the information recorded in the Notes log, visually scanning the Notes log for specific problems is difficult. Instead, you can use the Log Analysis tool to search for key words in the Notes log. The Log Analysis tool pulls documents matching your search criteria into another database that you can browse visually.

MONITORING THE NOTES LOG

At least one administrator should check the Notes log for each server once a day. The views available in the Notes log are

- ◆ Database—Sizes
- ◆ Database—Usage
- ◆ Mail Routing Events
- ◆ Miscellaneous Events
- ◆ Phone Calls—By Date
- ◆ Phone Calls—By User
- ◆ Replication Events
- ◆ Sample Billing
- ◆ Usage—By Date
- ◆ Usage—By User

13

These views are self-explanatory except for the Sample Billing view. You can use the Sample Billing view to charge individual departments or users for their usage of the Notes server. Figure 13.1 shows an example of a Sample Billing view.

Figure 13.1.
The Sample Billing
view of the Notes log.

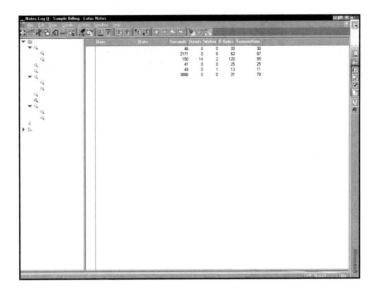

Server administrators and database managers should both be monitoring the Notes log to verify that

◆ Replication is working

◆ Sufficient disk space is available (especially for compaction of databases)

◆ Sufficient memory is installed in each server

◆ Dial-up and remote communications are working

The Notes log records the following information about Notes server activity:

◆ Sessions with servers or users

◆ Mail routing activity

◆ Replication activity

◆ Remote connections

◆ Dial-up activity

The Notes log records the following information about Notes workstations:

◆ Mail routing activity

◆ Replication activity

◆ Dial-up activity (outgoing only)

CREATING THE NOTES LOG

The Notes server creates the Notes log the first time the server is run. This default setting gives you one Notes log on each server. Some organizations may want one Notes log for the entire Notes network. You should share a Notes log across a network only if you have a very small network (fewer than five servers). The recommended approach is to create a single Notes log for each server and use the Log Analysis tool to copy data to a common database, rather than creating a common Notes log for all servers.

When the Notes log is created, the local server is defined as the manager of the database. The server administrator should immediately add the server administrator group to the access control list of the Notes log, giving the group manager access. If you want to define a different set of managers for different Notes logs, create multiple administrator groups rather than entering administrator names directly into an access control list. For details on adding names and groups to access control lists, see Chapter 18, "Administering Notes Security."

If Notes Setup is run from a remote workstation, the ID that was active during Notes setup will be defined as the manager of the Notes log. The server administrator should immediately add the server administrator group, giving manager access, and remove the person's ID from the access control list.

If you have a number of new administrators in your organization, consider editing the About documents for the Notes log. You should add the following information to the About document:

- ◆ The proper audience for the Notes log
- ◆ How to contact the manager of the Notes log

USING THE LOG ANALYSIS TOOL

The Log Analysis tool searches the Notes log for documents matching your search criteria and copies matching documents to the Analysis results database. An Analysis database will be created if one doesn't already exist. The Analysis database makes it easier for an administrator to monitor specific Notes resources.

To use the Log Analysis tool, follow these steps:

1. Choose File | Tools | Server Administration.
2. Select the server containing the Notes log you want to analyze.
3. Click the server's icon.
4. Select Log Analysis.

    The Server Log Analysis dialog box appears (see Figure 13.2).

Figure 13.2.
The Server Log
Analysis dialog box.

5. Click the Results Database button to display the Results Database dialog box (see Figure 13.3).

6. Select a server to store the results database.

   You should select a server on which you have rights to create a database.

Figure 13.3.
Use the Results
Database dialog box to
specify a results
database.

7. Enter a title for the results database. The default title is Log Analysis.

8. Enter a path and file name for the results database. The default setting is LOGA4.NSF.

9. Indicate whether you want to overwrite all entries in this database or add new entries. Because the purpose of the Log Analysis tool is to reduce the amount of clutter that an administrator needs to work through, the default setting is to overwrite this database.

10. Choose OK.

11. Enter the number of days back in time that the Log Analysis tool should search.

12. Enter the keywords for your search, separated by commas. If you are searching for potential errors, some good keywords are *cannot*, *error*, and *fatal*.

13. Click the Start button or the Start and Open button. The Start and Open button opens the Log Analysis results database for immediate browsing. Figure 13.4 shows an example of the Log Analysis output.

Figure 13.4.
A sample Log Analysis
output.

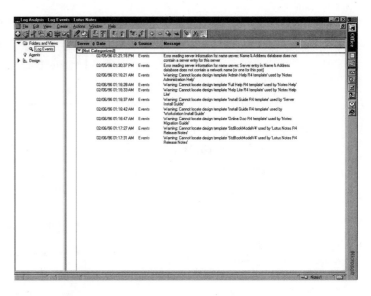

The Log Analysis view shows all the information in each document. The administrator doesn't have to open each document in the Log Analysis database to find possible problems or errors. The complete text of the message is contained in the view.

You can sort the output in the Log Analysis view by server, date, or message, in ascending or descending order. Simply select the proper arrow in the Server, Date, or Message column heading.

You can collect information from several server logs into a common Log Analysis database. This strategy is better than creating a single log for all servers on a network. Administrators have only one database to scan (the analysis database) instead of many logs, and server performance isn't degraded by the need to replicate the Notes log.

USING THE CERTIFICATION LOG

Immediately after installing the first Notes server in your organization, you should create a certification log (CERTLOG.NSF). The certification log is required for the use of the Administration Process. The certification log maintains a list of all registered and certified users and servers within your domain.

The certification log stores the following information from each user and server:

◆ Name, license type, and ID number
◆ Date the certificate expires

◆ Date the certificate was issued

◆ Name, license type, and ID number of the certifier ID file used when the user or server ID was created

You can open the certification log directly from the workspace or through the Server Administration panel (see Figure 13.5). Figure 13.6 shows a sample entry from the certification log.

Figure 13.5.
The certification log, By
Certifier Name view.

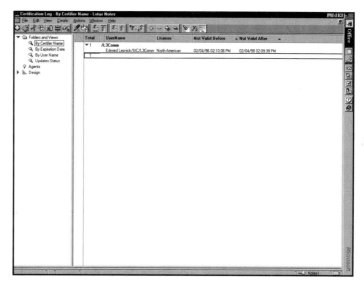

Figure 13.6.
A sample document
from the certifica-
tion log.

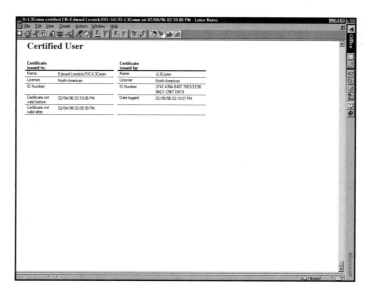

In addition to information on registered and certified users and servers, the certification log contains information on recertification requests in process. In-process recertification requests are ones that the Administration Process has not yet completed. You can view in-process recertification requests using the Update Status view.

The administrator must create the certification log manually. Notes doesn't create the certification log automatically. To create the certification log, follow these steps:

1. Choose File | Database | New.
2. Select the administration server on your network. Create database rights on this server to proceed.
3. Enter `Certification Log` for the title.
4. Enter `CERTLOG.NSF` for the name of the file. The certification log must use the file name CERTLOG.NSF (see Figure 13.7).

Figure 13.7.
Specifying the certifica-
tion log's file name.

5. Select Show Advanced Templates.
6. Select Certification Log from the list of templates.
7. Choose OK.
8. Add the certifier's group to the access control list, giving the group editor access. This setting enables certifiers to register new users and servers. You should remove the names of any administrators that appear directly in the certification log.

After you have created a certification log for a domain, you should create a replica of this file on all servers that will run the Administration Process.

UNDERSTANDING THE ADMINISTRATION PROCESS

The Administration Process automates the tasks of renaming users and servers. The Administration Process automatically updates the following databases whenever a name is changed in the Public Address Book:

◆ The Public Address Book

◆ Database ACLs

◆ User and server ID files

You can use the Administration Process to

◆ Migrate ID files from flat to hierarchical naming

◆ Recertify ID files

◆ Rename users or servers

◆ Delete users, servers, or groups from the Name and Address Book

The Administration Process works by scanning the Administration Requests database and responds to new requests. Requests are generated most often from the Name and Address Book.

You can create the Administration Requests database manually, or let the Administration Process create the database automatically. The Administration Requests database (ADMIN4.NSF) is based on the Administration Request template. You should maintain replica copies of the Administration Request database on all servers in your domain, and shouldn't have non-replica copies of Administration Requests databases on your network.

You don't need to run the Administration Process on every server that contains a copy of the Administration Requests database. This setup enables you to generate requests from any server, have those requests replicate to the server running the Administration Process, and have your requests automatically handled by the Administration Process. Minimize the number of servers in your domain running the Administration Process to simplify configuring the Administration Server property for the databases in your domain. Notes automatically adds Administration Process server task (ADMINP) to the ServerTasks setting in the NOTES.INI file. You should edit the NOTES.INI file and remove the ADMINP ServerTasks entry on all servers that will not be functioning as administration servers.

CONFIGURING THE ADMINISTRATION PROCESS

The Administration Process can run only on a Notes Release 4 server. To take full advantage of the Administration Process features, such as upgrading ID files from flat to hierarchical naming, the administration server should be hierarchically certified. To set up the Administration Process, follow these steps:

1. If you haven't done so, create the certification log database. See the earlier section "Using the Certification Log" for details on creating a certification log database.

2. Ensure that the ADMINP server program is set on the ServerTasks line in the NOTES.INI file.

3. Start the Notes server and workstation programs.

4. Modify the ACL in the Public Address Book. For each group of administrators that need to change user or server names or recertify users or servers, add the group name to the access control list, specifying at least author access with the ability to delete documents. Specify any or all of the following roles as appropriate for each administrative group:

   ◆ Group modifier

   ◆ Server modifier

   ◆ User modifier

   The ability to delete documents is required for all administrators who will have to remove users and servers from the network.

5. Modify the access control list of the Administration Requests database. Give author access to all administrators and administrator groups that will be requesting changes to user names and certificates.

After you have configured a server to be the administration server, you must specify for each database on the network which administration server has the right to update the access control list for that database. All replicas of the database should share a common administration server setting, to prevent replication conflicts when more than one administration server is updating a database's access control list. Each database must have a replica on one or more servers running the Administration Process. This strongly implies that you should configure your hub servers to be your administration servers also. If you aren't using a hub-and-spoke replication architecture, the easiest way to make sure that every database can be serviced by an administration server is to configure all servers to run the Administration Process.

You can specify an administration server for a single database or for a group of databases. To specify an administration server for a single database, follow these steps:

1. Select the database icon from your workspace.

2. Choose File | Database | Access Control.

   The Access Control List dialog box opens (see Figure 13.8).

3. Click the Advanced icon.

Figure 13.8.
Options for setting the
ACL for the adminis-
tration server.

4. Select the administration server for this database from the drop-down list. The list contains servers for the databases on your desktop. Click the Other selection in the drop-down list box to display other servers that are available, based on your current location.

5. Choose OK.

The following section includes a diagram that shows how the Administration Process updates database ACLs and server and user ID files. Administrators and certifiers submit requests for name changes and recertifications, using the Public Address Book. The Public Address Book automatically creates the appropriate requests in the local Administration Requests database. These requests are replicated to the administration server, where the Administration Process updates the Public Address Book. The Administration Process also updates the access control list for all the local databases that specify that server as their administration server.

You can set the administration server for a group of databases by using the Server Administration panel. Follow these steps:

1. Choose File | Tools | Server Administration.

   The Server Administration panel opens.

2. Click the database's icon.

3. Select Database Administration Server.

   The Set the Database Administration Server dialog box appears (see Figure 13.9).

4. Select one or more databases from the list. You can select multiple databases by holding down the Shift key as you select databases.

5. Type the name of the administration server for these databases. Double-check your typing to avoid typos. Enter the full name of the server.

6. Click Set.

   Notes posts a confirmation box when the databases have been updated.

7. Choose OK.

8. Choose Done.

Figure 13.9.
You can set the
administration server
for a group of data-
bases, using multiple
databases at one time.

USING THE ADMINISTRATION PROCESS TO CONVERT NAMES

The Administration Process automatically updates the Public Address Book, user and server ID files, and database ACLs in response to requests to change a user or server name or a certificate. The process is similar in all cases. (Note that the numbers in the following steps match those in Figure 13.10.)

Figure 13.10.
The steps carried out by
the Administration
Process when changing
a name or certification.

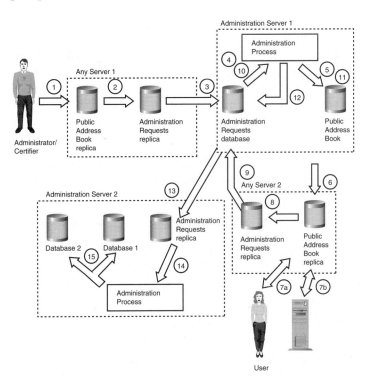

These are the steps:

1. A certifier uses the Public Address Book to request a change to a user's or server's name or certification.

To change the name or certification for a user, you open the People view in the Public Address Book, select the name(s) to be changed, and choose Actions | Rename Person to open the Certify Selected Entries dialog box (see Figure 13.11).

Note

The server used by the certifier in this step must have a copy of the Administration Requests database.

Figure 13.11.
Changing the certifica-
tion for selected entries.

In this dialog box, you can upgrade to hierarchical certification, change the common name, or change the certifier by using the Administration Process. You can change the common name of only a single user at a time. You can upgrade certification or change the certifier of groups of users at one time. Choose the button appropriate for this situation to display a file selection dialog box. Next, open the Certifier ID file that will be used to issue the new certificate for the users, type the password for the certifier file in the Enter Password dialog box, and choose OK. What happens next depends on the type of change you're making:

- If you are changing the common name of a user, the Rename Selected User dialog box appears. Enter the expiration date, first name, middle initial, last name, and qualifying organizational unit for the user. Select Rename.

- If you are requesting a move to a new certifier for selected entries, the Request Move for Selected Entries dialog box appears.

- If you are upgrading to hierarchical names, Notes posts the Upgrade Selected Entries to Hierarchical dialog box. Enter an expiration date and qualifying organizational unit (if any), and select the Upgrade button.

2. Notes automatically creates requests in the Administration Requests database.

3. The name change or certification requests replicate in the Administration Requests database on the administration server.

4. The Administration Process scans the Administration Requests database.

5. The Administration Process updates the entries in the Public Address Book for each user or server changed. The certificates are copied from the requests into the Public Address Book.

6. Changes to the Public Address Book replicate to all servers in the domain.

7. The ID file for the user or server is updated:

   7a. Every time a user accesses a server, Notes checks to see whether the change flag is set in that user's person document in the Public Address Book. If so, Notes compares the name and certification stored in the Public Address Book with the name and certification in the user's ID file. If they are different, Notes presents a warning to the user, showing the user's current name and new name. If the new name is correct, the user selects Accept, and Notes copies the new name and certificate into the user's ID file. If the user rejects the name change, Notes takes no further actions.

   7b. Servers regularly check their server documents to see if they should update their name or certification. If a server notices that its name or certification has been changed, Notes automatically updates the server ID file with the new name and/or certificate.

8. Notes creates a Rename Server in Address Book document or a Rename User in Address Book document in the local Administration Requests database.

9. The Rename request replicates back to the administration server for the Public Address Book.

10. The Administration Process scans the Administration Requests database.

11. All other entries in the Public Address Book are changed to reflect the new name or certification.

12. The Administration Process creates a Rename in Access Control List request in the Administration Requests database.

13. The Rename in Access Control List requests replicate to the Administration Requests database on administration servers throughout the domain.

14. The Administration Process scans the Administration Requests database.

15. The access control lists for all databases are changed to reflect the new name or certification.

All changes to the Public Address Book and database ACLs are replicated throughout the domain.

The user's ID is updated in step 7, but database access control lists are not updated until step 15. In the time between a user's ID being updated and database access control lists being updated, the user's name will be different from his name stored in a database ACL. If you are simply upgrading a user from flat certification to hierarchical certification, he will be able to access all databases, even before their access control lists are updated, if

◆ You have upgraded the servers to hierarchical certification

  and

◆ The servers use the same certification as the user

If you are changing the common name of a user or server, or switching from one hierarchical certifier to another, the user will not be able to access databases that explicitly mention this user in their ACLs. This problem is yet another reason for not explicitly including individuals' names directly in the ACL. If a user's name appears only in groups, which are in turn included in the ACL, he needs to wait only until the Public Address Book is updated in step 11 to gain access to all databases.

You can view the status of in-process requests in the certification log. Every time the Administration Process takes an action, it updates the certification log. For more details on the certification log, see the earlier section "Using the Certification Log."

This example is meant to illustrate the workings of the Administration Process, not to document all the steps required to convert a Notes network from flat naming to hierarchical naming. For complete details on converting from flat naming to hierarchical naming, see Chapter 12, "Migrating from Notes 3.x."

The Administration Process follows the same steps when recertifying hierarchical IDs. Steps 8 through 16 are skipped when there is no name change due to the recertification.

SCHEDULING THE ADMINISTRATION PROCESS

A significant amount of time can pass before the entire Notes network is updated in response to a request for a name or certification change. In particular, there may be a period of time during which users can't access databases on the network. The length of time required to update the Notes network depends on the replication schedule and the Administration Process schedule. To reduce the amount of time required, replicate the Administration Requests database and the Public Address Book more frequently and reduce the ADMINPInterval and ADMINPModifyPersonDocumentsAt settings in the NOTES.INI file.

The ADMINPInterval setting is the number of minutes between scans of the Administration Requests database. The ADMINPModifyPersonDocumentsAt setting is the hour of each day when person documents will be updated in the Public Address Book. You should schedule person document changes during off-peak hours. The default setting is midnight. Keep in mind that the ADMINPModifyPersonDocumentsAt setting uses a 24-hour clock, where 0 (zero) is midnight and 23 is 11:00 p.m.

THE PUBLIC ADDRESS BOOK

The Public Address Book is far more than a directory of users and servers. The Public Address Book stores the topology of your Notes network, your Notes replication architecture, and controls the way Notes mail is routed. The Public Address Book is also a powerful tool administrators can use to accomplish such tasks as these:

◆ Recertifying users and servers

◆ Updating configuration settings on remote servers

◆ Scheduling miscellaneous programs and tasks

The Public Address Book is the most important database in the Notes network. It's extremely important that you keep a backup copy of the Notes Name and Address Book available at all times to replace any that might become corrupted.

There is one Public Address Book for each Notes domain. In addition, each user can set up one or more Personal Address Books on their own machines. Each server needs a copy of the Public Address Book. Users (other than mobile users) don't need a replica of the Public Address Book on their client machines. Mobile users may need to have a copy of the Public Address Book on their machines to properly route mail. See Chapter 19, "Supporting Dial-Up Users," for a full discussion of the options available to mobile users.

CONTROLLING ACCESS TO THE PUBLIC ADDRESS BOOK

The Public Address Book is designed to be managed by many different administrators, possibly working at different locations. You can have your administrators specialize geographically or by tasks. Users also have an important role to play in maintaining their own person documents.

In addition to the normal database ACL access levels, the Public Address Book is shipped with eight roles that you can use to fine-tune the authority given to each administrator or user. As discussed in Chapter 3, "Understanding Security," roles don't protect the data in a database. Roles are a user interface convention intended to prevent accidents or errors. These are the eight roles for the Public Address Book:

- *UserCreator.* UserCreators can create new person documents.
- *UserModifier.* UserModifiers can update all person documents.
- *ServerCreator.* ServerCreators can create new server documents.
- *ServerModifier.* ServerModifiers can edit all server documents.
- *GroupCreator.* GroupCreators can create new group documents.
- *GroupModifier.* GroupModifiers can edit or delete existing group documents but cannot create new group documents.
- *NetCreator.* NetCreators can create all Public Address Book documents except person, group, and server documents.
- *NetModifier.* NetModifiers can edit or delete all Public Address Book documents except person, group, and server documents.

Although it's certainly possible to distribute responsibility for the Public Address Book across multiple regions and multiple administrators, your organization may choose to centrally administer the Public Address Book. Roles are more important for large organizations that administer the Public Address Book centrally. In this case, you have several administrators at one site, allowing the administrators to specialize. If your organization has administrators at multiple sites, or is medium-to-small in size, you may not have the opportunity to have your administrators specialize. There simply aren't enough administrators at any one site to divide up the tasks. In this case, you should consider relying more on the access control list's access levels, such as manager, editor, and so on, and not worry about assigning roles.

If your organization is going to use roles to control access to the Public Address Book, create a matching group for each role. For example, create a group called UserModifier for all users and administrators who have the ability to edit person documents.

The Creator roles must be assigned to all administrators who need to create documents, regardless of the administrator's access level to the Public Address Book (except for managers). The Modifier roles are useful only for tuning the ability of administrators or users with author access to the Public Address Book. Anyone with manager, designer, or editor access to the Public Address Book already has the ability to modify all documents. For each access level allowed in an access control list, you need to determine which users will have rights to the Public Address Book, as described in the following list:

◆ Manager access.

Manager access gives the ability to read or change all documents in a database, modify the replication settings, or delete the database. You should assign at least two people manager access to the Public Address Book.

◆ Designer access.

Designers are responsible for maintaining views, forms, fields, and all other design elements. Designers also have the ability to create full-text indexes or modify replication formulas. If you are going to use the standard Public Address Book, you don't need to give any administrator designer access. If you want to customize the Public Address Book, create a backup of the original template before making any changes.

◆ Editor access.

Editors have the ability to change or delete all documents in the Public Address Book. Editors who are also assigned to the creator roles have the ability to create documents. Most administrators will be given editor access to the Public Address Book. This enables them to maintain any document in the Public Address Book.

◆ Author access.

Users and administrators with author access to the Public Address Book can create any document for which they are assigned a creator role. The Public Address Book is also set up so that they can edit any document they create. Users are often given author access so that they can update information in their own person documents. Author access is also commonly used for administrators who have specialized tasks. Use author access in combination with roles to assign specialized duties to administrators.

◆ Reader access.

Readers can't edit or create any document in the Public Address Book. Users are given reader access if they are not to be involved in updating their own person documents.

◆ Depositor.

Depositor access is not typically used with the Public Address Book.

◆ No access.

The no access setting is not typically used with the Public Address Book.

Chapter 3, "Understanding Security," describes these access levels in detail.

The Public Address Book is a good example of how to use access levels, author fields, and roles to fine-tune access for a wide variety of users.

Every document in the Public Address Book contains an Administrators field that is used to delegate specific responsibilities for individual documents. Administrators is an author type field. Author type fields give the ability to edit a specific document in which the field appears. You can use the Administrators field to give users the ability to edit their own person documents without giving them the ability to edit any other person document.

You use the Administrators field to control access to a specific document. Use the modifier roles to give to a user the ability to edit a whole class of documents. The modifier roles are useful only for modifying the access level of users or administrators with author access.

The Administrators field, as with all author type fields, is useful only for modifying the access given to users with author access to the database. Users with reader access to a database cannot edit a document even if their names appear in an author type field. This means that all users must be given author access if you want them to edit their own person documents. You cannot give users reader access, list their names in the Administrator's field, and expect them to edit their own person documents.

When planning your administrator groups, you should consider these issues:

◆ Are responsibilities divided along geographic or departmental boundaries?

   Most organizations assign a local administrator for all large offices, who will be responsible for all users in that office. This is an example of dividing responsibilities geographically. Centrally managed organizations can divide administrator tasks by task type, using roles. You can also mix geographic, task, and departmental divisions. Even though you may have an administrator responsible for all users in a geographic location, you may reserve the right to create and edit server documents to an administrator at the central site.

◆ Will users edit their own person documents?

   There are several fields in a person document that every user is quite capable of filling in. Having an administrator fill in these fields for every user would be burdensome. If you choose not to allow users to edit their own person documents, typically these fields end up not being used. See the later section "Person Documents" for more details.

Groups that you set up for use in the Public Address Book should be created for use in access control lists only. These groups will not be used for mail routing or server access. Chapter 9, "Designing Your Notes Network," covers setting up groups and default access control lists in more detail.

Public Address Book Document Types

The Public Address Book contains eleven different types of documents that enable administrators to configure and manage the Notes network. The following list describes the documents in the Public Address Book:

◆ Certifier document.

Certifier documents store information about certifiers and cross certificates.

◆ Connection document.

Each connection document stores information about the connection between two specific servers.

◆ Domain document.

Domain documents contain information on how to route mail from one domain to another, and allow you to specify whether you should accept or deny mail from that domain.

◆ Group document.

Groups are simply collections of users, servers, and other groups. Groups can be used for specific purposes, such as mail routing or access control lists, or can be general-purpose.

◆ Location document.

Each location document specifies all the information needed to connect to your Notes network from that location. Location documents are primarily used by mobile users.

◆ Mail-in database document.

A mail-in database document specifies the file name, location, and mail address of a database.

◆ Person document.

Each user has his own unique person document.

◆ Program document.

Program documents can be used to schedule any type of program, not just Notes server tasks.

◆ Server document.

Every server has a server document that lists the domain, network, and access restrictions for that server.

◆ Server configuration document.

Server configuration documents can be used to edit the NOTES.INI file for both the local and remote servers.

♦ User setup profile.

Profiles list the passthru, dial-up, and Internet servers for a group of users. Profiles are used during user registration.

The following sections describe each of these document types and their uses in more detail.

CERTIFIER DOCUMENTS

Certifiers are responsible for issuing certificates that bond together user and server public keys and names. Certifiers and certificates are described in more detail in Chapters 3 and 18.

Certifier documents in the Public Address Book contain information about an individual certifier. The certifier's name, ancestor, contact information, and certified public key is contained in the certifier document (see Figure 13.12).

The public key contained in a certifier document is not displayed in Read mode. You must put a certifier document into Edit mode (by pressing Ctrl+E) to view the public key. You may need to read the public key to another certifier over the phone when you are setting up cross certificates with another organization.

Figure 13.12.
You must open a
certifier document in
Edit mode to view the
public key.

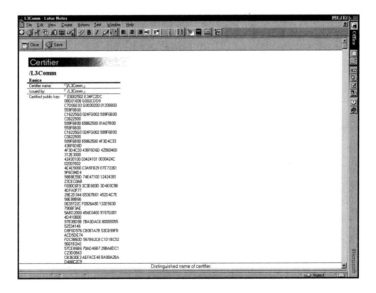

CONNECTION DOCUMENTS

Connection documents are used to configure replication and mail routing between two specific servers (see Figure 13.13). The servers don't need to be in the same domain or on the same Notes network. Using a connection document, you can specify the times, days, and intervals between scheduled connections for two servers. When two servers connect, by default Notes replicates all databases in common and routes all pending mail. You can cause Notes to connect to another server at an unscheduled time if the amount of pending mail exceeds a specified threshold.

Figure 13.13.
A typical server
connection document.

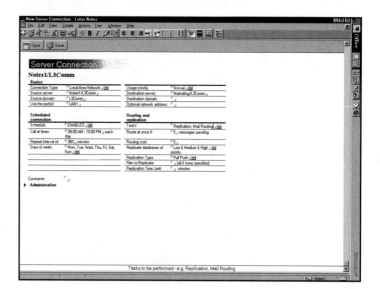

You can create multiple connection documents for a specific pair of servers. This system is useful if you want to schedule replication and mail routing separately. To create a connection document for replication only, deselect Mail Routing in the Tasks field. Similarly, to schedule mail routing without causing replication, delete the Replication entry in the Tasks field.

Chapter 14, "Administering Notes Mail," and Chapter 15, "Administering Replication," contain more information on configuring replication and mail routing.

DOMAIN DOCUMENTS

Notes offers a variety of different types of domains. Each domain is a logical set of servers. Any collection of servers can be included in a domain, whether they are on the same network, connected by modems, or not connected in any manner.

Foreign domains are typically used to route mail to non-Notes mail users. Each type of mail system that must connect to Notes needs its own foreign domain document. Lotus has created foreign domain documents for the most typical types of mail interconnections, including X.400, SMTP, and cc:Mail. For each foreign domain, you must specify a particular server that connects to the other mail domain. Typically, this is a gateway server running both mail systems, as well as a program that converts mail from one system to another. Figure 13.14 shows a typical foreign domain document.

Figure 13.14.
A typical foreign
domain document.

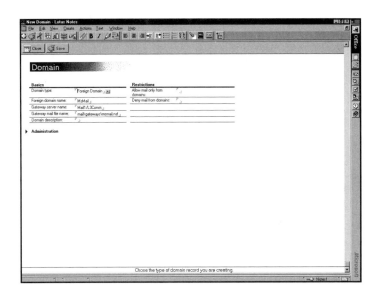

Non-adjacent and adjacent domain documents route mail between Notes domains. Non-adjacent domains are all domains that don't directly connect to a server in your organization's domain. Adjacent domains have at least one server that can connect directly to a server in your domain. For non-adjacent domains, you need to specify an adjacent domain that, in turn, knows how to route mail to the non-adjacent domain. Figure 13.15 shows a typical non-adjacent domain document

You need only specify the name of an adjacent domain. Notes automatically scans the Public Address Book for a server in the adjacent domain when it needs to route mail.

Global domain documents configure mail address conventions used in a worldwide domain. Global domains are useful when you are sending mail to Internet domains or X.400 mail systems.

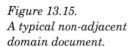

Figure 13.15.
A typical non-adjacent
domain document.

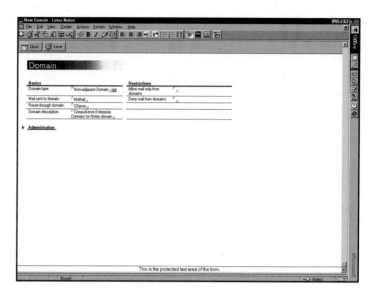

GROUP DOCUMENTS

Groups are collections of users, servers, and other groups. Groups are useful for reducing the amount of administrative effort needed to maintain a Notes network. You should use groups instead of explicitly listing individual user or server names.

The most difficult problem you will face with groups is the proliferation of group names in the Public Address Book. If you distribute management of the Public Address Book such that many people have the ability to create groups, consider creating a policy for naming groups. Your goal should be to have a group's name clearly define the group's reason for being. For example, if you want to create a group of administrators who can edit server documents in the Public Address Book, you might call the group PABServerModifiers. By prepending the initials PAB to the group name, you are indicating that this group is to be used specifically with the Public Address Book. You can come up with a set of prefixes and suffixes for groups that will clearly identify whether the group is for use by a particular department, database, access control list, mail addressing, or is a multi-purpose group.

Creating a group document is extremely easy. You simply need to specify the group name, type, and members. A useful option is to enter a detailed description of the group in the group document. Figure 13.16 shows an example of a group document.

Figure 13.16.
A group document in
the access control list.

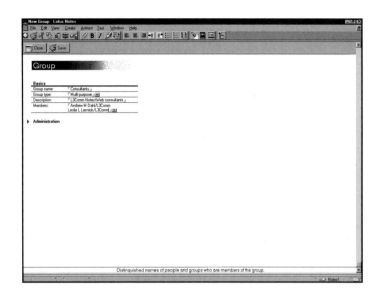

Pay particular attention to group types. Using group types helps clarify the purpose of the group, as well as reducing clutter on the Notes interface. The types that Notes provides are

- ◆ Multi-Purpose
- ◆ Access Control List Only
- ◆ Mail Only
- ◆ Deny List Only

Groups with the type Mail Only appear only in views and lists for addressing mail. This setting increases view performance as well as reduces the number of groups that a user needs to sift through when addressing mail. All the other types function in a similar manner. The Access Control List Only groups appear only in dialog boxes and views pertaining to access control lists. The Deny List Only type appears only in the server access list views.

LOCATION DOCUMENTS

Location documents are used by mobile users to instruct Notes on how to reach their Notes network. Each location to which a mobile user travels must have its own location document. Figure 13.17 shows a typical location document.

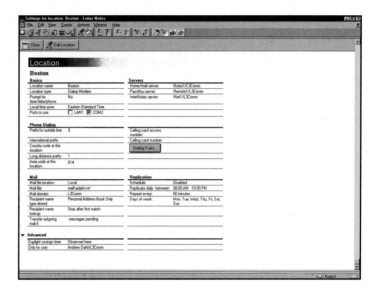

Figure 13.17.
A typical location
document.

Each location document specifies the mail file to be used at that location, a replication schedule (if applicable), and a set of servers accessible from that location. Chapter 19, "Supporting Dial-Up Users," provides detailed information on configuring location documents.

MAIL-IN DATABASE DOCUMENTS

The Notes mail router can place mail in any Notes database, not just mailboxes. Any Notes database can be a recipient of Notes mail. Before a database can receive mail, you must create a mail-in database document in the Public Address Book for that database. Figure 13.18 shows a typical mail-in database document.

You address mail to a mail-in database as you would any other mail recipient. You can include mail-in database addresses in groups or explicitly in any To field. Mail-in databases can respond automatically to mail by using macros.

Figure 13.18.
A typical mail-in
database document.

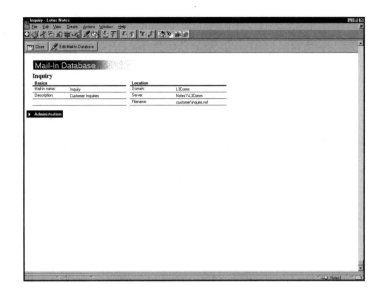

PERSON DOCUMENTS

Person documents contain information for mail routing, as well as generic address and phone number information. Figure 13.19 shows a typical person document.

Figure 13.19.
A typical person
document.

Most of the fields in a person document are self-explanatory. If you need to view the public key for a person, you should place a person document in Edit mode by pressing Ctrl+E.

Person documents are created automatically when you register a new user. By listing the user's name in the Administrators field at the bottom of a person document, you can have your users enter their own address and phone number information. When you first register a new user, that person's ID file is stored as an attachment to his person record (if you have elected to store ID files in the Public Address Book). The first time a Notes user accesses his home server, the ID file is detached from his person document and stored on his local hard drive.

PROGRAM DOCUMENTS

You can use the Notes Public Address Book to schedule tasks and programs on any Notes server. Common uses for program documents are to schedule backups and software updates. For each program, you need to provide a complete path and file name for the program, including any extensions, such as .EXE. You can specify the time of day and day of week for each program. Figure 13.20 shows a typical program document.

Figure 13.20.
A typical program
document for backing
up a server.

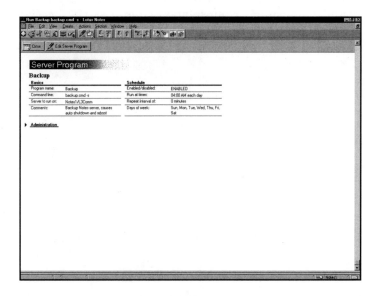

Using the Enabled/Disabled field, you can cause a program to be run according to the schedule, on system startup only, or to not run at all. If you select STARTUP ONLY, the program will run each time the Notes server is shut down and restarted.

13

Server Documents

The server document is the most complex document in the Public Address Book. Server documents contain information on the server's location, network configuration, access control, Agent Manager, mail routing, and administrator contact information. Server documents are created automatically when you register a server. Figure 13.21 shows a typical server document.

Figure 13.21.
A typical server
document in the Public
Address Book.

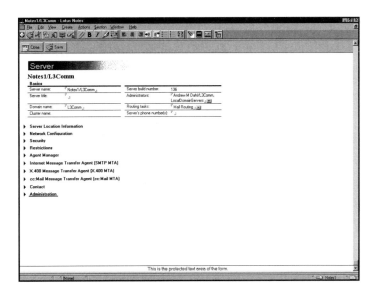

For information on filling in server location and network configuration sections, see Chapter 10, "Installing and Configuring Notes Servers." For details on the security and restrictions information, see Chapter 18. For information on the passthru fields in the Restrictions section, see Chapter 19. Information on configuring the agent manager is contained in the section "Using the Agent Manager," later in this chapter.

The administration section of a server document contains four fields: Owners, Administrators, Certified Public Key, and Change Request. The Change Request field is set by the Administration Process (described earlier in this chapter) when a server's name or certification changes. A server scans its own server document periodically, checking the Change Request field. If the Change Request flag is set, the Notes server will verify the information in the server document and then update the server ID file.

SERVER CONFIGURATION DOCUMENTS

Server configuration documents are one way you can edit parameters stored in the NOTES.INI file. You can use a server configuration document to change a parameter in every server's NOTES.INI file or to change a parameter for a single server. A single server configuration document can be used to set any number of NOTES.INI parameters. Figure 13.22 shows a typical server configuration document.

Figure 13.22.
A typical server
configuration
document.

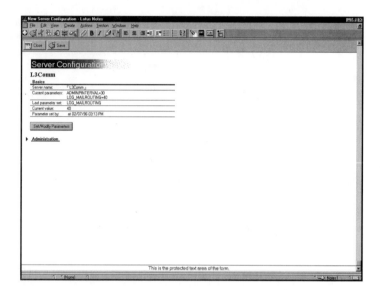

To create a server configuration document, follow these steps:

1. Open the Public Address Book.
2. Choose Server | Configurations | View.
3. Choose Add Configuration.

   Notes creates a server configuration document with a default server name of *.
4. Enter the server name for this server configuration document. The default setting (*) causes this server configuration document to apply to all servers in the domain.
5. Click the Set/Modify Parameters button.

   The Server Configuration Parameters dialog box opens (see Figure 13.23).
6. Click the little down-arrow button by the Next button.

   The Select a Standard Parameter dialog box appears.
7. Select the parameter you want to configure.

13

8. Choose OK.

Notes fills in the Item field with the parameter name and displays Help text in the bottom of the Server Configuration Parameters dialog box.

Figure 13.23.
The Server Config-
uration Parameters
dialog box.

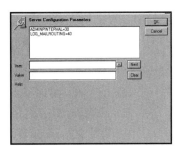

Tip

You can use the Server Configuration Parameters dialog box to help you understand specific NOTES.INI parameters. Detailed Help text is available in this dialog box for all NOTES.INI parameters.

9. You can repeat these steps to configure multiple parameters in a single server configuration document.

10. Choose OK.

The Current Parameters field in the server configuration document is updated with one line for each parameter you have specified.

11. Choose Save.

12. Choose Close.

The server configuration document replicates to all copies of the Public Address Book and causes the NOTES.INI files to be updated. NOTES.INI parameters set using the server configuration document take precedence over settings in the current NOTES.INI file. These settings will typically take effect within one minute of the time the server configuration document is placed in the Public Address Book on a server. You don't need to reboot the server for these new parameters to take effect.

A single parameter for a server can be set in more than one server configuration document. This can happen when you use one server configuration document to specify parameters for a group of servers and another server configuration document specifically for a single server. The parameter value from the server configuration for a single specific server takes precedence over a server configuration setting for multiple servers.

One way to configure multiple servers efficiently is to create a server configuration document for each type of dedicated server in your organization. For example, you may have a specific set of parameters for mail servers and another set for hub servers. Create a group document for each class of servers and place that group name in the Server field in the server configuration document.

Every time a server reboots, it scans the Public Address Book for server configuration documents that apply. Any new parameters are read into memory and the NOTES.INI file is updated. The server scans the Public Address Book for configuration settings every five minutes. Every time a server finds a new or modified configuration setting, it reads that setting into memory and updates the NOTES.INI file. Remote servers experience more of a delay, due to the time needed for the document to be replicated, the Public Address Book view to be updated, and the Public Address Book to be scanned. In all, you can expect a delay of an additional twenty minutes on top of the replication time before parameter changes take effect on remote servers.

You cannot edit every parameter in the NOTES.INI file using a server configuration document. You must enter some configuration changes using the server document. This system is necessary to maintain proper Notes security. The parameters that cannot be updated using a server configuration document are in the following list:

- Any parameter beginning with $
- ServerName
- ServerTitle
- AllowAccess
- DenyAccess
- CreateFile
- CreateReplica
- ADMINAccess
- AllowPassthruAccess
- AllowPassthruTargets
- AllowPassthruClients
- AllowPassthruCallers
- Type
- Form
- Names
- Domain
- MailServer

◆ MailFile

◆ Ports

◆ KitType

◆ ServerConsolePassword (you can set the ServerConsolePassword only directly from a server console)

If these fields aren't specified in the server document, a Notes server will use them.

Consider the following example, which shows how a Notes server uses different configuration documents to arrive at the actual parameter values used. In this example, there are three server configuration documents. One specifies parameters for all servers, using *, the second specifies parameters for a group of servers, and the third specifies parameters for a specific server.

```
All Servers Configuration Document
    Server Name = *
        LOG_MAIL_ROUTING = 10
        Update_No_Full Text = 1

Mail Servers Configuration Document
    Server Name = MailServers     (Group containing all mail servers)
        LOG_MAIL_ROUTING = 30
        Replicators = 2

Single Server Configuration Document
    Server Name = Mail1/L3COMM
        ADMINP_Interval = 30
        Replicators = 4
```

Notes will first read in the parameters from the All Servers configuration document. Notes then reads the server group configuration document and overwrites any parameter values from the All Servers document. Finally, Notes reads the Single Server configuration document and overwrites any existing parameter values. The final set of parameters used by Mail1/L3COMM is as follows:

```
LOG_MAIL_ROUTING = 30
    ADMINP_Interval = 30
    Replicators = 4
    Update_No_Full Text = 1
```

USER SETUP PROFILE DOCUMENTS

User setup profiles are used during user registration to automatically create connection documents for the servers listed in the profile. User profiles simplify the registration of multiple users by eliminating the need to provide common information repeatedly. Although you can create as many profiles as you want, each user can be associated only with a single profile.

When creating a new user setup profile, you specify the name and phone numbers of passthru and remote dial-up servers and the name of the Internet server for the class of users. You also can specify a mail domain for that set of users. All fields are optional except the name of the profile.

Notes creates all the location and connection documents needed by users to access the servers listed in the profile. These documents are stored in the Personal Address Books for the users.

GATHERING STATISTICS AND EVENTS

The Notes Event Monitor enables you to configure automatic notification for large numbers of errors and conditions. You also can use the Event Monitor to record statistics about activities on the Notes network, including replication events, changes to access control lists, and database usage. The Event Monitor works with two databases: Statistics & Events (EVENTS4.NSF) and Statistics Reporting (STATREP.NSF). The Reporter server task is responsible for generating statistics and events. When Notes is installed, no statistics or events are being monitored. You must configure the exact statistics and events that you want to track. Consider these issues when deciding what statistics and events to monitor:

◆ Create a set of events and statistics for each type of dedicated server.

◆ Assign responsibilities for handling alarms generated by the Event Monitor.

◆ Identify the key databases that need to have replication and access control lists carefully monitored.

◆ Assign responsibility for reviewing generated statistics for potential bottle-necks in the Notes network.

◆ Each server administrator should have access to the statistics and events generated by the servers under her control. This doesn't mean that you must have different Statistics Reporting databases for each server, but that the server administrators should have access to a common database.

Events are broken into categories. Each category has specific events broken into severity levels. The following list details the types of events:

◆ COMM/NET.

Events and statistics relating to communications and network traffic.

◆ Security.

Events and statistics concerning ID files and access to servers or databases. Some notifications generated by ACL-monitored documents also have this type.

◆ Mail.

Events and statistics concerning the mail router.

◆ Replication.

Events and statistics concerning replication. Some replication-monitored document events fall into this type.

◆ Resource.

Statistics and thresholds concerning system resource usage.

◆ Misc.

Generic events and statistics.

◆ Server.

Events and statistics concerning a specific server not covered in any other category.

◆ Statistic.

Events and statistics for alarms configured by an administrator.

◆ Update.

Indexing events and statistics.

You create an Event Monitor document in the Statistics & Events database (EVENTS4.NSF) for each type of event you want to track. You can have more than one Event Monitor document for each type of event, if you want to monitor different severity levels on different servers.

The Statistics & Events Database

The Statistics & Events database can contain:

◆ Event monitors

◆ ACL monitors

◆ Replication monitors

You can view all events and their associated message text by using the Names and Messages views in the Statistics & Events database. You can edit individual documents in these views to create your own message text or to add new messages specifically for your installation. Figure 13.24 shows typical names and messages—messages by text view—in the Statistics & Events database. As the figure shows, each message has an associated type and severity.

Figure 13.24.
Viewing message text in
the Statistics & Events
database.

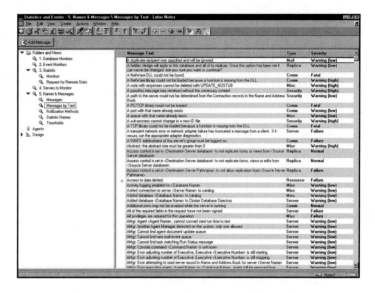

CONFIGURING EVENTS AND STATISTICS REPORTING

The Event Monitor and Reporter server tasks don't run automatically. An administrator must edit the ServerTasks setting in the NOTES.INI file. Add the entries Event and Reporter to the ServerTasks parameter to run the Event Monitor and Statistics Generator on a server. The first time the Event server task runs, it will automatically migrate Release 3 monitor documents from the Public Address Book and configure all the necessary databases and entries in the new Public Address Book. Specifically, the first time the Event task runs, it will take these steps:

1. Creating the Statistics & Events database (EVENTS4.NSF) if none exists.

2. Creating a Server to Monitor document for every server in the Public Address Book.

3. Migrating all Notes Release 3 monitor documents from the Public Address Book to the Statistics & Events database.

4. (Event Monitor) Adding an address for mailed-in events in the Server to Monitor document for the server running the Event server task.

5. For the database listed in the address on the Server to Monitor document, creating a mail-in database document in the Public Address Book.

6. Creating a mail-in database corresponding to the mail-in database document if none exists.

The Reporter server task automatically configures a Notes server the first time the task is run. The Reporter is responsible for tracking statistics on its server. A Reporter must have a mail-in database to receive statistics information. The mail-in database can be a local database, or one on a remote server that is used to collect information from multiple servers. The recommended configuration is to use a centralized Statistics Reporting database that receives messages from the Reporter tasks running on multiple servers in the network.

You should run the Event Monitor and Reporter server tasks one time from the console to automatically configure a server for statistics and events monitoring. After the server has been configured, you can tune the installation by editing the Server to Monitor documents in the Statistics & Events database. To edit a Server to Monitor document, follow these steps:

1. Open the Statistics & Events database.

   You can open the Statistics & Events database directly from your workspace or by using the Server Administration panel (for details, see the later section "Using the Server Administration Panel"). To use the Server Administration panel, select the database's icon and choose Configure Statistics Reporting.

2. Open the Server to Monitor view.

3. Open the Server to Monitor document for the server you want to configure.

4. Enter the address of the mail-in database that will receive statistics.

   Enter the address exactly as it appears in the Mail-In Name field in the mail-in database document in the Public Address Book for the Statistics Reporting database.

5. Enter a collection interval for the server.

   The collection interval is the interval between Reporter tasks. The collection interval controls how many documents will be created in the Statistics Reporting database. One document is created for each running of the Reporter task. Running the Reporter task more often creates more documents and causes the analysis to take longer to perform. The minimum interval you can specify is 15 minutes. The recommended interval is 4 hours for heavily loaded servers and once a day for infrequently used servers.

Tip

If you are experiencing problems on a specific server, increase the reporting frequency to 30 minutes.

6. Enter an analysis interval.

   Analysis reports summarize the individual statistics documents in the Statistics Reporting database. At each interval specified, the Reporter server task creates a report containing information such as averages and peak usages. The analysis reports are useful for planning server and network upgrades and for assigning users to lightly loaded servers. The analysis report also reports on database and templates.

7. (optional) Enter a description for the server.

8. Select Save Server to Monitor.

USING THE SERVER ADMINISTRATION PANEL

You can access the Server Administration panel from any workstation. The Server Administration panel centralizes the most common tasks that administrators need to perform. All types of administrators, including certifiers, server administrators, and database managers, can use the Server Administration panel. The following list details some of the tasks you can accomplish from the Server Administration panel:

◆ Registering a person or server

◆ Viewing entries in the Public Address Book, including groups, users, servers, and certificates

◆ Opening the Public Address Book

◆ Configuring servers by using server configuration documents in the Public Address Book

◆ Managing certificates, including certifying user and server ID files, issuing cross certificates, creating certifier ID files, and editing and placing multiple passwords on ID files

◆ Debugging mail routing problems

◆ Viewing critical administration databases, such as the Notes log, database catalog, Statistics Reporting database, and Administration Requests database

◆ Managing databases, including performing database analysis, compacting databases, managing full-text indexes, setting maximum database sizes, and specifying an administration server for databases.

◆ Accessing the remote console (described in the later section "Using the Server Console")

To access the Server Administration panel, choose File | Tools | Server Administration. In the list of servers, highlight the server you want to manage, and select the desired task from one of the drop-down menus accessed from the buttons to the right. Each of the tasks that you can accomplish by using the Server Administration panel is covered in detail in other chapters. Using the Server Administration panel to manage certificates and ID files is covered in Chapter 18. The Notes console, administration databases, and Public Address Book are covered in this chapter. Using the Server Administration panel to manage databases is covered in Chapter 17, "Administering Notes Databases." Analyzing mail problems with the Server Administration panel is covered in Chapter 14.

USING THE SERVER CONSOLE

At the server console, you can enter commands for immediate execution by the server. You can access the server console directly on the server or through the Administration Server panel. Figure 13.25 shows a typical server console listing.

Figure 13.25.
A typical server console.

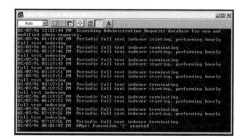

The difference between a server console and a remote console? Only those listed as administrators for a server can access that server by using a remote console.

The remote server console is shown in Figure 13.26. You access the remote server console from the Server Administration panel by selecting the Console button.

To enter a command using the remote server console, follow these steps:

1. Select the correct server from the drop-down list.
2. Enter the command in the Server Console Command field. You can retrieve commands you have already typed by selecting them from the drop-down list.
3. Choose Send.

    The response from the remote server, if any, appears in the Server Response field. You can scroll the Server Response field to view lengthy messages.

4. You can copy the server response into another document or to the Clipboard by using the Copy Response button.

Figure 13.26.
The remote server
console.

5. When you have completed your session on the remote console, click Done.

You can send results of a server command to an output file by typing the server command and then entering > *filename* on the same line before selecting Send.

When entering commands at the server console, keep the following points in mind:

◆ Press Enter to display the > prompt.

◆ You can access previously entered commands by using the up- and down-arrow keys.

◆ The Notes server continues to display messages while you are typing at the server console. If your server command becomes unreadable, press Ctrl+R to redisplay the current server command.

◆ All server commands have short abbreviations that can save an administrator a considerable amount of time.

◆ Server parameters containing spaces must be enclosed inside double quotes (" ").

◆ To prevent server console messages from scrolling by, press the Pause button or use Ctrl+Q to pause the server output. To resume server output scrolling, press Ctrl+R. The Pause key has no effect on NetWare servers.

Table 13.1 summarizes the server commands you can use at either the console or the remote console.

13

TABLE 13.1. SERVER COMMANDS.

Abbreviation	Example	Description
Broadcast	Broadcast *Message UserName(s)*	Sends a message to all users specified. The default is to send a message to all users currently attached to a server.
Drop	Drop *UserName*	Closes out a user's connection to a server. If you have entered `LogSessions = 1` in the NOTES.INI file, Notes reports confirmation when a session is dropped.
Exit	Exit	Shuts down the server.
Help	Help	Generates a complete list of server commands with brief descriptions.
Load	Load *ProgramName*	Executes a specific server task or launches any program that can be run from the current operating system's command line. When using Load to run Notes server tasks, you need to know the executable name for the server task. Chapter 16, "Administering Notes Servers," contains a complete list of the server tasks and their executable names.
Pull	Pull *ServerName*	Replicates database updates from the destination server to the current server. No updates are sent from the current server to the specified server.
Push	Push *ServerName*	Replicates database updates from the current server to the specified server. No updates are replicated from the specified server to the current server.
Quit	Quit	Shuts down the server.
Replicate	Replicate *ServerName*	Begins a replication session between the current server and the specified server. The current

continues

TABLE 13.1. CONTINUED

Abbreviation	Example	Description
		server pulls changes from the other server and then gives the other server an opportunity to pull changes. If the minimum interval between replications for these two servers has elapsed (see the replication schedule in the connection document), the other server pulls changes from the current server. Otherwise, the other server waits until the next scheduled replication. If the server is replicating when the Replicate command is entered, the command is queued until the current replication ends.
Route	Route *ServerName*	Immediately routes all pending mail to the specified server. The other server must be on another Notes network, because Notes always immediately routes mail within a network. Use the Route command when you are attempting to troubleshoot mail problems.
Set Configuration	Set Configuration *Setting*	Updates settings in a server's NOTES.INI file and server configuration documents. The Set Configuration Server command immediately updates the specified parameters for the server at which the command was entered. The Set Configuration command updates the server's configuration document in the Public Address Book or creates a server configuration document if none exists. You will need to reboot the server when using the Set

13

Abbreviation	Example	Description
		Configuration command to change the following parameters:
		◆ ServerTasks
		◆ ServerTasksAt
		◆ NSFBufferPoolSize
		◆ Domain
		◆ ModemFileDirectory
		◆ ServerKeyFileName
		◆ Ports
		◆ Names
Set Secure	Set Secure *CurrentPassword*	Prevents unauthorized access to a server console by requiring a password. A password-protected server console prevents users from using the Exit, Load, Quit, Set Configuration, and Tell commands. In addition, any command that launches a Notes server task cannot be launched from a password-protected console. The console remains protected until a second Set Secure command is entered, using the same password.
Set Statistics	Set Statistics *Statistics*	Resets the running total for statistics. You can use a wild card (*) to reset all statistics at once.
Show Configuration	Show Configuration *Setting*	Displays the current configuration value for the specified parameter. Any setting for the NOTES.INI file can be used. For a complete listing of parameters in the NOTES.INI file, see Appendix B.
Show Directory	Show Directory	Displays a list of all databases and templates in the data directory.

continues

TABLE 13.1. CONTINUED

Abbreviation	Example	Description
		This command works only with the Notes data directory.
Show Disk Space	Show Disk Space *Location*	Displays the number of bytes available on a specified hard drive, file system, or volume. *Location* is an identifier applicable to a specific operating system. Under Windows NT and OS/2, use a hard drive letter. Under NetWare, enter a volume label. Under UNIX, enter a file system name. The default setting displays information about the disk containing the Notes program directory.
Show Memory	Show Memory	The Show Memory command displays the total amount of virtual memory available to the Notes program. Under OS/2 and Windows NT, this is the total system memory installed plus swap space available. Under NetWare, this command displays the total amount of memory configured. The Show Memory command is not available under UNIX.
Show Port	Show Port *PortName*	Displays information about a specific communications port. *PortName* can be any configured port, including LAN and COM ports.
Show Schedule	Show Schedule *ServerName / ProgramName / Location*	Use Show Schedule to display information about programs related to a specific server, program, or location. Show Schedule shows the next program of the specified type to be run.

13

Abbreviation	Example	Description
Show Sessions	Show Sessions *ServerCommand*	Displays system information about the specified server command. The default is to show information about all current Notes sessions. Use the Show Sessions command when debugging a Notes installation.
Show Stat	Show Stat *StatisticName*	Displays information about disk space, memory utilization, and network activity. The statistic name can be any statistic available in the Statistics & Events database's Names and Messages—Statistic Names view. The default is to display information about all statistics.
Show Tasks	Show Tasks	Displays the status of all active server tasks.
Show Transactions	Show Transactions	Displays the current transaction statistics for a server.
Show Users	Show Users	Displays the list of all users currently connected to a server, along with the databases they have accessed and the elapsed time since the last database access.
Tell	Tell *ServerProgram Parameter*	Use Tell to shut down specific server tasks without shutting down the entire server. You also can use Tell to issue any command that will be accepted by a server task.

USING THE AGENT MANAGER

Agents are like personalized butlers that Notes users use to carry out specific tasks. Agents can be a significant drain on server resources. For this reason, it's important for a server administrator to restrict the amount of server resources that agents can use. You can restrict a user's ability to create agents, the times of day that agents can run, and the number of agents that can be running simultaneously.

The Agent Manager is responsible for launching all agents on a server. Before executing an agent, the Agent Manager verifies the authority of the person who created the agent. If the user has insufficient authority to run an agent, the Agent Manager rejects the request to run an agent. The Agent Manager then checks to see that all other restrictions, such as time of day and number of simultaneous agents, are not violated. If all these criteria are met, the Agent Manager launches the specific agent. All Agent Manager activity is recorded in the Notes log on the server where the individual agents are run.

To restrict the agents that can run on a particular server, follow these steps:

1. Open the Public Address Book.
2. Open the Server-Server view.
3. Open the desired server document in Edit mode (press Ctrl+E).
4. In the Agent Manager field, enter the users who are allowed to run private agents. The default setting allows all users to run private agents. Users listed in this field can create personal agents using either the Agent Builder or formulas. Users must have reader access to a database to create personal agents.
5. Enter the names of any users who are allowed to run restricted LotusScript agents. Any user not specifically listed in the Run Restricted LotusScript Agents field can't use restricted agents. Restricted LotusScript agents can execute only a limited set of calls. Restricted agents cannot access security features or the operating system.
6. Fill in the users who will be allowed to run unrestricted LotusScript agents. Any user not specifically listed in the Run Unrestricted LotusScript Agents field can't run unrestricted agents. Unrestricted LotusScript agents can execute any LotusScript call.
7. In the Refresh Agent Cache field, enter a time of day when you want to have the list of agents updated. The Agent Manager scans all databases and the Public Address Book at the specified time for new or deleted agents.
8. Specify a start and end time for your daytime operations. Users who can't run agents during the daytime also can't run agents between the start and end time specified.

9. The maximum number of concurrent agents allowed is 10. Up to 10 agents can run on a server at a single time. A database can execute only a single agent at a time, but multiple databases can have agents executing concurrently. Enter the maximum number of concurrent agents for your server in the Max Concurrent Agents field.

10. Enter the maximum number of minutes a single agent is allowed to run. Use this field to limit absolutely the amount of resources that are consumed by an agent. When an agent has been executing for the maximum number of minutes allowed, the Agent Manager terminates the agent without allowing it to complete.

11. Enter the maximum percentage of time an agent is allowed to poll before being delayed. This field specifies the maximum percentage of the CPU that can be used by a single agent. If an agent exceeds this threshold, the Agent Manager delays the further execution of the agent.

12. Repeat steps 9 through 11 for the nighttime parameters.

13. Choose Save.

14. Choose Close.

SUMMARY

Notes provides a variety of tools for administering the Notes network. Several key databases track statistics, events, and other information about the Notes network. The key databases with which all administrators should be familiar are the Public Address Book and Notes log. Other administrative databases, such as the Administration Requests database and the Statistic & Events database, are associated with specific server tasks that administrators must also know how to use.

With proper planning and a little bit of training, administering a Notes network need not be an onerous chore. The following chapters provide specifics on administering the various parts of the Notes network, including mail routing, replication, and security.

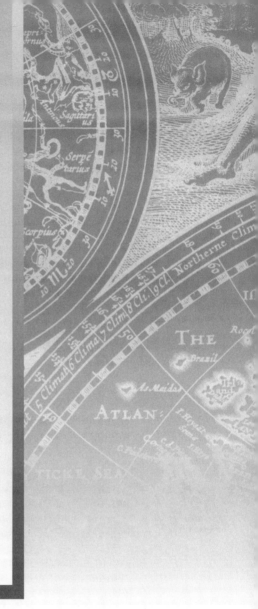

CHAPTER 14

Administering Notes Mail

E-mail by itself, without all the other features of Notes, has been known to change corporate culture. E-mail is the lifeblood of communication for many organizations today. Reliable, fast delivery of e-mail is the number one priority for Notes administrators. A lonely Notes administrator only need pull the plug on the mail server to hear the phone ring.

Notes Mail is designed to work with most existing e-mail packages (with the appropriate mail gateway package). The list of third-party mail gateways for Notes is so extensive that Notes has been proposed as a universal mail gateway, able to take mail from anywhere and route it anywhere. Notes Mail can connect directly to any MAPI- or VIM-compliant mail package as well as MHS, Profs (an IBM mainframe mail system), the Internet, and more. Connecting Notes to other mail systems continues to get easier with each release. The Notes e-mail system is called, naturally enough, *Notes Mail*.

NOTES MAIL CAPABILITIES

Notes Mail supports the asynchronous transfer of messages between unconnected servers and workstations.

By default, any document in any database can be mailed. Notes can deliver mail to any Notes database, not just mailboxes. The Notes administrator simply needs to set up an address for a database in the Public Address Book, and that database can receive mail. Personal mailboxes are simply Notes databases with views, forms, and agents tailored for e-mail. You could copy any or all of the features from the default personal mailbox to any other database. You need to set up a mail-in database document in the Public Address Book for any non-mailbox that is to receive mail. The mail-in database document defines a mail address for the database.

Notes supports encryption and electronic signatures (introduced in Chapter 3, "Understanding Security") for all databases, but these features are especially easy to use as part of sending and receiving mail. Administrators or users can configure mailboxes to encrypt incoming or outgoing mail. In addition, users can choose to sign a mail message. Signing a message enables the recipient to validate the identity of the sender and guarantees that a message wasn't altered in transit.

Notes mailboxes also come with agents for archiving mail, sending out-of-office notices, and populating Personal Address Books. Mail forwarding can be done for individual messages by users. Administrators can have all messages forwarded by entering a forwarding address in the person record for a user in the Public Address Book.

PLANNING FOR NOTES MAIL

Your primary consideration when planning for Notes Mail is reliability. The two most critical factors are ensuring that adequate disk space exists for personal mailboxes and configuring connection documents and foreign domain documents to enable mail routing between Notes and other networks or mail systems.

Every Notes user has a personal mailbox. Administering these mailboxes is easier when you group them together on one server. Having one mail server also reduces the number of connection documents that must be set up. The only users who shouldn't be using server-based mail are remote and mobile users. This type of user needs to have a copy of her personal mailbox on her workstation and dial into a server to replicate mail.

E-mail reliability is enhanced by minimizing the number of documents that must be configured in the Public Address Book. You should pay particular attention to the number of connection documents that must be maintained. You need a pair of connection documents to route mail between servers on different networks or in different domains.

At least one server in each Notes named network must have a connection document to a server on the other Notes named network to route mail between the two networks. This is true even when both networks are in the same domain. Notes is smart enough to route mail between networks if there is a single server connected to the other network. The router will automatically forward mail to the server that is connected to the other network. This system means that you never need more than one pair of connection documents to route mail between networks. You should pick two or three servers on each of your Notes networks to act as gateways to Notes networks, and specify more than one link between networks so that mail will be routed even if one of the connected servers fails. This method greatly reduces the number of connection documents and the chance for error.

A single connection document can be used to schedule both mail routing and replication. You can reduce the number of connection documents by taking advantage of this feature. If you want to route mail more often than you replicate, you will need to set up one pair of connection documents for mail routing and one for replication. Do this only if replication is taking a long time to complete. Setting up multiple connection documents between servers may cause overlapping connection documents. Overlapping connection documents that specify conflicting or duplicate information can confuse the router.

All servers in a domain must use a common Public Address Book for mail routing to work reliably. Make sure that all servers are regularly replicating the Public Address Book to keep connection and server documents updated.

Finally, restrict access to connection documents to a few administrators. This plan reduces the chance of error when you add or delete servers on the network. Use roles in the Public Address Book to specify the administrators with the right to create and modify connection documents.

All mail servers serving more than 50 users should set a quota on the size of individual mailboxes. To calculate a quota for mailboxes, you must determine the amount of disk space you can devote to mailboxes and then divide by the number of mailboxes you need. Leave some disk space unassigned, to handle users that must have additional disk space.

USING MAIL SERVERS

Administering Notes mail is simplified when you use *mail servers*—servers dedicated to mail. I recommend placing all personal mailboxes on a single server (large organizations will need multiple mail servers). Grouping mail on one server allows you to provide a consistent level of service to your users. Grouping mailboxes

◆ Isolates mail from other network and application problems

◆ Provides better, more predictable performance

◆ Minimizes network traffic

◆ Saves disk space

By isolating mail from the effects of other Notes databases, you ease performance monitoring and troubleshooting. A server running a troublesome application is no place for a mailbox. That person's mail is unavailable while the server is down. Server crashes are the main cause of corrupted databases. You can avoid corrupting personal mailboxes by grouping them on a single mail server. Mail servers also minimize the number of servers involved with routing mail. Any server on the same network as the mail server delivers mail directly to the mail server. In a hub-and-spoke environment, only the source server, the hub, and the mail server are involved. Fixing mail delivery problems is easier when fewer servers must be considered.

A poorly performing application will have minimal impact on your mail delivery when you are using a mail server. This wouldn't be the case if mail were intermingled with other applications. Other applications have more unpredictable loads due to index building and replication overhead. As you add applications and users to a Notes database server, performance may fall dramatically; as you add users to a mail server, performance degrades slowly (if at all). By monitoring memory and free disk space on your mail server, you can plan ahead for upgrades. You should be able to predict when you will need a second mail server by tracing mail performance as users are added.

Mail servers also minimize network traffic. Mail sent from one user to another user on the same home server is placed directly in the recipient's mailbox without any network traffic. For organizations sending large files, graphics, or multimedia presentations, this is a real concern. More organizations fall into this category every day. Plan ahead and save a headache later by using mail servers now.

Mail servers also allow you to save disk space. Notes stores messages delivered to more than one person just once. Instead of the actual message, a pointer is placed in each person's mailbox. If John and Sally have the same home server (their mailboxes are on the same server), a message addressed to both of them is stored a single time.

How Mail Routing Works

The router is the Notes task responsible for delivering mail. The router scans MAIL.BOX looking for new messages, and uses the Name and Address Book (NAB) to determine what action to take with the message. The router runs on all Notes servers, not just on a mail server. All Notes servers need a MAIL.BOX database and a copy of the NAB in order to route mail.

Mail routing is more complex when sending across domains or networks. Remember, all servers in a domain share a single NAB. Notes needs additional information when routing mail between networks and domains. This information is provided by connection records and nonadjacent domain records. The primary benefit of grouping servers together in a single domain is simplified mail routing.

A mail message is altered as it is delivered. The Notes workstation substitutes full hierarchical names for any short names used, and expands groups to their individual members. The router also modifies the message, adding fields to make troubleshooting easier and modifying recipient and originator addresses. Addresses are modified when sending between domains to provide complete path information for replies.

Mail Routing Within a Domain

Figure 14.1 shows mail being routed within a domain. A message is sent by being placed in MAIL.BOX on any server. The router scans MAIL.BOX, finds the message, and reads the SendTo field. (All Notes mail must have a SendTo field.) The recipient's person record in the NAB is used to find the correct home server. The server document for the home server is checked to see which network the server is on. The router connects to the home server and places the message in MAIL.BOX on that server. A field, RouteServers, is added to the message, showing that the message was created on the source server and was sent to the home server. The recipient and originator addresses aren't modified. The router on the home server places the message in the correct personal mailbox. Figure 14.2 shows how the message is modified at each step.

Figure 14.1.
Delivering mail within a domain on the same network.

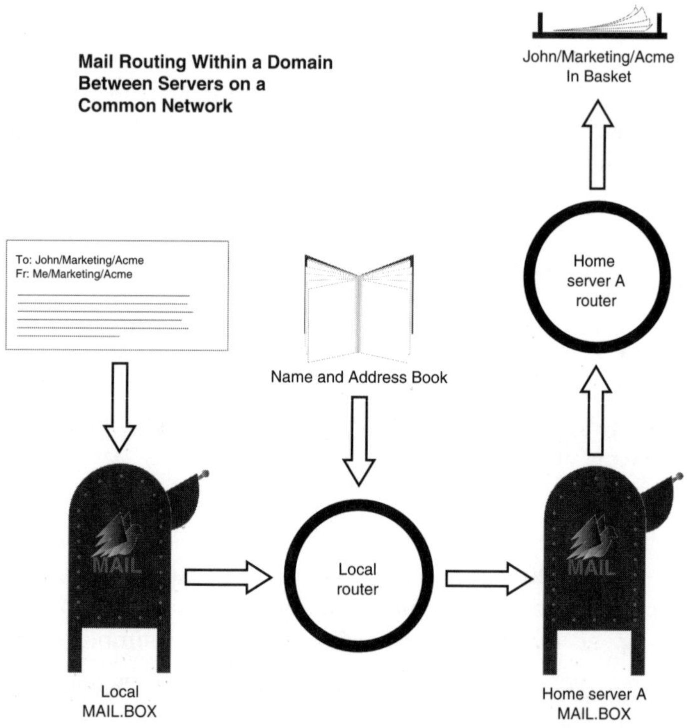

Mail Routing Within a Domain Between Servers on a Common Network

John/Marketing/Acme
In Basket

To: John/Marketing/Acme
Fr: Me/Marketing/Acme

Name and Address Book

Home server A router

Local router

Local MAIL.BOX

Home server A MAIL.BOX

In this scenario, three documents need to be correctly configured in the NAB: a person document for the recipient, and server documents for the source and home servers. Multiple recipient messages are handled in a similar manner. Only one mail message is sent per home server. The router doesn't send multiple messages, one per recipient, to a home server.

MAIL ROUTING BETWEEN DOMAINS

You can specify a destination in another domain by adding an "@ *domain*" to the recipient address. For example, to send mail to Benny/Transport/TCom in the TCom domain from the Acme domain, the address is Benny/Transport/TCom @ TCom. The router treats anything to the right of "@" as a domain name. If the domain name is different from the current one, the router looks through connection documents for any server in its domain with a connection to a server in the recipient domain.

Figure 14.2.
E-mail is modified
during delivery. Each
server may modify the
address and
RouteServers fields.

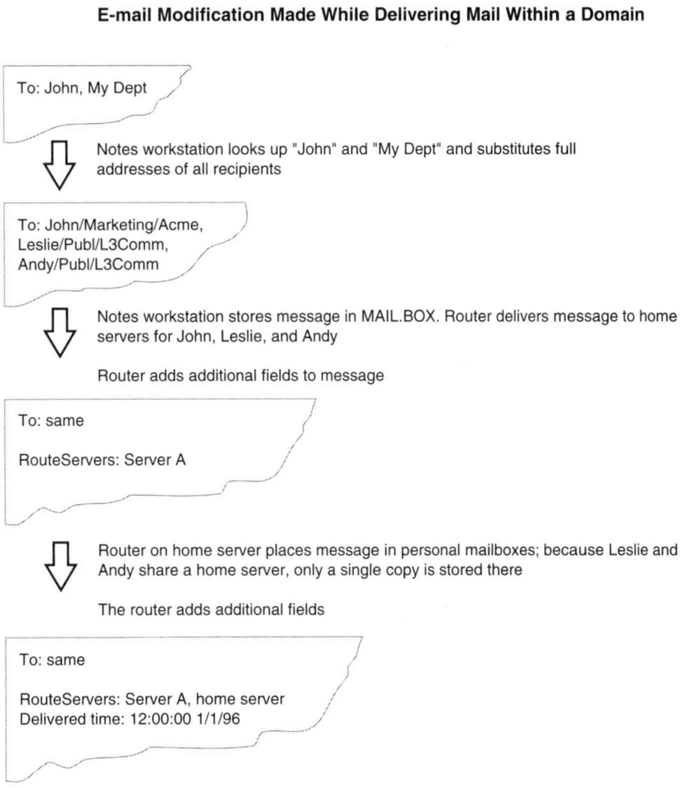

E-mail Modification Made While Delivering Mail Within a Domain

To: John, My Dept

⇩ Notes workstation looks up "John" and "My Dept" and substitutes full
addresses of all recipients

To: John/Marketing/Acme,
Leslie/Publ/L3Comm,
Andy/Publ/L3Comm

⇩ Notes workstation stores message in MAIL.BOX. Router delivers message to home
servers for John, Leslie, and Andy

Router adds additional fields to message

To: same

RouteServers: Server A

⇩ Router on home server places message in personal mailboxes; because Leslie and
Andy share a home server, only a single copy is stored there

The router adds additional fields

To: same

RouteServers: Server A, home server
Delivered time: 12:00:00 1/1/96

14

ADMINISTERING NOTES MAIL

If no direct connection is found between domains, nonadjacent domain documents are searched. Nonadjacent domain documents specify the next server in the path to the destination domain. This next server then must know how to deliver the message. Figure 14.3 shows the path a mail message takes when being delivered to a different domain (in this case, one that isn't directly connected). Figure 14.4 shows the connection documents needed to route mail from the TCom domain to the Acme domain.

Figure 14.4 shows the connection, server, and domain documents needed to route mail from the TCom domain to the Acme domain. Another set of documents is needed to route mail from the Acme domain to the TCom domain. In a real situation, there would be a pair of connection documents for servers B and C as well as for servers C and D. The Acme domain would need an adjacent domain record for the Lippi domain and a nonadjacent domain record for the TCom domain.

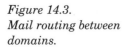

Figure 14.3.
Mail routing between domains.

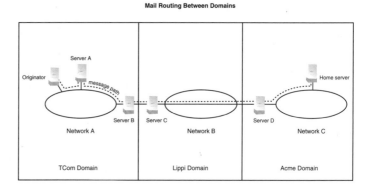

Mail is routed through the Lippi domain on the way to the Acme domain. The router in each domain adds its domain name to the originator name and deletes its domain name (if present) from the rightmost domain name list. This is done so that at any point during transmission, should an error occur, the message can be returned to the original sender. If the original recipient in Figure 14.3 is John/Marketing/Acme @ Acme and the original sender is MyName, the Recipient and Sender fields of the delivered message would be John/Marketing/Acme and MyName @ TCom @ Lippi.

The router doesn't expand names and groups to the left of the @. The destination domain expands any groups, but doesn't expand any simple names into full hierarchical names. Typos in a group name or recipient address aren't discovered until the router in the destination domain can't deliver the message. A recipient must have an unambiguous address when it is received by the destination domain. A single exact match must be found in the local Name and Address Book for either a person or a group, or the message will be returned.

The router efficiently handles multi-domain mail when multiple recipients are specified. Only a single copy of the message is sent to any destination domain. This isn't necessarily the case for gateways. Mail sent through a gateway is handled by the gateway and not the Notes router, so all bets are off when routing mail through a gateway.

MAIL ROUTING BETWEEN NETWORKS

A Notes network is any collection of servers that can connect directly to each other using a common protocol. Servers on different networks may or may not be in the same domain. Networks and domains are two different concepts.

Figure 14.4.
Connection, server and
domain documents
needed to route mail in
figure 14.3.

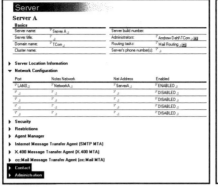

Server

Server A
Basics
- Server name: Server A
- Server title:
- Domain name: TCom
- Cluster name:
- Server build number:
- Administrators: Andrew Dahl\TCom
- Routing tasks: Mail Routing
- Server's phone number(s):

- Server Location Information
- Network Configuration

Port	Notes Network	Net Address	Enabled
LAN0	NetworkA	ServesA	ENABLED
			DISABLED
			DISABLED
			DISABLED
			DISABLED

- Security
- Restrictions
- Agent Manager
- Internet Message Transfer Agent (SMTP MTA)
- X.400 Message Transfer Agent (X.400 MTA)
- cc:Mail Message Transfer Agent (cc:Mail MTA)
- Contact
- Administration

Server

ServerB
Basics
- Server name: ServerB
- Server title:
- Domain name: TCom
- Cluster name:
- Server build number:
- Administrators: Andrew Dahl\TCom
- Routing tasks: Mail Routing
- Server's phone number(s):

- Server Location Information
- Network Configuration

Port	Notes Network	Net Address	Enabled
LAN0	NetworkA	ServerB	ENABLED
LAN1	NetworkB	ServerB	ENABLED
			DISABLED
			DISABLED
			DISABLED

- Security
- Restrictions
- Agent Manager
- Internet Message Transfer Agent (SMTP MTA)
- X.400 Message Transfer Agent (X.400 MTA)
- cc:Mail Message Transfer Agent (cc:Mail MTA)
- Contact
- Administration

Server

HomeServer
Basics
- Server name: HomeServer
- Server title:
- Domain name: Acme
- Cluster name:
- Server build number:
- Administrators: Andrew Dahl\Acme
- Routing tasks: Mail Routing
- Server's phone number(s):

- Server Location Information
- Network Configuration

Port	Notes Network	Net Address	Enabled
LAN0	NetworkC	HomeServer	ENABLED
			DISABLED
			DISABLED
			DISABLED
			DISABLED

- Security
- Restrictions
- Agent Manager
- Internet Message Transfer Agent (SMTP MTA)
- X.400 Message Transfer Agent (X.400 MTA)
- cc:Mail Message Transfer Agent (cc:Mail MTA)
- Contact
- Administration

Server

ServerC
Basics
- Server name: ServerC
- Server title:
- Domain name: Acme
- Cluster name:
- Server build number:
- Administrators: Andrew Dahl\Acme
- Routing tasks: Mail Routing
- Server's phone number(s):

- Server Location Information
- Network Configuration

Port	Notes Network	Net Address	Enabled
LAN0	NetworkA	ServerC	ENABLED
LAN1	NetworkB	ServerC	ENABLED
LAN2	NetworkC	ServerC	ENABLED
			DISABLED
			DISABLED

- Security
- Restrictions
- Agent Manager
- Internet Message Transfer Agent (SMTP MTA)
- X.400 Message Transfer Agent (X.400 MTA)
- cc:Mail Message Transfer Agent (cc:Mail MTA)
- Contact
- Administration

Server Connection

ServerC\Lippi to ServerD\Acme
Basics
- Connection Type: Local Area Network
- Source server: ServerC\Lippi
- Source domain: Lippi
- Use the port(s): LAN2
- Usage priority: Normal
- Destination server: ServerD\Acme
- Destination domain: Acme
- Optional network address:

Scheduled connection
- Schedule: ENABLED
- Call at times: 08:00 AM - 10:00 PM each day
- Repeat interval of: 360 minutes
- Days of week: Mon, Tue, Wed, Thu, Fri, Sat, Sun

Routing and replication
- Tasks: Mail Routing
- Route at once if: 5 messages pending
- Routing cost: 5

Comments:
- Administration

Server Connection

ServerB\TCom to ServerC\Lippi
Basics
- Connection Type: Local Area Network
- Source server: ServerB\TCom
- Source domain: TCom
- Use the port(s): LAN1
- Usage priority: Normal
- Destination server: ServerC\Lippi
- Destination domain: Lippi
- Optional network address:

Scheduled connection
- Schedule: ENABLED
- Call at times: 08:00 AM - 10:00 PM each day
- Repeat interval of: 360 minutes
- Days of week: Mon, Tue, Wed, Thu, Fri, Sat, Sun

Routing and replication
- Tasks: Mail Routing
- Route at once if: 5 messages pending
- Routing cost: 5

Comments:
- Administration

Domain

Lippi
Basics
- Domain type: Adjacent Domain
- Adjacent domain name: Lippi
- Domain description: TCom domain record for the Lippi Domain.

Restrictions
- Allow mail only from domains:
- Deny mail from domains:

- Administration

Domain

Basics
- Domain type: Non-adjacent Domain
- Mail sent to domain: Acme
- Route through domain: Lippi
- Domain description: TCom non-adjacent doamin record for the Acme domain.

Restrictions
- Allow mail only from domains:
- Deny mail from domains:

- Administration

Domain

Acme
Basics
- Domain type: Adjacent Domain
- Adjacent domain name: Acme
- Domain description: Lippi adjacent doamin record for the Acme domain.

Restrictions
- Allow mail only from domains:
- Deny mail from domains:

- Administration

Figure 14.5 shows mail routing between networks. A mail message must go through two intermediate hops before being delivered to the home server. The router compares the network lists in the server documents for the source server and home server. No match is found. The connection documents are then scanned to find a path to the home server (the connection documents are already loaded into memory, so scanning is very fast). The router is searching for any combination of connection documents that define a complete path to the home server. (To be completely correct, a Notes server actually scans all connection documents when booted and keeps an in-memory network diagram for use with routing messages.) For example, the router may find a server on its network with a connection to the home server, a server on its network with a connection to another server on the same network as the home server, or a server with a remote connection to the home server. The router can deliver the message successfully in any of these cases. If no complete path is found, the mail is returned as undeliverable.

In this scenario, at least five documents in the NAB need to be correctly configured: a person document for the recipient, and four server documents (one for each server). To deliver the message, all three networks need to be operational and the bridge between them needs to be working. Figure 14.6 shows the server documents needed to route mail from Server A to the home server in Figure 14.5. Normally, connection documents are needed to route mail from one named network to another. In this case, the intermediate servers are defined to be on two networks, making a connection document unnecessary. If either server B or server C wasn't on two networks, one or more connection documents would be needed to link at least one pair of computers from each named network. The moral of the story here is that you can reduce the number of connection documents by defining gateway servers that exist on two named networks.

Figure 14.5.
Mail routing between
servers within a
domain, but on sepa-
rate networks.

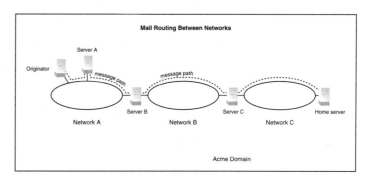

The mail message is modified as in Figure 14.6. RouteServers would list Server A, Server B, Server C, and the home server.

Figure 14.6.
Documents required to
route mail in Figure
14.5.

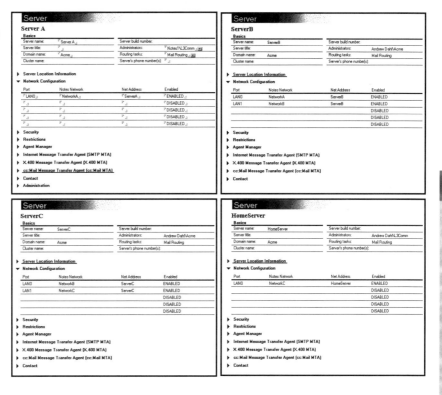

ALTERNATE ROUTE SELECTION

Notes maintains a history of connections that have recently failed, and will attempt to reroute mail around failed connections by searching connection documents for a different path. Alternate path selection focuses on finding different servers to use. Notes doesn't support automatically trying alternate ports to a single server. If Notes Server A attempted to connect to Server B using port LAN0 and failed, and COM2 was also configured as a connection to Server B, Notes wouldn't automatically attempt to use COM2 to connect to Server B.

The router always attempts to use the "least cost" route when delivering mail. Each connection has an associated cost; the cost of a route is the sum of the costs of the individual connections. The router can't use alternate, more expensive routes. Only routes that are equal in cost to the original route are considered. This prevents a flood of traffic across bridges or the use of multiple dial-up connections to route mail.

You can configure this cost in the connection document, or rely on the defaults. The default cost for LAN connected servers is one. You should change this to two for servers connected across a bridge. COM ports have a default cost of five. If multiple routes of identical cost exist, the server that comes first alphabetically is used.

RESTRICTING MAIL DELIVERY BETWEEN DOMAINS

Connection documents contain Allow Mail Only From and Deny Mail From fields. These fields can be used to cut off mail delivery from untrusted domains. These fields control mail coming from other domains, not domains that can be reached from your domain (if you don't want mail going to a domain, don't create a connection document for it). The router checks incoming mail against the entries in these fields. If there are domains listed in the Allow Mail Only From field, and the domain submitting the message isn't listed, the message is rejected. If there are domains listed in the Deny Mail From field, and the domain submitting the message is listed, the message is rejected.

SCHEDULING MAIL DELIVERY

Mail routing between servers on a network is immediate—you never need to schedule mail delivery between servers on a network. Servers on separate networks or domains use connection documents to specify a mail delivery schedule. You can have servers deliver mail periodically and/or deliver mail when the number of pending mail messages exceeds a threshold. You can have mail delivered automatically whenever two servers connect for replication, or specify a schedule just for mail delivery.

You should carefully plan mail delivery between modem-connected servers. Build a schedule that lets users exchange a message and reply within a half day. Trouble tickets generated in response to an alarm are delivered via mail—another reason to specify a connection interval of no more than a half day (two hours is better) between modem-connected servers.

You can always route mail immediately by using the Route command at the server console.

ROUTING AND MAIL PRIORITIES

Each Notes message has an associated priority. These priorities affect how mail is delivered between servers that aren't on the same Notes named network (mail always is delivered immediately if the destination is a server on the same Notes named network). Users can specify high, normal, or low priority when sending a message. High-priority messages are routed immediately regardless of what is in the server or connection documents. Normal-priority mail is routed at the next scheduled mail delivery time. Low-priority mail is routed only during off-peak hours. By default, low-priority mail is delivered between 12:00 a.m. and 6:00 a.m. Low-priority mail is seldom used in most organizations, so the default delivery times should be sufficient.

> *Warning*
>
> Make sure that your connection documents between modem-connected servers specifies a connection time between 12:00 a.m. and 6:00 a.m., or low-priority mail will never be delivered.

You can disable mail priorities on a server by setting the MailDisablePriority parameter in the NOTES.INI file to 1. This causes all mail to be routed using normal priority. Chapter 13, "Administrative Tools," discusses ways to edit NOTES.INI. Appendix B, "NOTES.INI Parameters," contains a complete list of mail-related parameters.

USING MULTI-THREADED ROUTERS

The router can be configured to enable mail transfer to multiple servers simultaneously. The router needs one thread for each server to which it is transferring mail. The default is to configure one thread per server port. Because a server can easily connect to more than one server using a LAN port, you may want to increase this limit. There is virtually no penalty to increasing this limit, as threads are created only when they are needed. To increase the maximum number of router threads, edit the MailMaxThreads parameter in the NOTES.INI file. Set this parameter equal to 32 or 64, depending on your operating system. UNIX systems don't support threads, so processes are used instead.

DETERMINING MAIL CAPACITY

Notes 3.x administrators report assigning anywhere from 50 to 500 users to a single mail server. Notes 4.0 should result in higher usage capacities. Because server capacity varies according to platform and usage, no definitive answer is possible. You should collect information during the pilot installation (discussed in Chapter 5, "Building a Deployment Plan") to determine an estimated mail server capacity in your organization. Monitor the following statistics to determine the usage pattern in your organization:

◆ Number of mail messages smaller than 1K (probable text messages)

◆ Number of mail messages larger than 5K (probable files or graphics)

◆ Average number of mail messages waiting to be delivered during peak hours

◆ Average delivery time for normal- and high-priority delivery during peak hours

◆ Percentage of time mail server is functioning

◆ Average number of recipients for a single message

These statistics can be tracked using information in the Notes log.

When configuring your mail servers, always allow room for growth. Over time, you will need to add more users and allow users to do more with their mailboxes.

SHARED MAIL

Shared mail reduces the disk space requirements for personal mailboxes. Messages addressed to multiple recipients are stored only a single time in the shared mail repository. Users' mailboxes contain links to mail stored in the shared database. Users never need be aware that their mail is stored in a shared mail database. They can view, edit, forward, and replicate their mailboxes without worrying about shared mail.

Shared mail can significantly reduce the disk space requirements on a mail server, but there is a price to be paid. Creating, deleting, and moving personal mailboxes takes one extra step. You must link new databases to the shared database and unlink mailboxes that are being moved or deleted.

CONFIGURING SHARED MAIL

Shared mail must be enabled by an administrator. The default is not to use shared mail. These are the steps in configuring shared mail:

1. Create a shared mail repository. This is done using the server console.
2. Edit the Shared_Mail parameter in the NOTES.INI file.
3. Configure personal mailboxes that won't use shared mail.
4. Link personal mailboxes to the shared repository.

The router creates a shared mail database and edits NOTES.INI for you. Make sure that the router is running on a server; then enter the following command at the server console:

```
Tell Router Use SharedDatabaseName
```

SharedDatabaseName is the full path name for the shared mail repository. The directory that you specify must be part of the Notes data directory tree. Otherwise, the router can't find the shared database when the server is rebooted.

The router will create the shared database and set the Shared_Mail parameter in the NOTES.INI file to 2. The router also creates MAILOBJ.NSF in the Notes data directory. MAILOBJ.NSF is a database pointer to the actual shared mail database. As there can be only a single MAILOBJ.NSF file, the router can store mail only in one shared mail database. You can always change this database, but you can never have two active at one time.

The Shared_Mail parameter controls which messages are placed in the shared database. A value of 2 tells the router to place all messages in the shared database. This setting can waste space by allowing messages addressed to a single user to be stored in the shared database. This can also cause the shared database to grow very large, slowing mail performance. By setting the Shared_Mail variable to 1, only mail addressed to more than one recipient is stored in the shared database. Other mail will be stored in personal mailboxes.

After you have created a shared mail repository, you can link mailboxes to the database. You can link individual mail files or entire directories. If you are going to process an entire directory, you should first exclude any mailboxes that won't use shared mail. To exclude a mailbox, enter this command at the server console:

```
Load Object Set -Never MailboxName
```

MailboxName is the file name of the mailbox, including the directory, that should be excluded. You can always reverse this setting with the following command:

```
Load Object Reset -Never MailboxName
```

You can link a mailbox to a shared repository with the following command:

```
Load Object Link MailboxName SharedDatabaseName
```

MailboxName can be either the name of a single database or a directory. For example, you could enter

```
Load Object Link c:\notes\data\mail shared.nsf
```

to link all databases in the mail directory to the database shared.nsf.

The Link parameter causes all messages in the mailbox that aren't already linked to another shared database to be linked to the shared database. All new messages also are linked. To link all messages, including those that are already linked to another shared database, use this command:

```
Load Object Relink Mailbox SharedDatabaseName
```

When linking a database to a shared mail database, if more than five messages are copied from the mailbox to the shared database, the mailbox is compacted. See Chapter 17, "Administering Notes Databases," for more detail on compacting databases. To prevent compaction of mailboxes, use this command:

```
Load Object Link -Nocompact Mailbox SharedDatabaseName
```

Mailboxes aren't compacted even if more than five messages are copied to the shared database.

You can check to see which mailboxes use shared mail with this command:

```
Load Object Info Mailbox
```

You can only check for a single mailbox at a time.

DELETING A SHARED MAIL DATABASE

You must unlink all personal mailboxes from a shared mail database before deleting it. Otherwise, users will be knocking down your door wondering where their mail went. To unlink all personal mailboxes, use the following command at the server console:

```
Load Object Unlink SharedMailDatabase.nsf
```

This will cause all shared messages to be copied to the personal mailboxes of all recipients. Because this action can cause a significant increase in the amount of disk space used, make sure that you have plenty to spare before trying this command.

You must wait 24 hours after unlinking personal mailboxes before deleting the shared mail database. This time allows the router to copy documents from the shared database back into the personal mailboxes.

PURGING SHARED MAIL

The Collect server task is responsible for purging messages from the shared database. After each recipient of a message has deleted the link from his or her personal mailbox, the Collect task will remove the message from the shared database. The Collect task runs daily at 2:00 a.m.

The Collect task also can be used to delete obsolete links in personal mailboxes. Links in personal mailboxes can become obsolete when a shared mail database is corrupted. Some messages in the shared mail database may not be recoverable, yet a user's mailbox still may contain links to the messages. The user can't read these messages. To remove these obsolete links from a database enter the following command at the server console:

```
Load Object Collect MailboxName
```

MOVING MAILBOXES

You may need to move personal mailboxes when people change jobs or when a mail server is overloaded. Follow these steps:

1. Make a replica of the user's mailbox on the new server. You should create a replica, not a totally new database.
2. Unlink the mailbox from any shared mail database. Enter this command at the server console:

```
Load Object Unlink MailboxName
```

3. Wait 24 hours after unlinking personal mailboxes. This time allows the router to copy documents from the shared database back into the personal mailboxes, and allows the Collect task to purge messages from the shared database that will no longer be used. Make sure that all messages have replicated to the new personal mailbox before continuing.

4. Edit the Home Server field in the user's person document in the Public Address Book. Change the server to the name of the new home server.

5. Have the user update any location documents in his Personal Address Book.

6. Replicate all messages to the new mailbox.

7. Select the original mailbox from your workspace.

8. Choose File | Database | Delete.

If the user is moving to a different mail system, enter a forwarding address in the user's person document and have the user forward all stored mail to himself.

USING MAIL GATEWAYS

Mail gateways are an unfortunate reality of life. Different mail systems use different mail addressing schemes, have different internal formats, and support different features. Mail gateways have higher administrative overhead and fewer features than a homogeneous e-mail system. Notes mail features lost with most gateways include encryption, nondelivery notices, high-priority mail delivery, and confirmation of delivery to the recipient. If possible, we recommend using a single e-mail system for internal use, whether that e-mail system is Notes or some other system. Notes can directly use any VIM- or MAPI-compliant mail system.

E-mail gateways all work in essentially the same way. A message is treated either as an entry in a database or as a file in a directory. Gateways are responsible for understanding the formats used by the two mail systems being connected. Mail system A writes out messages destined for a user of mail system B to a special database or directory, generally configured by the administrator. The AtoB gateway scans this database or directory, reads any new mail, performs all conversions, and places the message in a new database or directory, where mail system B takes over.

In Notes, gateways are configured as foreign domains. Other e-mail systems appear to Notes as a separate domain. The Notes administrator uses foreign domain documents to specify a particular database to which all e-mail is sent for users of a particular mail system. The gateway program for the other e-mail system must be configured to read this database. In order for this to work well internal to an organization, users of other mail systems should be listed in a "gateway" Notes NAB stored in a different directory from the main Public Address Book. All users need access to both of these Address Books. Non-Notes e-mail users also must be listed in the directory of the other e-mail package. In multiple-mail-package environments, double the amount of work of a single e-mail environment may be required to keep mail routing correctly configured. Directory synchronization is meant to solve this problem.

Directory synchronization is the process of posting updates automatically from one e-mail directory to another e-mail directory. This system removes the administrative burden of keeping multiple copies updated. Some directory synchronization products require that one or the other e-mail system be the master from which all changes originate. These gateways are suitable only for single departments in the process of converting mail programs. If you have multiple departments, each with its own e-mail package and its own administrator, assigning one as the master directory will be impossible. Before buying a gateway, make sure that it will work in your environment.

FOREIGN DOMAIN DOCUMENTS

You must create a foreign domain document for every mail gateway you install. The foreign domain record enables users to address mail to the gateway. Mail sent to users of the other mail system must specify the foreign domain. For example, if you have set up a gateway to Microsoft Exchange and given it the foreign domain name Exchange, to address mail to Peggy Sue, an Exchange user, enter `Peggy Sue @ Exchange` in the To: field.

To create a foreign domain document:

1. Open the Public Address Book.
2. Open the Server-Domains view.
3. Select Add Domain.
4. Select Foreign Domain from the drop-down list box.

Note

Check the documentation that came with the gateway product when filling out the fields in the foreign domain document. Some fields may have to contain specific values for your gateway to work.

5. Enter the foreign domain name.
6. Enter the gateway server name.
7. Enter the gateway mail file. This is the Notes database that will receive mail sent to the gateway.

RESTRICTING FOREIGN DOMAINS

You can restrict the domains that can send mail to this gateway by specifying a list of domains allowed to send mail or by specifying a list of domains that can't send mail. The default is to allow all domains to send mail. (There is no way to restrict who can receive mail from a gateway using a foreign domain document. See the documentation that came with the gateway for this feature.) Follow these steps:

1. (optional) Enter a list of domains allowed to send mail to this gateway.

2. (optional) Enter a list of domains not allowed to send mail to this gateway.

3. Ensure that the correct administrator groups for your organization are specified in the Administrators field.

4. Choose Save.

5. Choose Close.

You must have author access to domain documents to create a foreign domain.

MONITORING NOTES MAIL

Monitoring Notes mail is a matter of configuring the desired mail monitors on each server. Notes uses reconfigured agents to generate mail events and to provide mail statistics. Events are discussed in detail in Chapter 13. Events are generated by the Event server task. The Event task doesn't run by default; I recommend running Event on all servers. To run Event automatically at server startup, add Event to the NOTES.INI variable ServerTasks.

Note

> On servers running both the Event and Report tasks, run Event first, as it's the Event task that creates the Statistics & Events database used by both tasks. List Event first in the ServerTasks variable.

To configure which mail events to report and the database/server used to collect events, you create event monitor documents in the Statistics & Events database (EVENTS4.NSF).

When the Event server task has been run at least one time, you can create monitor documents to monitor Notes mail. To create a mail event monitor, follow these steps:

1. Open the Statistics & Events database.

2. From the Create menu, choose Monitors | Event Monitor.

3. Leave Event Notification enabled.

4. Specify the server for this event monitor. The default (*) causes all servers in the domain to report the specified event. The default is okay for some events; for other events, you may want to specify different threshold values for different servers.

5. Click the button next to Event Type, and press Enter to display a list of event types.

6. Select Mail.

7. Click the button next to Event Severity to display the Event Severity keyword list.

8. Now you must decide which events you want reported. Notes provides five severity levels: Fatal, Failure, Warning (high), Warning (low), and Normal. All events are classified into one of the five categories. Select the categories for the events you want reported. (This is a multiple-selection list; simply click all desired entries.) Table 14.1 summarizes Notes events by severity level.

You can't select individual events for reporting; you must select one of the five categories. You can edit message entries to minimize the number of unwanted or duplicate event reports received. See the next section for more details.

Select one or more severity levels. In general, select only higher severity levels, so that you aren't inundated with unimportant event messages. I recommend selecting Fatal, Failure, and Warning (high).

TABLE 14.1. NOTES MAIL EVENTS BY SEVERITY.

Severity	Event Description
Fatal	No Name and Address Book database found.
	Unable to allocate mail message queue item.
	Unable to locate Name and Address Book.
Failure	Error delivering to <server name> <mail file name>.
	Error transferring to <database name>.
	Groups cannot be nested more than 6 levels deep when mailing.
	Maximum hop count exceeded. Message probably in a routing loop.
	No route found to domain <domain name> from server <server name> via server <server name>. Check Server, Connection and Domain documents in Name & Address Book.

Severity	Event Description
	No route found to domain *<domain name>* from server *<server name>*. Check Server, Connection and Domain documents in Name & Address Book.
	No route found to server *<destination server>* from server *<initial server>*. Check Server and connection documents in Name & Address Book.
	Recipient's Name & Address Book entry does not specify a mail file.
	Recipient user name *<user name>* not unique. Several matches found in Name & Address Book.
	The number of documents and/or attachments in the selected messages exceeds the capacity of your mail system.
	There were too many recipients listed in the message.
	This recipient's public key has been disabled in the Address book.
	Too many recipients. Recipient addresses must total less than 2MB.
	User *<user name>* not listed in public Name & Address Book.
	Your Domain does not have access to route messages to the specified domain.
	Your mail system is unable to complete your requested action.
	*** UNKNOWN ROUTER ERROR ***
Warning (high)	Unsupported use of group name; Cannot send to a Group @ Domain nor auto-forward to a Group.
Warning (low)	A duplicate recipient was specified and will be ignored.
	Invalid SendTo or CopyTo field value.
	This recipient's public key could not be found in the Address book.
	This recipient does not have a North American license.
	You are already sending mail. You must complete sending it first.
	You do not have a mail system specified. Use Tools Setup Mail... to set it.
Normal	Mail held in outgoing mailbox for transfer to *<number of>* users.

continues

14

ADMINISTERING NOTES MAIL

TABLE 14.1. CONTINUED

Severity	Event Description
	Mail submitted for delivery. (1 Person/Group).
	Mail submitted for delivery. (*<number of>* People/Groups). New mail has been delivered to you!

9. Click the button next to Notification Method to display the Notification Type Keywords list. Your choices are Mail, Log to Database, Relay to Server, and SNMP Trap. (SNMP is a network management protocol supported by many network management products, such as NotesView by Lotus.)

Tip

> SNMP products allow administrators to view status and error information on the entire network through a single console. I recommend using an SNMP tool when managing large networks of servers.

I recommend using a centralized collection point for mail events. This plan speeds up identification and resolution of problems. Designate a single server as the collection point for all mail events on a network. The Event task writes all events directly to the STATREP.NSF database on the collection server. Avoid using mail to alert you of mail errors.

10. Select a method for reporting the events. I recommend Relay to Server. For remote servers, use Log to Database. Select SNMP only when you are using a product that supports SNMP alerts.

11. Click the button next to Notification Destination. The value entered here depends on the type of notification you are using. For Mail, the name of a user or mail-in database is needed. For Log to Database, specify a local database. This database should be based on the Stats and Events Report template. For SNMP Trap, specify a server to receive the traps. Be sure to spell the name correctly.

12. Press F9 to generate a brief description of the event.

The Notes administrator must check the Mail Event Reporting database at least twice a day. Consider specifying an agent that will mail the administrator a notice whenever more than three unread documents are waiting in the event reports database.

MINIMIZING EVENTS REPORTED

You can prevent a flood of the same message by editing the message document. Open the Statistics & Events database and select Names and Messages | Messages from the navigator. Open the message you want to alter and go into Edit mode (Ctrl+E). Set the minimum number of minutes between events by editing the Suppression Time field. For Fatal and Failure mail events, I recommend setting the suppression time to at least one minute except for route not found messages. Set the suppression time to at least 15 minutes for route not found-type messages. This setting gives the administrator time to fix any corrupted connection documents or reboot a Notes server (whichever is required). Route not found-type messages are also the ones most likely to multiply quickly, generating an event for each mail message being routed.

MAIL STATISTICS TO GENERATE

The statistics reporter automatically generates a variety of statistics, including the number of dead mail messages and the number of pending messages. Use the number of pending messages as a rough guide to mail performance. If you regularly have several mail messages pending, you may need to change your mail schedule or get a faster connection (if the server is remote).

LOGGING MAIL INFORMATION

Whenever a user is having mail problems, check the Mail Routing Events view of the Notes log. You can control how much information is logged by using the Log_MailRouting parameter in the NOTES.INI file. These are the possible values for Log_MailRouting:

- ◆ 10—Minimal. Logs only errors and warnings.
- ◆ 20—Normal. Logs all minimal information plus transfer and delivery information.
- ◆ 30—Informational. All normal information plus information on individual threads and processes. Provides more detailed information on transfer and deliveries.
- ◆ 40—Verbose. Logs everything.

See Chapter 13 for details on editing NOTES.INI.

TROUBLESHOOTING MAIL PROBLEMS

Gateways are the source of most mail problems. A little planning can eliminate mail problems caused by applications sending out notices. Other sources of mail problems are corrupted NABs or simple human error.

NONDELIVERY REPORTS

Notes generates a nondelivery report whenever it can't deliver a message. Most nondelivery reports are caused by typos in the Address field. Other possible causes include

- ◆ The recipient no longer exists.
- ◆ The recipient has changed names.
- ◆ The person document in the NAB is corrupted.
- ◆ Someone replied to a message that was sent from an application by an administrator using the server console. Because servers don't have personal mailboxes, the router can't deliver mail to them.

Nondelivery reports are returned to the originator of the message, not to the Notes administrator.

DEAD MAIL

Dead mail is mail that can't be delivered or returned to the sender. Mail that can't be delivered within 24 hours is placed in the dead mail pile. When a Notes user generates mail that can't be delivered, Notes returns that mail to the user; it isn't considered dead mail.

Common causes for dead mail include

- ◆ Mail is received through a gateway and is undeliverable, but the return address is no longer valid.
- ◆ The destination server was unavailable for 24 hours. This problem happens on weekends on a regular basis.
- ◆ There is no common protocol between the server where the message originates and the destination server.
- ◆ The message was generated by an application without a return address and is undeliverable.

Configure the Statistics agent to mail you notices of dead mail. Notes administrators should respond to dead mail within two hours. In addition to using a dead mail agent, you can check for dead mail by using the server console command SHOW TASKS or by opening MAIL.BOX on your servers.

You can usually determine the cause for dead mail by checking the message. To open a piece of dead mail, follow these steps:

1. Open MAIL.BOX.
2. Select the Dead Letters view.
3. Open the dead mail.

There are several questions to ask when tracking down the cause for dead mail:

◆ *Was the dead mail generated by an application?* Have the application generate a return address for all mail notifications. Create a mail-in database for use by all applications as the return address for any notifications they send. Mail sent by an application that is undeliverable will be placed in this mail-in database. Notes administrators should send a notice to the database administrator or application designer responsible for the application that generated the errant notice.

◆ *Was the dead mail received through a gateway?* This can happen when mail is sent through a gateway, is undeliverable, and is returned. If the gateway isn't configured properly, the sender address may no longer be valid on its second pass through the gateway. Check the configuration of your gateway or contact the manager of the other mail system.

◆ *Is there a connection document for the originator's home server domain in your NAB?* Mail routing is bidirectional. Another administrator may have created a connection document in a domain that enables mail to be sent to your domain. If you haven't created a connection document back to this domain, the mail router can't return undeliverable mail.

After determining the cause of the problem, correct one or both of the recipient and originator addresses and resend the message. To resend dead mail, follow these steps:

1. Open MAIL.BOX.
2. From the Actions Menu, select Release Dead Messages.

USER CAN'T CREATE OR SEND MAIL

Problems with creating or sending mail are usually caused by either a corrupt mailbox or the user not having added his mailbox to the desktop. A user can add his personal mailbox to his desktop by using File | Database | Open, selecting his home server, and selecting his personal mailbox from the list of databases.

14

USER CAN'T RECEIVE MAIL

Check that the home server listed in the user's person document in the NAB is the same as the one configured on the user's desktop.

SERVER NOT ROUTING MAIL

Use a mail agent to monitor the number of messages waiting to be delivered. Have a notice mailed to you whenever the number of waiting messages passes a particular threshold.

If you're lucky, this is caused by a network problem. The connection to the next server is down and mail is backing up. If you're unlucky, the MAIL.BOX on the server is corrupt and needs to be restored. This problem can also be caused by spelling errors in the server's server document in the NAB. Also check the spelling of the domain name in the NOTES.INI file on the server.

CORRUPTED NAB

If you suspect a corrupted NAB, try running Fixup before resorting to a rebuild. If you must restore the local NAB, create a replica from another server.

USING MULTIPLE NAME AND ADDRESS BOOKS

Notes users can create their own NABs in addition to the corporate NAB provided by Notes administrators. Each NAB must be listed on the NAMES line of NOTES.INI. Notes doesn't treat all NABs alike. The first NAB is the only one used when routing mail between servers. The second and any subsequent NABs are used only for recipient name lookup. Use multiple NABs to

- ◆ Provide convenient addressing for users in other domains
- ◆ Provide personal aliases for common addresses

Don't use multiple NABs to

- ◆ Resolve groups listed in database ACLs
- ◆ Resolve groups listed in server ACLs
- ◆ Resolve groups listed in a directory link file
- ◆ Determine the route to another server

Notes doesn't look in the second or subsequent NABs for server documents, connection documents, or groups. The NABs are searched in the order listed in

NOTES.INI for a full or partial match for each recipient. If a match is found, the current NAB is searched for any other alternate recipients. For example, if a match is found in the second NAB listed in NOTES.INI, Notes doesn't search the first or third NABs for alternate recipients.

To configure a workstation or server to use multiple Name and Address Books, follow these steps:

1. Choose File | Tools | User Preferences.
2. Click the Mail icon.
3. Enter the names of all Name and Address Books in the Local Address Books field.
4. Choose OK.

The NOTES.INI file will be updated to reflect the local Name and Address Books.

Mail Agents for Users

Users have a common set of concerns that you can preempt by providing the following mail agents. These agents are in the MAILAGNT.NTF template database on the CD for this book. I recommend making these a part of the standard personal mailboxes.

To include these agents in your standard personal mailboxes, follow these steps:

1. Copy MAILAGNT.NTF to your Notes data directory.
2. Open the database.
3. Make any necessary modifications as noted in the following sections.

Vacation Agent

A vacation agent is used to notify people that you are out of the office. The agent automatically sends this notice the first time mail is received from a user. You can also set up the mail agent to exclude certain addresses. If you subscribe to Internet mailing lists, use this feature to prevent out-of-office notices being sent to your lists.

To use the vacation agent, the user needs to change the dates the agent runs, enter her own vacation notice text, and enable the agent. The vacation agent is a standard part of a Notes mailbox. To enable a vacation agent, follow these steps:

1. Open your personal mailbox.
2. Choose Actions | Mail Tools | Out of Office.

    An Out of Office profile document appears, as shown in Figure 14.7.

Figure 14.7.
An Out of Office profile.

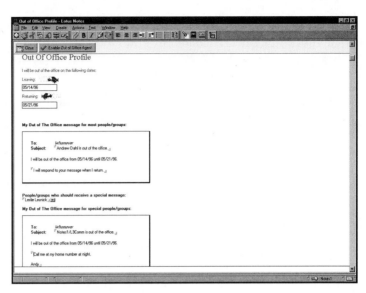

3. Enter a leaving date.

4. Enter a returning date. The returning date must be after the leaving date.

5. (optional) Enter a message that will be received by users who send you mail while you are away.

6. (optional) Enter the names of any users who should receive a special message.

7. (optional) Enter a message for the users listed in step 6.

8. (optional) Enter a list of addresses that shouldn't receive a notice. Be sure to include all Internet mailing lists to which you subscribe.

9. Select Enable Out of Office Agent.

    A prompt asks you for a server on which the agent will run.

10. Enter the name of the server. You must have the ability to create personal agents on the server you select.

11. Choose OK.

You can create multiple Out of Office profiles if you know you will be taking multiple trips.

FILING MAIL AGENT

Keeping mail organized is a universal problem. Finding a particular old message becomes a chore. Your users can avoid this problem by creating one or more agents to file messages automatically in folders. First, the user needs to create folders for each category of mail he receives. Create categories for major projects, for each person from whom you regularly receive mail, or for any Internet mailing lists to which you subscribe. A sample filing agent is included with MAILAGNT.NTF. Each user will need to create agents for his own particular categories.

To create a filing agent for the Key Measurements folder, for example, follow these steps:

1. Open your personal mailbox.
2. From the Create menu, choose Agent.
3. Give the agent a name, such as `File in Key Measurements`.
4. Select the Run option If New Mail Has Arrived.
5. Choose Add Search.
6. Select the condition Words and Phrases.
7. Enter any words that would indicate that the mail message should be filed in the folder. Here you would choose words like *profit* and *cycle time*. The success of this agent depends on the quality of the search criteria. You may need to experiment with the criteria over time to get the best results.
8. Choose OK.
9. Choose Simple Actions.
10. Choose Add Action.

    The Add Action dialog box opens.
11. Choose Move to Folder.

    The program displays a list of available folders.
12. Select the folder to which this message should be copied.
13. Choose OK.
14. Close the Agent Builder dialog box.

Keep in mind this caveat for the filing agent: Running multiple versions of this agent may cause confusing outcomes. If the search criteria overlap, causing a single mail message to be processed by more than one agent, the destination folder can't be predicted.

ARCHIVING MAIL AGENT

Instead of deleting old mail, archive it to another database. Archiving mail to a local database saves disk space on the server (which you may or may not want to do). The mail archive agent is configured once by users for their personal mailboxes.

Here's a caveat for the archiving agent: Archiving old mail to a local disk uses disk space faster. The archived mail probably isn't being backed up. Users still should prune their archived mail every six months or so, deleting unimportant messages rather than simply deleting the oldest messages.

To enable mail archiving, follow these steps:

1. Open your personal mailbox.

2. Select the messages you want to archive. If you don't want to archive any messages immediately, make sure none are selected.

3. Choose Actions | Mail Tools | Archive Selected Documents.

   A prompt appears, asking if you have really thought about this.

4. Choose Yes.

   If this is the first time you have archived mail, a second prompt tells you that an archive database will be created.

5. Choose Yes.

   The program creates a new archive profile document, as shown in Figure 14.8.

Figure 14.8.
An archive profile for a
user's mailbox.

6. (optional) Select Archive Expired Documents and enter the number of days after a document expires that it is to be archived.

7. (otional) Select Archive Documents Which Have No Activity and enter the number of days that can expire with the document not being accessed before it's archived. The default is 365 days. Heavy e-mail users should consider 180 days.

8. (optional) Select Generate an Archive Log Every Time an Archive Occurs. You can then elect to include document links.

9. Click the Local button if the archive database will be stored on the user's workstation. Click Server if the database will be on a server. Archiving mail to a workstation saves server disk space, but archived mail isn't backed up.

10. Enter a name for the archive database.

11. Choose Save Profile.

    A prompt appears when archiving is set up.

12. Choose OK.

13. Choose Close.

The program creates the archive database and enables the archive agent. To edit your archive profile, open the Archiving view in your personal mailbox.

ALTERNATE MAIL TRANSPORT SYSTEMS

You can install Notes and never use Notes Mail. All Notes workstations can be configured to use some other mail transport system. You can tell Notes to bypass its own mail system and use an alternate mail package by following these steps:

1. Choose File | Tools | User Preferences.

    The User Preferences dialog box opens (see Figure 14.9).

Figure 14.9.
The Mail Preferences
panel of the User
Preferences dialog box.

2. Click the Mail icon.

3. Select your mail program from the list or enter the name.

4. Fill in the mailbox name for your mail program.

You still get to use the Notes Mail interface when originating mail from a Notes workstation (although you don't have to do so). Notes uses whatever transport system you specify.

ENCRYPTING MAIL

You can encrypt individual mailboxes, individual messages, or all mailboxes on a server. Mail encryption prevents anyone except the recipient of a message from reading the message body. Message headers aren't encrypted.

For details on how to configure mail encryption, see Chapter 18, "Administering Notes Security."

SUMMARY

With Release 4.0, Notes Mail has come of age. Notes Mail directly supports advanced features such as encryption, electronic signing, mail forwarding, and out-of-office notices. Administrators can set up mailboxes that store message bodies in a shared mail database. Automatic monitoring and alarms also reduce the effort required to keep mail working.

Even with all these features, a little planning can pay off. You should consolidate user mailboxes onto a common server. This can reduce network traffic and increase the reliability of mail routing.

The source of most mail problems will be mail gateways. Mail gateways are programs that transfer mail from a Notes mailbox into a mailbox of another mail system such as SMTP mail (Internet mail). You should monitor mail gateways daily to catch any problems.

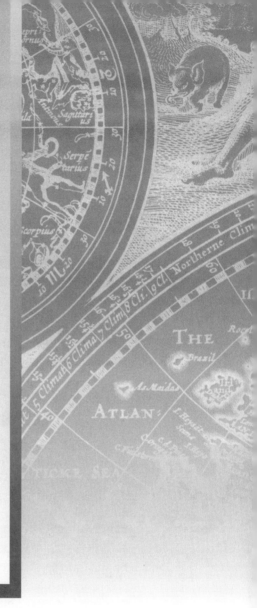

CHAPTER 15

Administering Replication

Replication is the process of updating databases on different servers. As an administrator, you will spend a significant amount of your time monitoring replications and fixing replication problems. A detailed understanding of Notes replication is invaluable when trying to accomplish these tasks. This chapter explains the reasoning behind Notes replication, how to configure replication, and the likely sources of error.

When attempting to understand replication, try to keep in mind the original intent of the Notes developers. Notes considers all replicas to be equal, and by default there exists no "master copy" of a database. When there is no master database, any change to a database will eventually propagate to all existing replicas of that database. The Replicator's task is to ensure that, over time, all replicas of a database are identical. As you venture further from a network of identical databases, the administrative effort required to monitor and correct problems increases. Common variations from a network of identical databases include master design databases from which all design changes originate, and personalized databases containing a subset of the data available in a master database. These examples are covered later in this chapter, following a look inside Notes replication.

INSIDE NOTES REPLICATION

Notes replication has a few traps for the unwary. This section describes the algorithms used during server-to-server replication. Client-to-server replication is similar, with the main difference being that a human generally selects specific databases and initiates replication, rather than having these steps performed automatically. If you are running into problems, following the steps outlined here may highlight probable causes of error.

Release 4.0

The Replicator task should be loaded when the Notes server is started. The Replicator remains idle until a scheduled replication is due or a replication request is received from the server console or from another server. If the replication request is received from another server, the Refuse Replication Requests flag is checked before beginning a replication. The Replicator builds a list of databases on the two servers, ignoring any that have an internal "Do Not Replicate" flag set. In Notes Release 4, this list of databases is kept in memory to speed up this step. The Replicator checks the replication history for each database that the two servers have in common. The replication history contains information about the last time these two databases were replicated.

Next the Replicator scans all the documents in both databases that were modified (changed, added, deleted) since the last replication. For each modified document, filtering criteria determine whether the modification should be replicated to the other database. The filtering criteria involve security settings, including

ReaderNames fields, and all the selective replication settings. Table 15.1 lists each type of modification, along with the security and selective replication settings checked by the Replicator. The Replicator looks only in the primary Name and Address Book when determining security access.

TABLE 15.1. FILTERING CRITERIA USED DURING REPLICATION.

To Replicate...	Security Settings Required	Selective Replication Settings Required
Form, view, or macro changes	Source server has designer or manager access in destination database	Form, view, macro replication is always enabled
Access control list changes	Source server has manager access in destination database	ACL replication is enabled
Deletion of data document	Source server must have editor access (or better) in the destination database; if document has a $Readers field, it lists the destination server	Source server has "Do not replicate deletions" disabled
Addition of new data document	Source server has author access or better to destination database; if note has a $Readers field, it lists the destination server	Data in document passes selection formula stored in destination database
Changes to an existing data document	Source server has editor access (or better) to destination database; if document has a $Readers field, it lists the destination server	Data in document passes selection formula stored in destination database

If the change passes the filtering criteria, the corresponding document (matching Note's ID) in the other database is checked.

Note

During replication, documents are identified by their Notes ID. Every Notes document has a world-wide unique ID. All replicas of a document share this unique ID, which contains enough information to uniquely identify each document and determine its last modification date.

After both documents pass the filtering criteria, the modification dates of the two documents are compared. A replication conflict occurs if more than one user, each accessing a different replica of the database, edited the same field in the same document since the last replication. You can configure the Replicator to accept the last change (discarding at least one of the changes) or flag conflicts for resolution by the administrator whenever a replication conflict occurs. If no conflict occurs, the modification is replicated to the other database. If both databases are in Release 4 format, only the modified fields are replicated. If either database is in Release 3.x format, the entire document is exchanged. When replication completes successfully, the replication histories of both databases are updated. A time stamp is entered in each replica, using the clock on the other server. If replication fails, no time stamps are issued and an entry is created in the servers' Notes log.

This method of replication offers several advantages over systems that rely on e-mail to propagate database changes:

◆ Scalability.

Because replication is handled by a separate bidirectional subsystem, Notes performs better in environments with large numbers of databases and servers. Using an e-mail scheme forces a change to flow through the e-mail system for each database/replica pair in the network. The number of messages rises geometrically with the number of databases and servers on the network; however, the load on the network rises linearly when a separate replication subsystem activates when two or more servers are connected. Lack of scalability is the Achilles heel of systems using e-mail for replication.

◆ Easier administration.

With Notes replication, a source server doesn't need to know about all replica databases on all destination servers, because the source server reacts to a request from a destination server. When using an e-mail system, the source server must actively send out changes to all replicas of the database, so some mechanism must exist that tracks all replicas of a database. Even if automated, this additional mechanism adds to the administrative burden and becomes a possible source of error.

◆ Simplified problem resolution.

Having separate subsystems for replication and mail routing enables administrators to isolate problems more easily. If you are having replication problems between two servers, yet mail continues to be routed between the two servers, you can eliminate many network and configuration problems. For example, you can eliminate the network software version number as a source of error if mail is being routed. Likewise, you can eliminate the server document as a source of error, as the two servers clearly know about each other.

Don't confuse Notes replication with transactions in a relational database management system (RDBMS). If a network connection is lost during replication, updates already performed aren't rolled back. No concept of a rollback exists in Notes. With an RDBMS, partial changes, which may span multiple disk writes, are either completed or rolled back. They are never left partially done.

Now that you understand the basics of Notes replication, examine the ways to configure Notes replication.

REPLICATING DELETIONS

You may wonder how the Notes Replicator knows that a note was deleted. Whenever a note is deleted, it is replaced with a *replication stub*. The replication stub contains only enough information to determine the unique note ID. A *deletion stub* is just another note with a special class. While the Replicator is scanning all modified notes, the Replicator checks all new deletion stubs. Of course, after the deletion has been replicated to all databases, the deletion stub is just wasted space on your hard disk. Notes rids the database of deletion stubs by purging and compacting a database. *Purging* marks the deletion stub as free space and *compacting* reclaims the free space in a database.

One way to get replicas out of sync with each other is to purge a deletion stub before it has replicated to all databases. If Notes replicates with a database containing a modified copy of the note after the deletion stub for that note has been purged, the note is copied back into the database. It's as if the note was never deleted! Care should be taken when setting purge intervals so that all deletions have time to replicate. The default setting of 90 days is appropriate for most databases. Set the interval to 30 days for highly active databases. Even if you are going to use selective replication to disable deletion replication, set the purge interval as if you were replicating deletions. This can save you heartache down the road should you ever want to start replicating deletions.

CREATING REPLICA DATABASES

Database replicas are identified by their replica IDs, not by file names. Although you don't need to force your replicas to share a common file name, I recommend that you do so. No other way is as convenient to determine when two databases are replicas of each other. Using common file names also prevents you from creating two replicas on the same server, something you should never do. Having more than one replica of a database on a server can lead to confusing and unpredictable results.

15

ADMINISTERING REPLICATION

Two ways exist to create replicas. The first is to copy the database file, using an operating system command. For example, you could use the COPY command from a command line to create a new database file. Because the new file is an exact duplicate of the old file, it contains the same replica ID.

The second way to create database replicas is to use the Notes client interface. Follow these steps:

1. Select the database icon from the workspace.

2. Choose File | Replication | New Replica.

   The New Replica dialog box opens, as shown in Figure 15.1.

Figure 15.1.
Creating a replica by
using the Notes client
interface.

3. Specify a server, database title, and file name for the new replica. You must change the server or the file name (or both).

4. If you're creating a replica on another server, you have the option of creating the replica immediately, or at the next scheduled replication. If the other server is connected via a LAN or WAN connection, creating the replica immediately is the best choice. If the server is connected via a modem, select Next Scheduled Replication.

5. Indicate whether the new replica should use the same ACL, and whether you want to create a full-text index for the new replica.

6. Choose the desired encryption options for the new replica. If you're creating a replica on a laptop, you should strongly consider encrypting the new replica. Click the Encryption button and specify Strong, Medium, or Simple encryption. Then choose OK. (The advantages and disadvantages of these options are discussed fully in Chapter 18, "Administering Notes Security.") I recommend using strong encryption and seeing whether performance is acceptable. If you find performance to be unacceptable, create a second replica, using medium encryption.

7. Choose a size limit for the new replica by clicking the Size Limit button. You can specify a 1, 2, 3, or 4 gigabyte limit.

8. Set the replication options by clicking the Replication Settings button. These options are explained in full in the following section.

9. Choose OK.

Notes creates your replica with the setting you specified.

CONFIGURING REPLICATION

You have many options to consider when configuring replication. You must choose a replication topology and a replication schedule. Notes also gives you many ways to customize replication. Most organizations don't need to use any of these options, but you may want to test each option to see how you might use it in your organization.

REPLICATION SCHEDULES

You can specify a time range or a specific time for replication to occur. When you specify a range, Notes begins to replicate at the start of the range and repeats replication after an interval that you specify. When you indicate a specific time for replication, Notes initiates replication at the specified time and, if unsuccessful, retries for up to one hour.

Replication schedules are set using connection documents in the Public Address Book. You can create multiple connection documents for each set of servers, with each connection document specifying a different time range, day of the week, or set of databases. If you use multiple connection documents for a pair of servers, make sure that the time ranges don't overlap. This error can lead to unpredictable results. I recommend using a single pair of connection documents for each pair of servers. Conflicting priorities and multiple time ranges lead to replication problems.

A few examples might help highlight the different ways to schedule replication. Figure 15.2 shows the most common type of replication (in my personal experience)—a time range with a repeat interval. In Figure 15.2, ServerA will connect to ServerB (the home server) at 8:00 a.m. If the connection is unsuccessful, ServerA will retry periodically until either a connection is made or the time interval ends. After a successful call, ServerA waits four hours before connecting again.

Two ways are available to schedule a daily replication. You can use a time range without a repeat interval, or a specific time without a repeat interval. When you specify a time, Notes retries for one hour after a failed connection. When you specify a time range, Notes retries for the entire time range. Figure 15.3 shows how to use a time range without a repeat interval. Figure 15.3 is identical to Figure 15.2, except that the repeat interval has been deleted. In this case, ServerA connects to ServerB only once a day. If unsuccessful, ServerA repeats the attempt until the time range expires.

Figure 15.2.
Scheduling a replica-
tion time range and
repeat interval.

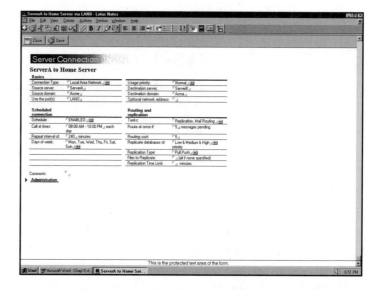

Figure 15.3.
When scheduling a
daily replication, you
can use a time range
without a repeat
interval.

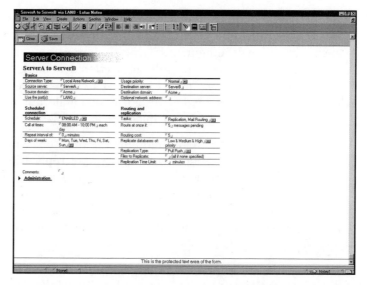

Figure 15.4 shows how to schedule a daily replication, using a specific time without a repeat interval. Use this technique when you are sure that a one-hour repeat interval is enough to guarantee a successful replication.

You also can provide a list of specific times at which replication will occur. Simply enter a list of times separated by commas in the Call at Times field. This technique is used most often for low- and medium-priority databases.

Figure 15.4.
You can indicate a
specific time when
scheduling a daily
replication.

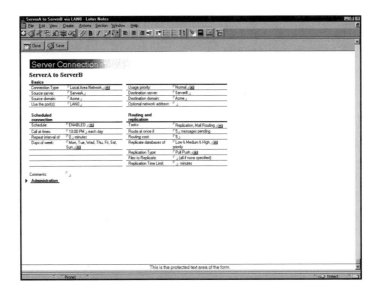

FORCING REPLICATION

You can initiate replication from the server console with the `Replicate`, `Pull`, and `Push` commands. `Replicate` forces a two-way replication. `Pull` replicates changes from the other server, and `Push` replicates changes from the current server.

REPLICATION TOPOLOGIES

Chapter 9, "Designing Your Notes Network," discusses the advantages and disadvantages of several replication topologies. The bottom line is that you should always use a hub-and-spoke topology for Notes replication. When you have fewer than five servers, the hub server also can serve as a database server for users. When you have six or more servers, you should use a dedicated hub server. A hub-and-spoke topology reduces the number of connection documents and thus is easier to administer. In a hub-and-spoke topology, the hub server initiates all replication with the spoke servers. The hub server is always listed as the source server and the spokes are always the destination servers.

When you choose a hub-and-spoke replication topology, you don't have to disregard special cases totally. For instance, you might have a large reference database that exists on only two servers. Instead of taking disk space on the hub server, you can schedule a replication directly between the two servers and specify that only the reference database be replicated. One exception exists to this exception. If you back up databases only from the hub server (as opposed to backing up each server), you need to place a replica of every database on the hub server.

MULTIPLE REPLICATORS

You can propagate data faster by using multiple Replicators. Notes Release 4 enables you to configure up to four Replicator tasks per server. Each Replicator can be updating databases simultaneously with the other Replicators.

CUSTOMIZING REPLICATION

Notes enables you to specify subsets of data to replicate, and you can control whether certain database properties are replicated to or from a database. These options are set using the Replication Settings dialog box and the connection document in the Public Address Book.

Using the Replication Settings dialog box (choose File | Replication | Settings), you can specify these options:

◆ Whether deletions, changes to the database title and catalog information, and changes to the Local Security property are replicated from the source database. By default, changes to the Local Security property aren't replicated, but changes to the database title, catalog info, and deletions are replicated. You can access these settings from the Send panel.

◆ Disabling replication for this database (use the Other panel).

◆ Specifying the replication priority for the database (use the Other panel).

◆ Specifying a CD-ROM publishing date (use the Other panel). The CD-ROM publishing date should be used only when you are distributing databases on a CD. If this setting isn't specified, Notes does a complete scan of the database during the first replication, even if no documents have been changed since the CD-ROM was cut. If you specify a CD-ROM publishing date, Notes scans for changes only in those documents that have changed since the publishing date. This setting can significantly reduce the load on your server when you are distributing large databases on CD-ROM. It also reduces the time needed during the first replication.

You need to specify these settings for each replica. They don't replicate from one database to another. You also can customize replication between a pair of servers, using the connection document. You can specify the replication type, the databases that should be replicated, and a time limit for replication.

The Replication Type field controls whether changes should be pushed to or pulled from each server. Choose from four options: Pull-Pull, Pull-Push, Pull Only, and Push Only. With Pull-Pull replication, the source server pulls changes from the destination server and then sends a request to the destination server to pull changes from the source server. With Pull-Push replication (the default), the source server pushes changes to the destination server and then pulls changes from the destination server. The Replicator on the destination server isn't involved. With Push Only and Pull Only, changes are replicated in only one direction. Push Only replicates changes from the source to the destination. Pull Only replicates changes from the destination to the source. Pull-Push replication is always used for hub-and-spoke topologies and is the default setting.

If you want to replicate a specific set of databases, you can specify the file names in the Files to Replicate field. If this field is blank, all databases in common are replicated.

The Replication Time Limit field limits the amount of time during which two servers can replicate. Simply enter the maximum number of minutes the two servers should spend replicating during one replication session. When the limit is reached, the source server ceases replication. This setting is useful when servers are replicating via modems. You can limit the number of minutes spent replicating during peak hours by setting a time limit. In this case, you should specify another off-peak connection document with no time limit, to guarantee that all changes are replicated within a day's time.

You also can customize replication by using selective replication, which is covered in the next section.

SELECTIVE REPLICATION

Selective replication copies portions of a source database to a destination database. One often unexpected side effect of selective replication is the deletion of documents in the source database. Selective replication deletes any documents that don't pass the selection formula for a database, and it doesn't just filter incoming documents—it deletes documents from the database containing the selection formula. Only documents modified since the selection formula was changed are affected, because the Replicator only processes documents that have been modified since the last replication. Think of selective replication as a method of pruning a database, not as a way of copying subsets of data. Any application using selective replication should ensure that any document created in a database passes the selection formula. Otherwise, your users will surely wonder why their data is being deleted.

Selective replication enables you to

◆ Independently enable/disable replication of views, forms, macros, and access control lists.

◆ Disable replication of deletions from the source database.

◆ Prune the data stored in a database, using arbitrary criteria. This option also reduces the amount of network traffic generated during replication.

◆ Truncate large documents and attachments. Use this setting to reduce the network traffic and disk space required for replicas.

Although selective replication appears to be a good way to create personalized databases, I don't recommend using it this way. Besides the overhead of creating a selection formula for each person, it's just too easy to end up with deleted documents. Use selective replication to disable the replication of views, forms, macros, and ACLs. Use design templates instead to replicate design changes.

To set up selective replication, you use the Replication Settings dialog box. Follow these steps:

1. Select the database icon from the workspace.

2. Choose File | Replication | Settings.

   The Replication Settings dialog box appears.

3. Click the Space Savers icon (it should already be selected). Alternatively, if you want to configure selective replication between a specific pair of servers, click the Advanced icon.

4. If you are specifying selective replication for a pair of servers, specify the source and destination servers using the When Computer and Receives From drop-down lists.

5. Select the Replicate a Subset of Documents check box.

   At this point, you need to decide whether you want to replicate documents from certain views, or you want to specify a selection formula. Replicate documents in a view only if you know that you want the documents in that view, and that this situation won't change even if the view selection formula changes. If you replicate based on a view simply to avoid retyping the selection formula, you may need to come back and update the selective replication setting whenever the view selection formula is updated.

6. If you want to replicate documents that appear in a view, select that view from the list of views. You can select more than one view.

   or

   If you want to replicate based on a selection formula, select the Select by Formula check box and enter the selection formula.

7. If you want to control whether to replicate design elements (forms, views, and so on), access control lists, agents, replication formulas, and deletions, click the Advanced icon (if you haven't already done so).

If you want these settings to apply to all servers, select All Servers in both the When Computer and Receives From drop-down lists.

8. Select the desired options under the Replicate Incoming section.

9. Close the dialog box.

REPLICATING DESIGN CHANGES

There are two methods for distributing design updates: replicating design changes directly from source database to destination database; or indirectly, using design templates. Figure 15.5 compares the data flow with these methods.

Figure 15.5.
A) Data flow through a
Notes network that isn't
using design templates;
B) Data flow through a
Notes network using
design templates.

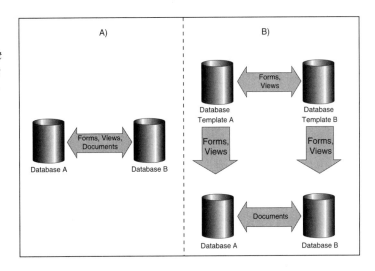

Introducing a level of indirection by using design templates offers several advantages. The primary advantage for most companies is that using design updates lets you set a more restrictive level of security on your databases. If you replicate design changes directly, all of your servers need at least designer access to all databases; if you replicate design changes with design templates, servers need only editor access to most databases and designer access only to templates. As designer access carries with it several privileges, restricting the number of databases allowing this access is beneficial. Of course, if you need to replicate ACL changes, you must give manager access to all servers and can't use this technique.

Design templates offer other advantages not related to replication, because they can serve as repositories of common forms, macros, and views. Design templates are also key in setting up special administrator views in databases, which relies on Notes' capacity for a single database to inherit designs from several templates.

15

ADMINISTERING REPLICATION

If your database design guidelines require the use of design templates, an administrator can easily create a design template containing any special administrative views and macros. To customize a database with special administrator views, follow these steps:

1. Create a new database, giving the database an .NTF extension.
2. Choose File | Database | Information. Select Design Information and enter a name for this template. Check the option Database Is a Design Template.
3. Create any special views, macros, or forms in the new template database.
4. Copy any desired views, forms, or macros to the database you want to customize.
5. Choose Design | Views; Design | Forms; and Design | Macros; and select the new views, forms, and macros from the list. Select Info and enter the name of the design template. Check the option Inherit from Template.
6. Choose File | Database | Replication and check the Selective Replication settings. Make sure that replication of views, macros, and forms is disabled.

You can now use your own custom views, forms, and macros without fearing that these items will replicate to and take up space on every server in the network. The method used to create master design databases is the same as the method for adding custom administrative views and macros, with the addition of two extra steps. Make sure that the master design server has designer access to all replicas of the design template. All other servers should have only read access to the templates on the master server. Any changes to the design made on any server other than the master design server will eventually be overwritten by the design stored on the master server.

Design templates offer benefits both to an administrator and an application developer. I strongly recommend using design templates for all key databases.

DISABLING REPLICATION

You can disable replication of a database with the Notes user interface or with the utility described in the following steps. If you use the Notes interface to disable replication, you can turn it back on at any time. The utility disables replication in a way that can't be undone with the Notes interface, although you can use the utility to turn replication back on. Use the utility when you want to permanently disable the replication of a database. Otherwise, use the Notes user interface.

To disable replication, use this utility:

1. Open an OS/2 command line.
2. Type `ReplSet database_name DISABLE` and press Enter.

To use this utility to re-enable replication, follow these steps:

1. Open an OS/2 command line.
2. Type **ReplSet database_name ENABLE** and press Enter.

Listing 15.1 displays the complete listing of the source for this utility under OS/2. Don't worry if you're not a C programmer. The actual utility is already built and ready to run on the CD included with this book (the executable name is replset).

LISTING 15.1. SOURCE LISTING FOR REPLICATION ENABLE/DISABLE UTILITY.

```
/*
 * Purpose: Turn replication ON/OFF for a given database
 *
 * Usage:
 *    Disable replication - ReplSet db_name ENABLE
 */

#include <stdlib.h>
#include <stdio.h>
#include <string.h>

/* Notes API include files */

#include <global.h>
#include <nsfdb.h>
#include <kfm.h>
#include <misc.h>

STATUS far PASCAL NotesMain(int argc, char *argv[])
{
 STATUS       error;
 DBHANDLE     db_handle = NULLHANDLE;
 DBREPLICAINFO replica_info;

 if (argc != 3)
 {
     printf ("Usage: replica database_name ENABLE¦DISABLE\n");
     return FALSE;
 }

 /*
  * Open the database.
  */

 if (error = NSFDbOpen (argv[1], &db_handle))
 {
     printf ("Error on Database Open." );
     return FALSE;
 }

 if (error = NSFDbReplicaInfoGet(hdb, &replica_info))
 {
```

continues

15

ADMINISTERING REPLICATION

LISTING 15.1. CONTINUED

```
        printf ("Could not get Replica Info");
        NSFDbClose (db_handle);
        return FALSE;
    }

    if (strstr (strupr(argv[2]), "ENABLE") != NULL)
        /* turn replication on  */
        replica_info.Flags &= !(REPLFLG_NEVER_REPLICATE);
    else
        /* else turn it off     */
        replica_info.Flags |= REPLFLG_NEVER_REPLICATE;

    if (error = NSFDbReplicaInfoSet(db_handle, &replica_info))
    {
        printf ("Could not set Replica Info");
        NSFDbClose (db_handle);
        return FALSE;
    }


    NSFDbClose (db_handle);

    return (NOERROR);
}
```

MONITORING NOTES REPLICATION

One of the toughest jobs for an administrator of a distributed system is knowing when a problem is occurring. Ideally, an administrator discovers and corrects any problems before users are aware of or affected by the problem. Products exist today, such as NotesView by Lotus, that can tell you if the Replicator task is alive and if it is reporting any errors. Ensuring that the Replicator task is running isn't enough. Users want access to data, and the Notes administrator must make sure that all databases are receiving updates and that all replication conflicts are resolved.

If you aren't using one of the automated monitors, you should check the Notes log's Replication Events view for each server at least daily. See Figure 15.6 for a snapshot of the Replication Events view.

The Replication Events view displays all the replication log entries in the log. Figure 15.7 shows a replication log entry, displaying the number of documents deleted, added, and modified, along with the total duration of the replication.

Figure 15.6.
The Replication Events
view of the Notes log
shows all Replicator
activity.

Figure 15.7.
A replication log entry
is created every time
two databases are
replicated.

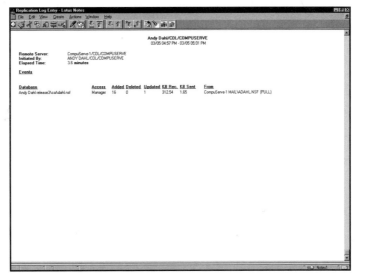

As an administrator, you will save significant amounts of time if, over time, you develop a history for each database in your network. This history should show the expected number of modifications per day/hour/week along with the expected duration time. Any changes in the replication pattern may signal problems. For example, if the duration of a replication declines dramatically while the number of modifications remains stable, someone may have selected Truncate Attachments in the Selective Replication dialog box.

TROUBLESHOOTING REPLICATION

Notes administrators eventually have to resolve inevitable replication problems. The good news is that most problems can be traced to incorrect security settings or incompatible network software. Before attempting to troubleshoot replication problems, be sure you have access to the following information:

◆ An accurate diagram of your network, showing all servers and routers

◆ The ACL for any affected database

◆ The Notes logs for the affected servers

◆ The replication history for any affected databases

◆ The selective replication settings for the affected databases

◆ The Name and Address Book for the domains involved

You should have direct access to this information or the cooperation of someone who can provide this information quickly.

Following is the general procedure you should follow when resolving replication problems:

1. Determine the recent changes to the server or the affected database, and ask yourself the following questions:

   a. Has the ACL changed?

   b. Have any modifications been made in the Name and Address Book to any groups in the ACL for the affected database?

   c. Have any new views, forms, or macros been added to the database?

   d. Have any changes been made to the network?

Note

Even if a change seems unrelated to the current problem, always consider the most recent change first, as it is most often the cause of any problems.

2. Determine as specifically as possible the symptoms of the problem.

3. Isolate the problem. Is only one server or database not replicating correctly (check the ACL)? Is a particular set of servers or users unable to access the server (check your routers or the Public Address Book)? Can you manually initiate either a pull or push replication from the server console (check your connection documents)?

4. Resolve the problem (correct the relevant ACL, install a software fix, update the Public Address Book).

Use the following list of symptoms and possible causes when trying to resolve replication problems. Try to match your situation with one of the symptoms described here. This list certainly isn't exhaustive, so you may not find an exact match with your current situation. Use this list only as a guide for thinking about replication problems. Also, refer to Chapter 19, "Supporting Dial-Up Users," for supporting dial-up clients.

◆ Symptom: No data or views are being replicated to a new server added to the network.

Possible Cause 1: If the servers are in different domains, the servers aren't cross certified. See Chapter 18, "Administering Security," for instructions on cross certifying servers.

Possible Cause 2: The server documents in the Name and Address Book list different network names. Network names must match exactly for servers in the same domain.

Possible Cause 3: The servers have no common replicas. This problem usually happens early in the rollout of a Notes network. Make sure that your application designers and users understand the difference between a database copy and a database replica.

Possible Cause 4: Incorrect software versions of the network software are installed on the new server. Get the latest software requirements list from Lotus and verify that all software is certified for use with Notes servers.

◆ Symptom: No data or designs are being replicated for a newly created database.

Possible Cause: The new database doesn't have the server listed in its ACL. Make sure that the new database has all destination servers listed explicitly, in a group, or in a role.

◆ Symptom: Design changes aren't being replicated.

Possible Cause 1: If you aren't using design templates, the ACL of the destination database doesn't grant designer access to the source server. Make sure that all destination servers give designer access or better to source servers.

Possible Cause 2: If you are using design templates, make sure that all destination servers have a replica of the design template. If a template exists, make sure that the source server is listed in its ACL.

◆ Symptom: Client machines can't replicate databases.

Possible Cause: On the client machines, you have a problem with the group definition for your local servers in the Name and Address Book. If you have servers defined in the group LocalDomainServers (the exact name isn't significant), you must copy this group to the Name and Address Book on all client machines. Remember, when resolving groups for security access, only the primary Name and Address Book is used. Because LocalDomainServers isn't included automatically in client Name and Address Books, you must explicitly copy it into the client's Address Book. If all clients share a replicated Name and Address Book, this isn't a problem. To support mobile users, you must list all dial-in servers explicitly in the ACL of all databases. I recommend using a naming scheme for all dial-in servers and using wild cards in the ACL. For example, if your organization has three dial-in servers, name them this way:

> server-dial1/Acme
>
> server-dial2/Acme
>
> server-dial3/Acme

Add `server-dial*/Acme` to all ACLs. Now you can add new dial-in servers without changing the ACL in every database or requiring every mobile user to copy an updated server group document to the Name and Address Book.

◆ Symptom: Two servers connected via modems no longer replicate.

Possible Cause: You have problems with your modem configuration. Check the Phone Calls view in the Notes log to gather more information. You also should check the connection documents for the two servers. If the servers are in separate organizations, make sure that the proper cross certificate has been issued for each server.

◆ Symptom: Replications are losing the connection while replicating (not including dial-up).

Possible Cause: Does this problem arise at a specific time of day? If so, you probably have an overloaded network. If there is a router connecting the source and destination servers, it is a likely candidate. This is especially true if mail continues to be routed between the two servers. Network groups often are unaware of the unique demands Notes replication places on a network. Notes replication isn't like e-mail or file transfers; it's more similar to a remote procedure call. A packet is sent to the other server, requesting a replication. The server generally will take time to process this request before it sends any data to the requesting server. During this time, watchdog messages are sent to the requesting server to keep the connection alive. On a heavily loaded server or network, these watchdog messages are sometimes delayed, causing the connection to drop. Playing with the settings on the router can often solve this problem.

If none of the situations described here helps solve your problem, visit the Lotus Web site (www.lotus.com) and search their online help reference.

RESOLVING REPLICATION AND SAVE CONFLICTS

Notes doesn't enforce any kind of locking on documents. Two situations can arise where an administrator needs to tell Notes what to do. Multiple users can simultaneously edit the same field in the same document in the same database. In this case a *save conflict* occurs. A *replication conflict* occurs when multiple users edit the same field in the same document on replica copies of a database. In both of these situations, Notes can't tell which change to accept. Instead, Notes saves both changes and marks them for review by an administrator. Notes creates two documents, a main document and a response document, and places a diamond next to the response document. When a save conflict occurs, Notes stores the first document saved as the main document and all others as responses. When a replication conflict occurs, Notes makes the document with the most changes the main document (ties go to the first document saved) and all others are saved as responses.

The database manager for a database needs to monitor the database regularly for conflicts. Dealing with replication and save conflicts isn't difficult; open both documents, decide which change should be saved, copy the correct information to the main document, and delete the responses.

You also can design databases so that conflicts are minimized or eliminated. For example, you can have all edited documents saved as responses. But you shouldn't turn on this option just to avoid conflicts. If conflicts become a problem on a particular database, have the application developer write a macro that handles conflicts automatically.

SUMMARY

Replication is a great tool. When it works, it helps you propagate changes to remote sites, load-balances servers at headquarters, and enables mobile users to work while disconnected from the network. Notes replication contains several features that make it efficient and easy (relatively speaking) to administer. When you configure replication, use the simplest approach. I always recommend using hub-and-spoke topology, even for the smallest networks. Keep the number of connection documents to a minimum, don't use selective replication unless you really must, and avoid changing the default replication settings without a very good reason. If you follow the guidelines outlined in this chapter, replication won't be a burden on your administrative staff.

CHAPTER 16

Administering Notes Servers

This chapter lists all the sundry tasks a server administrator must perform that aren't covered in Chapter 15, "Administering Replication," and Chapter 14, "Administering Notes Mail." The server console and the Name and Address book, two critical administrative tools with which you must be familiar before reading this chapter, are covered in Chapters 12, "Migrating from Notes 3.x," and 13, "Adminstrative Tools." In this chapter you will learn about

- ◆ Server administrator responsibilities
- ◆ Tasks that can be run on a server
- ◆ How to administer remote servers
- ◆ Strategies for backing up a Notes server
- ◆ How to change a server name, domain name, operating system, or administrator
- ◆ How to monitor a network port

Responsibilities of Server Administrators

Server administrators are the focal point of a Notes support team. Server administrators are responsible for coordinating the activities of the various database administrators and application developers who, in turn, are responsible for databases residing on Notes servers. In addition, the server administrator is responsible for the overall reliability and performance of the Notes network.

The server administrator should have a clear understanding of all of the tasks that are running on the servers under his care. In addition to the server tasks that run as part of the Notes server, the administrator should know how to start and stop any add-in programs developed by in-house developers, and how to administer any third-party products running on the server, and should be aware of any agents that are run on one of his servers.

Note

With the advent of R4, tracking agents becomes more difficult. You can limit agents on a database-by-database basis; if you don't, knowing what's running and when is more difficult. Close cooperation between application developers and administrators is essential; monitoring can't be easily automated.

The server administrator must monitor all aspects of a Notes server on a regular basis to ensure reliable operation of the Notes network. Table 16.1 lists the tasks to be monitored.

TABLE 16.1. ADMINISTRATIVE TASKS SCHEDULE.

Task	Daily	Weekly	Monthly
Mail routing	x		
Replication	x		
Modems	x		
Memory usage			x
Free disk space	x	x	x
Swap file size (OS/2 only)	x		
Server capacity			x
Backup server	x	x (offsite)	x (offsite)

In addition to the tasks outlined above, the server administrator should run the database Fixup task to correct corrupted databases as needed. If Fixup fails to correct the problems with a database, you will need to restore from a backup.

Chapter 17, "Administering Notes Databases," and Chapter 13 detail the tools available to the server administrator to accomplish these tasks. In summary, the databases that are central to a server administrator's job include

◆ The Notes log

◆ The Statistics and Reporting database

◆ The server mailbox

◆ The Name and Address Book

In addition to these databases, the server administrator should be comfortable using the Server Administration panel, server console, remote console, and administrative agents.

Other chapters cover some of these tasks in detail. See Chapter 15 for details on configuring and maintaining Notes replication. See Chapter 14 for details on configuring and maintaining Notes Mail.

USING DATABASE LIBRARIES

A database library is a specialized form of a database catalog. The database library is meant to include references to databases that have some common features. For example, you may create one database library for marketing databases and a different database library for research databases. Each reference to a database contains a brief abstract about the database, database title and replica ID, and buttons that enable a user to access the database and add it to her workspace. Users need only reader access to use a library.

You use the DBLIB4.NTF template to create database libraries. The person who creates a library is automatically entered as a librarian and given manager access to the database. Figure 16.1 shows a small library database.

Figure 16.1.
A library of Notes
databases.

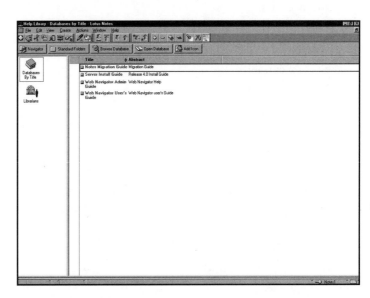

Release
4.0

If you choose to use libraries, specify at least one librarian to maintain each library. The librarian may or may not be the server administrator. Only librarians can add database references to a library; users can't add a database to a library. When a user attempts to add a database to a library, the librarian receives an e-mail message with a reference to the database to be added, enabling the librarian to publish the database for the user.

The librarian for a database should be someone with an interest in or knowledge of the topic areas covered by the library.

To create a database library, follow these steps:

1. Choose File | Database | New.
2. Select Database Library as a template.
3. Enter a server, a database title, and the file name for the new library.
4. Choose OK.

If you are going to create libraries on your server, create a special subdirectory where users can find the libraries. The person who creates the library is given the status of librarian. To add more librarians, follow these steps:

1. Select the library database icon.
2. Choose View | Librarians.
3. Open the librarians document.
4. Enter the name of the new librarian.
5. Close and save the librarians document.

You add entries to a database library in two ways: select and add a database of your own volition, or add a database as a result of a user request. To add a database entry, follow these steps:

1. Add to your workspace the database icon for which you are going to create a new entry.
2. Select the icon of the database.
3. Choose File | Database | Publish.
4. Select the library to contain the new entry.
5. Choose OK.
6. Enter a description of the database in the Abstract field of the new database entry.

You can create a new database entry in a library as the result of a request from a user. You, the librarian, will receive a message in your In Box requesting that you create the new database entry. This allows librarians to control the entries in their library without being responsible for generating all the ideas for the databases to be referenced. Of course, if you choose to deny a user's request, you should respond to the mail message explaining the reasons for the rejection. To add a database entry based on a user request, follow these steps:

1. From the mail message, select the database link for the database to be added to the library.
2. Choose File | Database | Publish.
3. Select the library to receive the new database entry.
4. Choose OK.

Note

If the name of the library doesn't appear in the selection list, you need to add the icon for the library database to your workspace.

5. Enter a description of the database in the Abstract field of the new database entry.

6. Notify the user that you have created the database entry.

As a librarian, you always have the option of deleting a database entry from a library. To delete a library, perform the following steps:

1. Open the library database.

2. Select the database entries you want to delete.

3. Press the Delete key.

MANAGING FULL-TEXT INDEXES

As a server administrator, you may not expect to be involved in maintaining full-text indexes. Full-text indexes are primarily the job of a database administrator, who is responsible for creating and deleting full-text indexes for individual databases. Database managers can also update full-text indexes for their databases. The server administrator can update the indexes of all databases in one batch operation by using the UPDALL server task. It's the server administrator's responsibility to update full-text indexes on a regular basis.

You can run the UPDALL task in three ways: from the server console, from a program document, and from the NOTES.INI file. From the console, you run UPDALL by typing the following command (you can run UPDALL from a program document by entering this same information in a program document):

```
Load UPDALL parameters
```

These are the parameters:

◆ -f

Updates full-text indexes but not database views.

◆ -s

Updates all full-text indexes with immediate or hourly as an update frequency.

◆ -m

Updates all full-text indexes with immediate, hourly, or scheduled updates frequencies. This argument is unnecessary if UPDALL is being run from a program document in the Name and Address Book.

◆ -h

Updates all full-text indexes with immediate or hourly frequencies.

◆ -l

Updates all full-text indexes and views.

◆ -x

Deletes and rebuilds all full-text indexes.

The default behavior for UPDALL when no parameters are specified is to update all views and full-text indexes on the server. The parameters -v, -r, and -c also can be used with UPDALL to update views on specific databases. See Chapter 17 for details. For details on creating a program document to run UPDALL, see Chapter 13.

Full-text indexes aren't updated automatically as the content in a database changes. Updating a full-text index is a significant drain on system resources and should be done during off-peak hours. You can control the update frequency for each full-text index on your server, but you should coordinate the updates with the database managers in control of the databases on your server. You should require database managers to justify specifying an update frequency other than daily or scheduled. This policy prevents database managers from wasting the server CPU by updating full-text indexes during peak periods. You can select from the following update frequencies:

◆ Immediate
◆ Hourly
◆ Scheduled
◆ Daily

For details on each of these settings, see Chapter 17.

The third way that you can run UPDALL is by adding an entry to the NOTES.INI file. When you use the NOTES.INI file, you run the UPDALL task on a daily basis. You can control the time of day when UPDALL runs by editing the ServerTaskAt setting. The default setting is 2:00 a.m.

You also can control whether UPDALL updates views and full-text indexes or just views. To have UPDALL update only views, add this line to NOTES.INI:

```
Update_Full_Text=1
```

16

COMPACTING DATABASES

Compacting databases is primarily the responsibility of database managers. Chapter 17 describes in detail the process of compacting databases. As a server administrator, you need to do the following:

- ◆ Ensure that there is enough disk space on the server to run Compact on the largest database on that server
- ◆ Control when compacting occurs

You can run Compact from the server console, from a program document, or from the NOTES.INI file. Using the console, you can compact all databases or just databases with wasted (free) space. To run Compact from the console, type

```
Load Compact parameter
```

where *parameter* is -s percent.

You can specify a minimum percent of free space that will trigger a database compact. Databases with less internal free space than the specified minimum won't be compacted. You should compact all databases with more than ten percent free space. The default behavior when you specify no parameters is to compact all databases on the server.

You can use either the Database Properties dialog box (click the I tab) or the Server Administration panel to compact a single database. Follow these steps to use the Server Administration panel:

1. Choose File | Tools | Server Administration.
2. Select the server containing the database to be compacted.
3. Select the database icon.
4. Choose Database | Compact.
5. Select the database from the list presented.
6. If a database contains a corrupted view, choose Discard View Indexes.
7. Choose Compact.

Figure 16.2 shows the steps that Notes follows when compacting a database.

Because Compact creates a copy of a database before reclaiming free space, you will need enough free disk space on your server to hold a duplicate copy of the largest database on your server.

You can also use the Compact routine to change a database from Release 4.0 to Release 3.x format. At the server console, enter this command:

```
load compact databasename -r
```

Figure 16.2.
The database compac-
tion process.

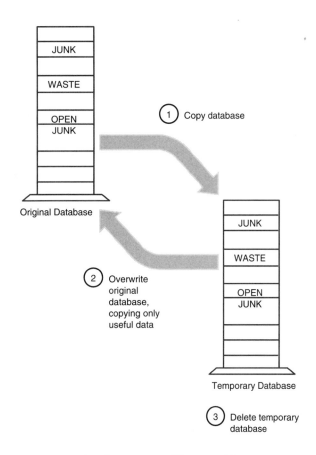

For details on using Compact to revert databases, see Chapter 17.

MONITORING MODEM COMMUNICATIONS

Historically, modems have been one of the most trouble-prone areas of Notes. A significant amount of setup is required to run a modem successfully, including modem files and scripts. The server administrator needs to ensure on a daily basis that modems are functioning properly. You can monitor modems as described in the following sections.

MONITORING MODEM ACTIVITY WITH THE NOTES LOG

The Miscellaneous Events view of the Notes log contains records that can indicate modem problems. By default, only successful modem connections are recorded. To monitor additional information that can help you correct modem problems, follow these steps:

1. Choose File | Tools | User Preferences from the workstation program running on the server or client to be configured.

2. Click the Ports icon.

3. Highlight the COM port corresponding to the modem that you want to monitor. Your screen should resemble Figure 16.3.

Figure 16.3.
Configuring ports in
the User Preferences
dialog box.

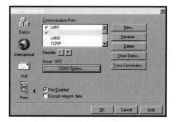

4. Click the COM*x* Options button.

The Additional Setup dialog box opens (see Figure 16.4).

Figure 16.4.
Set COM port options
by using the Additional
Setup dialog box.

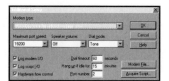

5. Select the options Log Modem I/O and Log Script I/O.

6. Choose OK.

You should check the Notes log for modem problems every day. In addition to the Miscellaneous Events view, you can use the Phone Calls view to see details by individual phone calls.

VIEWING MODEM STATISTICS WITH THE REPORTER TASK

The Reporter server task generates a number of useful modem statistics. To view statistics generated by the Reporter task, follow these steps:

1. Open the Statistics Reporting database (STATREP.NSF).

2. Choose View | Communications.

VIEWING MODEM STATISTICS FROM THE SERVER

You can review the current modem statistics from the console by typing this command:

`Show Portportname`

To view modem statistics from the workstation program on the server, follow these steps:

1. Choose File | Tools | User Preferences.
2. Click the Ports icon.
3. Choose Show Status.

You can configure the Event server task to generate alarms that indicate possible modem problems. For complete details on setting up and configuring event monitoring, see Chapter 13. For details on alarms and statistics specific to modem ports, see Chapter 19, "Supporting Dial-Up Users."

TRACING SERVER CONNECTIONS

You can collect information that will help you troubleshoot connection problems by tracing a server's attempts to connect to another Notes server. The trace connection feature allows you to see the steps taken to connect to a specific server, using a specific port. You can choose to display the trace information and/or record the information in the Notes log. To enable the trace connection feature, follow these steps:

1. Choose File | Tools | User Preferences from the server (using the Notes Workstation program on the server) or workstation you want to trace.
2. Click the Ports icon.
3. Select the port you want to trace.
4. Click the Trace Connection button.
5. Select the server to which you want to connect.

   The Trace Connections dialog box appears (see Figure 16.5).

Figure 16.5.
Setting the information
to be collected by the
trace connection
feature.

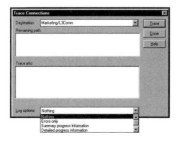

16

ADMINISTERING NOTES SERVERS

6. Specify the information you want to record in the Notes log. You can select any of the following settings:

   ◆ Nothing

   ◆ Errors only

   ◆ Summary progress information

   ◆ Detailed progress information

   ◆ Full trace information

7. Click the Trace button.

   The Trace dialog box displays the steps Notes is taking to make the connection. If the connection attempt is unsuccessful, the Remaining Path box will contain all servers in the connection path.

Tip

Try tracing connections to various types of servers (LAN-connected, different Notes named networks, different domains) to get an understanding of how Notes uses connection and server documents in the Public Address Book.

You also can use the CONSOLE_LOGLEVEL setting in the NOTES.INI file to control the amount of information displayed on the status bar when you trace a connection. See Appendix B, "NOTES.INI Parameters," for complete information on the CONSOLE_LOGLEVEL setting.

MONITORING KEY SERVER STATISTICS

As a server administrator, you must guarantee that your server has enough memory and disk space to provide reliable and predictable service to your end users. These are the key statistics you should monitor:

◆ Server memory

◆ Disk space

◆ Server load

◆ Server performance

Chapter 7, "Determining Hardware and Software Needs," shows the recommended amount of memory for each platform. Memory is critical to the stability and performance of a Notes server; you should monitor the amount of memory being used by a server at least daily, and evaluate your need for additional memory on a weekly basis.

CHECKING MEMORY ON OS/2

To check the amount of memory being used by a Notes server under OS/2, use the `Show Memory` command at the server console. If your Notes server doesn't have adequate memory installed, you should see a large swap file. The OS/2 swap file (c:\os2\system\swapfile.dat) serves as a temporary storage area for programs and data that can't be held in memory. If your server swap file is greater than 2 megabytes in size (the default initial size), your Notes server is memory-constrained. You can probably live with a swap file up to 20 megabytes in size, although any swapping is detrimental to server performance. An OS/2 application server, such as a Notes server, should never need to swap memory to disk. This recommendation is in direct contrast to recommendations for OS/2 workstations, where some swapping is quite acceptable. If your swap file grows beyond 20 megabytes and you feel that you have enough memory in the server, check with IBM to ensure that there are no current problems with OS/2 causing large swap files.

You can view the size of the swap file by using the `dir` command at an OS/2 command prompt or by using the Notes Statistics Reporting database. If you are using the Reporter task, you can look up the size of the swap file in the Statistics Reporting database.

You can also check the size of the swap file from the console by typing this command:

```
show stats
```

The `show stats` command displays the amount of free memory in the `Mem.Availability` statistic. The `Mem.Availability` statistic has three possible values: painful, normal, and plenty. The value of `Mem.Availability` determines the amount of disk caching that Notes automatically configures. The amount of memory that Notes sets aside for disk caching is controlled by the NSF_BUFFER_POOL_SIZE setting in the NOTES.INI file. Under low-memory conditions, Notes automatically shrinks the amount of memory set aside as a cache. The size of the cache can range from 192K under painful memory conditions to 6M under plentiful memory conditions.

You can't increase performance in low-memory conditions by increasing the size of the disk cache. If you attempt to reserve memory for disk caching in low-memory situations, you will, in fact, slow the server. If your disk cache is being swapped to disk, as would happen under low-memory conditions, you are forcing Notes to write data to disk twice instead of once. Notes writes data to the cache, causing a disk write, and then transfers the data from the cache to the actual database, causing a second disk write.

16

CHECKING MEMORY ON WINDOWS NT

Use the Microsoft Windows NT Diagnostics program to view the amount of memory available on a Windows NT machine.

CHECKING/FREEING DISK SPACE ON THE SERVER

For each server that you administer, you should maintain a schedule of anticipated disk space needs. You should be able to anticipate the number of users who will be added to mail files, and the amount of disk space you would need to set aside for those additions. Work with application developers and database managers to track the projected needs of their databases on a monthly basis. Monitor the Notes server's available disk space on a weekly basis to ensure that you have enough disk space to meet future requirements. You can monitor free disk space using the console or the Reporter task. From the console, type this command:

```
show disk space
```

The Reporter task (covered in Chapter 13) collects information on free disk space in the Disk Statistics section of the System Statistics report in the Statistics Reporting database.

Note

For rough formulas that you can use to calculate disk space requirements, see Chapter 7.

If you need additional disk space on a server, you can add disk space or delete items from the server. To free disk space, you can delete or move databases or possibly run the Compact program. System administration databases are primary disk hogs, as they collect historical information. You should consider archiving or deleting sections of the Notes log, database catalog, and Statistics Reporting database.

To reduce the size of the Notes log, you can disable modem logging if you aren't experiencing modem problems. You also can limit the size of the Statistics Reporting database by limiting the number of servers and statistics that are tracked. Limiting the size of the Notes log and the Statistics Reporting database should be considered temporary solutions at best. Even though you can turn off modem logging, eventually you will need to log modem activity again. If you haven't taken the steps necessary to acquire additional disk space, you will spend a considerable amount of administrative effort to solve problems because you can't track modem activity.

Instead of attempting to limit the size of Notes databases, consider moving non-administrator databases to servers with available free space. Chapter 17 details the steps you should follow when moving a database.

You also should carefully review the disk space being used by non-Notes resources on the server. It may be possible to slim down the installation of your operating system and supporting utilities.

MONITORING THE NUMBER OF USERS AND TRANSACTIONS

In addition to monitoring the amount of memory and disk space being used by Notes, you should monitor the number of users and transactions a Notes server is servicing. You can monitor these statistics with the Statistics Reporting database, or from the console by typing this command:

```
show stats
```

The statistics you should monitor are

◆ `Sessions.InUse`

This statistic is in the Communications section of the report. If the number of sessions in use is equal to the maximum number of sessions you have configured for this server, you need to increase the maximum number of sessions specified in the network configuration file.

◆ `Server.Users.Peak`

The `Server.Users.Peak` statistic is in the System section of the report. If peak usage of this server is consistently higher than similar servers within your organization, consider transferring some of the databases or mail files to other servers.

◆ `Server.Trans.PerMinute`, `Server.Trans.PerMinute.Peak`, `Server.Trans.Total`, and `Server.Users`

These statistics are in the System section of the report. Server transactions are a reflection of the number of documents being accessed on the server. If the load on a server is greater than the average load of servers in your organization, consider transferring some databases or mail files to other servers.

◆ `Command.Blocks.Available`

The `Command.Blocks.Available` statistic is in the Communications section of the report. If users are having trouble connecting to the server, check the statistic. A low number indicates that Notes is running out of memory to support additional connections.

16

ADMINISTERING NOTES SERVERS

Monitor the performance of your server by attempting to use different applications on the server as well as monitoring specific server statistics. You can monitor these statistics from the console command by typing

```
show stats
```

or from the Statistics Reporting database (if you are running the Reporter task). The statistics that can indicate performance problems are

◆ `Server.Sessions.Dropped`

The `Server.Sessions.Dropped` statistic is in the System section of the report. Seek to minimize the number of sessions that Notes drops. Dropped sessions could be an indication that the maximum number of sessions is reached on a regular basis, or that you need more memory, a bigger disk, or to move or clean up databases.

◆ `Transmissions.Retried`

The `Transmissions.Retried` statistic is in the Communications section of the report. This statistic is particularly important for dial-up users. Retransmissions are generally caused by noisy phone lines or faulty modems. If you are getting a large number of retransmissions over a LAN, check the network cabling or interface card.

◆ `Errors.Retransmitted.Packets`

The `Errors.Retransmitted.Packets` statistic is in the Communications section of the report. The higher the number of retransmitted packets, the slower your network performance.

CONVERTING THE OPERATING SYSTEM OF A SERVER

Many organizations that use OS/2 as a Notes platform may be considering switching to Windows NT, as Windows NT gains more acceptance and more products are written for that platform. Regardless of the operating system you are currently using or the one you want to use, you can perform the following steps to change the operating system of a server:

1. Back up the server's ID file, DESKTOP.DSK, and NOTES.INI.
2. Install the new operating system and run the notes Install process to place the new server program files on the new server.
3. Replace the new server's files with the three you backed up in step 1.
4. Install any add-in tasks that will run on the new server.
5. Start the new server.

If you don't have two server machines available at a single point in time, completely back up the old server before installing the new operating system. After installing the new operating system, make any custom changes based on your backed-up files.

Tip

> If you suspect that hardware problems are causing your Notes system to be unreliable, set up a new server machine to replace the current machine. Follow the steps in this section, but just use the same operating system!

CHANGING THE NAME OR DOMAIN OF A SERVER

The most common reason for changing a server name is to upgrade a server from flat naming to hierarchical naming. You also may want to rename a server when you dedicate the server to a different task or relocate the server to a new geographical region. In any case, whenever you change the name of a server, you must recertify that server ID. See Chapter 18, "Administering Notes Security," for details on renaming and recertifying the server IDs. Before changing a server's name, be sure that you understand all the implications of a name change. When a server's name is changed, every reference to the server must be changed throughout your entire network. All ACLs, connection documents, database formulas, and LotusScript programs must be checked and updated (the Administration Process can help with some of these tasks; see Chapter 18 for details). Users have to update their database icons for databases on the server.

The primary reason to change the domain name of a server is to consolidate multiple domains into a single domain. Domains are simply logical collections of servers. There are no limitations on which Notes servers may or may not be in a single domain. Servers may be on the same network and be in separate domains; servers on different networks can be in the same domain.

Make sure that you have a copy of the Name and Address Book from the new domain available before changing the domain of a server. To change the domain of a server, follow these steps:

1. Edit the server's NOTES.INI file. Change the DOMAIN= setting to the name of the new domain.

   You also can edit the NOTES.INI file by using the console, with this command:

   ```
   SET CONFIG "DOMAIN=domain name"
   ```

2. Copy the server document from the original Name and Address Book to the new domain's Name and Address Book.

3. Change the domain name for the server in the server document.

4. Edit all connection and network documents that reference this server to reflect the change in domain name.

5. Move all mail-in database documents for mail-in databases on this server.

6. Move all person documents for all users who have this server as their home server to the new domain's Name and Address Book. Update each person document and enter the new domain name.

7. Servers in domains other than this server's new domain should update any remote connection documents that mention this server. Replicate all changes to the Name and Address Books for both domains.

8. Check all your applications to see whether they assume any particular domain names.

9. Restart the server.

REMOVING A SERVER

Administration is easier when fewer servers exist to monitor. When larger, more robust, more scalable servers (like SMP machines) become available and more affordable, you should have opportunities to consolidate several servers into a single server. When consolidating servers, remove all references to servers that are being removed from the network. As with changing a server's name, make sure that you understand all the implications of removing a server before proceeding. When you remove a server from the network, you must delete every reference to the server throughout your entire network. Check and update all ACLs, connection documents, database formulas, and LotusScript programs (the Administration Process can help with some of these tasks; see Chapter 18 for details). Users must update their database icons for databases on the server.

To remove a server, follow these steps:

1. Move all databases to a new server. Follow the guidelines in Chapter 17 when moving a database.

2. Make backups of all critical files from this server in case you decide you need to rebuild the server in the near future.

3. From a different server, edit the Name and Address Book for the domain. Delete the server document, delete the server from all groups, delete any connection documents that mention this server, and erase the server's ID file.

4. Edit the Name and Address Books from other domains that communicated with this server's domain. Delete the server from any groups, and delete any connection documents mentioning this server.

5. Replicate any changes to the Name and Address Book.

Let the server continue to operate for a short period of time, to allow all users a chance to migrate their references to any databases on the new server.

CHANGING A SERVER'S ADMINISTRATOR

You may need to change a server's administrator when someone changes jobs or leaves the company. By planning ahead, and having at least two administrators for every Name and Address Book, you can ease the transition. You should attempt to replace the administrator as soon as possible. To change a server's administrator, follow these steps:

1. Edit the server document in the Name and Address Book. Enter the name of the new administrator and remove the name of the previous administator.

2. Remove the previous administrator from any administration groups.

3. If the administrator's name appears explicitly in the Name and Address Book ACL, remove it.

4. Remove the administrator's name from any server access lists in which it appears.

5. Replicate any changes to the Name and Address Book.

If you are changing the server's administrator because the administrator left the company, you should follow the guidelines in Chapter 18. If the administrator has simply changed positions, you may need to assign a new home mail file. Follow the guidelines in Chapter 14 for guidelines on changing a person's home mail server.

CONTROLLING ACCESS TO A SERVER

Administrators control access to a server by editing the server access lists contained in a server document for that server. Chapter 18 contains complete information on server access lists. In summary, there are four primary server access lists:

◆ Allow access

◆ Deny access

◆ Create database access

◆ Create replica access

Following are the valid entries for a server access list:

◆ The names of users or servers

◆ Groups listed in the local Name and Address Book on the server

◆ Views in the local Name and Address Book

◆ Wild-card entries

If you make a change to a server access list, you should restart the server to put the changes into effect. If you change groups or wild-card entries, however, those changes are recognized without restarting the server.

Only those people listed as administrators in the server document can use the remote server console for the server.

Tip

> The use of server access lists can hurt performance on your server. If you are using server access lists, every access by every user must be checked against each list. If you want to use server access lists while minimizing the performance impact, create a group for each server, containing frequent users for that server. List this group first in all access lists to speed access for users that frequently use a server.

MAINTAINING REMOTE SERVERS

Administration costs are eased when you locate all of your servers in a single office, but this setup isn't possible for all organizations. Chapter 5, "Building a Deployment Plan," provides guidelines for placing remote servers.

The primary tool for a server administrator to administer a remote server is the remote server console. To use the remote server console, an administrator's name must appear in the Administrators field or in a group in the Administrators field for that server. Chapter 13 covers the remote server console in detail.

Although the remote server console is your primary tool for managing remote servers, sometimes you may want to reboot a remote computer or access the file system on that computer. The tools you should consider, in addition to the remote console, are

- ◆ A remote reboot utility
- ◆ Telnet
- ◆ FTP
- ◆ Remote-control software

REBOOTING WITH A REBOOT UTILITY

For many operating systems, you can build your own reboot utility. For example, under OS/2, the SETBOOT command (which can be entered at any command line) reboots the server. You could place the SETBOOT command in a batch file and launch the batch file from a program document. The following code line is an example of a batch file that you could use for this purpose. This batch file reboots an OS/2 server from drive C:.

```
SETBOOT /IBD:c
```

Commercially available reboot utilities are available, such as the Notes Shutdown and Reboot Utility from CleverSoft (http:\\WWW.Cleversoft.COM\Cleversoft). The Cleversoft reboot utility is also available through CompuServe (Go LOTUSC).

REBOOTING WITH TELNET OR FTP

Telnet and FTP are TCP/IP utilities that give you access to an operating system command line and transfer files. If you install Telnet and FTP servers on a Notes server, make sure that they are password-protected and that these servers can't be accessed by external companies. There are several known ways to gain access to a server that is running Telnet or FTP server programs. Notes security can be compromised if non-administrators have access to the operating system and file system.

BACKING UP SERVERS

You should back up your Notes servers on a daily basis. The goal of your backup plan should be to minimize the amount of data lost in a system crash, and the effort required to restore the Notes network to working order.

Unlike most major relational database products (such as IBM's DB2 or Oracle), with Notes you can't guarantee that no data will be lost when a database is corrupted. The best defense you have against losing up-to-the-minute data is keeping at least one replica copy of each database. You can keep replica copies of key databases updated on an hourly basis, minimizing the number of changes that would be lost in a system crash. The replica would have all changes except those that happened since the last replication. But you can't rely solely on replication for your backups, because a damaged database can sometimes replicate its damaged parts to other databases. Part of your backup plan must include backing up to tape.

Tip

In many circumstances, corrupted databases can replicate their corrupted portions to other replicas. Like a virus, a problem with one database can quickly spread to other replicas. The only solution to this problem is to monitor your databases frequently, and keep a non-corrupted backup.

The recommended method for creating backups depends on your network topology and uptime requirements. If you have a hub-and-spoke topology, the hub is a natural place to keep a replica of every database in your network. While this strategy might seem like a natural solution, proceed carefully before blindly replicating all databases to the hub. The hub is often the first server to become overloaded. To maximize your chances of having a non-corrupt database you can use to restore, decide which databases are truly mission-critical, and back up these databases as *infrequently* as possible (to avoid replicating corrupted documents) to an off-site, secure server.

In any case, you may not be able to back up databases directly from the hub server if you have a requirement to provide service 24 hours a day, 7 days a week, because Notes keeps several key files open while the server is running. Even though there are several tape backup products that can back up open files, if you want to guarantee absolutely that your backup isn't corrupted, you must shut down the Notes server before backing it up. Many organizations have backed up Notes servers for years without shutting them down, with no problems. Though there are no guarantees, you can decide whether the risk is great enough to warrant the expense of either shutting down the server or buying a dedicated backup server.

The following list details the basic elements of a backup strategy:

◆ Use a backup utility that can back up open files even if you intend to shut down the server during a backup.

◆ Back up on a daily basis.

◆ Once a week, store a copy of the backup tape off-site, to guard against the danger of fires, earthquakes, and other natural disasters.

◆ Be sure to back up all Notes databases, template files, ID files, and NOTES.INI files.

◆ Keep an up-to-date copy of the Public Address Book available on at least three servers or workstations. The Name and Address Book is the most likely database to become corrupted, as well as the most critical database for the operation of your Notes network. Your Notes network is dependent on having an up-to-date copy of the Public Address Book. In addition to having a convenient copy of the Public Address Book, you also should keep a taped backup.

◆ Have at least one replica of each production database. This strategy is your best defense against losing all the updates to a database since the last backup.

Don't forget to test your restore procedures, using an actual backup of a Notes database. You should test by restoring a database, a whole directory, and a whole drive from your taped backups.

Organizations serious about minimizing downtime of their Notes servers should maintain a *hot backup server* that can be called into duty when a Notes server's hardware fails. A hot backup server is very much like a hub server, except that the hot backup server is available to be a substitute for any other server that fails.

A hot backup server should contain replica copies of all the databases on the network. This setup enables you to substitute the hot backup for any database on your network. A server's identity is determined by the local NOTES.INI file and the local ID file. To substitute the hot backup for another server, shut down the hot backup, replace its NOTES.INI and ID files with a backup copy from the failed server, and reboot the hot backup server. Remember to keep a copy of personal mailboxes on the hot backup server, or you can't substitute the hub backup server for a home server. This problem is especially crucial considering the fact that a home server, a server that stores users' mailboxes, is often the most critical server in a network.

Understanding Server Tasks

The Notes server is actually a collection of tasks that run under the control of the main server program. You can configure the server program to run any of these tasks at server startup, at a specific time, or on command. If you want to run a task at a specific time, you can use the ServerTaskAt setting in the NOTES.INI file or create a program document in the Public Address Book. You also can run your own custom command programs from program documents in the Public Address Book. The types of programs that you can run include

◆ Windows batch files

◆ Notes Server API programs

◆ OS/2 command files
◆ UNIX shell scripts or programs
◆ Any Notes server task

Table 16.2 contains a summary of each server task, its program name, and its purpose.

TABLE 16.2. A SUMMARY OF SERVER TASKS.

Server Task	Program Name	Description
Administration Process	AdminP	Propagates name changes for users and servers. Used for maintaining ACLs and migrating from flat to hierarchical naming.
Agent Manager	AgMgr	Responsible for running database agents for databases on a server.
Chronos	Chronos	Maintains full-text indexes that have update frequencies of hourly, daily, or weekly.
Database Cataloger	Catalog	Updates the database catalog.
Database Compactor	Compact	Reclaims disk space by eliminating unused space in databases.
Database Fixup	Fixup	Fixes corrupted databases.
Designer	Design	Copies changes from database templates to all databases that inherit changes from that template.
Event	Event	Generates server events reports.
Indexer	UPDALL	Updates all views and/or full-text indexes for all databases on a server.
Object Store Manager	Object	Maintains mail-in databases and mail files that use shared mail.

Server Task	Program Name	Description
Replicator	Replica	Propagates changes to databases to other Notes servers.
Reporter	Reporter	Generates statistic reports to the Statistics Reporting database.
Router	Router	Routes mail.
Statistics	Stalog	Generates database statistics to the Notes log.
Stats	Stats	Used at the console with the Show Stats command to view current server statistics.

Chapter 13 gives complete details on how to run these tasks from program documents, the NOTES.INI file, and the server console.

SWITCHING SERVER IDS

The Notes workstation program defaults to the server ID when used on a Notes server. An administrator may wish to switch to his administrative ID to read or send mail, as a requirement for using some applications, or to maintain a correct audit trail. You could switch IDs for a single session or permanently.

To use your own ID, choose File | Tools | Switch ID and select your personal ID file. When you have completed your task, remember to switch back to the server ID.

You can permanently change the default ID for the workstation program on a server by editing the NOTES.INI file. You may want to do this if the administrator is using a server as his workstation (not recommended) or if a particular administrator often needs to switch IDs at a server. To specify a different default ID for the workstation program, add the following lines to the NOTES.INI file:

```
ServerKeyFileName=Server.ID
KeyFileName=User.ID
```

Where *Server.ID* is the server ID file and *User.ID* is the administrator's ID file.

On a Macintosh, specify the path. For example:

```
KeyFileName=NOTES:ADAHL.ID
```

On UNIX, specify the full path and name for the ID name. For example:

```
KeyFileName=\HOME\NOTES\SERVER.ID
```

On NetWare, specify the mapped network drive corresponding to the directory containing the ID file. For example:

`KeyFileName=G:\NOTES1.ID`

On Windows, specify the full path and file name, including the drive letter. For example:

`KeyFileName=C:\NOTES\USER.ID`

On OS/2, specify the path, file name, and drive letter. For example:

`KeyFileName=C:\NOTES\DATA\USER.ID`

Note

See Chapter 13 for ways to edit the NOTES.INI file.

CATALOGING DATABASES IN A DOMAIN

You can use the catalog server process in conjunction with the database catalog (CATALOG.NSF) to build a list of all databases in a domain. The catalog server task runs, by default, at 1:00 a.m. every day. The catalog server task scans all databases on the server, deletes entries from the database catalog for any databases that have been deleted from the server, and adds entries to the database catalog for new databases. Database managers and designers can prevent a database from being listed in a catalog by using the Design Property dialog box. Follow these steps:

1. Open the database from your workspace.
2. Choose Design | Design Properties.

   The Design Properties dialog box opens.
3. Select Database from the drop-down list.
4. Click the Design tab. You should see the dialog box in Figure 16.6.

Figure 16.6.
The Design tab of the
Database Properties
dialog box.

5. Deselect the List in Database Catalog check box.

As a server administrator, you should coordinate the contents of the database catalog with the individual database managers in your organization. If a database catalog grows to an unusable size, screen out databases that don't need to be in a catalog.

To create a catalog of databases in an entire domain, create replicas of the database catalog on every server in the domain.

Don't use the database catalog as your sole notice to users that a database is going to be moved or deleted. See Chapter 17 for details on moving Notes databases.

Summary

The server administrator is the coordinator of all activities for your Notes servers. Other administrators, database managers, and certifiers should coordinate their activities through the server administrator. The server administrator is responsible for maintaining a reliable Notes network.

The server administrator needs to back up the server regularly, monitor access to the server, and update the design of databases, with input from application developers.

The next two chapters detail the responsibilities of database administrators and certifiers. A Notes server administrator should have an understanding of every task that a database administrator or certifier performs.

16

Administering Notes Servers

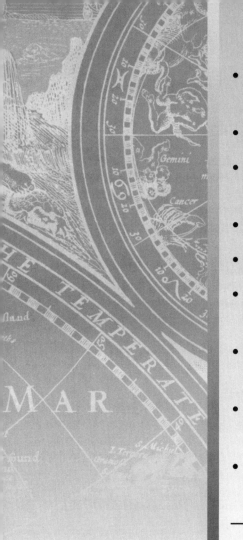

CHAPTER 17

Administering Notes Databases

Each database should have a database manager assigned to it. The database manager is responsible for the maintenance of the database. The database manager is responsible for these tasks:

◆ Controlling access to the database

◆ Creating replicas of the database

◆ Monitoring database usage, size, and so on

◆ Deleting or moving the database

◆ Installing and updating the database

Chapter 8, "Preparing Your Organization," discusses the role of database manager in detail. This chapter shows you how to carry out database manager tasks. Security tasks such as changing the access control list are covered in Chapter 18, "Administering Notes Security."

INSTALLING A NEW DATABASE

You should have a well-defined process for installing new databases on your production servers. This process should be written and available through a Notes database to your application designers, administrators, and users. Chapter 8 covers in detail a recommended process for installing new databases. This chapter will simply summarize the steps that you should follow.

Installing a database on your production servers involves all of the following tasks:

◆ Design reviews. Reviewing the database for conformance to standards and getting the approval of users.

◆ Complete environment testing. Testing the database in the actual production environment.

◆ Setting the access control list and other security settings. Be sure to have an administrator create any groups needed for this database.

◆ Creating all replicas of your database. If you are using a backup server, remember to create a replica of the database on your backup server. If you need a replica on another production server, don't forget to place a replica on the hub server.

◆ Creating replicas for any design templates involved.

◆ Making sure that you have configured any Address Book settings, especially mail-in database documents. If the application uses e-mail anywhere, create a database to receive undeliverable mail sent by this application. Create a mail-in database document in the Public Address Book for the dead mail database. The database manager is responsible for regularly checking the dead mail database for the application.

◆ Notifying users of the new database through the use of mail, a database catalog, or your own company database listing.

◆ Distributing any encryption keys that are used by the application.

◆ Providing training to your users and help desk on the new application.

Keep in mind that the amount of testing that each application gets is dependent upon the importance of the application. If you work in a large organization, you may allow a large number of users and application designers to create their own databases. It is quite possible that not all groups will use the same process. However, your important databases and critical applications should go through a formal release process.

PURGING DATABASES

Purging a database is the process of removing old documents. The Purge server task removes old documents and deletion stubs from the database. The *purge interval* controls both the number of times Purge is used on a database and the minimum age of documents that will be removed. Purge runs against a database every one-third of the purge interval and removes all documents and deletion stubs older than the purge interval. For example, if you set the purge interval at nine days, Purge is run against this database every three days, and any documents or deletion stubs older than nine days will be deleted each time Purge runs. Make sure that your purge interval is long enough to guarantee that deletion stubs have replicated to all other servers. You can set the purge interval independently for each database.

Keep in mind that Purge runs against all documents in a database. If you have a database that mixes highly dynamic data with reference information that doesn't change, Purge will delete your reference information, making the database less useful. As an administrator, you have the option of disabling Purge and/or running Purge only against deletion stubs. You cannot prevent specific documents from being purged. Because of this limitation, you should not mix static and dynamic information in a single database.

You set the purge interval for a database by using the Database Properties dialog box. The Database Properties dialog box is the central management point for a database while using the Notes client.

To set the purge interval for a database, follow these steps:

1. Click the database icon on the workspace.

2. Right-click the database icon to open the Database Properties dialog box.

3. Click the Basics tab.

4. Click the Replication Settings button.

   The Replications Settings dialog box appears, as shown in Figure 17.1.

Figure 17.1.
Use the Replication
Settings dialog box to
view or change replica-
tion settings.

5. Select the Remove Documents Not Modified check box.

6. Enter the purge interval that you want for this database in the Days entry field.

7. Select the appropriate action that should be taken when a document is to be purged. If you don't want the purging process to delete documents, just to remove deletion stubs, deselect the Remove Document Not Modified check box.

8. Choose OK.

A purge interval of 90 days, the default setting, is adequate for most databases. Use a shorter interval if the database is growing and performance problems due to large indexes are causing complaints.

COMPACTING DATABASES

Over time, as you add or delete documents from a database, white space creeps into your database. This space causes the database to be larger than it otherwise needs to be. *Compacting* is the process of reclaiming the white space. For example, when a document is deleted, it is replaced with a deletion stub. The space used by the original document is now wasted. It is unlikely that another document will be created that exactly fills the wasted space. Over time, small unused chunks of wasted space appear in a database. Compacting a database removes this wasted space. The most active databases are the ones that need the most compacting. The Notes log and Public Address Book are prime examples.

You can compact a database either from the desktop or on a Notes server. By default, the Compact task is configured to run as one of your nightly jobs. You should run Compact at least once a month.

When Notes compacts a database, it first makes a duplicate copy of the database, so you must have at least enough disk space to hold two copies of the database. Compact then copies useful information from the copy back to the original database and throws away any excess. The temporary copy is then deleted.

Compact can run only against closed databases, which means that you must shut down the server to compact these databases. A database that is in use either by the Notes server or by a user cannot be compacted. If a user attempts to open a database while it is being compacted, he will get a message indicating that the database is being compacted. When building your server schedule, be sure to schedule the compacting process during your off-peak hours to minimize conflict with end users. Check with your Notes administrator to see if she has configured Compact to run automatically at night. (This is usually the case.) In this event, all you need to do is make sure that your database is being compacted anytime it has more than 10 percent white space.

Note

Server administrators need to remember that certain databases kept open all the time, such as the Address Book and log, can't be compacted while the Notes server is running. In this case, the administrator would need to shut down the server, start up the workstation on the server machine, compact these databases manually, and then restart the server. (I repeatedly emphasize the point about not compacting open databases throughout this book; attempting to compact open databases is often the cause of overnight tasks not running correctly.)

To compact a Notes database from the desktop, follow these steps:

1. Click the database icon.
2. Right-click the database icon to display the Database Properties dialog box.
3. Click the Info tab.
4. Select the Percent Used button. If the Percentage Used statistic for a database falls below 90 percent (10 percent space wasted), you will want to compact the database.
5. Click the Compact button to compact the database.

See Chapter 16, "Administering Notes Servers," for details on scheduling the Compact server task.

You can also use the Server Administration panel to compact a database. This is the procedure:

1. Choose File | Tools | Server Administration.

    The Server Administration panel appears.

2. Select the server that hosts the database you want to compact.

3. Click the database icon.

4. Choose Compact Database.

    A file selection dialog box appears.

5. Select the database to be compacted.

6. Choose Compact.

7. Repeat steps 5 and 6 for any other database you want to compact.

8. Choose Done.

One side effect of compacting a Notes Release 3.x format database is that the database is converted to Release 4.0 format. Give your Release 3.x databases an extension of .NS3 to prevent Compact from changing the format.

You also can use the Compact command to revert a Release 4 format database to Release 3 format. Enter the following command to change a database to Release 3 format:

```
Load Compact DatabaseFileName -r
```

MANAGING INDEXES

Every view or folder for your database is backed up by an index. The view or folder displays the information currently in the index. If you want your users to view up-to-date information, you need to keep your indexes updated.

Building indexes is one of the most server-intensive tasks in Notes, but you have some options for updating indexes:

◆ Update all indexes on all databases automatically overnight, using the UPDALL task (the typical method).

◆ Have an index updated automatically every time a user accesses it.

◆ Have an index updated automatically every time a user accesses it—but no more often than once in a set number of hours, where you can choose the number of hours.

◆ Have the index updated manually.

You can use any combination of these settings. (Note here that I am talking about indexes for use in folders, not for full-text searching.) You can set the index update properties independently for every view and folder by following these steps:

1. Open the design for the view.
2. Choose Design | View Properties.

   The View Properties dialog box opens.
3. Click the Advanced tab (the icon looks like a hat with a propeller).
4. Select the desired setting from the Refresh Field drop-down list.

To build an index from the server console, type this command at the server console:

```
Load UPDALL databasename
```

Pay particular attention to the indexing settings on databases with more than 10,000 documents or with databases that have more than a combined 1,000 additions and deletions in a day. These databases take considerable time to keep updated. If you have them updated automatically at user access, users end up waiting.

MANAGING FULL-TEXT INDEXES

A full-text index is used differently than the indexes for folders. A full-text index is a search tool, not a presentation tool. A database must have a full-text index before you can perform full-text searches on the database. For example, in a Human Resources database of résumés received, assume that you want to find a person who has experience in Notes, OS/2, and NetWare. You would perform a full-text search against the Human Resources database by searching for the words *OS/2, Notes,* and *NetWare*. All documents that contain all three of these words are returned. A full-text search is far more powerful than this simple example. Check your Notes documentation for full details on performing full-text searches. The focus here is on maintaining these indexes with minimal effort.

A full-text search is actually a collection of files stored in a subdirectory relative to the database. If you were to look at the hard disk, using a program like File Manager (under Windows), you would see that Notes creates a new subdirectory when it creates a full-text index. The name of the subdirectory is based on the database name. If the database is named HResources.NSF, the full-text index will be in the directory HResources.FT. All the files comprising the full-text index are stored in this directory.

Tip

A full-text index takes considerable disk space. The more items from the database that you include in the index, the more powerful the searches you can perform. You can include the text from each document as well as attachments in your full-text index. But you will need to balance the disk space available and the search needs for each database.

You need manager or designer access to create a full-text index on a server database. No special access is required when creating a full-text index on your local machine. The only exception to this is if the local replica of the database was created with the Uniform Access Control option selected. In this case, you also need manager or designer access to create a full-text index on a local copy on the local machine.

Note

Notes licenses technology from the Verity Corporation for the full-text search. Verity licenses this same technology to a variety of other database companies.

ESTIMATING THE SIZE OF A FULL-TEXT INDEX

Before creating a full-text index, make sure that you have adequate disk space. A full-text index can be up to 75 percent of the size of the text in your original database, depending on the content of the database and the options selected. The size of the full-text index depends primarily on two factors:

- ◆ The amount of text in your database, as opposed to nontext items such as bitmaps and graphics. If you are going to index attachments, this percentage should be based on the percentage of text contained in your database, along with all your attachments.

- ◆ The full-text options chosen. The options that are critical to the size of the full-text index are Word Breaks Only and Word, Sentence and Paragraph Breaks. If you select the Word Breaks Only option, the full-text index can be up to 50 percent of the size of the text in your original database. If you select Word, Sentence and Paragraph Breaks, your full-text index can be up to 75 percent of the size of the original database.

If you are concerned about the size of the full-text index, the Notes administrator can use the NOTES.INI variable FTMaxINSTANCE to control the number of words that Notes will index from a single document. If you include the line

```
FTMaxINSTANCE=2,000
```

Notes will index no more than 2,000 words per document. The default is 100,000 words per document. See Chapter 13, "Administrative Tools" for details on editing NOTES.INI.

Use the following formula to estimate the size of the full-text index:

$$database\ size \times percentage\ of\ text \times options\ factor = \text{full-text size}$$

where your options factor is .5 if you select Word Breaks Only, and .75 if you select Word, Sentence and Paragraph Breaks.

To create a full-text index, perform the following procedure:

1. Open the Database Properties dialog box by right-clicking the icon for the database.
2. Click the Full Text tab. Figure 17.2 shows the Database Properties dialog box with the Full Text tab selected.

Figure 17.2.
Creating a full-text
index with the
Database Properties
dialog box.

3. Choose Create Index.
4. Select the desired options. (The options are described following these steps.)
5. Choose OK.
6. If you are building a full-text index in a local database, Notes presents a dialog box asking whether you want to create the index immediately. Choose OK.

When creating a full-text index, you can choose from several options. You can create a case-sensitive index, index all attachments, index encrypted fields, and/or choose to exclude selected words. The following list describes these options:

◆ Case Sensitivity.

If you select this option, Notes will index each word each time a different capitalization scheme is used. For example, *Notes* and *notes* will be indexed separately if you use a case-sensitive index. Selecting Case-Sensitive Index can increase the size of your full-text index by up to 10 percent.

◆ Index Attachments.

Text in any attachments is included in the index when you select this option.

◆ Index Encrypted Fields.

With this option, only people with the correct decryption key can search the index. Every server with a full-text index will need access to the proper decryption key in order to include encrypted fields in the full-text index.

◆ Stop Word File.

Using a stop word file is a way to minimize the size of your full-text index, because none of the words in the stop word file are included in the index. Selecting this option can decrease the size of your full-text index by up to 20 percent. Although Notes ships a default stop word file, you can create your own; in the text file, simply list the words that you want to exclude from your full-text index. One easy way to create a customized version of a stop word file is to copy the DEFAULT.STP file and then edit it, adding or deleting words as desired. You will need to copy your customized stop word file to all servers that will hold a replica of this database. Because stop word files don't replicate, if you don't put a copy of your customized stop word file on each server, the indexes on your other servers will be considerably larger than the index on your original source server because the other servers don't remove the words in your customized stop word file from their full-text indexes.

You should be familiar with the words in a stop word file before selecting this option. The stop word file shipped with Notes includes *like, the, and,* etc. You can review the words in a stop word file with any text editor.

◆ Word Breaks Only.

If you choose this option, you can perform searches on a word-by-word basis. This option results in a smaller full-text index, but you can no longer use proximity operators in your full-text searches.

◆ Word, Sentence and Paragraph Breaks.

Selecting this option enables you to use proximity operators. Proximity operators find documents that contain multiple words in the same sentence or paragraph; for example, if you are searching a Human Resources database for people with Notes administration experience, you can search for the words *notes administrator* to find all documents that contain the words *notes* and *administrator* in the same sentence.

Full-text indexes can take a considerable amount of time to create. For very large databases with 80,000 to 100,000 documents or more, a Pentium computer can easily take 20 minutes to an hour to create the full-text index.

Replicating Full-Text Indexes

Full-text indexes don't replicate, but the fact that a full-text index should be created does replicate to all replicas of a database. The servers must have designer access in order to replicate the fact that a full-text index should be created. A full-text index is built on the replica copy when the UPDALL server task runs again.

Setting Full-Text Index Update Frequency

You can set a full-text index maximum update frequency after the full-text index has been created. Check with your Notes administrator before setting the frequency of your index update. The Notes administrator can use the NOTES.INI file variable Update_Suppression_Time to limit the update frequency. For example, the administrator can insert the line

```
Update_suppression_Time=5
```

to limit index updates to no more than one every five minutes. To control the full-text index update frequency, follow these steps:

1. Display the Database Properties dialog box.
2. Click the Full Text tab.
3. Select the desired update frequency. Your options include immediate, hourly, daily, and scheduled:
    ◆ Immediate. This is the default setting, which updates the full-text index (after you close the database) any time a document has been added, deleted, or updated.
    ◆ Hourly. The full-text index is updated every hour, using the server Agent Manager process.
    ◆ Daily. The full-text index is updated every night by the UPDALL task.
    ◆ Scheduled. The full-text index is updated according to a schedule set in the Name and Address Book. To use scheduled updates, you have to create a program document in the Name and Address Book for the UPDALL server task. Check with your Notes administrator before relying on the UPDALL task to update your full-text indexes. The Notes administrator can use the NOTES.INI setting UPDALL NOFULL TEXT to prevent full-text indexes from being updated by the UPDALL task.

Tip

Choose your options carefully when creating a full-text index. If you later decide to change the options on your full-text indexes, you will need to delete and re-create your full-text index with the new options.

DELETING A FULL-TEXT INDEX

You may be tempted to go to the directory and use a program such as File Manager to delete a full-text index. However, if you do, Notes simply rebuilds the index the next time the UPDALL task runs. To delete an index permanently, you need to use the Database Properties dialog box. Simply display the dialog box, click the Full Text tab, and choose the Delete Index button.

MOVING A DATABASE

When a server runs out of disk space, or you need to balance loads between multiple servers, you will want to move databases from one server to another. The database manager needs to work with the Notes administrator to determine when and where a database will be moved. The Notes administrator needs to make sure that proper connection documents are set up so that the database continues to replicate after it has been moved. You have two ways to notify your users of the database move:

◆ Send all users of this database a special mail message that includes a button to launch a Notes macro (you must program this button yourself).

◆ Replace the original database with a "database moved" notice.

No matter which method you use, make sure that your database continues to replicate after moving it from one server to another.

To move a database, you need to create a replica on the new server, delete the original database, update any Address Book documents, and notify users of the move. Before deleting the original database, make a note of the full file and path name. You will need this information to notify users of the move. To move a database, follow these steps:

1. Select the database icon on the workspace.

2. Choose File | Database | New Replica.

   Notes creates a new replica database. You can wait for the next replication to have the new replica initialized, or force a replication with the Replicate command.

3. After a new replica has been initialized, delete the original database by selecting the original database icon on the workspace and choosing File | Database | Delete.

4. For each replica copy of this database, remove the original server from the access control list, and add the new server's name to the access control list. If you are using group names (for example, LocalDomainServers and OtherDomainServers) or wild cards (such as */Server/Acme), you shouldn't need to perform this step.

5. Update the Address Book. Be sure that you have the proper connection documents in place so that the new server can replicate changes to the database. Also, if the database was a mail-in database, you need to update the mail-in database document with the new location.

Of course, you can always skip steps 1 and 2 and use operating system commands to copy the file from one server to another.

These steps are ordinarily performed by the Notes server administrator.

USING MAIL TO NOTIFY USERS

If you know which users have been accessing the database on the original server, you can notify them with a mail message. A "database move" mail message contains some explanatory text and a single button. All users need do is select that button and the new database is added to their workspace. The button has a simple formula that adds and opens the new database.

USING A MOVE NOTIFICATION DATABASE

If you are not sure which users have been accessing a particular database, you can use a *move notification database* to notify users. A move notification database replaces the original database and simply tells the users about the move, providing a button to add the new database to the workspace.

You should create the move notification database after you have already created and initialized the replica on the new server. To create a move notification database, follow these steps:

1. Choose File | Database | New Copy to create a new copy of MoveDB.NSF. Enter the full path and file name of the original database in the Destination Database field.

2. Compose a move notification form and fill in each of the fields that apply. Specify both the location and name of the original database and the location and name of the new database. The formula for the button is as follows:

```
File := @Subset( @DbName; -1 )
ServName := "CN=NewServer/O=xxx/C=yyy";
@Command( [AddDatabase]; ServName : File );
@Command( [FileOpenDatabase]; "CN=OldServer/O=xxx/C=yyy" : File );
@Command( [FileCloseWindow] );
@Command( [FileCloseWindow] );
@Command( [WindowWorkspace] );
@Command( [EditClear] );
```

This formula uses only Release 3 features and works with both Release 3 and Release 4 databases. This method helps when you need to rename databases from an .NSF extension to an .NS3 extension (to prevent the compactor from changing the database's format).

When users attempt to access the database from the workspace, this notification document appears. All the user needs to do is click the button; Notes adds the new database to the workspace and deletes the icon for the move notification database from the workspace.

USING THE DATABASE ANALYSIS TOOL

The database analysis tool collects statistics from all the sources a database manager would otherwise need to check manually. Information is collected from the replication history, Notes log, and User Activity dialog box. The analysis tool collects information about

◆ Replication events

◆ Design changes

◆ Database accesses

◆ Mail messages received

To collect information using the database analysis tool, follow these steps:

1. Choose File | Tools | Server Administration.

   The Server Administration panel opens.

2. Select the server containing the database you want to analyze. (You can use any replica of the database.)

3. Click the database icon.

4. Choose Database Analysis.

   The Database Analysis dialog box opens, as shown in Figure 17.3.

5. Click the Source Database button.

   The Database Selection dialog box appears.

6. Select the database you want to analyze. You can choose a database on any server.

Figure 17.3.
The Database Analysis
dialog box.

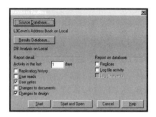

7. Choose OK.

8. Click the Results Database button.

 Notes posts the Results Database dialog box.

9. Specify a results database. If the database doesn't exist, Notes will create it, using the Database Analysis template (DBA4.NTF). You should specify a database on the local machine to optimize performance.

10. If you want to collect information from several analysis runs, select Append to This Database. Otherwise, select Overwrite This Database.

11. Choose OK.

12. Select the information you want to include in the analysis report.

13. Specify the number of days' worth of documents to search.

14. Choose Start to begin analyzing the database. Choose Start and Open to automatically open the analysis database once the collection routine finishes.

The analysis routine can take several minutes to complete.

The analysis report contains the following views:

◆ *By Date.* All information sorted by date.

◆ *By Source.* All information sorted by the server at which the event happened.

◆ *By Source DB.* All information sorted by the database that generated the event.

◆ *By Event.* All information sorted by event type.

Each document in the report contains the following information:

◆ Date and time of event.

◆ Event type. The event type is one of the following:

　◆ *Activity events* track user database accesses as they are recorded in the User Activity dialog box.

　◆ *+Activity events* track user database accesses as they appear in the Notes log.

- ◆ *Data Note events* track changes to data in the database.
- ◆ *Design Note events* track changes to the ACL, views, forms, subforms, navigators, and other design elements.
- ◆ *Mail Router events* track documents that were mailed to the analyzed database.
- ◆ *Replicator events* track the replication history as recorded in the database's Replication History dialog box.
- ◆ *+Replicator events* track replication events as they appear in the Notes log.

- ◆ Information Source. This can be the analyzed database (Replication History), User Activity dialog box, or the Notes log.
- ◆ Source Database. The database from which information in the document was generated.
- ◆ Server. The server that hosts the source database.
- ◆ Destination. The name of the database that received updates from the source database.
- ◆ Destination machine. The server hosting the destination database.
- ◆ Description. A description of the event.

You should add the Analysis Report database to your workspace if you use the same one repeatedly. Set up one report database and collect information from all of your databases in it. If you manage several hundred databases, you will need to overwrite the existing database each time you run an analysis to avoid cluttering the analysis database.

FIXING CORRUPTED DATABASES

Database corruption occurs most frequently as a result of a server crash. Databases that are open when a Notes server crashes can have partially written documents or views. Databases that are open all the time, such as the Public Address Book and the Notes log, are the most likely databases to be corrupted.

Each database contains an internal flag that indicates that it was improperly closed. This flag doesn't automatically mean that the database is corrupted. When Notes encounters a database with this flag set, it runs the Fixup utility. The Fixup utility scans every field in every document in the database, checking for corruption. Corrupted documents can usually be fixed without loss of data, but sometimes a document is deleted. Document deletions due to corruption are not replicated to other copies of the database.

Notes can encounter the improperly closed flag in one of two ways. Notes checks the flag every time a database is opened. You also can have the Fixup utility scan all databases on a server, looking for improperly closed databases. The default Notes server configuration runs Fixup every time the server is started.

Fixup first checks the Notes log and then checks other databases. This scheme enables Fixup to log all activity on databases other than the Notes log. When run at system startup or as a result of opening a database, Fixup doesn't rebuild corrupted views. You must run Fixup manually on a database to fix corrupted views.

You can run Fixup manually from the server console by typing this command:

```
Load Fixup DatabaseName parameters
```

DatabaseName is an optional database file name, including the path. The default is to scan all databases in the Notes data directory tree. Fixup cannot handle open databases, so make sure that no one is accessing a database when you run Fixup.

Table 17.1 describes the Fixup parameters.

TABLE 17.1. FIXUP COMMAND PARAMETERS.

Parameter	Description
-L	Logs every database suspected of being corrupted. The default is to log only actual problems.
-V	Fixup doesn't check any views. This option reduces the time Fixup takes to run.
-I	Check only documents that have changed since the last time Fixup was used on this database.
-N	No purge of corrupted documents. Corrupted documents are left intact so that you can attempt to salvage information. Fixup will need to be rerun on this database.

Fixup logs messages to the Notes log. At a minimum, each corrupted document or view generates a message in the log. You can determine the extent of damage to a database by reviewing the log after Fixup completes.

Running Fixup can take a very long time on servers with large databases or a large number of databases. Running Fixup on hub and mail servers can easily take 20 minutes to an hour. A server is unavailable while Fixup is running after a reboot. This means that if a large mail server crashes, users will not be able to access their personal mailboxes for up to an hour. To reduce the time it takes Fixup to run, run multiple fixups. You can run two Fixup tasks for each processor in the machine. It wouldn't help to try to run more, because Fixup uses a large amount of CPU time. To increase the number of Fixup tasks, set the Fixup_Tasks setting in NOTES.INI to the desired number. Don't set this value at more than twice the number of CPUs in a system.

You should run Fixup manually only when you strongly suspect that databases have been corrupted or when you want to fix corrupted views. You can also schedule Fixup, using a program document in the Public Address Book. Fixup will fix corrupted views when run as a scheduled program. Because Fixup consumes so much system resources, you must avoid running it during peak hours. Run Fixup daily only if you have open time during the night when no other process is running and users will not be accessing the server.

Fixup is your best friend when it comes to corrupted databases. Always start by running Fixup when you suspect corruption. But Fixup isn't the only tool. Replacing a corrupted database at the file level, using a replica, is often faster than running Fixup. If you do copy a replica over a corrupted database, you will lose any updates that weren't yet replicated. You should always keep an online replica of key databases such as the Notes log and the Public Address Book. You can also use replicas as a way to restore documents purged by the Fixup task. Use the server console to force an immediate replication. Pull updates from the replica to the fixed database by entering the command

```
Pull servername
```

where *servername* is the server hosting the replica.

Pulling changes, rather than performing a full replication, will minimize the amount of time taken by this unscheduled replication.

If more than a few documents were purged, you should consider replacing the whole database file.

You can also restore purged documents by copying them from a replica. This technique is obviously useful only when a few documents need to be restored.

FIXING CORRUPTED VIEWS

When a view is corrupted, you can use Fixup (as described in the preceding section), or rebuild the view from scratch. You can rebuild a view from the server console by using UPDALL from the user interface by using Shift+F9 (to rebuild the current view) or Ctrl+Shift+F9 (to rebuild all views), or by creating a new replica of the entire database.

From the server console, enter

```
Load Updall DatabaseName -R
```

to rebuild all views in a database.

When all else fails, create a new replica of the database and replicate all documents from the original database. View indexes are never replicated, so the replica will rebuild all views from the original data. You should create a new replica only when the other techniques have failed, because all documents will be marked unread.

LIMITING DATABASE SIZE

You can set a database quota to limit the size of a database. When a database reaches its maximum size, users will not be able to add documents. The only exception to this rule is personal mailboxes. When a personal mailbox reaches its quota, the router can continue to deliver mail, but the user will not be able to file new messages.

Notes server administrators set the database quotas for databases on their servers, but they should do this only after consulting with the database managers of the databases.

You must be listed in the Administrators field in the server document in the Public Address Book to set database quotas.

To set a quota for a database, follow these steps:

1. Choose File | Tools | Server Administration.

   The Server Administration panel appears.
2. Click the database icon.
3. Choose Database Quotas to display the Set Database Quotas dialog box, as shown in Figure 17.4.

Figure 17.4.
Set limits on database
size by using database
quotas.

4. Select a database from the list.
5. Select the Quota radio button and enter a maximum database size. The maximum must be greater than the current size.

6. (optional) Select the Warn if > radio button and enter a threshold value. When the database size first exceeds the threshold, a warning appears in the Notes log. The threshold has no other effect.

7. Choose Set.

8. Repeat this procedure for all databases to receive a quota.

9. Choose Done.

Consider placing quotas on personal mailboxes. This strategy lets you plan upgrades to the mail server. If you set quotas on mailboxes, make sure that users know how to archive mail that they want to save.

SUMMARY

The duties of a database administrator overlap those of a server administrator. The server administrator can often process many databases at once, avoiding the need to have database administrators deal with a single database at a time. The tasks that can be accomplished by both a database administrator and a server administrator include

- ◆ Building indexes
- ◆ Compacting databases
- ◆ Configuring an administration server

Because of this overlap, most organizations combine the roles of database administrator and server administrator. When these roles are split, administrators must constantly coordinate with each other. In this scenario, server administrators must coordinate the activities of all the database managers who have databases on the server.

The one activity that justifies separating the role of database manager is the need to control access to data. When the database manager's primary responsibility is managing the ACL, a nontechnical manager can play the role of database manager. The best choice in this situation is the manager responsible for the data contained in the database.

Database managers must always take responsibility for monitoring a database's performance, ACL, and replication conflicts, and for fixing a database that has been corrupted.

- Managing Access Control Lists

- Controlling Server Access

- Providing Physical Security for Servers

- Managing Certificates

- Notes Encryption

- Protecting Documents, Forms, and Views

CHAPTER 18

Administering Notes Security

The everyday work involved in administering Notes security, such as managing access control lists, issuing IDs, and monitoring database access, are a considerable part of an administrator's job. Chapter 5, "Building a Deployment Plan," shows you how to plan your Notes network to minimize the overhead caused by the security system. You also should review Chapter 3, "Understanding Security," and Chapter 4, "Advanced Security Issues," before reading this chapter. This chapter details the tasks involved in administering Notes security. Specifically, this chapter discusses

◆ Each administrator's responsibilities

◆ Managing access control lists (ACLs)

◆ Managing certificates

◆ Managing ID files

◆ Handling employee terminations properly

◆ Migrating to hierarchical names

◆ Monitoring access

◆ Protecting database designs

◆ Protecting Notes databases

◆ Protecting Notes documents

◆ Protecting data stored on laptops

◆ Encrypting data

This chapter doesn't discuss in detail the concepts of access control, authentication, and encryption. These topics are covered in Chapter 4. This chapter provides the information you need to actually carry out your day-to-day tasks.

SECURITY ROLES AND RESPONSIBILITIES

Each type of administrator (server administrator, database administrator, certifier) has a role to play in Notes security:

◆ The server administrator is in charge of one or more servers within the organization, and determines who has access to the servers and the access levels allowed. The server administrator controls access to servers along with the authentication used by servers. The server administrator also determines which users have the ability to create and delete databases and replicas. Server administrators also can control access to specific directories in the data tree.

◆ The database administrator's primary responsibility is to maintain the access control list for one or more databases.

◆ Certifiers are responsible for creating user and server IDs. The certifier, because of his ability to create new identities, has the most sensitive position within the administration staff.

In small organizations, many of these roles are played by a single person. You should realize that giving a single person this much power is a clear security risk. Large organizations split these roles among several people. The recommended way of splitting these roles is to give certifiers no other responsibilities or access. For example, a person with access to your company's certificates shouldn't be either a server administrator or a database administrator. On the other hand, combining the role of server administrator and database administrator is okay.

MANAGING ACCESS CONTROL LISTS

Access control lists grant specific privileges to users and control which data replicates between servers. Access control lists are everywhere within Notes. Individual documents, databases, and servers can have their own ACLs. Each Notes database and server has an ACL. If you have 100 databases spread out over 5 servers, your administrators have at least 105 ACLs to manage. In large organizations, several thousand databases are not uncommon.

Managing access control lists efficiently should be a primary goal when designing your Notes network and applications. This section details each of the tasks that you need to accomplish when managing ACLs and shows you how to minimize the amount of effort needed to manage large numbers of ACLs.

DATABASE ACLS

All database-level ACL options are accessed by using the Access Control List dialog box. You administer ACLs in two ways. You can manually change an ACL for a single database by using the Access Control List dialog box, or you can manage the ACLs for all databases by taking advantage of the administration server. The Access Control List dialog box enables you to view and change names and roles, monitor changes to the ACL, and cause all database replicas to use the same access control list. Figure 18.1 shows a typical access control list.

Figure 18.1.
A typical access
control list.

Figure 18.1 shows that Andrew Dahl has manager access and the ability to delete documents. Each name listed in an access control list has an associated type access level and some specific abilities, and may be assigned one or more roles.

Each name in the access control list must be the name of a user, server, group, or the replica ID of a database. In addition, you can use the reserved word Anonymous to specify the access level for the general public. Anonymous differs from "default" in that noncertified users accessing the Notes system are given the Anonymous access level, while certified users are given the default access level.

Notes assumes, unless told otherwise, that names in access control lists use the same organizational unit certificate as the server that houses the database. For example, if the name David Malone appears in an access control list on the server Marketing/L3COMM, Notes assumes that the full name for David Malone is David Malone/L3COMM. If the user is certified with a different organizational unit certificate than that of the server that houses the database, you must specify the full name for the user. Because you can't always know in advance the servers that will house a particular database, you should always specify full names in the access control list.

Although server names can be specified directly in access control lists, you should always use groups to include servers in ACLs. Notes specifies two groups that are meant to control server access to a database. These groups are LocalDomainServers and OtherDomainServers. You add the name of a server to an access control list to control which information is replicated from this database to a replica on the other server. Listing a server in an ACL doesn't affect which information is replicated from the other server to the local database. As with user names, you have the option of specifying just the common name for a server, or the full hierarchical name. To ease your overall administrative burden, specifying the full name of a server in access control lists is better. Using the full name for servers provides tighter security and eliminates possible problems down the road.

Groups are a convenient way of collecting several users or servers, and are a key element in easing the administrative burden. All groups that you list in an access control list must be present in the Public Address Book.

You should never list specific names in an access control list. All users and servers should be placed in groups, using the Public Address Book. Only group names should appear in access control lists. The only exception to this rule is if your organization uses the Memo to Database Manager feature. The Memo to Database Manager feature is a convenient way for any user to send a memo to the database manager for that particular database. For this feature to work, you must specify the user's name directly in the access control list, and the user must have manager access.

ACCESS LEVELS

Chapter 3 contains a complete description of the various access levels that you can grant to users and servers. In summary, these levels are

- Manager.

  Managers have complete access to an entire database, except for encrypted data and hidden designs. Managers have all the rights of a designer plus the ability to change ACLs. Managers can optionally have the ability to delete documents.

- Designer.

  Designer access is meant for anyone with the responsibility of changing or updating views, folders, or forms.

- Editor.

  Editor access is for people who need to create, change, or delete documents.

- Author.

  Author access allows users to create but not edit documents.

- Reader.

  Reader access is for people who need only to view data.

- Depositor.

  Depositor access enables users to create documents, but not view, edit, or change any documents. Depositor access is designed for use with a server's mailbox. The router deposits messages into MAIL.BOX, but isn't allowed to view, change, or delete documents in the mailbox.

- No access.

  As the name implies, users with no access aren't allowed even to open the database.

Each of these access levels can be refined for a particular server, user, or group of users. The privileges that can be set on a per-name basis are detailed in Chapter 3. In summary, the optional settings are

- Create documents.

  Managers, designers, editors, and depositors always have the ability to create documents. Authors may optionally have the ability to create documents. Readers never have the ability to create documents.

- Delete documents.

  The delete documents privilege can be assigned to managers, designers, editors, and authors. Readers and depositors never have the ability to delete documents.

◆ Create personal agents.

Managers and designers always have the ability to create personal agents. Editors, authors, and readers may optionally have the ability to create personal agents. Depositors are never allowed to create personal agents.

◆ Create personal folders/views.

Managers and editors always have the ability to create personal folders or views. Editors, authors, and readers may optionally have the ability to create personal folders and views. Depositors can't create personal folders and views.

◆ Create shared folders/views.

Managers and designers always have the ability to create shared folders and views. Editors may optionally have the ability to create a shared folder or view. Authors, readers, and depositors can't create a shared folder or view.

◆ Create LotusScript agents.

Managers always have the ability to create LotusScript agents. Designers, editors, authors, and readers may optionally be given the ability to create LotusScript agents. Depositors never have the ability to create LotusScript agents.

The following sections detail each of the tasks involved in managing ACLs.

ADDING NAMES TO AN ACCESS CONTROL LIST

Chapter 3 discusses the issue of adding specific names to an access control list. The recommended approach to ACLs is to add only group names to an ACL. The steps for adding a name to an ACL are identical, regardless of whether the name is a user, server, or group. To add a name to an access control list, follow these steps:

1. Highlight the database icon from the workspace.
2. Choose File | Database | Access Control.
3. Click the Add button.
4. You can type the name you want to add, or look up the name in the Name and Address Book. Using the Name and Address Book prevents typographical errors and is the recommended approach. To get a name from the Name and Address Book, click the Person button, select the name you want, click Add, select and add any other names you want, and then choose OK.
5. Set the access level and optional privileges for the names you have added to the access control list.

6. Choose OK.

If you have trouble making changes to the access control list, check the access level of your current ID. You need manager access to change an ACL.

DELETING NAMES FROM AN ACCESS CONTROL LIST

You may want to delete a name from an access control list for a variety of reasons. Always remove the name of the designer that created the database when you place a database into production. You should also remove the name of anyone who has left the company from all access control lists in which that name appeared. The need to remove names of people who have left the company is one of the primary reasons you should avoid listing specific names in an access control list. To delete a name from an access control list, follow these steps:

1. Highlight the database icon from the workspace.
2. Choose File | Database | Access Control.
3. Highlight the name you want to remove.
4. Click the Remove button.
5. Choose OK.

If you have trouble making changes to the access control list, check the access level of your current ID. You need manager access to change an ACL.

CHANGING NAMES IN AN ACCESS CONTROL LIST

The primary reason you will need to change names in an access control list is that the user has changed departments and his or her fully qualified name has changed. For example, when Leslie Lesnick moves from Marketing to Consulting, her fully qualified name could be changed from Leslie Lesnick/Marketing/L3COMM to Leslie Lesnick/Consulting/L3COMM. When a user's name changes, you need to update all ACLs in which the name appears, and recertify the user. You can do this manually, or automatically by using the administration server agent. To manually change a name in a ACL, follow these steps:

1. Highlight the database icon from the workspace.
2. Choose File | Database | Access Control.
3. Select the name you want to change.
4. Choose Rename.
5. You can type the new name or use a lookup in the Name and Address Book. Using the Name and Address Book lookup can help you avoid typographical mistakes. To get a name from the Name and Address Book, click the Person

button, select the name you want, click the Add button, find and add any other names you want, and choose OK.

If the name appears in a large number of access control lists, it's easier to have an administration agent automatically update all ACLs to reflect the new name in the Name and Address Book. Using the administration server to update ACLs guarantees that all changes to the Name and Address Book are reflected in the access control lists for all databases in your organization. To have a database ACL updated using an administration agent, you must specify an administration server for the database. The server that you select must be running the Administration Process. You don't need to specify an administration server for every replica of a database if you have configured your servers to replicate ACL changes. If you haven't set up servers to replicate ACL changes by giving the servers manager access to all replicas of this database, you need to specify an administration server for each replica of the database. To have your database ACLs automatically updated by an administration agent, follow these steps:

1. Select the database icon from the workspace.
2. Choose File | Database | Access Control.
3. Click the Advanced icon.
4. In the Administration Server portion of the dialog box, select the Server radio button.
5. Select an administration server from the drop-down list.
6. If the administration server doesn't appear in the drop-down list, select Other and type the name of the administration server. All servers listed in the Name and Address Book appear in the drop-down list; if you don't see the server you want, check the local Name and Address Book.

The Administration Process automatically updates all group documents in the Name and Address Book, as well as the ACLs of all databases specifying an administration server, with the new full name for the user. The administrator only needs to change the person document for the user on the administration server. The Administration Process notices the change and does the rest. For details on the administration server, see Chapter 13, "Administrative Tools."

UNDERSTANDING USER TYPES

The user types feature enables an administrator to specify the exact type (user, server, group of users, group of servers, mixed group) for each name in an ACL. This feature, while not a true security feature, helps prevent security mistakes. For example, by specifying the type Mixed Group for a name, you prevent someone from accessing a database by creating a user ID with the same name as the group listed in the ACL. This feature doesn't prevent someone with the power to create IDs from gaining access to a database—he could create an ID that's listed as part of the group, and use that ID to access the database. But it does help prevent you from accidentally giving the wrong access level to a user.

You can assign any of the following types to a name in the access control list:

◆ Person

◆ Server

◆ Mixed group

◆ Person group

◆ Server group

◆ Unspecified

The default type for all names is unspecified. The administrator or database designer needs to take steps to force a type to be assigned. You can assign a type to each name manually or you can force Notes to look up each name in the Name and Address Book and automatically specify a type. To manually change a user type, follow these steps:

1. Select the database icon from the workspace.

2. Choose File | Database | Access Control.

3. Select the name in the access control list for which you want to specify a user type.

4. Select the appropriate type from the User Type drop-down list.

5. Choose OK.

If you have a large number of databases, or a large number of names in a particular database's ACL, use the Name and Address Book lookup to save time and avoid mistakes. To force Notes to assign types that match the entries in the Name and Address Book, follow these steps:

1. Select the database icon from the workspace.

2. Choose File | Database |Access Control.

3. Select the Advanced icon.

4. Click the option Look Up User Types for (Unspecified) Users.

5. Choose OK.

Notes looks up the type for each name in the ACL that doesn't have a type. All groups are specified as mixed; if you want to specify a person or server group, you need to manually specify a type for each of those groups.

RESOLVING DUPLICATE ENTRIES IN AN ACL

A user or server may be listed more than one time in an ACL. There are three situations in which this can happen:

◆ A name appears explicitly in an ACL and as a member in a group.

In this case, the name will be assigned the access level associated with the explicit listing. For example, consider an ACL containing the entries Leslie Lesnick and the group Marketing (which also contains Leslie Lesnick). If Leslie Lesnick is assigned editor access and the group Marketing is assigned manager access, Leslie will receive editor access.

◆ A name appears in two or more groups.

In this case, the highest level of access is granted. The only exception is when one of the groups is assigned no access. Any part of a group that is assigned no access will receive no access, even if listed in another group that has a higher level of access.

◆ A name appears in an ACL and in one or more access lists for views or forms.

The access level specified in the ACL always takes precedence over access specified through view properties or form properties. Even if a person is listed as having create access on a form, that person can't create a document if listed as a reader in the ACL.

ACCEPTABLE ENTRIES IN AN ACL

There are four acceptable types of entries in a database ACL:

◆ User names
◆ Server names
◆ Group names
◆ Replica IDs

You can place the name of any user in an ACL. If the user is listed in the Name and Address Book on the server on which the database resides, you can use the short name or the full name. If the user isn't listed in the local Name and Address Book, you must specify the full name for the user. Avoid explicitly listing user names whenever possible. Groups are easier to manage than individual names. You also should use wild cards (for example, */Marketing/L3Comm) rather than individual names. Wild cards are useful only when you have a hierarchical naming scheme.

Servers appear in ACLs to control which data replicates to and from the server. LocalDomainServers and OtherDomainServers are two default groups that Notes provides in each access control list. These groups have manager access so that all servers can replicate changes to an ACL.

Groups can hold multiple users or servers and are useful for specifying access level to a class of users or servers. All groups must be listed in the Public Name and Address Book. Notes needs access to the group document in order to resolve the individual names within a group. You can specify short names or full names for members of a group. The only exception is when a name appears in a group that is in turn included in another group. In this case, you must specify the full name exactly as it appears in that person's ID file. Because of this restriction and the fact that you can't tell in advance which groups will be nested inside other groups, you should always use full names when including them in a group.

Applications must often retrieve data from another database. This is done by using the @DbColumn or the @DbLookup functions. The database from which you want to retrieve data must have the current database's replica ID in its ACL. For this technique to work, the two databases must exist on the same machine, and the database that's retrieving data must have at least reader access to the other database.

Because replica IDs are long sequences of gibberish, avoid typing them into an ACL. Instead, cut-and-paste a replica ID from a database information box to the ACL of the other database. You can determine the replica ID of a database by following this procedure:

1. Choose File | Database | Properties.

2. Click the Information tab.

    The replica ID is listed near the bottom of the dialog box.

You only need to specify replica IDs when the default access for a database is depositor or no access. If the default access is reader or higher, all entities, including other databases, will be able to query data from the database.

MONITORING ACL CHANGES

The database manager for a database should keep track of all changes to an ACL. You can perform this task in two ways: regularly check the ACL log, or have changes mailed to you automatically.

To force all ACL changes to be sent to your mailbox, follow these steps:

1. Open the Statistics & Events database. The Statistics & Events database must have the file name EVENTS4.NSF.

2. Choose Create | Monitors | ACL Monitor.

3. Make sure that the monitor is enabled.

4. Specify the full path and file name for the database you want to monitor (for example, Consulting/Contracts.NSF).

5. Select an Event Severity of Normal to have all changes reported.

6. Enter the mail address, including any domain names necessary, of the person who should be notified via mail. To avoid typographical mistakes, look up the address in the Name and Address Book.

7. To monitor the ACL of all replicas, enter an asterisk (*) for the server name. Otherwise, enter the specific name of the server that you want to monitor.

8. To have Notes fill in the description automatically, press F9.

9. Choose Save ACL Monitor.

To disable ACL monitoring for a database, follow these steps:

1. Open the Statistics & Events database.

2. Choose View | Database Monitors.

3. Open and edit the ACL monitor document for the database and server you want to disable.

4. Make sure that Monitor Disabled is selected next to Enabled/Disabled.

5. Choose Save ACL Monitor.

If you are monitoring a large number of databases and receiving many notifications in your e-mail, consider setting up a mail-in database to receive ACL changes. In addition to setting up a custom mail-in database, you can use the Statistics Reporting database (described in Chapter 17, "Administering Notes Databases").

Even if you are having all changes to an ACL sent to your e-mail or a central database, you need to check the ACL log regularly to prevent someone from temporarily disabling ACL monitoring, making a change to an ACL, and then re-enabling ACL monitoring. To view all ACL changes to a database, follow these steps:

1. Select the database icon from the workspace.

2. Choose File | Database | Access Control.

3. Click the log icon.

   The date, time, and a brief description of all changes appear in the Change History box.

USING ROLES

Roles are useful for controlling access to specific design elements within a database. You don't use roles to assign specific access levels, such as manager or designer, to names. Instead, you use roles in the read or edit access lists for views and forms. Chapter 3 discusses reasons why you may want to use roles. Strictly speaking, roles aren't necessary. You can accomplish the same goals by using groups in the Name and Address Book. These are the advantages of using roles:

◆ As with groups, modifying a role is easier than modifying several individual names.

◆ Roles help the designer remember specific security features that are important to a database. Roles appear in the Access Control List dialog box, but groups appear only in the Name and Address Book.

Note

The author recommends that you use roles sparingly, if at all. Roles aren't useful in protecting the data in a database, only in protecting the views and forms in a database. The only ways to protect data in a database are with access levels and encryption. Because roles aren't useful in protecting data, the administrative overhead involved in maintaining roles usually outweighs any benefit gained from roles.

When creating a role, use a name that reflects the purpose of the role. To create a new role, follow these steps:

1. Select the database icon from the workspace.
2. Choose File | Database | Access Control.
3. Click the Roles icon.
4. Click Add.
5. Type the name of the role.
6. Choose OK.

No mechanism exists for automatically looking up roles specified in the access lists of the forms and views of a database. Always double-check the spelling of a role when you create a new role.

Notes databases have five roles already specified in the ACL. You may want to eliminate these roles to avoid clutter in the ACL. To remove a role, follow these steps:

1. Select an icon from the workspace.
2. Choose File | Database | Access Control.
3. Click the Roles icon.
4. Select the role that you want to remove.
5. Click the Remove button.
6. Choose OK.

Roles are useful only after you have assigned users to a role and used those roles in specific access lists for views and forms. To assign users to roles, follow these steps:

1. Select the icon from the workspace.
2. Choose File | Database | Access Control.
3. Select a name to be added.
4. Select the roles to be assigned to this name. A check mark appears next to each role as you select it.
5. Repeat steps 3 and 4 for each name to be assigned one or more roles.
6. Choose OK.

You use the same process to delete users from roles, except that you deselect users in step 4.

No easy mechanism exists for viewing the names assigned to a specific role. Instead, you must review each name in an ACL to determine if it is part of a role. To view the members of a specific role, follow these steps:

1. Select the database icon from the workspace.
2. Choose File | Database | Access Control.
3. Select a name in the ACL. All roles assigned to this name have a check mark.
4. Repeat step 3 for each name in the access control list.
5. Choose OK.

USING THE DEFAULT ACLS

Notes provides a default ACL for every database. The default ACL specified by Notes may not be appropriate for your organization. Chapter 5 shows how to develop an ACL that's right for your organization. Most organizations could benefit by using the following default ACL (covered in detail in Chapter 5):

- Terminations
- Administrators
- Managers
- Default
- Anonymous
- OtherDomainServers
- LocalDomainServers

Using the Terminations group in all ACLs is particularly important. All organizations have people who will leave the organization and should be denied access to Notes resources.

Tip

> You may think that preventing access to the server is sufficient to protect your data. It is, if you never mess up a server ACL. Use the Terminations group in each ACL anyway, as a backup mechanism.

SOLVING ACCESS CONTROL PROBLEMS

Problems in your access control lists show up in one of two ways. The database administrator may receive complaints about data not replicating or about documents that are unavailable. In these cases, the most likely problem is that too low an access level has been given to a user or server. While annoying, this problem often is less severe than giving users or servers too much access.

The primary goal of any security system is to prevent unauthorized access to confidential information. A database manager is unlikely to receive a complaint from a user that too much data is available or that the user has access to confidential data when he shouldn't have access. Discovering access control problems that allow access to confidential data requires constant monitoring of both the ACL and user accesses to a database. Chapter 17 shows you how to monitor access to a database.

ENFORCING LOCAL SECURITY

Manager access is the default level of access provided to anyone accessing a local database. This case is true even if the user has a lower access level for the copy of the database stored on the server. This issue can lead to confusion among users, who make changes to their local copies that aren't replicated to the server. To avoid these problems, you can force local copies to restrict users to the rights that they have in the ACL. Follow these steps:

1. Select the database icon from the workspace.
2. Choose File | Database | Access Control.
3. Click the Advanced icon.
4. Select the option called Enforce a Consistent Access Control List Across All Replicas of This Database.
5. Choose OK.

Local security is another feature that looks and smells like a security feature, but is actually used only to build good interfaces. Don't rely on the local security feature to protect data stored on laptops. You must encrypt databases if you want to protect the data from users who have file-system-level access to a database. See the later section on encryption for details on encrypting databases.

CONTROLLING SERVER ACCESS

Controlling access to servers is the first line of defense for your Notes network. Server access control is set by using the server document in the Name and Address Book. The server document in the Name and Address Book contains four key access control lists:

◆ Allow Access
◆ Deny Access
◆ Create New Databases
◆ Create Replica Databases

In addition to controlling access by using access control lists, you can force a Notes server to verify public keys or allow anonymous connections (described shortly).

ALLOWING AND DENYING ACCESS

To specify a list of users or servers that can access this server, follow these steps:

1. Open the server document for the server.
2. Expand the Restrictions section of the form.
3. In the Access Server field, enter the names of users or servers that should be allowed access.
4. Save the server document.

The names in the Allow Access list are the *only* names that will be given access. You can specify a list of users or servers that shouldn't have access by entering their names in the Not Access Server field.

The acceptable entries for a server access list are

◆ User names.

User names can appear in any of the server access control lists.

◆ Group names.

Group names can appear in any of the access control lists. Groups must be listed in the Public Address Book before they can be used in a server access list.

◆ Wild cards.

Wild cards can appear in any of the server access lists. You can specify a whole branch of a hierarchical certification tree by using wild cards. For example, if you want to allow all marketers access to a database, enter `*/Marketing/L3COMM` in the access list.

◆ Asterisks (*).

You can use an asterisk in the Access Server and Not Access Server fields. Use an asterisk in either of these fields to indicate that all names in the Public Address Book should be used. Entering an asterisk in the access server list is the same as selecting "Yes" for the option Only Allow Server Access to Users Listed in This Address Book.

◆ Views in the Public Address Book.

You can specify the name of a view in either the Access Server or Not Access Server field. This setting is the same as specifying a group containing all the names listed in the particular view. If you use cascaded address books, Notes searches each of the address books in order until it finds a matching view name. You can use this feature to ease the administration of groups that can be programmatically selected. The administrator can set up a custom view in the Personal Address Book with a selection formula that selects the proper list of names. This strategy requires less administrative effort than maintaining a large group. For example, if you want to give access to all users listed in the Name and Address Book, you can add the entry `People`, the name of the view listing all person documents, to the Access Server field in the server document.

Carefully plan your use of server access lists, because performance implications exist. Every server access is checked against the corresponding server access lists.

These checks can result in lower performance and capacity. To increase performance for frequent users of the server, consider creating a group called FrequentUsersOf*x* (where *x* is the name of the server). By listing frequent users of this server in a group and placing this group first in the Access Server field, you decrease the load placed on the server by these users. Notes looks in the first group and finds a matching name, without the need to search through the entire Name and Address Book.

Note

You can restrict the user's ability to create new databases or replicas by entering the names of people in the Create New Databases or Create Replica Databases fields.

USING ANONYMOUS CONNECTIONS

You can give the general public access to a Notes server by allowing anonymous connections. When you allow anonymous connections to a server, anyone with a Notes client can access the server. Users are given access to individual databases using the Anonymous class in database ACLs. Unauthenticated users receive whatever access is assigned to the word Anonymous in an ACL. If you don't specify an access level for Anonymous, anonymous users receive default access. To enable anonymous connections, follow these steps:

1. Open the Name and Address Book.
2. Open the server document for the server that will allow anonymous connections.
3. Type **Yes** in the Allow Anonymous Connections field in the Security section.
4. Save the server document.

RESTRICTING ACCESS TO DIRECTORIES

You can prevent people from even knowing of the existence of a database, by placing that database in a secure directory. You can create a secure directory by following these steps:

1. Create a directory that isn't part of the Notes data path.
2. Place a directory link from the Notes data path to the new directory.

A directory link is a text file with a .DIR extension. The first line in the file should be the full path name of the secure directory. All other lines in the file are treated as an access control list for the new directory.

3. Specify an access control list for the new directory.

Following is an example of a directory link:

```
c:\notes\securedb\
Andrew Dahl/Consulting/L3Comm
*/Acme
```

Caution

Minimize your use of directory link files; you must maintain the access control lists in these files by hand. The Administration Process doesn't update these files when users are deleted or have name changes.

PROVIDING PHYSICAL SECURITY FOR NOTES SERVERS

You can't maintain a highly secure Notes network in the absence of physical security for servers. All servers must be physically secure to guarantee Notes security, especially if all servers have manager access in database ACLs. Even if unsecured servers don't have manager access to all resources on the Notes network, they still represent a security hole. If you don't provide physical security for your servers, you have to rely completely on database encryption to prevent people from gaining access to confidential information through the local console. Physical security implies a locked, ventilated room. You can enhance physical security by taking these actions:

◆ Not using the Notes server as a file server.

   If you allow access to the file system of a Notes server, you run the risk of someone copying a database and gaining access to confidential information. For maximum security, Notes servers shouldn't be file servers, allow Telnet or FTP access, or be part of a distributed file system such as NFS.

◆ Use keyboard-lock passwords that are common now on all server platforms.

   If nothing else, these locks can slow someone attempting to gain access to a console.

◆ Set a password for the server ID.

Password-protecting the server ID prevents someone from manually restarting the server and thereby bypassing a locked keyboard. A password-protected server ID requires an administrator to be present when the server boots. For this reason, most organizations don't password-protect their server IDs.

◆ Use the SET SECURE command to protect the server console and restrict the tasks that can be done from the local console.

For details on the SET SECURE command, see Chapter 13.

Don't use database encryption to enhance physical security. Doing so would require that all administrators accessing the server from the local console have access to the ID file that was used to encrypt the database. This method causes a situation where multiple administrators use the same ID file, completely destroying your ability to maintain an audit trail for your Notes servers. You have no way of knowing which administrator is making modifications to an ACL, because everyone uses the same ID. Therefore, encrypting a database on a server that is physically secure ends up making your Notes environment less secure, by creating a loophole for the people most likely to cause security problems—your administrators.

NOTES SERVERS AS FILE SERVERS

With most of the network operating systems supported by Notes, you can use the server that Notes is running on as a file server. In fact, in the NetWare version of Notes, you have to turn off file serving if you don't want your server to be both a Notes server and a file server. You should never use a Notes server as a file server, for the following reasons:

◆ Using Notes servers as file servers is a security risk.

Forgetting to secure the directories containing the Notes system and databases is just too easy.

◆ Performance suffers for the Notes server, the file server, or both.

◆ Running Notes as both a file server and a Notes server can add instability to your network environment.

If you use a Notes server as a file server, a bug in a Notes add-on program or third-party Notes program running on the machine may cause the entire server to crash, bringing down your network file server with it. File server crashes can quickly cost an organization more than the cost of buying another server machine.

RESTRICTING ACCESS TO SERVER PORTS

You can specify a list of users, servers, or groups that are allowed to access a server by using a particular port. This scheme is useful when you want to set aside a particular port for a specific set of servers, or restrict access to dial-in ports. To create an access control list for a port, follow these steps:

1. Create a group called AccessPort*x* (where *x* is the name of the port), listing all users and servers with access to the port. Use nested groups whenever possible.

2. Enter the line `ALLOW_ACCESS` = `AccessPortx`. Alternatively, if you want to deny access to a port, use the keyword `DENY_ACCESS` and create a group called DenyAccessPort*x*. You must restart the server to make these changes effective.

If you use both a port access list and a server access list, a name must be listed in both the port access list and the correct server access list to access the server.

MANAGING CERTIFICATES

Notes security is based on possession of ID files. ID files contain public and private encryption keys unique to each user in a Notes system (probably the world). Notes authenticates a user's identity by ensuring that the user has the correct private key. Notes authentication is concerned only with identifying users, not controlling access to resources. Notes uses lists of names to control access to resources, and must therefore have some mechanism of binding encryption keys to names. Otherwise, users could simply change the name stored in the local ID file and gain access to any database or server. Certificates are the mechanism for binding names and encryption keys. Certificates bind together a specific name and a private key. Certificates are issued by a certifier—a third party that both the server and client trust. By stamping an ID file with a certificate, a certifier validates the key/name pair contained in the ID file. A Notes server or client accepts a name if the other party also has a certificate issued by a trusted certifier. In Notes, a certifier is trusted only if the local ID file contains a certificate from that certifier.

Chapter 3 contains more details on the various types of certificates that Notes supports, such as organizational, organizational unit, flat, and cross certificates.

CREATING CERTIFIER ID FILES

To issue certificates, a certifier must have possession of a certifier ID file. Certifier ID files are similar to other ID files. They have a pair of encryption keys and a name. Certifier ID files, with one exception, must also contain a certificate that validates the key/name combination. The one exception is the organization-level certifier ID. The organizational certifier is the root of the certificate hierarchy. Each level in the certificate hierarchy is certified by the level above. For example, Columbus/Marketing/Acme is certified by Marketing/Acme. Marketing/Acme is certified by Acme. Acme has no predecessor.

Before you create the certifier ID files used to stamp user and server ID files, you should read Chapter 5, which contains details about creating a naming structure for your organization. After you create a naming structure for your organization, the next step is to create the certifier ID files that match your naming structure.

ORGANIZATIONAL CERTIFIERS

The first certifier ID file that you create is the organizational certifier ID file. The organizational certifier ID file is created automatically when you install the first server in your organization. You can also create a new organizational ID by following these steps:

1. Choose File | Tools | Server Administration.
2. Click the Certifiers icon.
3. Select Register Organization.
4. Specify the correct registration server by clicking the Registration Server button and choosing the correct server from the drop-down list.

   The registration server must be available on the network before you can proceed. The registration server does the actual work of creating the ID file and updating the Name and Address Book.
5. (optional) Specify a country code for this organization. Country codes are useful when communicating internationally.
6. Specify your organizational name. The name you use here should be the exact name you chose for the root of your naming scheme.
7. Enter a password for the new certifier ID file.
8. (optional) Specify the mail address of the certifier who will be authorized to stamp user and server ID files, using this new certifier ID file.

9. (optional) Select Other Certifier Settings if you want to add a comment or location to this ID file, or you want to specify a license type or minimum password length.

10. Click the Register button.

11. Enter a name for the new ID file.

12. Choose Save.

After creating the organizational ID file, keep it in a secure place.

Caution

> Never use an organizational certifier to stamp an ID file of a user or server. Doing so makes providing a high level of security throughout your Notes network more difficult.

ORGANIZATIONAL UNIT CERTIFIERS

The only reason you should use the organizational certifier is to create organizational unit certifiers. Because of the sensitive nature of the organizational certifier ID, you should specify multiple passwords and store the file in a safe place. To use the organizational certifier file to create organizational unit certifier ID files, follow these steps:

1. Choose File | Tools | Server Administration.

2. Click the Certifiers icon.

3. Select Register Organizational Unit.

4. Enter the password for your current ID file.

5. Specify the correct registration server. The registration server must be available on the network for this process to continue. The registration server does the actual work of creating the ID file and updating the Name and Address Book.

6. Specify the correct organizational certifier.

7. Specify the name of the organizational unit, using the exact name planned in your naming structure.

8. Enter a password for the new organizational unit certifier file.

9. (optional) Specify the mail address of the certifier who will be authorized to stamp ID files, using this new file.

10. (optional) Select other certifier settings if you want to add a comment or location to this ID file, or you want to specify a license type or minimum password length.

11. Click the Register button.

Notes creates the certifier ID file.

Repeat the process of creating organizational unit certifiers until you have finished creating the certifiers for your entire naming structure. Keep in mind that you can create an organizational unit certifier file by using another organizational unit certifier file, not just with an organizational certifier ID file. For example, to create the Acme/Marketing/New Products organizational unit certifier ID, you would specify Acme/Marketing as the certifier which will stamp the new certifier ID file.

SPECIFYING MULTIPLE PASSWORDS

All but the smallest organizations should protect all certifier ID files with multiple passwords. You use these same steps to add multiple passwords to any type of ID file, not just certifier ID files. To add multiple passwords, follow these steps:

1. Choose File | Tools | Server Administration.

2. Click the Certifiers icon.

3. Select Edit Multiple Passwords.

A file selection dialog box appears.

4. Select the ID file you want to edit.

The Edit ID File Password List dialog box opens. Figure 18.2 shows the dialog box.

Figure 18.2.
Use the Edit ID File
Password List dialog
box to add or remove
passwords.

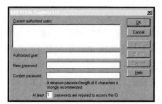

5. Enter a user/password combination for this file. The user entries are for administrative convenience only—to help you remember who knows the various passwords. The user entries aren't required when trying to access the ID file.

6. Click Add.

7. Repeat steps 5 and 6 for each user/password combination.

8. Choose OK.

You must manually update the user names stored on multiple-password ID files when administrators change jobs or leave the company. The Administration Process doesn't automatically perform this task.

RECERTIFYING USERS AND SERVERS

Every user and server must have a certified ID file. The certifier is responsible for issuing certificates to users and servers, and should always perform these steps herself. Never give access to a certifier ID file to *anyone* other than the authorized certifier.

Note

This section assumes that users have already received an ID file and are requesting a new certificate. For directions on issuing the initial certificates for a user, see the later section "Managing ID Files."

Before certifying a user, the certifier must guarantee that the name on the ID file is in fact the name of the person who will use the ID file, and that the name is unique. You can double-check the validity of an ID file by comparing the ID number stored with the file you have to the one stored on the user's workstation. You can have users check the ID number of the ID on their individual workstations by choosing Tools | User ID.

A certifier issues a certificate for the following reasons:

◆ A certificate has expired for a current user or server.

◆ You are migrating from flat names to hierarchical names.

◆ You need a cross certificate to communicate with other organizations.

◆ A user or server has changed names.

◆ A user or server has a new public/private key pair.

◆ A certifier has left the company and you are reissuing all certificates created by that certifier.

You have several ways to accomplish the task of certifying ID files. Certifiers can receive ID files from administrators one at a time or en masse, or a user can request a new certificate. The communication between the certifier and user can take place via Notes Mail or floppy disk, as described in the following sections.

RECERTIFYING GROUPS OF USERS

Certifiers can recertify groups of users simultaneously, using the Public Address Book. You must be using the Administration Process to recertify groups of users. Chapter 13 contains information on the Administration Process.

To recertify a group of users, the certifier follows these steps (which must be carried out at the server with the Public Address Book):

1. Open the Public Address Book.

2. (recertifying users) Open the People view.

   (recertifying servers) Open the Servers-Servers view.

3. Select the users or servers you want to recertify. All selections must have been certified with the same certifier ID file.

4. (recertifying users) Choose Actions | Recertify Person.

   (recertifying servers) Choose Actions | Recertify Server.

5. Open the certifier ID file used to certify the selected servers or users. You must use the same certifier that was originally used to certify the ID files.

6. Enter the password for the certifier ID file.

   The Certify ID dialog box opens.

7. (optional) Change the expiration date.

8. (optional) Enter an expiration date for a subset of users.

9. Choose Certify.

CERTIFYING THROUGH NOTES MAIL

You recertify individual users or servers through Notes Mail or by using floppy disks. No matter which method you use, the process involves the creation of a safe copy of an ID file that is certified and returned to the user. A *safe copy* is an ID file without the private key. Because private keys are the cornerstone of Notes security, they never should be sent over the network. Safe copies enable a certifier to issue certificates to users and servers without having access to the private key.

A user can generate a request for a certificate at any time by using Notes Mail, in three steps. The user generates a request, the certifier issues a certificate, and the user merges the certificate into his real ID file.

GENERATING A CERTIFICATE REQUEST

To generate a request for a certificate, the user follows these steps:

1. Choose Tools | User ID. You may need to enter a password before proceeding.

   The User ID dialog box opens.

2. Click the Certificates icon. Figure 18.3 shows the resulting dialog box options.

Figure 18.3.
Users can request new
certificates by using the
User ID dialog box.

3. Choose Request Certificate to display the Mail Certificate Request dialog box (see Figure 18.4).

4. Fill in the correct address for the certifier.

5. Choose Send.

Figure 18.4.
Fill in the address
of the certifier.

Because many users don't know the address of their certifier, consider providing this information in a How To database that users can check.

Notes sends a safe copy of the user's ID file to the certifier, using Notes Mail. As Figure 18.4 shows, the request is signed by the user making the request (the Sign check box is selected and grayed). This system safeguards the ID file attached to the mail message while it's being sent. If anyone manages to tamper with the file in transit, Notes warns the certifier when she receives the message.

ISSUING THE CERTIFICATE

The certifier issues a certificate for a request received via Notes Mail by following these steps:

1. Open the message containing the request.

2. Verify the identity of the user and the ID number in the ID file received.

3. Choose Actions | Certify Attached ID File.

4. Open the correct certifier ID file.

   If the ID file already contains a hierarchical certificate, the Certify dialog box opens. The certifier can replace the existing certificate (which changes the user's name) or issue a cross certificate (covered a little later).

5. Choose Recertify.

    The Certify ID dialog box displays different options, based on whether a hierarchical or flat certificate is being created. Figure 18.5 shows the options for issuing hierarchical certificates; Figure 18.6 shows the options for issuing flat certificates.

Figure 18.5.
Options for issuing
hierarchical certi-
ficates.

Figure 18.6.
Options for issuing flat
certificates.

6. (optional) Change the certificate expiration date. The suggested default is two years. If you are certifying many users at one time, change the date to avoid having to recertify all users at the same time two years in the future.

7. (optional) Enter a minimum password length (hierarchical only). Eight characters is the recommended minimum.

8. (flat certificates only) Deselect Trust Other Certificates Signed by This Certifier if you are certifying an ID file from a different organization.

9. (optional) Change the registration server by clicking the Server button. (The registration server must be available on the network before you can proceed.) The registration server is the server that does the actual work of changing the user's entry in the Name and Address Book.

10. Choose Certify.

    Notes generates a certificate for the ID file. The Mail Certified ID dialog box appears.

11. Enter the user's name in the To field.

12. (recommended) Select the Sign check box.

13. Choose Send.

    Notes mails the certified ID file to the user.

If the certification causes a user's name to change, the Administration Process automatically updates the Name and Address Book and any database ACLs to the new distinguished name of the user. See Chapter 13 for details on configuring the Administration Process.

ACCEPTING THE CERTIFICATE

When the user receives the certified ID file, he needs to merge the new certificate with his ID file by following these steps:

1. Open the message.
2. Choose Mail | Accept Certificate.

    For hierarchical certificates, the Accept New ID Information dialog box opens. For flat certificates, Notes posts the Merge Certificate into Your ID File dialog box.

3. (hierarchical) Choose OK.

    (flat) Choose Accept.

The user should update any backup copies of his ID file after receiving the new certificate.

CERTIFYING VIA SNEAKERNET

You should use Notes Mail to fulfill user requests for certificates whenever possible. If the network isn't available, you can use the process outlined in the following short sections. Three steps are required: the user saves a safe copy of his ID to a floppy disk (and gives it to the certifier), the certifier issues a certificate, and the user merges the certificate into his ID file.

CREATING A SAFE COPY OF THE ID FILE

To create a safe copy of the ID file, the user follows these steps:

1. Choose File | Tools | User ID.

    The User ID dialog box opens.

2. Choose More Options. Figure 18.7 shows the additional options that appear.
3. Choose Create Safe Copy. Notes displays a file selection dialog box.
4. Enter a name for the safe copy.

Figure 18.7.
Creating a safe copy of
an ID, using the User
ID dialog box.

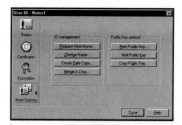

Tip

Using your name as part of the file name for the safe copy helps the certifier keep files organized.

5. Choose Save, and save the safe copy to a floppy disk.
6. Give the floppy disk to the certifier.

ISSUING THE CERTIFICATE

The certifier stamps an ID file that she received on a floppy disk by following these steps:

1. Choose File | Tools | Server Administration.
2. Click the Certifiers icon.
3. Choose Certify ID.
4. Open the desired certifier ID file.
5. Enter the password for the certifier ID file.
6. Open the safe copy of the ID file to be certified.

   The Certify ID dialog box opens. The dialog box changes, based on whether a hierarchical or flat certificate is being created. (Refer to Figures 18.6 and 18.7 to see an example of each version.)

7. (optional) Change the certificate expiration date. The suggested default is two years. If you are certifying many users at one time, change the date to avoid having to recertify all users at the same time two years in the future.

8. (optional) Enter a minimum password length (hierarchical only). Eight characters is the recommended minimum.

9. (flat certificates only) Deselect Trust Other Certificates Signed by This Certifier if you are certifying an ID file from a different organization.

10. (optional) Change the registration server by clicking the Server button. (The registration server must be available on the network before you can

proceed.) The registration server is the server that does the actual work of changing the user's entry in the Name and Address Book.

11. Choose Certify.

    Notes generates a certificate for the ID file.

12. The ID file is returned to the user, who then follows the steps in the next section, "Merging the Certificate."

If the certification causes a user's or server's name to change, the Administration Process automatically updates the Name and Address Book and any database ACLs to the new distinguished name of the user. See Chapter 13 for details on configuring the Administration Process.

MERGING THE CERTIFICATE

When the user receives the safe copy with the new certificate, he needs to copy the certificate into his ID file. Administrators should perform this function for server ID files, using the workstation program running on the actual server. In either case, follow these steps:

1. Insert the floppy disk with the certified safe copy into the disk drive.

2. Choose File | Tools | User ID.

   The User ID dialog box appears.

3. Choose More Options.

4. Choose Merge a Copy.

5. Open the certified safe copy on the floppy disk.

6. Choose Done.

The user should make new backups of his ID file after receiving a new certificate. If the ID file is for a server, the administrator for the server should keep a backup in a safe place.

ISSUING CROSS CERTIFICATES

Cross certificates enable communication between two hierarchically certified organizations. Both organizations must use hierarchical certifiers to use cross certificates. A cross certificate is the stamp of approval from your local certifier that the other organization's certifier is trustworthy. After your certifier issues a cross certificate for another organization, your users and servers trust the certificates issued by that other certifier.

Notes uses certificates during authentication. Because authentication is bidirectional (each party authenticates the other), both organizations must issue cross certificates. Both parties attempting to communicate (user and server, or two servers) must trust the certifier that issued the certificate for the other party.

The cross certificate is created by your certifier and stored in your organization's Public Address Book. When a user or server from the other organization attempts to access one of your servers, the server looks in the PAB for a cross certificate. If it finds one, authentication succeeds, and the server checks the appropriate ACLs to see if access should be given to the user or server.

To limit the number of users from the other organization that gain access to your Notes network, issue cross certificates using organizational unit certifiers. If you issue a cross certificate for an organizational certifier ID file, you are saying that you trust all the certifiers in that entire organization. By insisting on the use of an organizational unit certifier, you need to trust only that certifier and his descendants. You also can cross certify individual users and servers. (Certifying specific users and servers requires more work on the part of the certifier but limits access to specific users and servers.)

Cross certificates enable your users and servers to authenticate users and servers from the other organization. They do nothing to control access to servers. Use server access lists to limit the servers and users from the other organization that can access your Notes network.

You can exchange cross certificates with another organization manually (using Notes Mail, floppy disks, or the telephone) or automatically.

AUTOMATIC USER CROSS CERTIFICATION

After a certifier creates a cross certificate for another organization, the users must copy-and-paste the cross certificate into their Personal Address Books. Many users won't understand how to do this, or why they should. And you may not have given users reader access to the Name and Address Book, preventing them from copying the cross certificate even if they know how. You can avoid the need to copy cross certificates by having users from your organization automatically create a cross certificate when they first access the other organization's server. This strategy helps only when the server being accessed already has a cross certificate for your organization. Otherwise, the other server rejects all connections.

When a user accesses a hierarchically certified server from another organization for which she doesn't have a cross certificate, Notes presents a warning that explains a little about authentication and asks if the user wants to authenticate the identity of the server being accessed. The user can respond to the warning message in one of three ways:

◆ Choose Yes.

Notes creates a cross certificate for the root certifier for the server being accessed. The user now automatically accepts any certificate from the other organization.

◆ Choose No.

No cross certificate is created; instead, Notes gives the user the option of using Anonymous access. The original warning appears again the next time the user accesses the server.

◆ Choose Advanced Options.

The user can create a cross certificate for the certifier ID used to stamp the server's ID file. This cross certificate can be stored in the Public Address Book for other users to access. This method is the easiest way for a certifier to create a cross certificate for the other organization when he can directly access a server (usually using a modem or over the Internet).

This same warning appears when users receive mail signed by a user from another organization. (Notes is really asking if you want to trust the signature.)

CROSS CERTIFYING VIA TELEPHONE

Certificates bind together public keys and names. A name is just a text string. A public key is just a long string of nonsense text. The process can be a little tedious, but you can transfer names and public keys over the phone (by talking). Notes takes advantage of this fact and allows a certifier to talk on the phone to an administrator from another organization and create a cross certificate.

To create a cross certificate over the phone, follow these steps:

1. Choose File | Tools | Server Administration.

   Notes displays the Server Administration panel.

2. Click the Certifiers icon.

3. Choose Cross Certify Key to display a file selection dialog box.

4. Select the certifier ID file you want to use.

5. Enter the password for the ID file.

6. Enter the name of the organizational unit certifier ID file you want to cross certify.

7. Enter the public key for the organizational unit certifier ID file. The public key is available in the Server-Certificates view of the Name and Address Book. Open the certificate document for the certifier in Edit mode to view the public key.

8. Choose Certify.

Notes creates a public key and stores it in the Public Address Book.

REQUESTING A CROSS CERTIFICATE VIA NOTES MAIL

When using Notes Mail or floppy disks to generate a cross certificate, the process takes two steps. First, each administrator generates a request for a cross certificate and issues a cross certificate. Notes stores a copy of the cross certificate in the Name and Address Book. For example, if you use the L3Comm certifier ID file to cross certify the Acme certifier ID file, the L3Comm-issued cross certificate ends up stored in Acme's Name and Address Book. Any user certified with the Acme certifier ID File can copy-and-paste the cross certificate from Acme's Public Address Book into his Personal Address Book, and access your servers.

Use Notes Mail when you have the ability to route mail to the other organization. Exchanging cross certificates by using mail is far less burdensome than any of the other methods.

REQUESTING A CROSS CERTIFICATE

Each administrator follows these steps to generate a request for a cross certificate:

1. Choose File | Tools | User ID.

   The User ID dialog box opens.

2. Click the Certificates icon.

3. Choose Request Cross Certificate to display a file selection dialog box.

4. Select the ID file you want to cross certify.

   The Mail Cross Certificate Request dialog box appears (see Figure 18.8).

Figure 18.8.
Using Notes Mail
to request a cross
certificate.

5. Enter the address of the certifier in the other organization.

6. Choose Send.

   Notes mails a safe copy of the ID to the other certifier.

CROSS CERTIFYING AN ID

When a certifier receives a request for a cross certificate, he can issue a certificate by following these steps:

1. Open the message containing the request.
2. Choose Actions | Cross Certify Attached ID File. Notes displays a file selection dialog box.
3. Select the certifier ID file you want to use.
4. Choose Certify.

    Notes creates a cross certificate and stores it in the Public Address Book.

Users who need access to your servers must copy-and-paste the cross certificate from the Public Address Book into their Personal Address Books. Servers already have a local copy of the Public Address Book and don't need the cross certificate pasted into a Personal Address Book.

REQUESTING A CROSS CERTIFICATE WITHOUT NOTES MAIL

When you first cross certify with another organization, you probably don't have a way to route mail. If you have some other way of exchanging files, such as via the Internet or floppy disk, follow the steps in the next few short sections to exchange cross certificates. You can also create cross certificates over the phone.

CREATING A SAFE COPY

Each administrator should create a safe copy of the ID file to be cross certified. Follow these steps:

1. Choose File | Tools | Server Administration.

    Notes displays the Server Administration panel.
2. Choose Administration | ID to display a file selection dialog box.
3. Select the certifier ID file for which you want to create a cross certificate.

    The Enter Password dialog box opens.
4. Enter the password for the certifier ID file.

    The User ID dialog box appears.
5. Choose More Options.
6. Choose Create Safe Copy.
7. Enter a file name for the safe copy. The default name is SAFE.ID. You can help eliminate confusion by using the name of your organization somewhere in the file name.

8. Choose Save.

9. Send the safe copy to the certifier at the other organization.

ISSUING THE CROSS CERTIFICATE

A certifier issues a cross certificate for a safe copy of a certifier ID file by following these steps:

1. Choose File | Tools | Server Administration.

   Notes displays the Server Administration panel.

2. Click the Certifiers icon.

3. Choose Cross Certify ID File. Notes displays a file selection dialog box.

4. Select the certifier ID that you want to use to certify the cross certificate (the certifier ID file from your organization).

5. Enter the password for the certifier ID file.

   Notes redisplays the file selection dialog box.

6. Select the safe copy received from the other organization.

7. (optional) Select a registration server. The registration server is the server where the cross certificate is stored in the Public Address Book. The registration server must be available on the network before you can create the cross certificate.

8. (optional) Change the expiration date. The default is ten years.

9. Choose Cross Certify.

   Notes adds the cross certificate to the Name and Address Book on the registration server.

If you used "local" as the registration server, you must copy the new cross certificate to the Public Address Book before servers and users in your organization can communicate with the other organization.

MANAGING ID FILES

ID files are the basis of Notes security. Your primary goal in managing ID files is to keep them secure. Users inevitably have an important role to play, although administrators can take steps such as keeping backup copies that minimize user responsibilities.

Following are the basic ID tasks:

◆ Registering new ID files

◆ Distributing ID files

◆ Recertifying ID files (covered in the preceding section)

The following sections cover creation and distribution of ID files.

DISTRIBUTING ID FILES

You should decide how you want to distribute ID files before you create any files. During the creation process, Notes asks how you want to distribute ID files. You have three options for distributing ID files: floppy disk, the Name and Address Book, or both. You have these options no matter how you decide to create ID files (one at a time, or in batches). At some point during the creation of IDs, Notes presents the Register Person dialog box. By selecting the Other icon in this dialog box, you display the options shown in Figure 18.9.

18

ADMINISTERING NOTES SECURITY

Figure 18.9.
Specifying how you
want Notes to distrib-
ute ID files.

The default selection is to store new ID files in the Name and Address Book. This method is the preferred way of distributing ID files to users, who then store the ID files on their local hard drives. When a user first accesses Notes, the ID file is cut from his person document and stored on his hard drive. You must give the user the correct password for the ID file. Notes requires a password at least one character long when storing ID files in the Name and Address Book.

You also can choose to store the new ID file on a floppy disk. You may choose this option because you are storing all ID files on a file server, or to create an initial backup of the user's ID file. If you are creating a backup copy, select both the In Address Book and In File options on the Other panel of the Register Person dialog box. If you are storing ID files on a file server, select just the In File option. You can override the default file name (a:\user.id) by selecting the Set ID File button.

REGISTERING NEW USERS

Registering users is the process of creating ID files for users. You can create ID files one at a time, or in batches (using a file as input). For each user you plan to register, you must have the following information:

◆ The common name assigned to the user

◆ The certifier ID file to use

♦ A password for the ID file

♦ The license type for the user

♦ The mail system for the user

♦ The user's home server

In addition to these items, you can optionally set up a location and administrator for each user. If you are registering multiple users at one time, you should specify a unique name for each ID file created.

USER PROFILES

You can save considerable time when setting up new users by using user profiles. A user profile lists the passthru, dial-up, and Internet servers common to a group of users, and the mail domain for a group of users. The information from the user profile is entered automatically into the person document created for each user. Notes also creates the connection documents needed for users to reach the listed servers.

You create user profiles by using the Name and Address Book. Follow these steps:

1. Open the Name and Address Book.

2. Select the Server-Setup Profiles view.

3. Click the Add Setup Profile button.

   Notes displays the User Setup Profile form (see Figure 18.10).

Figure 18.10.
The User Setup
Profile form.

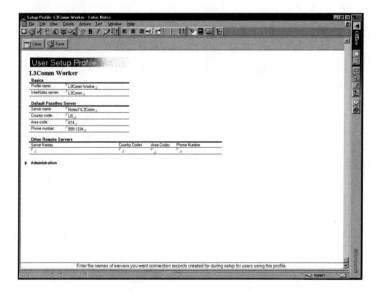

4. (optional) Enter the name of the InterNotes server.

5. (optional) Enter the name and phone number of the default passthru server.

6. (optional) Enter the names and phone numbers of all remote servers.

7. (optional) Enter the mail domain name for these users.

8. Choose Save.

9. Choose Close.

You should create a user profile for each department or geographic region in your organization.

REGISTERING A SINGLE USER

Follow these steps to register a single user:

1. Choose File | Tools | Server Administration.

   The Server Administration panel opens.

2. Click the People icon.

3. Choose Register Person.

   The Enter Password dialog box appears.

4. Enter the password for the certifier ID file.

   The Register Person dialog box is redisplayed.

5. (optional) Specify a registration server. The registration server's Name and Address Book will be updated with the new person record and ID file. The specified registration server must be available on the network before you can complete registration.

6. (optional) Specify a new certifier ID.

7. Specify a security type. See the later section "International Compatibility" for details on the differences between North American and international security.

8. Specify an expiration date. The default is two years.

9. (optional) Specify the profile you want to use.

10. Choose Continue.

    The Register Person dialog box reappears (see Figure 18.11).

11. Click the Mail icon.

12. Specify the type of mail system for the user.

13. Specify the home server for the user.

Figure 18.11.
Registering a
single user.

14. Click the Other icon.

15. Choose to store the ID file in the Name and Address Book, in a directory, or both. For details on making this selection, see the earlier section "Distributing ID Files."

16. (optional) Enter a location for this user.

17. (optional) Enter the administrator for the user's location.

18. (optional) Add a comment about the user.

19. Choose Register.

You can repeat these steps starting at step 5 for every user you want to register.

REGISTERING MULTIPLE USERS

Notes can register many users at one time, using a file as input. The file contains one line for each user, with all the information on that one line. Each entry contains the following information, in order, separated by semicolons:

- ◆ last name
- ◆ first name
- ◆ middle initial
- ◆ organization
- ◆ password
- ◆ ID file directory
- ◆ ID file name
- ◆ home server name
- ◆ mail file directory
- ◆ mail file name
- ◆ location
- ◆ comment
- ◆ forwarding address

The following listing shows an example of a user registration file.

```
Dahl;Andrew;;L3Comm;password;c:\notesids;adahl.id;notes1;mail;adahl.nsf;;;;
Lesnick;Leslie;L;L3Comm;password;c:\notesids;llesnick.id;notes1;mail;llesnick.nsf;;;;
```

After you have created a registration file, use it to register multiple users by following these steps:

1. Choose File | Tools | Server Administration.

   Notes displays the Server Administration panel.

2. Click the People icon.

3. Choose Register from File.

   The Enter Password dialog box opens.

4. Enter the password for the certifier ID file.

   The Register Person dialog box appears.

5. (optional) Specify a registration server. The registration server's Name and Address Book will be updated with the new person record and ID file. The registration server specified must be available on the network before you can complete registration.

6. (optional) Specify a new certifier ID.

7. Select a security type. See the later section "International Compatibility" for details on the differences between North American and international security.

8. Specify an expiration date. The default is two years.

9. (optional) Specify the profile you want to use.

10. Choose Continue.

    Notes posts a file selection dialog box.

11. Open the text file containing the user information.

    The Register People from Text File dialog box appears.

12. Enter a minimum password length for the users. Make sure that all the passwords specified in the file meet this requirement.

13. Specify a license type for the users.

14. (optional) Specify a user profile for the users.

15. Click the Mail icon.

16. Specify the type of mail system for these users.

17. Specify the home server for the users.

18. Click the Other icon.

19. Choose to store ID files in the Name and Address Book, in a directory, or both. For details on making this selection, see the earlier section "Distributing ID Files."

20. Choose Register.

Notes creates ID files for all users listed in the file. When the ID files are complete, Notes displays a confirmation message with the number of users registered.

BACKING UP ID FILES

Some controversy exists about whether you should create backups of ID files. In organizations that don't make heavy use of multiple certificates or encryption keys, backing up an ID file can ease the administrative burden associated with lost ID files and forgotten passwords. If your organization has a large number of users accessing databases that require special encryption keys, on the other hand, keeping current versions of ID files backed up may require more work than occasionally re-creating an ID file.

Caution

> Backup ID files are a potential security hole. An administrator with access to the backup ID file can use it to impersonate the user who owns the ID file. You can alleviate this security hole by requiring multiple passwords on backup copies of IDs. (The user who owns the ID should be one of the people who knows a password.) Of course, if the administrator is also the certifier for your organization, no additional security holes are created by allowing him to keep backup copies of ID files. An administrator who is also a certifier can just as easily create a brand-new ID file.

CHANGING A USER'S NAME

The most common reason for changing a user's name is that he has transferred to a new department. One of the key considerations when creating a naming structure is to minimize the name changes that will be required.

If you're changing the user's name from flat to hierarchical, see Chapter 17 for details on changing from flat to hierarchical naming.

To change the common name for a user, you must have access to the correct certifier ID file for the user(s) being renamed. Follow these steps:

1. Open the Name and Address Book.
2. Select the People view.
3. Select the person document for the user to be renamed.
4. Choose Actions | Rename.
5. Choose Change Common Name.

   Notes displays a file selection dialog box.
6. Open the certifier ID file for the user.

   The Enter Password dialog box appears.
7. Enter the password for the certifier ID file.
8. Change the user's first name, last name, or middle initial as desired.
9. Specify an expiration date for the new certificate.
10. (if needed) If a user exists with this name, certified by the same certifier ID file, specify a unique qualifier for this user to differentiate between the two users. Enter the qualifier next to the New Qualifying Org. Unit option. This qualifier will appear between the user's common name and the certifier name.
11. Choose Rename.

The Administration Process propagates the name change to all documents in the Name and Address Book and database ACLs that list this server as an administration server. See Chapter 13 for more details.

When the user next connects with a server, the user's local copy of his ID file will be updated with the new name.

NOTES ENCRYPTION

Lotus licensed the public key cryptography technology from RSA CryptoSystems, a company in California. RSA is short for Rivest Salmir and Adelman, the professors at MIT who developed the public key algorithm. RSA technology is currently the most widely used public key system. RSA claims a patent on all public key systems, although challenges to that patent were pending when this book was written. Notes can use public key encryption to

◆ Encrypt fields within a document
◆ Encrypt entire databases
◆ Encrypt data sent over a network port
◆ Encrypt the bodies of mail messages

Perhaps the most common use of public key encryption in Notes is hidden from users. Public key encryption is a critical part of Notes authentication. Chapter 3 covers Notes authentication in detail.

ENCRYPTING MAIL

Administrators or users can cause outgoing mail, incoming mail, or saved mail to be encrypted automatically. Notes encrypts only the body of a message, not the header information, such as the To, From, and cc fields. Notes can only encrypt mail sent to recipients for which Notes can find a public key in the Name and Address Book. Because no global public key storage currently exists for Notes, most organizations can send encrypted mail only to other users within the organization. You can't send encrypted mail to non-Notes Mail users, because they can't decrypt the message. Even if a non-Notes Mail user has an entry in the Public Address Book, he can't decrypt the message, because his mail system can't use the Notes Mail ID file to retrieve the private key, which is needed to decrypt the message.

Encrypt outgoing mail when you want to ensure that only the recipient can read the message; a mail message in transit may pass through several servers, and the path that the message takes isn't controllable by the user.

Only users can encrypt outgoing mail. To encrypt outgoing mail, follow these steps:

1. Choose File | Tools | User Preferences.
2. Click the Mail icon.
3. Select the Encrypt Sent Mail check box.
4. Choose OK.

When you enable encryption of sent mail, Notes generates a different encryption key (known as a *session key*) for each message sent. Notes encrypts the message body, using the session key. Notes then encrypts the session key, using the recipient's public key, and sends both the encrypted message and the encrypted session key to the user. Notes automatically decrypts the message when the recipient reads the message. Because only the intended recipient has the private key needed to decrypt the message, only he can read the message.

Encrypting incoming mail prevents administrators or any unauthorized person from reading mail after it arrives in your mailbox. Encryption of incoming mail can be set up either by users or administrators. The administrators have the option of setting up encryption for an individual user or for all users on a mail server. A user can encrypt incoming mail if he has editor access to his person document in the Name and Address Book by following these steps:

1. Open the person document in Edit mode.

2. Select Yes for the Encrypt Incoming Mail option.

3. Choose Save.

If the user doesn't have editor access to his person document, the administrator must perform these steps for him.

Administrators can turn on encryption of incoming mail for all users on a mail server by following these steps:

1. Add the following line to the NOTES.INI file:

```
Mail_Encrypt_Incoming=1
```

2. Save the NOTES.INI file.

3. Reboot the server.

The following steps detail the encryption process for incoming messages:

1. Generating a new encryption key for each message.

2. Encrypting the message with the key.

3. Encrypting the key, using the recipient's public key stored in the Name and Address Book.

4. Storing the encrypted key with the encrypted message in the user's mailbox.

A user can encrypt all mail saved in her mail file, including drafts of unsent messages and messages saved after sending. This option has the same effect as turning on encryption of incoming mail—it prevents administrators and others with access to mail files from reading mail in the user's personal mailbox. To enable encryption of saved mail, users can follow these steps:

1. Choose File | Tools | User Preferences.

2. Click the Mail icon.

3. Select the Encrypt Saved Mail option.

4. Choose OK.

Only documents saved after this option is enabled are encrypted. Messages already in the mailbox aren't encrypted.

FIELD-LEVEL ENCRYPTION

Database designers can include encryptable fields in documents. Notes automatically encrypts all encryptable fields in a document, if an encryption key is stored with that document. Because only a single encryption key can be stored with a document, all encryptable fields within a document are encrypted by using the same key. Encrypted fields can be read only by a user who has the correct encryption key stored in her ID file. Users without the correct key can't read the data in an encrypted field. You can enable encryption for a field by following these steps:

1. Open the form containing the field.
2. Right-click the field to display the Field Properties dialog box.
3. Click the Options tab.
4. Select Enable Encryption for This Field from the Security Options drop-down list.
5. Close the Field Properties dialog box.

Encryptable fields display red brackets; non-encryptable fields have gray brackets.

DISTRIBUTING ENCRYPTION KEYS

If your organization has databases that are set up to encrypt fields within documents, you need a mechanism for distributing encryption keys to users. You can distribute encryption keys by sending encrypted mail to the users who require the encryption keys. Users can merge the encryption keys into their ID files.

SPECIFYING ENCRYPTION KEYS FOR DOCUMENTS

All encryptable fields in a document are encrypted as soon as an encryption key is associated with the document. The designer can indicate a specific set of keys, using the Form Properties dialog box. To associate default keys with a document, follow these steps:

1. Open the form definition for the document.
2. Right-click to display the Form Properties dialog box.
3. Click the Security tab.
4. Select the appropriate encryption key from the Default Encryption Keys drop-down list. If no keys are listed, the current ID file has no encryption keys stored in it. Before being able to associate a specific key with a document, you must create that key and store it in the designer's ID file.
5. Choose OK.

PORT ENCRYPTION

You can encrypt data sent over a specific port. This tactic is most useful when Notes servers communicate over a public network, such as the Internet. Port encryption prevents unauthorized users from monitoring Notes data traffic. Notes servers detect encrypted data sent via a port and automatically decrypt the data. Encrypting data sent over a port doesn't have a significant impact on performance, although it eliminates the chance of using any kind of data compression (lack of data compression is a problem common to all encryption schemes). To encrypt data sent over a port, follow these steps:

1. Choose File | Tools | User Preferences.
2. Click the Ports icon.
3. In the Communication Ports list box, select the port that you want to encrypt.
4. Select the Encrypt Network Data check box.
5. Choose OK.

ENCRYPTING DATABASES

Laptop users often carry replicas of sensitive information as they go about their everyday tasks. Thefts of executive laptops are a common occurrence. To protect your data, you should encrypt all databases stored on laptops. Encrypting a database makes it more difficult for a company that steals the laptop to read the data in Notes datbases, although Notes encryption is far from unbreakable. If the user's ID is also stored on the laptop, a hacker needs only to guess the password in the ID file to gain access to encrypted databases.

You must have manager access to a database to turn on encryption. Notes provides three levels of encryption for databases:

◆ Simple.

   Simple encryption is the fastest encryption method, but prevents only casual users from gaining access to the data in a database. You can compress a database if it's encrypted using simple encryption.

◆ Medium.

   A medium level of encryption provides quick access to data, while forcing unauthorized users to spend at least some effort in decrypting the database. Databases encrypted by using the medium setting aren't compressible.

◆ Strong.

   Accessing databases encrypted with strong encryption is slower, but strong encryption offers the greatest amount of security. Databases encrypted by using strong encryption aren't compressible.

You have to decide for each database the level of encryption needed. To encrypt a database, follow these steps:

1. Choose File | Database | Properties.
2. Click the Encryption button.
3. Select the option Locally Encrypt This Database.
4. Select the desired level of encryption from the drop-down list.
5. If you want to encrypt this database for someone other than yourself, click the For button and select the name from the list that appears.
6. Choose OK.

Database encryption is intended to prevent unauthorized users who copy a database file by using operating system commands from gaining access to confidential information. Database encryption isn't meant as a wholesale substitute for field-level encryption. An encrypted database can be decrypted only by a single user. Encrypted fields can be decrypted by anyone with the proper key. When Notes encrypts a database, it generates a random encryption key and uses that key to encrypt the database. The encryption key is then encrypted by using the public key from the Public Address Book for the name you specified in the Database Properties dialog box. Notes then appends the encrypted key to the database. When a user attempts to open the database, Notes checks to see whether the local ID file contains a private key capable of decrypting a database.

ELECTRONIC SIGNATURES

Chapter 4 covers electronic (digital) signatures in detail. In summary, an electronic signature is the digital equivalent of a handwritten signature, a mark that can be made only by a single individual. Electronic signatures have the additional feature of guaranteeing that the document hasn't changed since it was signed. Notes enables you to add an electronic signature to a field or section of any form. The signing of fields and sections is controlled by the database designer. To enable signing of a field or section, follow these steps:

1. Open the form containing the field or section.
2. Right-click the field or section and display the Field Properties dialog box.
3. Click the Options tab.
4. Select Sign If Mailed or Saved from the Security Options drop-down list.
5. Choose OK.

Notes also allows signing of e-mail messages. The user can decide whether to electronically sign mail that he sends. To turn on signing, follow these steps:

1. Choose File | Tools | User Preferences.
2. Click the Mail icon.
3. Select the Sign Sent Mail check box.
4. Choose OK.

This selection causes all mail sent from this user to be signed. Users also can decide to sign individual messages by selecting Sign as a delivery option.

The validity of electronic signatures is completely dependent on the security of ID files. Electronic signatures are assumed to be unique because ID files are assumed to be unique. If an unauthorized person has a copy of an ID file, he can use it to forge signatures.

INTERNATIONAL COMPATIBILITY

Notes licenses come in two flavors: International and North American. The U.S. government restricts the type of encryption technology that can be exported. In previous versions of Notes, the International version used weaker encryption than the North American version. This system meant that data encrypted using a North American license couldn't be read by someone with an International license. This is no longer the case. With Lotus Notes Release 4.0, both International and North American licenses use 64-bit keys to encrypt data and are therefore completely interoperable.

The International licenses generate keys of which 24 bits are given to the U.S. government. This leaves only 40 bits of protection from the U.S. government, a trivial decryption exercise for the U.S. government. Everyone other than the U.S. government must decrypt the full 64 bits, a much harder task (although still clearly possible).

PROTECTING DOCUMENTS

You can add access lists to individual documents, to control who can edit or read a document. A user with author access to a database can edit a document only if his name appears in a field of type Author. If you want to allow a user with author access to edit documents he creates, you must include his name in a field of type Author. You can do this by programming a macro that executes when the user saves the document. The macro should contain the line

```
"Fieldxxx := @name([abbreviate]:author list)
```

where *Fieldxxx* is the name of the field of type Author.

18

You can restrict who can read a document by including a field of type Reader in the document. Any user not listed in the field can't read the document, and any server not listed in the field can't replicate the document. If you are going to use reader fields, and you want documents with reader fields to replicate correctly, include the group LocalDomainServers in all reader fields. This action gives all servers reader access and the capability to replicate the document.

Tip

> The simplest form of limiting access to a database is simply not to tell anyone about the existence of a database, and not list the database in a database catalog. Hiding databases is an effective technique, although not truly a security technique. The primary method of protecting a database is the access control list.

PROTECTING FORMS AND VIEWS

Protecting design elements such as forms and views is a useful user interface feature, but isn't an effective way to protect data. Forms and views simply filter data. If the user has access to another form or view that displays the underlying document, he can still gain access to the data. If you want to protect the data in a database, you must rely on access control lists, encryption, and Author/Reader fields.

Roles are the primary method of protecting design elements such as forms and views. For some background on roles, see Chapter 3. In summary, roles are groups of users associated with a particular database. Roles require additional administrative effort and aren't used in most organizations. You don't need to use roles to protect forms and views. Instead, you can use any group that appears in the access control list.

PROTECTING FORMS

To specify the users who have the right to read documents created using a particular form, follow these steps:

1. Open the form definition.
2. Right-click anywhere in the form and display the Form Properties dialog box.
3. Click the Security tab.

4. To specify individuals allowed to read documents created with this form, make sure that the All Readers and Above check box is deselected.

5. Select from the list box only those names and groups that should be able to read documents created with this form.

To limit who can create documents with a form, make sure that the All Authors and Above check box is deselected. You specify the exact users and groups allowed to create documents by including them in the access control list and selecting them in the list.

PROTECTING VIEWS

You can limit the users allowed to read documents that appear in a view by using the View Properties dialog box. Follow these steps:

1. Open the view definition.

2. Choose Design | View Properties.

3. Click the Security tab.

4. Make sure that the All Readers and Above check box is deselected.

5. Select the appropriate names and roles from the list.

Users with the ability to create personal views can create a view that displays the same documents as the protected view. The personal view could then be used to access any of the protected documents. Don't rely on view access lists to protect data from view.

HIDING DATABASE DESIGNS

If you are distributing applications to third parties or building products for distribution, you will want to hide the design of your databases. Organizations may also want to hide the design of their internal databases, because this strategy also has the effect of disabling all changes. To hide a database design, follow these steps:

1. Create a master template for the database.

2. Create a new database, based on the master template.

3. Select the new database icon from the workspace.

4. Choose File | Database | Replace Design.

5. Select the master template and make sure that the Hide Formulas and LotusScript check box is selected.

6. Choose Yes.

This action prevents anyone without access to the master template from viewing the design or making any changes to the design. Hiding a database design institutes the following settings:

◆ Users can't view the settings for design elements.

◆ Users can't modify, add, or delete fields, forms, subforms, views, folders, or navigators.

◆ Users can't view or change formulas or LotusScript programs.

◆ Users can't change any of the database open properties (the set of actions performed by Notes when a database is opened).

◆ Users can't display a synopsis of the design.

◆ Users can't create a replica that has a non-hidden design.

You can always unhide a design in the future by replacing the design with the master template, after disabling the hiding of formulas and LotusScript programs.

PREVENTING PRINTING, COPYING, AND FORWARDING

Sometimes you want to allow reader access to sensitive data, while taking reasonable efforts to control the spread of this information. You can discourage people who have reader access to data from printing, copying, or forwarding it to other users. Follow these steps:

1. Open the form definition.

2. Right-click somewhere in the form and display the Form Properties dialog box.

3. Click the Security tab.

4. Select the option Disable Printing, Forwarding, Copying to Clipboard.

5. Save the form.

SUMMARY

Notes provides an extensive list of security features that enable you to protect databases, documents, and design elements. You can protect against users gaining access from the server console or against eavesdroppers on telecommunication lines. For further background on Notes security features, see Chapters 3 and 4.

Issuing IDs and certificates and managing access control lists are the primary jobs involved in Notes security. Notes administrators, database managers, and certifiers all play a role in administering Notes security. Certifiers are responsible for issuing certificates for ID files. Database managers are responsible for maintaining the ACLs on the databases that they control. Notes administrators are responsible for limiting access to Notes servers and supporting the other two roles. Proper planning and coordination can minimize the overhead needed to maintain a secure Notes system.

- Designing a Remote Network

- Configuring Dial-Up Servers

- Configuring Dial-Up Clients

- Training for Mobile Users

CHAPTER 19

Supporting Dial-Up Users

One of Notes' major advantages is its integrated ability to support remote and dial-up users. The typical mobile user is a salesperson or executive traveling around the globe on a regular basis. Notes is designed to support the needs of this user with no extra software required. Notes is being used increasingly to connect organizations, telecommuters, and virtual companies into powerful workgroups and teams.

Supporting disconnected remote sites poses special challenges to a Notes administrator. Because running a completely hands-off remote server is impossible, every geographic site must have at least a minimal level of talent available to help support a Notes installation. In addition, a number of challenges face you when configuring Notes remote support, including

◆ What type of connection to use for each remote site—modems, ISDN, permanent connections, direct connections to a single remote server, remote LAN connections, or Notes passthru

◆ How to support replication and mail routing for remote and mobile users

◆ How to upgrade software on remote servers and workstations

◆ Troubleshooting problems with remote hardware

This chapter shows you how to handle these issues, configuring your remote servers and clients to minimize the number of problems. For a complete discussion of network design, see Chapter 9, "Designing Your Notes Network."

DESIGNING A REMOTE NETWORK

The first step in designing your remote network is determining the needs of your users. You should use interviews and questionnaires, and review any logs of current activity, to help you determine their needs.

The next step is to decide which type of connections to support for each class of user. After the connection type is known, assigning servers to tasks is straightforward.

DIAL-UP ISSUES

Dial-up users face several issues requiring special attention by Notes administrators and trainers. Poor performance is a problem. Dial-up users with a 14.4 or 28.8 modem will have noticeably slow performance when connecting with a remote server. Dial-up users should avoid replicating large attachments whenever possible.

Each dial-up user has two ways of accessing data: replicating databases to the laptop, or connecting to a server every time she needs to access a database. This decision is made by the mobile user for each database access.

Each approach has advantages and disadvantages:

◆ The advantages of online access are that it saves disk space on the laptop, mail is routed immediately, and information is current. The disadvantages of online access are the higher telephone costs for long-distance calls, the requirement of more server modems to support a set of mobile users, and the fact that mobile users can't work while the server or network is down.

Mobile users are likely to be dialing in after hours from a motel room. Considering time zone differences, dial-up users often are trying to connect while a server is down for maintenance.

◆ The advantages of replicating data to a laptop include better performance when accessing databases, the fact that users can work while the server or network is down or when a phone isn't available, and lower telephone costs. The disadvantages of creating replicas on laptops are that users can't check addresses when creating mail without a replica of the Public Address Book on their laptops, and that mobile users must be trained in how to create and maintain replicas.

The Notes administrator needs to consider all these factors when deciding what connection type to support for each server or user.

In most cases, the increased flexibility and performance mobile users get from working from local replicas justifies replicating data to laptops. At a minimum, mobile users should have local replicas for frequently used or critical databases.

Online access is appropriate for large databases, such as reference databases or databases with large attachments, that don't lend themselves to replication.

CHOOSING CONNECTION TYPES

The first consideration when designing remote network topology is what type of physical connection to support between your remote offices, mobile users, and headquarters site. If you're just installing Notes for the first time, your remote offices likely are already connected using some networking software. You need to evaluate whether Notes can ride on top of that software. In addition, different remote users may have different communications needs. For each remote location or type of user (mobile user, telecommuter), you need to decide which of these physical connection types to support:

◆ Dial-up connections.

Notes supports workstation-server and server-server connections directly over modems using the XPC protocol. Although the XPC connection offers the least functionality, it has the advantage of not needing any software in addition to Notes.

◆ Passthru connections.

Release 4 servers can serve as conduits for connections to other Notes servers. This method enables workstations or servers connected via modem directly to another server to access other Notes servers on the network. A passthru connection gives access to all Notes resources on a network, but doesn't give access to non-Notes resources. Passthru connections don't require any software in addition to Notes.

◆ Remote LAN services.

Passthru and dial-up connections give users access to Notes resources. You may want to have a remote client connected to a network. The advantage of connecting to a network is that all servers on the network, not just Notes servers, are then visible to the workstation. The client still connects by using a modem, but runs a LAN protocol over the modem connection. Notes doesn't directly support dialing in to a network. You must install a third-party package that supports this feature.

◆ Connections using alternate networks.

A number of private networks exist that you could use to connect your remote offices and headquarters. For example, you could have CompuServe or Sprint install network connections directly into your headquarters or remote sites. The protocol used over these connections varies, but is commonly X.25. To support these type of networks, you must install communications software appropriate for the network, as well as the Notes driver for the network.

USING REMOTE LAN PACKAGES

Notes administrators can support dial-in users by using Notes XPC with passthru or with a networking package that allows users to dial in to a network rather than to a single server. When using a network-based dial-in, a network appears to users as it would connected locally on a LAN. All network resources are available, including printers, file servers, and Notes servers. TCP/IP (via PPP or SLIP) is a common protocol used when providing network-based dial-in. Microsoft RAS is another popular remote access service. When selecting remote LAN servers, you need to balance ease of administration, ease of use, and security concerns.

Allowing PPP access to your TCP/IP network can open several security breaches. A variety of ways to break into TCP/IP servers are known. Check with your telecommunications group or security consultant if you're concerned about security issues involved with allowing TCP/IP dial-in.

Remote LAN connections appear to applications as normal network applications after a connection has been established. Making that connection requires a few extra steps. Notes can automate these extra steps (user ID, password, and so on) for some remote LAN packages.

Once you've decided to use remote LAN software, the major issue left to decide is exactly what protocol and package to use. The protocol you should use is whatever protocol you are currently using on your network. For example, if you are currently running an SPX network, use a remote LAN software package that supports SPX over dial-up. The most common dial-up support today is PPP supporting either SPX or TCP/IP. Windows NT's remote access software is also a popular choice for remote access to servers—maybe more popular than any other remote software program.

The hardest part about configuring Notes to use remote LAN software is installing and testing the remote LAN software. Troubleshooting Notes connections becomes a matter of deciding whether you have a third-party software problem, a Notes configuration problem, or a Notes bug.

Using Passthru Connections

Passthru allows a Notes server to serve as a conduit for Notes clients. Clients can dial in to a single server and access other servers on the network. Passthru makes available only Notes resources. The Public Address Book allows you to create a secure environment using passthru. The Name and Address Book enables you to specify, for each passthru server, which servers can be accessed using passthru, as well as the servers that can be reached using a passthru connection (no matter which passthru server is used).

When supporting remote or mobile Notes users, Notes passthru is the best option. Setting up Notes passthru is considerably easier than other types of connections and allows complete access to all Notes resources on the network. In addition, the integrated security features are easy to manage and require no special training.

Remote or mobile users who are already set up to use a network dial-in should continue to do so. Users who need access to non-Notes resources also need to use a network dial-in package.

Once you've weighed the various advantages and disadvantages of different connection types and decided that passthru is the appropriate type of connection to support your dial-up users, you still need to decide how to implement passthru for your organization. Are you going to allow all your Notes servers to be accessed using passthru, or restrict access to only a few servers? It's easier to manage security in an environment where you limit the number of servers that can be accessed using passthru, but you run the risk of users being unable to access databases they need.

After you've identified the servers that are accessible using passthru, you need to designate one or more servers as the passthru server. All the servers that dial-up modem users can access by using passthru should have a network connection to at least one passthru server. For a higher degree of reliability, you should have at least two passthru servers set up for each network. You can designate a current server to do double duty as a passthru server. The only server that shouldn't also be used as a passthru server is your hub server. Hub servers never should be accessible to end users. For more details on hub servers, see Chapter 9.

After you've designed your network topology for passthru, decide whether to restrict passthru to a certain set of users. Restricting users who can use passthru provides some limited increase in security, because it prevents people who have a forged copy of an ID from accessing your Notes network if that ID isn't enabled for passthru. Your passthru servers contain access control lists that allow you to control the users who can use passthru.

POLICIES AND PROCEDURES

Every bit as important as the protocols and software you choose to support remote access for dial-up users are the policies and procedures you put in place. You can greatly simplify the task of administering and troubleshooting remote-access problems by following a few simple guidelines:

◆ Use a 1-800-number hunt group.

Hunt groups appear to the outside world as a single number. When a user dials in to a hunt group, the telephone call is forwarded to the first available line. This system allows you to make maximum use of your telephone lines. Without a hunt group, you need to assign numbers to users, attempting to split up the load across multiple phone lines. A hunt group enables you to avoid this division of phone numbers.

◆ Clients must call the server.

Notes requires that all remote access be initiated by a client. All remote users must be trained to access servers on a regular basis. Workstations based in home offices can easily have a schedule set up to initiate calls to the server.

These two techniques will greatly simplify your life as an administrator without burdening your users. They are highly recommended.

Configuring Dial-Up Servers

Now it's time to get down to the nitty-gritty—the step-by-step instructions for setting up remote access. Whether you are going to use passthru servers or remote LAN software, set up remote servers, or mix-and-match these strategies, you need to decide how many modems you will place on every server that is directly accessed by mobile users.

Determining the Number of Modems

For each server providing remote access in your Notes network, you need to determine how many modems are required. Too few modems means that your users can't get access to the network, and too many modems means that you have wasted money. To estimate the number of modems you need, estimate the number of minutes that users need to be connected in a given day, week, or month. Chart out the expected demand over the course of a day, so you know what your peak usage is likely to be. These are the factors that determine the number of minutes users are connected and your peak usage:

- ◆ Do users replicate databases or browse online?
- ◆ How much data must be replicated to laptops?
- ◆ How many databases are accessed by mobile users?
- ◆ When do users typically access Notes resources?

You should plan to provide a high level of servers to mobile users. The cost of a busy line can be quite high. If your mobile users use Notes for serious applications, they need assurance that they will be able to connect to the network as needed. A few busy numbers doesn't sound all that bad from an administrator's point of view, but it can quickly lead to frustration among users. If this situation eventually leads to an underused Notes platform, any money saved on phone lines and modems has been far more than offset by lost productivity.

Configuring Servers for a Passthru Network

All passthru servers must be Release 4 hierarchically named servers. After you have laid out your network by deciding which servers can be accessed as passthru servers and which servers will be passthru servers, actually setting up passthru is extremely easy. There are three steps in configuring passthru servers:

1. Setting up destination servers.
2. Setting up passthru servers.
3. Configuring a server to use passthru.

SETTING UP DESTINATION SERVERS

To allow a user to access a server by using passthru, follow these steps:

1. Open the server document for the server in Edit mode.
2. Open the Restrictions section of the server document.
3. In the Access This Server field, enter the users and servers that are allowed to access this server by using passthru. You can use names, groups, and wild cards or an * in this field. When the Access This Server field is blank, no one is allowed to access this server by using passthru.
4. Make sure that the following fields are blank for a destination server:
   - ◆ Route Thru
   - ◆ Cause Calling
   - ◆ Destinations Allowed
5. Choose Save.
6. Choose Close.

For a destination server to be accessible, both the destination server and the passthru server must be configured properly. The user or server attempting to access must be listed explicitly in the Access This Server field for the destination server. In addition, a passthru server must be set up to allow access to this server for the server or client calling.

If a passthru server lists this server as a legal destination but the destination server itself isn't set up to accept passthru connection, all passthru connections are denied. The server document for the destination server takes precedence over the server document in the passthru server.

SETTING UP PASSTHRU SERVERS

Before setting up passthru servers, compile a list of all destination servers that can be reached from this passthru server. Consider allowing access to all servers on the same network as the passthru server, but be more critical about allowing servers that can only be reached by modem from this server. To set up a passthru server, follow these steps:

1. Open the server document for the passthru server in Edit mode.
2. Expand the Restrictions section of the document.
3. In the Route Thru field, enter the names of all users and servers that are allowed to use this passthru server to access another destination server. Legal entries include user names, server names, groups, and wild cards.

Anyone not specifically listed in this field is denied access to this passthru server.

4. If you are allowing this passthru server to dial out to other servers to complete a connection, enter in the Cause Calling field the names of all servers that this server will call to complete a passthru connection. Legal entries include user names, server names, group names, and wild cards. If this field is blank, this passthru server can't dial out to complete a passthru connection.

5. In the Destinations Allowed field, enter the server names for all destination servers that can be reached by using this passthru server. Legal entries include server names, group names, and wild cards. If this field is blank, any server can be reached by using this passthru server.

6. Choose Save.

7. Choose Close.

The passthru restrictions that you set up in the Restrictions section don't affect general access to the server. For a user to use a passthru server, he must be listed in the Access Server field of the server document. The passthru restrictions also in no way affect access over a network to a server.

CONFIGURING A SERVER TO USE PASSTHRU

Both workstations and servers can be configured to reach a destination server by using a passthru server. Configuring workstations to use passthru is covered in the section "Configuring Dial-Up Clients," later in this chapter. To have a server use passthru when connecting to a destination server, you need to create a passthru connection document for these two servers in the Public Address Book. If the server can't directly access the passthru server on its local network, you need to create a connection document connecting this server to its passthru server as well.

You can set up a default passthru server that a server will use whenever it can't find another way to connect to a server, or you can define passthru servers to be used and/or indicate specific passthru servers to reach specific destination servers. To set up a default passthru server, perform the following steps:

1. Open the server document.

2. Open the Server Location Information section.

3. Enter the default passthru server in the Passthru Server field.

4. Choose Save.

5. Choose Close.

To configure a specific passthru server for a specific destination server, you need to create a connection document that specifies the proper passthru server. See Figure 19.1 for an example of a passthru server connection document linking two servers.

Figure 19.1.
A passthru server
connection document
linking two servers.

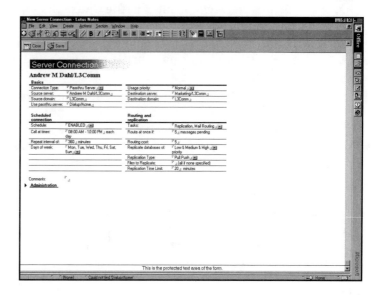

To create a passthru server connection document linking two servers, follow these steps:

1. Open the Server Connection view in the Public Address Book.
2. Choose Add Connection.
3. Select Passthru Server for the connection type.
4. Fill in the Source Server and Source Domain fields.
5. Fill in the Destination Server and Destination Domain fields. The destination server is the server that hosts the databases of interest.
6. Enter the full hierarchical name for the passthru server you want to use to contact the specified destination server.
7. Set up a schedule for connecting the two servers. Decide whether you are going to enable or disable this connection at a specific time, enter the time of day during which the schedule is valid, enter the number of minutes between calls in the Repeat Interval Of field, and select the days of the week for which this connection record is valid.

8. Configure the Mail Routing and Replication fields with the following settings:

   ◆ Specify the tasks to be accomplished when two servers are connected.

   ◆ Enter a threshold for the maximum number of mail messages that can be pending before a connection is initiated.

   ◆ Enter a cost factor for this connection. The default of 5 represents an asynchronous connection to the destination server.

   ◆ Specify the database priorities to replicate.

   ◆ Specify the replication type. Pull-Push replication is the desired method of replicating.

   ◆ Specify the databases to be replicated. Enter the full relative file name for each database.

   ◆ In the Replication Time Limit field, enter the maximum number of minutes for a single call.

9. Choose Save.

10. Choose Close.

If the source server can't directly connect to the passthru server on the same Notes named network, you must create a connection document linking the source server to the passthru server. In addition, there must be a connection linking the passthru server to the destination server.

CONFIGURING REMOTE SERVERS

A remote server is any Notes server dedicated to serving dial-up users. Remote servers differ from passthru servers in that remote servers host the databases themselves. The major disadvantage to remote servers is that you must create a replica of every database needed by any dial-up user.

If you already have remote servers set up, you can continue to use them for some time. The major issue facing you in this case is when to migrate to a passthru server.

Passthru servers are generally a better choice than setting up remote servers to serve dial-up users. The one exception to this rule is servers that are accessed by external organizations. To control security and limit the databases accessed by external organizations, use a remote server and create replicas of databases they are allowed to access. Servers available to the outside world that also allow anonymous access should be set up as remote servers rather than passthru servers.

CONFIGURING REMOTE LAN SERVERS

Remote LAN software must be obtained from a third party; it isn't shipped as part of Notes. Follow the instructions on your package. Make sure that your remote LAN connections are working before attempting to make a connection via Notes.

CONFIGURING DIAL-UP CLIENTS

Dial-up clients should use at least a 14.4 modem (28.8 is better, of course). Setting up a dial-in client involves

◆ Creating a replica of the corporate Public Address Book on the laptop (if the laptop has enough space—I'll discuss this in a minute)

◆ Enabling an asynchronous COM port

◆ Configuring the modem in Notes

◆ Creating a remote connection document for a server in the Personal Address Book on the laptop

◆ Configuring mail and replication settings

Dial-up clients can be set up to

◆ Directly connect to another server

◆ Use passthru to connect to a Notes network

◆ Connect using a remote LAN service

The client must be configured slightly differently for each of these options.

CONFIGURING COM PORTS

The first thing you need to do is to install a modem on the laptop. Make sure you use a modem that is supported by Notes. You can contact the Lotus Web site (www.LOTUS.COM) for a current list of supported modems. Make sure that the modem is working before proceeding with the Notes configuration. After installing and testing the modem, enable a Notes asynchronous COM port by following these steps:

1. Start the Notes workstation.
2. Choose File | Tools | User Preferences.
   The User Preferences dialog box appears.
3. Click the Ports icon.
4. From the list of Communication Ports, select the COM*x* port on which you installed the modem. If you installed the modem on a COM port that isn't

listed, click the New button and type the name of the port. The rest of these instructions assume that you've installed your modem on COM2.

5. Choose Port Enabled.

6. (optional) You can encrypt data sent over a modem by checking the Encrypt Network Data box.

7. Select COM2 Options.

   The Additional Setup dialog box opens.

8. From the Modem Type drop-down list, select the type of modem installed in the laptop. If you don't see your modem listed, contact Lotus to see whether one exists, or select the Auto Configure setting.

   The Modem Type list box lists all files with an .MDM extension in your Notes data/modems directory. Place any new or custom modem driver files in the Notes data/modems directory and then return to this dialog box.

   If you can't find an exact match, choose the closest match. For example, if you have U.S. Robotics Sportster and you can't find that model listed, try other U.S. Robotics modems before settling on automatic modem selection.

   You also can create a custom modem file. Follow the earlier steps under "Configuring Dial-In Servers" to edit your own modem file.

9. Set the port speed, speaker volume, and dialing mode.

10. Select the logging options. You can elect to log all modem I/O and script I/O. You should enable logging when you initially install a modem to aid in detecting any possible errors. Because logging modem I/O can consume a significant amount of disk space, however, you should disable logging modem I/O as soon as you know that the modem is working reliably.

11. Enter a dial timeout in seconds.

12. Enter the number of minutes that can go by with no user activity before a line is disconnected.

13. The behavior of the Hang Up If Idle option is determined by the settings on both the server and the client. The call is terminated at the lesser of the two settings. If the server is set to hang up after 10 minutes and the client is set to hang up after 20 minutes, the call is terminated by the server after 10 idle minutes.

14. (optional) Select Hardware Flow Control. This option is selected by default. Deselect this option if either the client modem or the server modem doesn't support hardware flow control.

15. Enter a port number for the modem.

16. For an asynchronous COM port, the port number is the same as the COM number. For example, the port number for COM2 is 2.

17. (optional) You can reorder COM ports by using the Reorder up/down arrows. Notes attempts to make a connection using ports starting at the beginning of the list and working down. Ports disabled at the current location are ignored. To reorder a port, highlight the port and use the up arrow to improve its priority or the down arrow to lower its priority.

18. Enable a modem port for all remote locations for the laptop.

19. Choose OK.

20. (optional) Specify a script to be used.

    A script file is a set of commands that allow Notes to complete a connection. Modem files allow Notes to manipulate the local modem. Script files allow Notes to navigate a network. For example, your modem can dial into an Internet service provider, but a script file is required to enter the user name, password, and server address. You specify a script file by selecting the Require Script option and selecting the proper script from the list.

    Notes is shipped with some sample script files to help you understand how to create script files. Check with your service provider for scripts, or check on CompuServe or on the Lotus Web site for scripts for common public networks. You also can create your own script file, using the samples as a guideline.

When you have completed configuring the Notes asynchronous communication port, you need to set up a dial-up server connection.

Personal Address Book Documents for Dial-Up

Mobile users must have a location document for each geographical location where they work. For each location, you need to tell Notes how to connect to the Notes servers in your network. You also need to specify from each location exactly which tasks should be accomplished. You can specify mail routing, replication, or both. You also can customize your replication based on location. You can specify, for each location, which databases to replicate, when to replicate, and whether you want to replicate only partial documents.

Dial-up modem connections include any connection that uses the modem on a laptop. This includes directly connecting to a Notes server, as well as connecting to a remote LAN service. The configuration of the location document is identical in either case. The server connection documents specified for a location differentiate between a direct connection, a passthru connection, or a remote LAN service connection.

CREATING LOCATION DOCUMENTS

The Personal Address Book for mobile users must contain a location document for every geographical location from which the user works. A location document contains information about default servers to use from that location, connection information such as phone numbers or the network to use, and schedules for connecting to a server.

Notes automatically creates four location documents in the Personal Address Book when the workstation is installed. Most mobile users can get by with just personalizing these four documents. The following list describes the four default locations:

◆ Office.

The office location document is used when the mobile user is connected to the same network as his Notes servers.

◆ Home.

The home connection document specifies how to connect to headquarters from a home office.

◆ Travel.

A travel document should be created for each time zone to which a person travels on a regular basis.

◆ Island.

An island is anywhere that a user doesn't want to connect to a Notes server.

You can optimize each location document for the type of connection available. For example, you could set up your mail file in the office location document to be server-based, while the home and travel location documents specify workstation-based mail.

Location documents also let you specify information, such as calling cards, that can be used only from certain locations. For example, you probably will use calling-card information only when traveling and calling in from hotels.

Location documents contain information that is configurable using the Replicator page from a Release 4 workspace. See the later section "Configuring Replication" for more information on configuring replication for mobile users.

CREATING LOCATIONS USING USER PROFILES

Creating a single location document is a relatively easy task. Mobile users need to be trained in creating location documents and can carry a great deal of the load. Administrators should provide users with as much information as possible.

Administrators supporting a number of mobile users are faced with the task of configuring several hundred location documents. The administrators can simplify the process of creating these location documents by using user setup profiles. Each profile specifies a set of default servers for a user. For complete information on user setup profiles, see Chapter 18, "Administering Notes Security."

CREATING LOCATION DOCUMENTS MANUALLY

Location documents must be stored in the mobile user's Personal Address Book. To create a location document, follow these steps:

1. Open the user's Personal Address Book.
2. Open the Locations view.
3. Create a new location by clicking the Add Location button.

   or

   Edit a current location by highlighting it and then selecting Edit Location.

See the following sections for information on filling in location documents for each type of location supported.

CONFIGURING LOCATIONS

Three types of location documents exist with which you should be familiar: Remote Locations, Office Locations, and Disconnected (Island) Locations. The Notes Install program creates a sample of each of these location documents when the workstation program is installed. The following sections describe how to edit each of these documents for your organization.

CONFIGURING NETWORK CONNECTIONS

Locations where you have a LAN connection to your Notes servers should have a network location document. You typically have only one network-based location document for your home office. To configure a network-based location document, follow these steps:

1. Open the Personal Address Book.
2. Open the Locations view.
3. Highlight the office connection document, if it exists. Otherwise, choose Add Location.
4. Type a meaningful name for the location.
5. Select Local Area Network as the location type.

6. Leave the default setting of No for the Prompt for Time/Day/Phone option, as you won't be using phone dial-up from this location.

7. Fill in the correct time zone.

8. Check each of the ports that you want to use at this location. Generally, you select just your LAN connections for a network-based location document.

9. Fill in the full hierarchical name for your default servers.

10. Specify the location of your mail file. For network-based connections, you should generally use server-based mail even if you have a local copy of your mail file.

11. Enter the file name for your mail file. If you don't know the file name, contact the administrator responsible for mail.

12. Fill in the desired action for Recipient Name Type Ahead. Recipient name type ahead is the feature that allows Notes to fill in a recipient's name while you are typing.

13. Enter a replication schedule for this location. Generally, for network locations you specify a frequent replication schedule so that your local replicas will be updated while you are in the office.

14. Open the Advanced section.

15. If this location document is for use by a specific set of users, fill in the Only for User field. You can use wild cards or group names to specify groups of users.

16. Choose Save.

When completed, your network location document should look similar to Figure 19.2.

Configuring Islands

An island is any location with no connection to your Notes servers. From an island, users must work with local replicas. There is certainly less information to fill in when configuring an island location document. See Figure 19.3 for a sample location document.

To create an island location document, follow these steps:

1. Open a Personal Address Book.

2. Open the Location view.

3. If the island location document exists, edit it or click the Add Location button.

4. Type a meaningful location name.

5. Select No Connection as the location type.

6. Specify the file name for the local copy of the mailbox.

7. Fill in the desired values for Recipient Name Type Ahead and Recipient Name Lookup.

8. Open the Advanced section and enter the names of all users who should use this location document. The default asterisk makes this location document available to all users.

Figure 19.2.
A network-based
location document.

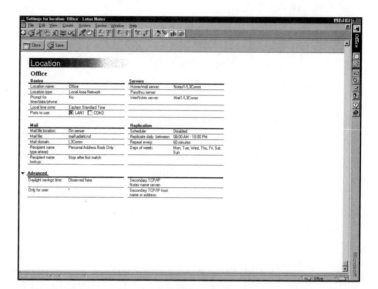

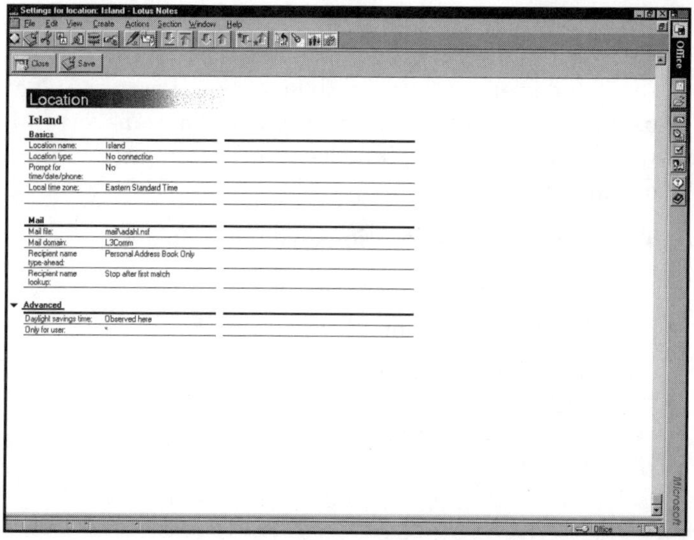

Figure 19.3.
An island location
document.

Each laptop user needs only a single island location document to support all locations from which no connection to a Notes server is desired.

CONFIGURING CONNECTION DOCUMENTS

Once you have set up your location documents, you are ready to specify the connection information for each server for each location. If you have a large number of locations from which you work and/or a large number of servers to which you connect remotely, you may have a large number of connection documents. You need a connection document for each server for each location, so that you can specify on a server-by-server basis when to connect via modem and when to connect via a LAN-based protocol.

If mobile users are using passthru servers, you need only specify a connection document for a passthru server. Destination servers that can be reached from the passthru server don't need connection documents. Whenever a user attempts to access a server for which no other connection document exists at the current location, Notes attempts to connect to the passthru server. The passthru server for a location is specified in the location document. You can specify multiple passthru servers for a location by creating extra server connection documents for a location with a connection type of passthru.

CONFIGURING DIAL-UP MODEM CONNECTIONS

Setting up a connection document that directly connects a mobile user to a server is a very simple process. You simply need to create a server connection document that specifies the server name and phone number and a dial-up modem connection type. Figure 19.4 shows a typical dial-up modem connection document.

To create a dial-up modem connection document, follow these steps:

1. Open the Personal Address Book.
2. Open the Server Connection view.
3. Edit a current connection document or create a new one by choosing Add Connection.
4. Select Dial-Up Modem for the connection type.
5. If you will always be dialing long distance when connecting to the server over modem, enter Yes for Always Use Area Code. Otherwise, enter No. If your location document is set up to prompt you automatically for area code and dialing information, leave this field as No, because you will have an opportunity to fill in that information when you connect.
6. Fill in the full hierarchical name for the server.
7. Fill in the country code, area code, and phone number for the server.
8. Open the Advanced section of the document.

9. Select the locations from which this connection document is valid. For dial-up modem connection, you generally select home and travel connections.

10. Specify the users that are allowed to use this connection document.

11. Specify a priority for this connection document. The default for a dial-up modem connection is Low Priority. This setting allows LAN connections to take precedence over dial-up connections.

12. Enter the modem port number for this laptop.

13. Fill in any log-in script and script arguments needed to access the server from the particular location.

14. Choose Save.

15. Choose Close.

Figure 19.4.
A typical dial-up modem connection document.

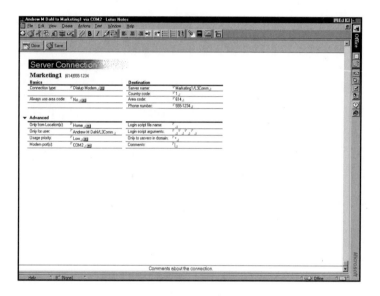

Generally speaking, you need only a single dial-up modem connection for each server. You can use the same connection document from all remote locations, as the phone number for a server generally doesn't change based on the travels of a user.

CONFIGURING PASSTHRU CONNECTIONS

You can set up a default passthru server for a location and/or a specific passthru server for each destination server. A destination server is any server hosting a database that you need to access. Connection documents that specify a specific passthru server for a destination server take precedence over the default passthru server specified in the location document. The passthru server in the location document is used only when no other connection to a server is in the Personal Address Book. All passthru servers must have a connection document that tells Notes how to connect to the passthru server. This is true whether the passthru server is specified in the location document or in a server connection document.

Notes attempts to use the server to which you are currently connected as a passthru server when

- No connection document is specified for your destination server.
- There is no default passthru specified for the current location.
- The destination server isn't located on the same physical network as the laptop.
- You are currently connected via an XPC dial-up modem connection to a server.

If the attempt to use the current server as a passthru server fails, your attempt to access the destination server will fail.

To set a default passthru server for a location, enter the full hierarchical name of the passthru server in the location document. Typically, this field already will be filled in by the administrator, using a user setup profile. The profile causes the correct location and connection documents to be created in a Personal Address Book.

To specify a different passthru server for a destination server, follow these steps:

1. Open the Personal Address Book.
2. Open the Server Connection view.
3. Edit a current connection document or create a new connection document by selecting Add Connection.
4. Select Passthru Server as the connection type.
5. Enter the full hierarchical name of the destination server. The destination server is the server hosting the database that you want to access.

   You can use wild cards in the Destination Server Name field to create a connection document for a group of servers. For example, if you have several servers certified by L3COMM, such as Marketing/L3COMM, Mail/L3COMM, and Notes 1/L3COMM, you can create a connection document that specifies a passthru server for all three of these servers by entering */L3COMM in the Destination Server Name field. Connection documents that use wild cards have a lower precedence than connection documents that specify a full name for a destination server. If you had a fourth server (such as Legal/L3COMM) that should use a different passthru server, you still could create a connection document, specifying the full name for Legal/L3COMM.

6. Specify the full hierarchical name of the passthru server to be contacted when attempting to reach the destination server.

7. Open the Advanced section of the document.

8. Specify the locations for which this passthru connection document should be used. Typically, passthru servers are used from home and travel locations.

9. Specify the users for whom this connection document applies.

10. Specify a usage priority for this connection document. Leaving the default at Low causes Notes to attempt to use network-based connections for this location when feasible.

11. (optional) Enter some descriptive comments for this server connection.

12. Choose Save.

13. Choose Close.

When you are done, your server connection should resemble Figure 19.5.

Figure 19.5.
A typical passthru
server connection
document.

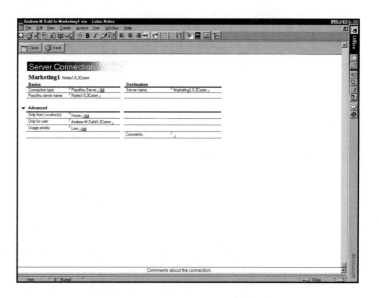

Don't forget to create another connection document that tells Notes how to contact the passthru server. The connection to the passthru server can be a LAN, a remote LAN, or a dial-up modem connection.

CONFIGURING REMOTE LAN CONNECTIONS

Remote LAN software fakes out the applications running on your machine so they believe that they are physically connected to a LAN—though they are connected via modem. All network resources available on a LAN can be made available via modem, using remote LAN software. Remote LAN software packages are available from third-party vendors and aren't part of Lotus Notes. Some remote LAN software packages can be controlled by Notes; Notes can initiate a connection or hangup. Other types of remote LAN software can't be controlled by Notes; a user would have to start a connection manually, start Notes, and then manually disconnect when finished.

If you have a package that can't be controlled by Notes, set up normal network connection documents for your Notes workstation, as Notes will behave exactly as if it were connected on a network. If you are using a remote LAN software package that can be controlled by Notes, set up a remote LAN service connection document. The few parameters needed by the remote LAN software can be entered into the connection document. Figure 19.6 shows an example of a remote LAN service connection document.

Figure 19.6.
A remote LAN service
connection document.

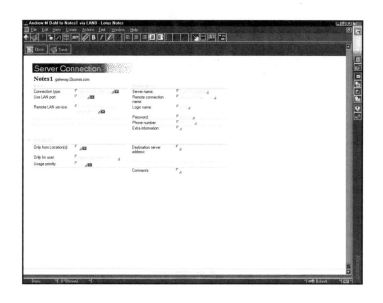

To create a remote LAN service connection document, follow these steps:

1. Open the Personal Address Book.
2. Open the Server Connection view.
3. Edit a current location document or create a new one by selecting Add Location.
4. Select Remote LAN Service for the connection type.
5. Specify the port that you have configured to use the protocol supported by the remote LAN software. This is typically a LAN port, not a COM port.

19

SUPPORTING DIAL-UP USERS

6. Specify the type of remote LAN software you are using. Notes 4 supports Microsoft Remote Access Service. Check with Lotus for a current list of supported software.

7. Enter the full hierarchical name of the destination server.

8. Enter the name of the computer that acts as a gateway to the network. This computer in many cases isn't a Notes computer. You need to enter the name of this computer as it is known to your remote LAN software, so that your remote LAN software knows how to connect.

9. Enter the login name and password to be used by the remote LAN software.

10. Enter a phone number for the remote gateway.

11. Open the Advanced section of the document.

12. Specify the locations that should use this connection document.

13. Specify the users who should use this connection document.

14. Specify usage priority for the connection document. Normally the default of Low is appropriate.

15. Enter the server address of the destination server, if required by your remote LAN software.

16. Choose Save.

17. Choose Close.

Before attempting to test a remote LAN service, you should have installed and configured the remote LAN software and tested it to make sure that you can make a connection. After you have completely installed and tested your remote LAN software, configure and test your Notes connection.

CONFIGURING ADDRESS BOOKS

The Address Book is the heart and soul of Notes. So what do your laptop users do when they are on the road? Without access to the Public Address Book, they have to rely on their puny Personal Address Books. All your carefully crafted groups go right out the window. You have seen what a user must do, just trying to configure location documents. The user also needs to be able to configure group documents—not just for the users with whom he wants to communicate, but for servers.

Personal Address Books come with two empty default groups that mobile users need to maintain. The group OtherDomainServers is a list of all servers from other domains with which the laptop user needs to communicate. LocalDomainServers is the list of servers within an organization with which the laptop user needs to communicate. Because these are documents in the user's Personal Address Book, they can't be replicated from the Public Address Book. A mobile user needs to edit these documents manually to add and delete servers as needed.

This situation raises the question, "Why not just put a copy of the Public Address Book on all laptops? It already contains all the groups users will need for security and mail routing and it could be updated through replication." Notes has built-in support that enables users to have both a copy of the Public Address Book and their own Personal Address Book on their laptops. So why not put a copy of the Public Address Book on all laptops? Users still would have to edit their own location documents and the two server groups. The server groups are needed so that the design changes replicate properly to replicas on the laptop; even if you keep a copy of the Public Address Book on a laptop, the client won't check it when determining access. The Public Address Book also can be quite large in many organizations, but with laptops nowadays typically ranging from 800 megabytes to 1 gigabyte, that's less of a concern than in the past.

The one advantage that you can get from keeping a replica of the Public Address Book on a laptop is that the user will know instantly if he has a typo in a mail recipient's name. The client can resolve groups and user names against the Public Address Book without having to wait to connect to the headquarters location. In the absence of a copy of the Public Address Book, the client simply assumes that a mail message is addressed correctly and sends it off. The first server to receive the message checks it against the Public Address Book, finds the typo, and sends back a nondelivery report. The user may not get the nondelivery report until the next time he is connected, and then may not be able to send the reply immediately. All in all, the time lost due to a simple typo can be unacceptable. So, if you've got the disk space available on the laptop, add a copy of the Public Address Book and configure it as a cascaded address book.

Tip

To set up cascaded address books, you simply need to edit the Names setting in the NOTES.INI file. Add the file name of the Public Address Book after the file name for the Personal Address Book, separated by a comma.

Make sure that the replication schedule for the laptop includes the Public Address Book, so that groups will be updated on a regular basis.

CONFIGURING REPLICATION

Laptop users who need to work while not connected to the home office must create replicas of all the databases they need. This fact implies that mobile users need a replication schedule to keep their databases updated. The goals you should have when setting up a mobile user replication schedule are as follows:

◆ Keeping critical information updated on a regular basis

◆ Minimizing phone charges

The basic strategy you should follow is to replicate high-priority databases such as the mailbox with every connection, while limiting the replication of large databases or low-priority databases to network-based locations. You also can limit your phone charges by setting up a maximum replication time or by replicating partial documents only. This strategy assumes that mobile users will be in the home office on a regular basis so that they can perform full replications.

You can limit replication time from either the client or server. You can set up your dial-up or passthru servers to limit replication time by editing the ReplicationTimeLimit setting in the NOTES.INI file. You also can edit a connection document on the server and enter a number in the Replication Time Limit field. The default when this field isn't filled in is to complete replication no matter how much time it takes.

One important part of replication for mobile users is the replication of design changes. You must give servers with which you replicate at least designer access to all replicas on your laptop. The easiest way to do this is to add all servers to the LocalDomainServers group in the Personal Address Book. This assumes that your organization is using LocalDomainServers and OtherDomainServers in database access control lists, and that these groups are given manager or designer access to databases. If your organization is using some other group name, create the appropriate group and enter servers into it.

Mobile users can develop a detailed replication plan for each location, using the Replicator page from the workspace. The Replicator page is always the last tab on a workspace, and changes depending on your location. To configure a Replicator page, follow these steps:

1. Choose File | Mobile | Choose Current Location.

   The Choose Location dialog box opens.

2. Select your location and click OK.

The Replicator page is now customized for the selected location. All database replicas on your laptop are automatically listed in the Replicator page. You can choose to replicate a database by selecting it from the list. The Replicator page also lets you initiate or hang up calls on demand as well as send mail.

CONFIGURING MAIL

Mail is the lifeline that connects mobile users to their organizations. Users need constant access to e-mail to create, send, or read the latest messages. Mobile users ideally should have access to their e-mail at all times. This system requires maintaining a replica copy of the mailbox on the laptop. If the laptop was configured as a mobile station during the initial setup, a replica of the user's mailbox has already been created on the laptop. Otherwise, you need to create a replica manually on the laptop. See Chapter 15, "Administering Replication," for details on creating replicas.

You can specify a different mail file for every location. For non-network-based locations, specify the local replica of your mailbox. This strategy enables you to create new messages offline and have them mailed the next time you connect. While in the office, you should use server-based mail so you have access to the latest e-mail. The mail file is configured in the location document.

Users should copy commonly used groups from the Public Address Book to the Personal Address Book. This plan enables the Notes client to check for typos even while not connected to a network.

Training for Mobile Users

Mobile users have to perform several tasks that are normally performed by an administrator, including

- Creating replicas
- Monitoring disk space
- Creating connection documents in the Personal Address Book
- Creating group documents in the Personal Address Book

Training for mobile users thus overlaps somewhat with training for administrators. It's important that mobile users know how to perform these tasks. Users should know how to create replicas on their laptops, and so must understand the concept of replication. Make sure that users enforce local security, so that they aren't confused when using local copies. For more details on local security, see Chapter 18.

Mobile users maintaining local replicas of databases should check disk space on a regular basis. Some databases can grow quite large. You need to make sure that mobile users purge local copies on a regular basis so that they don't run out of disk space.

Mobile users also need to know how to maintain an address book so that they can address mail and connect to servers. Because mobile users don't have access to the Public Address Book while disconnected, they need to copy parts of the Public Address Book to their Personal Address Books. Mobile users should copy all group documents for mail that they want to send, as well as server documents for servers to which they want to connect.

SUMMARY

Supporting mobile users can be quite a challenge. Even in a perfect environment, mobile users don't receive the same level of service as LAN-based users. Mobile users have extra hurdles, including mail routing and replication. Dialing in over a 14.4 or 28.8 modem doesn't make life particularly easy when replicating large databases. Because mobile users don't have direct access to the Public Address Book, they often have to spend more time maintaining the Personal Address Book than network-based users.

There's no doubt about it: supporting mobile users is more time-intensive than supporting LAN-based users. Some planning can help you minimize the amount of effort required to support remote users. You should carefully analyze the needs of your organization and mobile users when deciding how to support remote access to Notes resources. Your basic choices, which can be mixed-and-matched as desired, are

- ◆ Dial-up modem servers, containing replicas of all databases used by mobile users
- ◆ Passthru servers that allow access to other Notes servers on the network
- ◆ Remote LAN services that give access to all computer resources on the network, not just Notes

No matter which topology you choose, the extra cost involved in stringing phone lines and installing modems can be substantial. Some analysis of the number of connections needed should be done with an eye toward adequately supporting your peak usage demands. One way to make the best use of your phone lines and modems is to use a hunt group, which can be supplied by your local telephone company.

One more word to the wise: Buy name-brand modems. Modems are one of the most trouble-prone areas in Notes. The amount of administrative effort required to set up and configure no-name modems will far more than offset the slight cost advantage. Buy the fastest name-brand modems, and consider using multi-port modems for large installations.

CHAPTER 20

by Rob Wunderlich

Connecting Notes to the Internet with InterNotes

Somewhere between Notes R3 and Notes R4, the Internet became an overnight sensation. Despite the fact that the Internet has been around for 25 years, the sudden rush of software companies to embrace the Web became a literal stampede.

The Internet revolution at first seemed to challenge Notes. But Lotus moved quickly to integrate Notes and the Internet—to have them work together instead of competing with each other. That was when the InterNotes family of products came into being.

This chapter focuses on Notes and the Internet—from publishing to browsing to mail. The text even spends a minute to talk about other opportunities, such as the global Notes connections offered by CompuServe, the Lotus Notes Network, and WorldCom.

The job for the Notes administrator has taken on a whole new dimension, as Notes servers are now talking to the world via the Internet.

Note

A quick comment here about Internet connectivity issues. For the purpose of this chapter, the assumption is that your organization is already talking to the Internet in some fashion. Although fascinating topics, it's beyond the scope of this book to discuss the pros and cons of SLIP versus PPP, T1 versus ISDN hookups, and so on.

For the InterNotes products to operate, you need a live (not dial-up) Internet connection. This chapter assumes that your organization is hooked up and you've managed to deliver the Internet to the Notes 4 server. If you haven't done that already, this chapter will be interesting theory, but little else. InterNotes features don't work on a dial-up connection.

A WORD ABOUT LOTUS AND THE INTERNET

The Internet aspect of Notes is probably the area most likely to undergo changes over the life of Notes 4 and, as such, some of the details in this chapter are subject to change. Particularly from an administrator's viewpoint, a manual add-in today may well become an "automatic feature" tomorrow—so don't be surprised if some of the details that follow seem like the "good old days!"

Lotus is continually refining its Internet strategy; as more features are developed, they will be rolled into interim versions of Notes 4. Likewise, today's add-in products will likely be rolled into the main product.

A perfect example of this changing scene is the InterNotes Web Publisher. Originally a $7,500 separate product, it became a $3,500 separate product, then a "free" separate product (assuming the correct combination of support contract and/or product version) and then a free product, included in the package.

One of the best ways to keep abreast of Lotus' evolving Internet strategy and product line is to check in frequently with the InterNotes home page (http://www.lotus.com/inotes/). This Internet site is a great source of information about the Lotus Internet product line, features downloadable beta versions of products, and so on, as well as numerous links to Lotus Business Partners and others who've employed the InterNotes products and can offer assistance.

From an outsider's perspective, Lotus appears to be succeeding in the attempt to integrate Notes with the Internet. Its position is going to continue to grow and change (much as the products themselves), and as the Internet itself evolves, Lotus and the InterNotes products will evolve right along.

The InterNotes Family

There are four individual members of the InterNotes family:

- ◆ InterNotes Web Publisher—A Notes server application that provides Web site content from Notes databases and captures information from Web visitors into Notes databases.
- ◆ InterNotes News—Notes server application that captures Usenet news articles and enables Notes users to participate in newsgroups from Notes databases.
- ◆ Web Navigator—A Notes client feature that allows direct Internet access from within Notes itself.
- ◆ InterNotes "Web" or "Web Retriever"—The server task that facilitates the Navigator.

Although each of these products has merit, the product garnering the most critical acclaim is the InterNotes Web Publisher. This chapter looks at each of the individual products, but the Web Publisher comes first and gets the most attention.

In addition to the InterNotes family of products, some of the following text takes a look at Internet gateways for mail and other public offerings.

Web Publisher Close-Up

Now that you have met the InterNotes family, spend some time with the main product, InterNotes Web Publisher.

From an administrator's perspective, Web Publisher is wonderful, because it enables "normal people" to create content for a Web site. After the administrator has configured the InterNotes server correctly, everybody else does the work!

WHAT DOES WEB PUBLISHER DO?

In the most simple explanation, Web Publisher publishes Notes databases as HTML-coded documents and makes them available to specialized servers on the World Wide Web (the Web). Web servers are a special subset of machines hooked to the Internet; they're often called HTTP servers because they offer hypertext links between documents.

Web Publisher, by default, turns the database's About document into a home page, and the database's views become the way to navigate through the documents.

Web Publisher publishes new documents and modifications to existing ones, as well as removing individual documents or even entire databases from a Web site. Because it supports Notes doclinks, a Notes user can easily reference another Notes document with a simple doclink. It also supports file attachments, Notes tables, and even full-text indexes (enabling Web visitors to search a database). Perhaps most remarkably, Web Publisher enables users to paste a bitmap onto a Notes document, and it automatically converts it, regardless of original format, into GIF format for publication on the Web.

The transformation of a document in Notes to a Web-published document is seamless, automatic, and painless. The document on the Web appears virtually identical to the original document in Notes (see Figures 20.1 and 20.2).

Figure 20.1.
A document in the
Notes database.

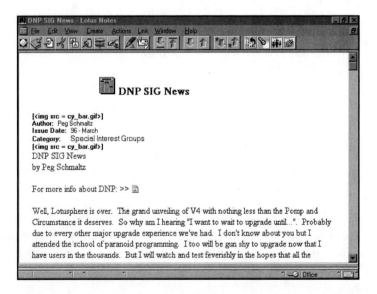

Figure 20.2.
The same document
published via
InterNotes (shown
through Netscape
Navigator).

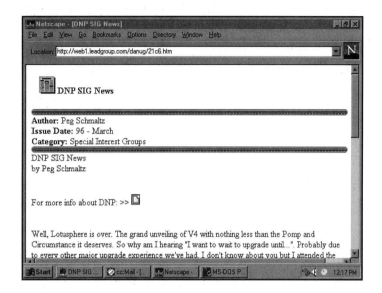

The two versions of the document are startlingly similar; both contain headings, graphics, text, and even the doclink is supported on the Web.

This document was published on the Web via InterNotes, yet other methods could have been employed. The biggest difference is that you can compose it, edit it, and even delete it in Notes. In essence, the content side of the database is easy—if you're familiar with Notes, you're a potential content provider. And the changes are done automatically in Notes.

If you've ever tried keeping a Web site current, you know that even the slightest change requires major work. Fire up the HTML editor, load the document, make the change, save the document, FTP it to your Web site, and so on. InterNotes Web Publisher handles all this work automatically.

There are two versions of InterNotes Web Publisher: Web Publisher 2.1, a Notes 3.x version, and Web Publisher 4.0, a Notes 4.x version. Each runs as a server add-in task and obviously requires the appropriate version of Notes server to be running. Although the functionality of the two is similar, Web Publisher 4.0 has some notable additional capabilities:

◆ It supports publishing Navigators as image maps.

◆ Link hotspots can be used for URLs.

◆ You can use and publish subforms, both computed and named.

◆ You can use bullets and numbered lists.

◆ Formulas can detect whether the user is viewing the document in Notes or on the Web.

◆ You can publish folders as well as views.

HARDWARE REQUIREMENTS

You're adding an additional server task, as well as most likely adding the Web site server itself. At the very least, the Web Publisher server should be a 486 or better machine, with an absolute minimum of 32 megabytes of memory (64M is better, and more than that if you can afford it—operating systems thrive on a lot of memory).

Depending on the eventual usage you envision for the server, the hard drive should probably start at 1 gigabyte and go up from there.

SOFTWARE REQUIREMENTS

Both Web Publisher versions require an OS/2 or Windows NT Notes server. For InterNotes Web Publisher 2.x, the OS/2 version requires Notes Server for OS/2 3.31 or better; the NT version requires Notes Server for NT 3.2 or better. For InterNotes Web Publisher 4.x, the requirement is Notes 4.x on either platform.

The operating system must be OS/2 Warp 3.0 or Windows NT Server 3.1 or 3.51. The Notes 4.x server is certified at those levels, along with its various add-in server tasks. Whatever the operating system, the necessary network and/or Internet connections must be in place, along with whatever gateways and so on may be needed. Just like a typical Notes server, the box itself needs to be configured for whatever protocol and network are in place. The assumption is that the box is up and running, communicating with the network and the Internet.

In addition, the Notes 4 server must be installed and running. Typically, this Notes server is similar in setup to other Notes servers in your organization. See the discussion later about the "skeleton server."

Caution

Keep in mind that, if you're placing this server on the Internet, it's in a position to be accessed by the outside world. Couple that with the fact that Notes 4 allows anonymous access, and there's a huge potential security problem.

If you haven't thought through the security aspects, *don't set up the server*. Setting up a Notes server outside your firewall isn't to be taken lightly; serious security considerations exist. In addition, keep in mind those unsavory types in the world who would like nothing better than to use a Notes/Web server to shoehorn their way into your network.

See the later discussion about the skeleton server for thoughts about security.

Typically, the Web Publisher server is also the Web *site* server (that is, the box that serves the HTML documents to the Internet). Therefore, in addition to the operating system and the Notes server, a Web HTTP server also must be in place.

Several well-known and easily configured Web servers exist: Netscape (`http://www.netscape.com`) offers a robust Web server for Windows NT and UNIX, O'Reilly and Associates (`http://www.ora.com`) offers a product called Web Site for NT and Windows 95. The major PC magazines frequently run comparison articles; check recent issues.

Tip

> A quick search at Yahoo (`http://www.yahoo.com`) or WebCrawler (`http://www.webcrawler.com`) for *Internet, servers* yields a lengthy list of products you can check out. There are sites for the major commercial publishers, as well as many shareware products. In most cases, you can download a demo version to try for 30 or 60 days.

The Web Publisher hardware and software requirements are met when

◆ The hardware component is purchased and of sufficient horsepower.

◆ The operating system of the box itself is in place and running smoothly.

◆ Connectivity with the local network and/or Internet is working.

◆ The Notes server is installed and running.

◆ The Web site server is installed and running.

INSTALLING WEB PUBLISHER

Web Publisher has two separate server components, as well as several "client" pieces. First, the server side.

Whether you obtained InterNotes Web Publisher on floppy disk or via download, it must be installed. (Because the downloadable version must be unpacked before it's installable, copy the downloaded executable into a temporary directory and unpack it there—usually by simply clicking on the file.)

Either way, you type **INSTALL** or click on the INSTALL.EXE executable and the install program takes over. It asks only the location of your Notes program directory, data directory, and your Web server's CGI directory. (In an install just before this book went to press, a revised installation script *didn't* prompt for the CGI location— the author was back to manual copying.)

When you install Web Publisher, it copies several files into the server's executable directory (notably, the Web Publisher and INOTES server tasks) and into the server's data directory: the Web Config database, Web Guide (online documentation), and Web Toolkit—a series of "how to" documents about HTML and the Web, not specifically about Web Publisher. In addition, the program installs sample databases, including the full-blown Mercury Sports Web demo (worth its weight in gold, to see what the Lotus people who really know what they're doing have put together). There are templates specific to InterNotes as well.

Some manual tasks need to be done before you're up and running, as described in the following sections.

HANDLING THE INOTES.EXE FILE

Double-check that the INOTES.EXE executable has been copied correctly into your server's CGI directory. During the install routine, you were asked in what directory to put CGI. The default is to put it in the CGI-BIN directory, but your server may or may not have such a directory (Web Site, for example, has CGI-DOS, CGI-WIN and CGI-SHL directories, but no CGI-BIN). Consult the online documentation for a chart that shows the correct directory depending on what Web server you're using.

Because the INOTES program is a DOS-based executable, it must be dropped into the CGI directory on your machine that handles DOS programs (for example, *not* CGI-WIN). If you're not sure, copy it into more than one directory and experiment (it doesn't cause any harm where it isn't needed).

Note

INOTES, incidentally, is the server task that gives InterNotes its interactivity. That is, INOTES enables visitors to your Web site to fill out forms and so on that are deposited back in your Notes database. Without INOTES, Web Publisher would be strictly a one-way street, publishing Notes databases to the Web. With INOTES, it's a two-way street, publishing to the Web, but also capturing information from the Web. A Web discussion database wouldn't be possible without INOTES.

Tip

Check in frequently with the Lotus InterNotes Web site (http://www.lotus.com/inotes/) for the latest information about things such as CGI mappings. There's a lively discussion database, and any problems you're having with such subjects has probably already been discussed at length.

In addition, the Lotus InterNotes Web site has a series of Tech Notes that give tips and tricks, as well as answers to common questions. This Web site, not surprisingly, is run totally by InterNotes, so you'll also have a chance to take a close look at a full-blown InterNotes site.

EDITING THE WEB PUBLISHER CONFIGURATION DATABASE

A second important task in installing Web Publisher is to edit the Web Publisher Configuration database. Two types of documents need your attention: The WebMaster Options Form and the database publishing records.

The WebMaster Options form, shown in Figure 20.3, is where the overall InterNotes configuration is set. Database publishing records, shown in Figure 20.4, tell InterNotes what to publish. Notice that the record in Figure 20.4 lists how often to publish, which specific views to publish, heading font mappings, and so on.

Figure 20.3.
A WebMaster document in the configuration database.

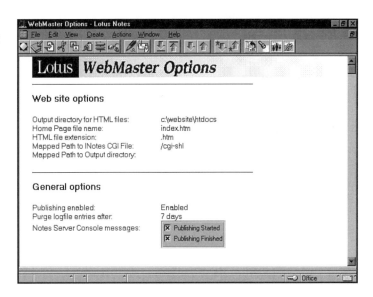

The WebMaster Options form is relatively straightforward, although the fields for mappings can be a bit confusing. Simply give InterNotes (via the WebMaster form) the following types of information:

◆ In what directory to publish

◆ The default name for the home page (the file name Web Publisher will give the "home page" in each database it publishes)

◆ The HTML extension you're using (typically HTM or HTML—it's often easiest to use HTM if you work with a normal Windows client, because it won't support the longer extension)

◆ The location of your CGI directory (that is, where you or the install program placed the INOTES executable) and the mapped output to the HTML directory

◆ Whether or not publishing is enabled (you may opt to turn off publishing during heavy server-load times), when to purge log files, and whether to have server console messages

Figure 20.4.
A database publishing record for the DANUG database.

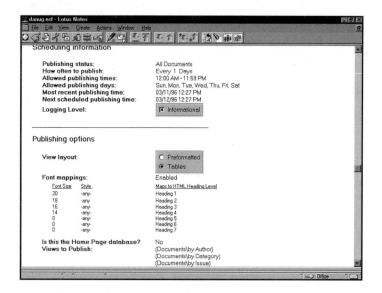

Note that both the CGI and HTML listings require mappings relative to the Web server's document directory, rather than a system mapping. That is, if your directory structure had the Web server's executables in the directory C:\WEB and the CGI files in C:\WEB\CGI-BIN, your CGI entry would be simply /CGI-BIN. In the preceding example, the actual CGI directory is C:\WEB\WEBSITE\CGI-SHL, but relative to the server's home directory, the path is .../CGI-SHL.

The other documents that need to be created are database publishing records, which tell InterNotes what to publish. You need at least one for every database you intend to publish.

Database publishing records give InterNotes information about the database(s) you want to publish. Specifically, you tell InterNotes information including the database to publish (the file name, complete with path, if necessary), how often to publish it, which views to publish, and so on.

You could conceivably publish once every second, although that hardly makes sense. A lively Web discussion database might be appropriate to publish once every minute or two, but a product information database might make sense to publish once a day.

Tip

You can have multiple database publishing records for a particular database. As such, it might make sense to have one record for updates only that publishes every five minutes, but another that publishes all documents once a day. In this manner, new or modified documents would find their way to the Web quickly, but all documents would be refreshed on a daily basis, in case forms or formulas are time-sensitive (such as a document that says the time created was 10:05 a.m. today).

The database publishing record is also where you specify to Web Publisher how to handle HTML headings. In the HTML world, font sizes aren't specified; information is sent that merely says, "This is Heading #1." The font mappings section of the publishing record enables the programmer to specify which font sizes in Notes equate to which heading marks in the HTML document. The default setting is that anything with a 20-point font or better is mapped as an H1 heading (the largest), and so on. If you've created styles in your Notes database, you can specify them in the publishing record as well.

You can specify which views you want to publish. A developer could create two similar views in a database—one for use in Notes, another for publishing to the Web. The second view could be hidden in Notes, yet specified in the Views to Publish field, so that Web Publisher publishes the second view. This scheme is a great way to include formulas with icons (a formula that displays a "new" bitmap next to documents that are less than a week old, for example), or put other bits of HTML code into a view that would make little sense if seen from Notes itself.

Warning

Be careful about answering Yes to the "Is this the home database?" question. If you say Yes, InterNotes may wipe out your main home page. A good rule of thumb is to set up the WebMaster Options form with DEFAULT.HTM as your home page file name, and leave INDEX.HTML as the name of your actual main home page. This way,

> even if you answer this question incorrectly, you won't blow up your entire site.

MODIFYING NOTES.INI

The third manual task is to modify the server's NOTES.INI file to include WEB PUBLISHER and INOTES on the ServerTasks line (see Figure 20.5). The server needs to be "bounced" at this point, or WEB PUBLISHER and INOTES need to be loaded at the console (type **LOAD WEB PUBLISHER** and **LOAD INOTES** at the console).

After you've modified the NOTES.INI file, each time you restart your server both WEB PUBLISHER and INOTES will load automatically as a server task. Note that if you change the information on the WebMaster Options form, you need to shut down WEB PUBLISHER and INOTES (type **TELL WEB PUBLISHER QUIT** and **TELL INOTES QUIT**) and then restart those two processes.

Figure 20.5.
A portion of a server's
NOTES.INI file,
showing server task
entries.

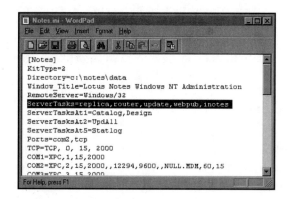

At this point, everything should be up and running.

TROUBLESHOOTING

Typically, some troubleshooting is necessary the first time you attempt to publish something. The path is wrong, INOTES is in the wrong directory, you specified incorrect databases or views, and so on. A lengthy amount of troubleshooting may be necessary to get it working correctly initially, but once your configuration is in place, everything should publish just fine.

Tip

> If you have checked everything there is to check and everything seems perfect, but Web Publisher and InterNotes aren't doing what you think they're supposed to be doing, shut down the entire box (not just the Notes server, but turn off the entire machine). Both NT and OS/2 are notorious for hanging onto things in a memory cache long after they should have let them go.
>
> There have been many times when, during a troubleshooting session, I had a problem mysteriously disappear after rebooting the machine, not just bouncing the server.

If something is seriously wrong, try retracing your steps, paying close attention to error messages you may be getting. Post questions on the Lotus InterNotes discussion database; they get answered quickly.

One additional consideration is that what looks great in Notes may not work on the Web. Typically, Notes databases have views laden with column headings and so on, and on a Web site those headings make things look cluttered. You may find that everything works perfectly, but you're not happy with the result for aesthetic reasons.

DECIDING WHAT TO PUBLISH

You can control what is published by Web Publisher, assuming that you don't want every view and every document in your database to be exposed to the public.

For purposes of this discussion, assume that you're working in a product information database. Not all the product information you're currently storing in this database is for public consumption; some info is strictly for sales people, some strictly for the production department. You have several ways to restrict what is published to just the product information that *is* for the public.

One way is to build a form with a field called Approved, and then build a view with a selection formula that only accepts documents marked Approved. You could then publish only that view. This way, you would have all the documents in a central database, but only documents that showed up in certain views would be made public. One benefit of handling publication control with this method is that the documents become available quite quickly once they're marked Approved (no need to wait for a replication to take place in the middle of the night, and so on).

In addition, the particular view you've chosen to publish might be formatted specifically for Web publishing, and you might have gone so far as to hide it from the view of your Notes users. A column in a view might contain some code like this to display an icon if the document is newer than 10 days:

```
REM "setting temporary variables to work with";
NewDate := @Adjust(@Today; 0; 0; -10; 0; 0; 0);
UpdatedDate := @Adjust(@Modified; 0; 0; -10; 0; 0; 0);
REM;
REM "Here's the statement that does the work";
REM "It'll display a NEW bitmap if the document is newer than ten days old";
REM "or an UPDATED bitmap if modified in the past ten days";
REM;
@If(@Created >= NewDate; "[<img src=../graphics/new.gif>]";
➥@If((@Modified >= NewDate) & (UpdatedDate > @Created);
➥"[<img src=../graphics/updated.gif>]"; ""))
REM;
```

If you publish the database with a formula like this in a hidden view, the Web version of the database correctly identifies which documents are new. If you left this formula in the column in a view visible to a Notes user, he would see the formula, although the Notes version could substitute the word NEW for the IMG code (see Figure 20.6). Note that for a formula like this to work effectively, you need a database publishing record set to publish all documents at least once a day.

Figure 20.6.
The view resulting from
the formula.

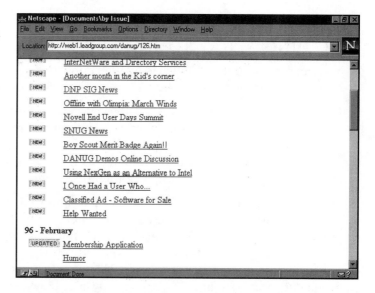

Another way to achieve control is to have two copies of the database, one on an internal production Notes server and the other on your InterNotes server. Using a method similar to the preceding method, you can create a selective replication formula that restricts any document not marked Approved from appearing in the

InterNotes database. The benefit of this strategy is the increased security of knowing that only the public documents are available to be published.

Yet another way is to eliminate the selective replication and substitute a mail macro that, for example, runs once a day and sends all approved documents to the second database. This scheme is more complicated, but virtually assures that only the appropriate documents are transmitted and published.

Warning

Before attempting any of these methods in a database containing sensitive information, do a dry run with some innocuous documents. Just as you would test agents (or macros), make sure that your formulas select the correct documents and replicate them (or display them, or whatever) properly. Nothing is worse than to see the opposite set of documents on a Web site!

Web Publisher 4.x also enables you to write formulas that can detect whether they're running in Notes, by using a new, Notes 4-specific @function, @UserRoles. This function returns a list of all roles that the current user has in a database. If Web Publisher evaluates this function, one of the values returned is $$Web. (The current revision of the product returns $$Web Publisher, but Lotus suggests testing for a string of just $$Web because future versions may change.)

Using @UserRoles, you can build a formula that displays a computed subform or various HideWhen options, based solely on whether this document was in Notes or on the Web.

Here's a sample chunk of code, borrowed directly from a Lotus technote, to illustrate:

```
REM "This formula evaluates to TRUE if the page is on the Web, FALSE if not";
REM;
@Contains(@Implode("x":@UserRoles; "<>"); "<>$$Web" );
```

Such a formula could control the display of computed subforms, HTML code, HideWhen formulas, input translation and validation, default values (if you're in Notes, default to your UserName, else default to "Please Type Your Name Here"), and even keyword formulas.

Using Objects, Attachments, Doclinks, and Popups

InterNotes also caters to the use of attachments, objects, document links, and other Notes features. The most obvious of these is the ability to convert graphics (see the discussion later in this section about graphics), but there are many other examples as well.

Notes has often been called the database where we put stuff for which we don't have databases. As such, Notes often becomes the depository for files, forms, and more. With an InterNotes database, those items can be put into normal, everyday Notes documents, and Web Publisher takes care of the dirty work. For example, if you have a .WAV file, you can embed the object in a Notes document, and Notes will interpret it correctly, leaving a file in the HTML output directory and a hotlink on the document itself.

Likewise, InterNotes automatically takes care of file attachments, creating a link at the bottom of a Web document that can be clicked to download the file. From a user perspective, this method is considerably easier than hard coding an HTML document and then transferring the file to whatever directory the Web visitors can access.

LINKING TO OTHER DOCUMENTS

Servers on the World Wide Web are called *HTTP servers* (HTTP stands for *Hypertext Transport Protocol*). One of their main features is the capacity to offer links between documents. These links, called *hypertext links*, enable users to click on a highlighted word to cause the server to send the new document, graphic, or whatever to the user's browser.

Typically, to facilitate that exchange within normal HTML coding, you'd have to put in a Uniform Resource Locator (URL), a direct reference to the other document (for example, `http://web1.leadgroup.com/lnu/index.htm`). With an InterNotes database, you merely need to create a doclink within Notes from the document you want to link. Figures 20.1 and 20.2, shown previously, feature doclinks in action.

One key benefit of using doclinks is that the user doesn't need to know anything about the directory structure of the HTTP server. She simply needs to be able to create a doclink within Notes itself.

Popups provide another way to create links. To create a link to another Notes document, you can highlight some text and create a text popup (Create | Hotspot | Text Popup). The text of the popup is the URL of whatever you want to link, surrounded by brackets. You could enter the preceding reference as the text of a popup like this: `[http://web1.leadgroup.com/lnu/index.htm]`. Notice the brackets surrounding the URL of the document. This method is particularly useful if you want something other than a strict document reference—for example, `[mailto:webmaster@leadgroup.com]` inserted as a popup to create an automatic mailto reference.

Yet another way to create links is to put the URL in brackets next to whatever you want to have create the highlighted link. For example, you can insert a graphic and next to the graphic put in a URL in brackets. Notes displays the graphic with a blue box around it; clicking the graphic triggers the link to the new document.

With Web Publisher 4, you can use navigators as image maps. A navigator in Notes is the same thing as an image map on the Web—they're both graphic images with embedded hotspots that trigger links when certain regions are clicked.

Navigator support is a last-minute addition to Web Publisher 4; check the online documentation and the Lotus Web site for updated information.

GRAPHICS

One of the truly frustrating things about working on the Web is the limitations placed on graphics. They must be in one of two formats for Web browsers to access them—GIF or JPG. Because neither format is supported by typical user graphics tools (Windows Paintbrush, for example, supports neither format), rendering graphics in Web documents is a chore.

Web Publisher makes life much simpler by enabling users to simply paste a graphic—Windows .BMP or .PCX file, scanned image, or whatever—in a Notes document. Web Publisher takes care of the rest. As Web Publisher publishes the Notes document, it automatically "tears off" the graphic, converts it to GIF format, places a copy of the .GIF file in the appropriate directory on the Web server, and creates a link in the document to display the graphic in the right spot. If you can import or paste it into a Notes document, you can publish it to the Web. This is a tremendous benefit, as users have no need for graphics packages other than Paintbrush or Paint.

You can create forms with company logos, bars, and other graphic elements, and Web Publisher translates all those items into nice-looking Web documents. Again, the samples in Figures 20.1 and 20.2 show some of the graphic elements transferring nicely between Notes and the Web.

Tip

If you have a graphic element that you'll use repeatedly within a database (such as a corporate logo), use HTML code in your Notes form, rather than pasting the graphic directly into your Notes document.

The rationale behind this plan is that Web Publisher sees the graphic in each document in your database as a different graphic, and re-publishes it for each document. If you have a 50-document database, you'll have 50 identical GIF files. As users move between your documents, their browsers must reload that graphic each time, slowing the access. If you merely reference the graphic, the browser will have cached the graphic image, and the document comes up much more quickly.

The downside to this method is that some HTML coding is necessary in your Notes form, although minimal, and on the Notes side it looks clumsy unless you are extremely good with formulas and extremely careful with HideWhen statements.

HTML CODING IN FORMS

Even though one of the key benefits of employing InterNotes is the ability to avoid HTML coding, in many places a little HTML code is worth the effort. In the graphics arena just discussed, referencing a graphic with an HTML tag makes sense, rather than forcing the user to reload the same image.

Likewise, you can do subtle things with HTML code placed on Notes forms to make the form nicer visually once published to the Web. A perfect example is document backgrounds. Although this seems to have shifted dramatically over the past year or two, many Web sites have adopted a style of "embossed" logos for backgrounds on their documents, or of various graphic textures or plain colors.

Although Web Publisher doesn't support backgrounds directly, there's no reason not to put the appropriate HTML codes in your Notes form to facilitate a background when viewed on the Web.

Any HTML code you want to put in a Notes form or document needs to be surrounded by brackets, so the HTML code for centered text, <CENTER>, would appear in a Notes form as [<CENTER>]. Web Publisher understands that anything within brackets is HTML code and translates it appropriately, making it invisible when published.

To drop in a logo for a background, you use a line such as this:

```
[<BODY BACKGROUND= "graphics/logo.gif">]
```

To use a color for a background, you use a line like this:

```
[<BODY BGCOLOR="#ffffff">]
```

One of the HTML codes you may want to use that Web Publisher doesn't currently support by itself is centered text, so you can add the [<CENTER>] tag before a heading to turn on centering and the [</CENTER>] tag after the heading to turn it off again.

Tip

Many books have been published on HTML coding, but online references are also available. Quite a few seasoned HTML coders have put together how to sites on the Web. Try a Yahoo or WebCrawler search on *HTML* to see what you can find.

As has become apparent, you've suddenly gone from simply publishing a Notes database as is to making major alterations for the Web. You can simplify the situation in several ways:

◆ First, if you're working strictly with one database and merely choosing which view to publish, write a form formula in both MainView (the Web version—notice that there is no space between the words) and Main View (the Notes version) that displays different forms for the same documents. You could then have a Web version of your main topic form with HTML code, but the form formula in the other view brings up a clean version for Notes users' consumption.

◆ Another option is to have different forms altogether, in two different databases. One database is used strictly for publishing purposes; it has the HTML-coded forms. The other database has the clean version of the form. The Notes users use the second database, and you set up the access control between the two so that they readily transfer new and modified documents, but design changes don't replicate.

◆ The advent of the new @UserRoles function mentioned earlier in this chapter also offers the developer the ability to control the display of subforms and so on. By using this capability creatively, you can display certain subforms only on the published documents, not on their Notes-side counterparts.

◆ Yet another consideration is creative use of HideWhen. You can use HideWhen to create a different look for forms being filled out and documents being read, although they're the same form. Which brings us to interactive forms (see the next section).

Using Interactive Forms

Many sites on the Internet are interactive in one form or another. You can order products, ask questions, request more information, and so on. The trouble in many of the existing systems is that the information gathered is dropped into a big DAT file on a UNIX server and you practically need a masters degree in computer science to decipher and use the information. Wouldn't it be nice to be able to capture information from a Web site and drop it directly into your prospects database in Notes?

With the advent of Version 2, Web Publisher became interactive. That is, not only can InterNotes publish *to* the Web, but it also can capture information *from* the Web. Better yet, the captured data is dropped directly into a Notes database.

The simplest example of this feature is an information request such as the Mercury Sports sample database that ships with InterNotes. In the Mercury Sports example, an interactive form is published to the Web, enabling visitors to the Web site to request information, order products, ask for a salesperson to call, and so on. If taken to the next level, a workflow application could be built in Notes, automatically routing that new document to the appropriate person. If the Web visitor checked "request information," the document gets routed to the mail room for fulfillment. But if "have salesperson call" was checked, it goes directly to the sales coordinator. The Mercury Sports sample database is a combination lead-generation, product information, and product ordering database.

In addition to that type of database, interactivity has a myriad of other uses. You can set up a discussion database, enabling Web visitors to participate in a discussion, or have a class registration database or automatic fax-back system. You can create an online help system with Knowledge Base documents already in place, yet enabling users to ask questions or request further information.

Full-text search falls under the heading of interactivity, too. You can index your Notes database and enable Web visitors to type search criteria, just as users can within Notes, and they'll receive a list of documents in the database that meet their criteria.

Caution

Searches work only if all the various components are on the same machine. That is, the Notes server, InterNotes Web Publisher, the Web server, and the database must all reside on the same physical computer.

Users have the same search options during Web searches that they have during a normal Web search (complex query statements, limiting the number of responses, and so on).

Unfortunately, while you can publish *to* the Web simply by filling out a database publishing record and telling Notes to do it, making things interactive takes a bit more intervention on the part of the developer.

Suppose that you are putting together the simple product information request form from the Mercury Sports sample database. Several steps are involved in making that form interactive:

1. Build the form itself in Notes. The form can be a normal Notes form, and you can do all the normal things you might do with a form in Notes: for example, input validations (`@If(Name—""`, `"Please Enter a Name"; @Success`), input translations (`@ProperCase(Name)`), and default values. You can do a number of subtle extra things to the Notes form to customize its appearance on the Web. For example, you can control the size of text fields by specifying a row and column length in the Help Description field. Figure 20.7 shows a field description that results in a field with a sizable input box.

Figure 20.7.
The Help Description
field is set to control the
size of the field in the
published Notes
document.

2. Give the form the synonym $$WEB. After the form has been created, the $$WEB synonym tells Notes that this form is to be made available to the Web. You may have multiple forms in a database with the $$WEB synonym. Typically, as this form is heavily formatted for Web use, you deselect the Include in Compose Menu option so that the form is available only on the Web.

   Notes creates an HTML form with the real name of the form. If your form is called Product ¦ $$WEB, for example, Notes creates an HTML document called PRODUCT.HTM that you can reference.

3. Create the HTML links to this form. That is, you need to access this form from the Web site. The easiest way to do this is to create a text popup hotspot on the home page that references the HTML name for the document. For example, if you have a sentence like `"Information Request,"` with the word *information* highlighted as a popup, and the text for the popup is `"[PRODUCT.HTM]"`, Notes can display a Product Info form when the popup is clicked (see Figures 20.8 and 20.9).

Figure 20.8.
The interactive form
in Notes.

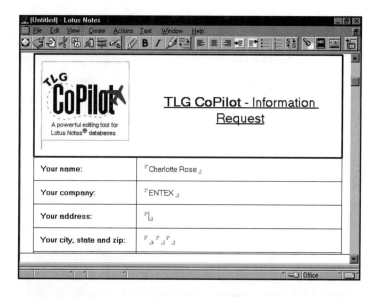

Figure 20.9.
The interactive form
shown on the Web.

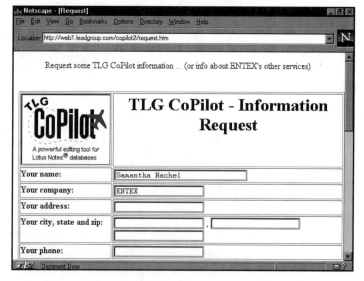

Many subtleties are involved in making a Notes database truly interactive:

◆ You can create a "response formula" that displays a "Thanks for your request" message after someone saves a request.

◆ You can include a search bar in a home page document, enabling people to search for documents in your database.

◆ You can create a discussion database, with true parent-child relationships between documents.

◆ Most importantly, you can create a complete workflow application in Notes so that, when someone enters information on your Web site, Notes handles routing to get the information where it needs to go.

Lotus has done an admirable job of documenting the nuances of creating a truly interactive Web site in both the documentation and the information available at the Lotus Web site. Read the documentation and give it a try; check the Web site for troubleshooting information.

Tip

The interactive forms portion of InterNotes Web Publisher is the most likely area for problems. Sometimes, although everything seems like it should work, it doesn't. Be ready for some long hours on simple forms, and try these suggestions:

◆ Take the entire machine down and bring it back up again—the box, not just Notes. Sometimes you may have fixed the problem, but Notes or the operating system has cached the wrong information and isn't reading the corrected form.

◆ Remember to constantly reload the document in your browser when testing. Your browser is also likely to keep documents cached.

◆ Triple-check the Lotus InterNotes Web site to see whether it lists any problems with the particular setup you're using. I was having a problem and found that O'Reilly's Web Site product handled environment variables differently than InterNotes was expecting, and interactive forms weren't working until a later InterNotes version.

◆ Feel free to post an "I need help" message on the LNOTESL newsgroup, the Lotus Web site, or CompuServe. I guarantee that whatever problem you're having, you're not the first!

THE SKELETON SERVER

Although the intention of neither this book nor this chapter is to delve heavily into Web security, ignoring the subject altogether would be a serious oversight. You must be aware of several things when you place any machine outside your organization's firewall. First, any actual connection between that machine on the outside and your network on the inside needs to be secured. Second, the machine *itself* needs to be secured. Third, the software, databases, and so on on that machine need their own security.

The first issue becomes a matter for the firewall experts. One of the easiest ways to virtually guarantee a secure connection from your outside server is to set up a "poor man's firewall," a modem setup. Hook up your outside machine to the Internet via a network card, but hook it up to another internal Notes server via a modem. Notes can communicate via LAN ports or COM ports; someone reaching your InterNotes server is coming in over the Internet on the LAN port. They may conceivably be able to do some damage on that machine, but they can't configure the box to do damage to your network over a modem that's attached only to the COM port of an internal Notes server. There's no shared protocol. It's about as safe as you can get.

In our office, we took this method a step further. We literally hooked up the "outside" machine to an "inside" machine via a LapLink cable. There wasn't even a real modem; the LapLink cable serves as a null modem (the transmit and receive pairs are reversed). The phone number you put in the connection document: "Ring."

The second issue is equally complicated. How do you secure the box itself? There are a couple of obvious things to do. Run Notes, the Web server software, and any other applications as NT services rather than as desktop applications. This strategy protects them further. Set up an extremely limited user population on that machine, and be sure the password is something other than "password." Use user limitations to make sure that unauthorized people won't be wandering around the machine if they should happen to stumble in.

The third issue is largely a matter of common sense, but needs to be mentioned in this context. Because there is a Notes server on this "outside" machine, it should be a "skeleton server." That is, the public Name and Address Book should be stripped of all documents other than those critical to making that machine run. Specifically, eliminate all connection documents other than the one the machine needs to communicate with the inside world. Eliminate all person documents other than the administrator. Eliminate unnecessary groups, servers, and certificates (and be sure to change your replication settings appropriately, so that you neither replicate out your deletions nor accept those type of documents).

Keep the mission-critical, company secret databases off this server. Use selective replication formulas to replicate only subsets of databases; keep the internal stuff off this machine.

Check your ACLs carefully. Eliminate individual names, and triple-check the default access on every database and database template. Be sure to break the replica IDs of anything out there, even if it's Help itself.

By doing this, if someone *should* figure out a way to break into Notes itself, they would not find much.

USING A HOME PAGE DATABASE

Creating a home page database, in its fullest implementation, would be two-fold.

First, create a database as your site's main home page. Use this database strictly as a jumping-off point for the other databases you want to publish. This part is relatively easily done. Create an About document with a two-column table: a skinny left column to hold a series of icons, and the right column a series of database names. Highlight both the icons and the database names with text popups containing the URLs of the individual databases.

The example in Figure 20.10 was insanely easy to create, maintain, and update. When the user reaches the Web site, a Notes About document answers. It's a spiffy document, complete with backgrounds and other graphics, but was created completely within Notes itself.

Figure 20.10.
The home page docu-
ment created from a
Notes About document.

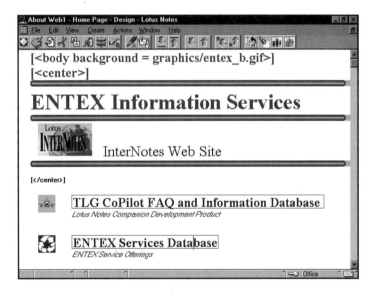

The second part of the home page database idea is a perfect opportunity for enabling users to create personal home pages in this database. The database obviously won't be used for anything other than InterNotes publishing. Why not enable users to create personal home pages there, using Notes? Offer them a Create menu option with a single option: Home Page. The Home Page form consists of three fields: an Author Name field, a Date field, and a Rich Text field into which they can put anything they want. Users can insert pictures, stories, files, jump links—anything.

With a little planning and some end-user education, you can give every person in your organization the ability to post information to the Internet.

LIMITATIONS OF WEB PUBLISHER

When writing about a product that does so much, you risk the reader thinking it does everything. It doesn't; there are some limitations as to what it can do. As the entire InterNotes family matures, some of these restrictions may go away, but here's a quick sampling of Web Publisher limitations:

- ◆ Certain HTML codes aren't supported (Web Publisher won't center text, for example).
- ◆ Many HTML extensions aren't supported (Netscape, Microsoft, and others have proprietary extensions that their browsers recognize—Web Publisher doesn't).
- ◆ Certain Notes functions and formulas are rendered ineffective (@DbLookup and @DbColumn, for example).

OTHER INTERNOTES PRODUCTS

Despite the amount of excitement generated by the InterNotes Web Publisher product, it's only one member of the family. Two other client-oriented products deserve mention: InterNotes News and InterNotes Web Navigator.

INTERNOTES NEWS

One of the most talked-about aspects of the Internet is the newsgroups. You can subscribe to a newsgroup on literally every imaginable subject. One problem with newsgroups—or Usenets, as they're also called—is managing the flood of material that comes through. Users typically lose the threads because things don't arrive sequentially, and often separating the worthwhile information from the worthless is difficult.

Lotus took aim at the newsgroup problem with InterNotes News, a product that grabs newsgroups and dumps the content into a Notes database. Users can read and respond to articles from within the familiar confines of Notes.

One main selling point of both InterNotes News and the Web Navigator is that they allow Internet connectivity through the Notes server. Individual users no longer have to be connected directly to the Internet to access the services; the server has the TCP/IP connection, not the user.

Another key benefit is that administrators can control the newsgroups to which users have access, by filling in a configuration database similar to that of Web Publisher. It enables administrators to subscribe to individual newsgroups, create custom Notes databases, and control their replication. ACL settings further the administrative options by restricting which users have access to the Newsgroup database.

Additionally, you can create full-text indexes for InterNotes News databases, meaning that users can search for material of interest, rather than having to dig through all the text. They can create macros and mail-forward scenarios to assist in disseminating the news through the organization.

InterNotes News is a server process combined with new database templates. If your server has Internet access, you can set up InterNotes news in a half hour. Just as with Web Publisher, InterNotes News is a server add-in task. You can load it manually at the server console (by typing LOAD INNEWS) or you can add INNEWS to the ServerTasks line in your server's NOTES.INI file.

After you have installed the software and have InterNotes News running, you need to set up a few configuration documents:

◆ News Gateway form
◆ News Server form
◆ News Connection form
◆ News Database form

Each of these forms, in succession, creates a step of the setup needed to get Usenet news to your Notes server. The Gateway form determines which Notes server functions as the news gateway. The Server form tells the gateway machine which new server to connect to, either within your own organization or at your Internet provider. The Connection form tells Notes how often to make a connection with the news server, and the Database form tells Notes in which database to store retrieved articles.

Once InterNotes News is running, new Usenet articles are added automatically to the various Notes databases you've specified. At that point, you can create a full-text index to facilitate searching the database, create signature files to facilitate postings on the newsgroups, add macros to filter and/or block certain subjects, and even send mail back to the author of an article.

InterNotes News is merely an easy way to get Internet news into Notes, but, like the other InterNotes products, it eliminates much of the confusion of the Internet, substituting the familiar ground of Notes.

INTERNOTES WEB NAVIGATOR

The final member of the InterNotes family has two parts: the Web Navigator (the client portion of the program), and "Web" or "Web Retriever" (the server add-in task). See Figure 20.11 for an example of the Web Navigator's main screen.

Figure 20.11.
The InterNotes Web
Navigator's main
screen.

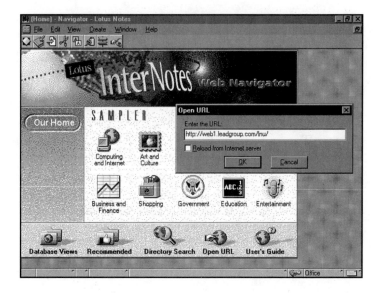

Just as InterNotes News dumps Internet newsgroup content into Notes databases, Web Navigator (WebNav) brings Web site content into Notes databases. When a user accesses an Internet site via Web Navigator, Notes retrieves and converts the content into Notes documents in the Navigator database. Subsequent users can access the content from the Notes database, and users can create doclinks to Web pages, and so on. Users can even create "Web tours," where they can track a certain series of Web pages as they're visited and "replay" the series.

In action, Web Navigator is similar to any other browser, enabling users to open URLs, back up through previously visited Web pages, and so on. As you can see in Figure 20.12, the Web page looks virtually identical viewed through Web Navigator as through other browsers.

A key Web Navigator selling point is the capacity to access Internet Web sites without needing to bring TCP/IP to each client workstation. Administrators also can deny access to certain Web sites, thus limiting users' access to "questionable" spots on the Web.

20

CONNECTING NOTES TO THE INTERNET

Figure 20.12.
Viewing a Web page
through Web
Navigator.

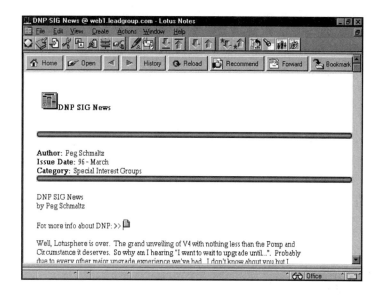

In addition, you can create agents or macros to regularly visit competitors' or suppliers' sites, sending colleagues a doclinked summary on a regular basis, showing changes. The full-text search feature of the Navigator database allows searching of Web sites for content.

A side benefit of having Web Navigator running is that URLs included in any Notes document (mail, discussions, news articles) are highlighted and can be accessed with a click of the mouse.

Installing Web Navigator is a simple task. Web Retriever needs to be installed on the Notes server as a server add-in task (modify NOTES.INI to add WEB on the ServerTasks line). Web Retriever automatically ships with Notes 4, as does the Web Navigator database template, but they must be added manually.

Tip

Lotus maintains a special section of its Web site strictly for information about the InterNotes Web Navigator. You can open the URL of this site directly (http://www.lotus.com/webnav.htm), or click on the Go to template resource site reference in the Administration document.

This site offers new Navigator templates, tech tips, and other information that you'll find useful. Recommended reading.

THE WEBNAV CLIENT

The InterNotes Web Navigator client is actually a central shared database. This database resides on a Notes server connected to the Internet and running the WEB server task. The client doesn't need TCP/IP; users can connect to the InterNotes server via whatever network protocol they normally use. (Also, a user can access the Internet via modem when dialing in to an InterNotes server.)

Each time a user accesses a Web page, WebNav translates it into a Notes document and dumps it into a Notes database. If several users access the same site, their access to the page is increased because they access a local Notes database instead of transferring all the data over the Internet.

The steps to configure WebNav on a client are simple. First, in your Personal Address Book, edit the current location document to include the name of the InterNotes server (use the hierarchical name). Next, choose File | Tools | User Preferences and select the Basics option Make Internet URLs into Hotspots. This setting enables you to simply click and open a Web page if someone sends you a URL reference in a document or mail.

When you first open WebNav, you'll see a Notes navigator that assists you in your travels on the Internet. Administrators can modify this document easily, to give one-click access to the organization's home page, certain vendor or customer sites, and so on.

In addition, clicking the Database Views entry on the Home navigator causes Notes to open another navigator that enables users to create their own bookmarks and so forth.

Users can mark a site as "recommended" by clicking a button on the action bar as they browse Web sites, and even give the page a rating. The page can be "live" (accessed just then), or they could be looking through the database to see what other people had visited. To see the pages others have marked as recommended, click the Recommended Views icon from the Home navigator.

Users also can create a "Web Tour"—a collection of Web pages. Essentially, it's a history of Web pages you've visited that you can share with others. You save the history of the sites you've been visiting, and enter the title of your tour. You can modify the tour, changing the order of the URLs, adding or deleting sites, and so on.

Currently, the feature set of the Web Navigator browser is similar to other browsers, but it adheres fairly closely to the vanilla HTML coding standards. It doesn't support some of the new extensions such as background graphics, but it does a passable job. By default, WebNav looks in its own database before accessing the Web, but administrators can set the configuration to automatically refresh pages stored in the database.

WebNav Administration

There are several important requirements for the WebNav server:

◆ Typical robust Notes server specs: 486 or better, 32 megabytes of memory, and at least a 1 gigabyte hard disk

◆ Notes 4 server (WebNav is strictly an R4 process), though not limited to NT and OS/2

◆ TCP/IP connection to the Internet (either leased line or via a proxy Web server connected via an Internet provider—dial-up doesn't work)

Because WebNav ships with Notes 4, it's available for use out of the box. Simply typing **LOAD WEB** at the server console starts it. (To automate this process each time the server restarts, enter WEB on the ServerTasks line in NOTES.INI. Once WEB is running, a SHOW TASKS command at the console reports that Web Retriever is loaded.)

You need to take care of some configuration items:

◆ Specify the location of the Web Navigator database by specifying an InterNotes server. Typically, this would be done on the client workstation in the location documents, but if those fields are blank Notes checks the server document in the Public Address Book.

◆ Because WebNav is a Notes database, you need to specify the ACL for WebNav. Both the local InterNotes server and other LocalDomainServers are recommended to have manager access to the database.

When WebNav is installed, a configuration document is created in the WebNav database, with defaults for the maximum size of the database and so forth.

Controlling Access to Certain Sites

Administrators can grant or limit access to certain Web sites easily, using the WebNav administration document.

There are two fields in the administration document, Allow Access and Deny Access, that enable the administrator to control users' ability to navigate in WebNav. An implied "all" in the blank Allow Access field enables users to access all sites, unless restricted by entries in the Deny Access field.

You can use wild cards, specific IP addresses, or site names. For example, to use wild cards to allow access to FTP or WWW servers at a site, use the setting `*.site.com`. Organizations can screen out specific Web sites with a listing like `www.playboy.com` in the Deny Access field.

The combined client and server portions of Web Navigator bring various Web services such as FTP, Gopher, and HTML to the Notes client—directly into Notes databases.

The combination of InterNotes News with Web Navigator rounds out the InterNotes family, allowing access to both Web sites and newsgroups from within the Notes 4 client. Users can have full Internet functionality without needing the additional protocol on each desktop, and can access Internet resources from the familiar confines of Notes.

OTHER INTERNET ASPECTS OF NOTES 4

This chapter has dealt almost exclusively with the InterNotes family of products thus far, but several other aspects of combining Notes and the Internet bear discussion: specifically, using the Internet to connect Notes servers, connecting to the Internet for mail, and using other global services such as CompuServe or WorldCom.

CONNECTING OVER THE INTERNET

Connecting two Notes servers via an Internet connection is no more difficult than connecting them via any other LAN port. The difference is that you use port TCPIP, and that port is connected to the Internet.

If you want your server NOTES1/ACME to connect with SILVER/LOTUS, you need a standard connection document. But, instead of the usual naming conventions, the new server document spells out the IP address of the server. That is, in the Destination Server Address field, you type the IP decimal address of the server (199.98.194.45), or a specific DNS server name (web1.leadgroup.com).

A key benefit of using the Internet for server communications is that replication and mail routing can use the relatively high speeds and low cost of an Internet connection, rather than relying on modem connections.

Additionally, a new feature with Notes 4 is the capacity to specify who can use what connection. With this feature, a Notes administrator can set up Internet replication between corporate servers, yet the servers wouldn't communicate with the outside world using the Internet. The group LocalDomainServers could be inserted into the Only For field, and the Internet would be available only for the servers to talk to each other. This is also an appropriate use for a passthru server. The passthru server could be used as a communications hub for remote users, allowing passthru to other company servers using the local network protocols.

Caution

Be very careful with any box that can be accessed from the outside world. See the earlier discussion about the skeleton server. If a passthru server can be accessed from the Internet via TCP/IP on a LAN port, your entire network could be compromised.

Be sure that the machine itself is secure, and that you've bulletproofed the setup. The Notes installation also should be a stripped-down version of your normal Notes setup.

Setting up remote users via the Internet shouldn't compromise your entire network!

Some firms set up one complete InterNotes machine—a Notes server with Internet connectivity—to be used for Web publishing, navigating, Internet mail gateway, and remote access.

Users can access the outside world via the InterNotes server, but TCP/IP doesn't have to be delivered to every desktop.

INTERNET MAIL

Some areas of Notes Internet strategy are still in progress, and the SMTP gateway—otherwise known as Internet mail gateway—is one of those areas.

As this book goes to press, Lotus has yet to release the SMTP gateway for R4. But here are the announced features:

- ◆ It's an MTA—Message Transfer Agent—rather than a simple gateway.
- ◆ It's an extra cost add-on program.
- ◆ It runs on limited platforms (Lotus is promising OS/2 Warp, HP-UX, and NT for R4).
- ◆ It requires an Internet mail server or service provider.
- ◆ It can be set up on a special communications server, or run on normal production Notes servers, provided they're connected.

OTHER GLOBAL CONNECTIONS

In addition to directly hooking up your Notes servers to the Internet, you can take advantage of several companies offering global connectivity. Although AT&T decided to pull the plug on the ill-fated AT&T Network Notes initiative, both

CompuServe and WorldCom have global Notes connectivity options that are alive and well. IBM is set to release its own public Notes network in the near future. Couple those with Lotus' own Notes Net, and whatever ends up coming out of Iris' fledgling Notes.Net startup, and the future seems open to options other than connecting via the Internet.

CompuServe and WorldCom have similar charters: hosting your firm's databases on their servers. Although at first glance this may seem unnecessary, the objective is to offer a one-stop administrative option. You simply give CompuServe or WorldCom your database; they handle all the cross certifications, replications, and so on.

CompuServe and WorldCom offer both a private and a public service. They'll host your organization's database(s), but also other public databases such as Notes discussions, and so on. CompuServe is currently publishing its very popular forums to its Notes network.

CompuServe is also an attractive option due to the myriad local access numbers CompuServe already has in place around the globe. Users would be hard-pressed to be in a location without a local CompuServe phone number, and many of the databases CompuServe has on its normal service are also available on the Notes service.

For companies with large constituencies, multiple databases, and limited administrative staff, these firms offer the answer. Additionally, firms that want to reach a lot of other firms find this a blessing: you place your database on one of the public networks and tell people to find it there, rather than cross-certifying everyone with whom you do business. If you want to charge for access to your Notes database, you should definitely be using one of these services.

Lotus had been underwriting the Lotus Notes Net for the past couple of years, but a recent restructuring made it more of a pay-for-play situation like the other commercial Notes services. Notes Net was originally intended as a mail and replication function for Lotus' many Business Partners, but soon spread to third-party vendors, customers, and the like.

Notes Net is in the process of evolving, and there's more of an emphasis on public databases than ever before.

All these public Notes offerings have the same intent: to offer a solution to the administrative chores that accompany working with the outside world. Additionally, depending on your setup, they can offer Internet connectivity.

SUMMARY

Suddenly, Notes and the Internet seem to be joined at the hip. The InterNotes family of products—Web Publisher, InterNotes News, and Web Navigator—offer Notes users, developers, and administrators an impressive arsenal of tools to work with the Internet.

Web Publisher allows Notes databases to be published to the Web, as well as capturing information from visitors to your Web site. Web Navigator gives Notes users a built-in browser, and InterNotes News brings newsgroup articles into a Notes database.

The InterNotes family brings full Internet integration to Notes 4. The products will continue to mature and evolve, and as the market continues to evolve additional capabilities will be added.

Couple the InterNotes products with the SMTP MTA, use of the Internet for replication, and the public services, and it becomes hard to see where Notes ends and the Internet begins. For administrators, it's yet another hurdle to jump. Keep checking with the Lotus Web site; it's your best source for up-to-date information.

- Country Codes

- NOTES.INI
  Parameters

PART V

Appendixes

APPENDIX A

Country Codes

This appendix provides the country codes you use when creating your hierarchical certificate ID files. Country codes are optional, but recommended for noninternational firms. Using country codes helps to ensure that your mail addresses are unique worldwide. Having unique certificate names is important when you want to communicate with external organizations. A full hierarchical name using a country code looks like this:

```
CN=Andrew Dahl\OU=Consulting\O=L3Comm\C=US
```

Code	Country	Code	Country
AD	Andorra	BS	Bahamas
AE	United Arab Emirates	BT	Bhutan
AF	Afghanistan	BU	Burma
AG	Antigua and Barbuda	BV	Bouvet Island
AI	Anguilla	BW	Botswana
AL	Albania	BY	Byelorussian SSR
AN	Netherlands Antilles	BZ	Belize
AO	Angola	CA	Canada
AQ	Antarctica	CC	Cocoa (Keeling) Islands
AR	Argentina	CF	Central African Republic
AS	American Samoa	CG	Congo
AT	Austria	CH	Switzerland
AU	Australia	CI	Cote d'Ivoire
AW	Aruba	CK	Cook Islands
BB	Barbados	CL	Chile
BD	Bangladesh	CM	Cameroon
BE	Belgium	CN	China
BF	Burkina Faso	CO	Colombia
BG	Bulgaria	CR	Costa Rica
BH	Bahrain	CS	Czechoslovakia
BI	Burundi	CU	Cuba
BJ	Benin	CV	Cape Verde
BM	Bermuda	CX	Christmas Island
BN	Brunei Darussalam	CY	Cyprus
BO	Bolivia	DD	German Democratic Republic
BR	Brazil	DE	Federal Republic of Germany

Code	Country	Code	Country
DJ	Djibouti	HK	Hong Kong
DK	Denmark	HM	Heard and McDonald Islands
DM	Dominica	HN	Honduras
DO	Dominican Republic	HT	Haiti
DZ	Algeria	HU	Hungary
EC	Ecuador	ID	Indonesia
EG	Egypt	IE	Ireland
EH	Western Sahara	IL	Israel
ES	Spain	IN	India
ET	Ethiopia	IO	British Indian Ocean Territory
FI	Finland	IQ	Iraq
FJ	Fiji	IR	Iran (Islamic Republic of)
FK	Falkland Islands (Malvinas)	IS	Iceland
FM	Micronesia	IT	Italy
FO	Faroe Islands	JM	Jamaica
FR	France	JO	Jordan
GA	Gabon	JP	Japan
GB	United Kingdom	KE	Kenya
GD	Grenada	KH	Kampuchea, Democratic
GF	French Guiana	KI	Kiribati
GH	Ghana	KM	Comoros
GI	Gibraltar	KN	Saint Kitts and Nevis
GL	Greenland	KP	Dem. People's Rep. of Korea
GM	Gambia	KR	Republic of Korea
GN	Guinea	KW	Kuwait
GP	Guadeloupe	KY	Cayman Islands
GQ	Equatorial Guinea	LA	Lao People's Dem. Republic
GR	Greece	LB	Lebanon
GT	Guatemala	LC	Saint Lucia
GU	Guam	LI	Liechtenstein
GW	Guinea–Bissau	LK	Sri Lanka
GY	Guyana	LR	Liberia

continues

Code	Country	Code	Country
LS	Lesotho	NZ	New Zealand
LU	Luxembourg	OM	Oman
LY	Libyan Arab Jamahiriya	PP	Panama
MA	Morocco	PE	Peru
MC	Monaco	PF	French Polynesia
MG	Madagascar	PG	Papua New Guinea
MH	Marshall Islands	PH	Philippines
ML	Mali	PK	Pakistan
MN	Mongolia	PL	Poland
MO	Macau	PM	St. Pierre and Miquelon
MP	Northern Mariana Islands	PN	Pitcairn
MQ	Martinique	PR	Puerto Rico
MR	Mauritania	PT	Portugal
MS	Montserrat	PW	Palau
MT	Malta	PY	Paraguay
MU	Mauritius	QA	Qatar
MV	Maldives	RE	Réunion
MW	Malawi	RO	Romania
MX	Mexico	RW	Rwanda
MY	Malaysia	SA	Saudi Arabia
MZ	Mozambique	SB	Solomon Islands
NA	Namibia	SC	Seychelles
NC	New Caledonia	SD	Sudan
NE	Niger	SE	Sweden
NF	Norfolk Island	SG	Singapore
NG	Nigeria	SH	St. Helena
NI	Nicaragua	SJ	Svalbard and Jan Mayen Islands
NL	Netherlands	SL	Sierra Leone
NO	Norway	SM	San Marino
NP	Nepal	SN	Senegal
NR	Nauru	SO	Somalia
NT	Neutral Zone	SR	Suriname
NU	Niue	ST	Sao Tome and Principe

Code	Country	Code	Country
SU	USSR	US	United States
SV	El Salvador	UY	Uruguay
SY	Syrian Arab Republic	VA	Vatican City State (Holy See)
SZ	Swaziland	VC	Saint Vincent and the Grenadines
TC	Turks and Caicos Islands		
TD	Chad	VE	Venezuela
TF	French Southern Territories	VG	Virgin Islands (British)
TG	Togo	VI	Virgin Islands (U.S.)
TH	Thailand	VN	Vietnam
TK	Tokelau	VU	Vanuatu
TN	Tunisia	WF	Wallis and Futuna Islands
TO	Tona	WS	Samoa
TP	East Timor	YD	Yemen, Democratic
TR	Turkey	YE	Yemen
TT	Trinidad and Tobago	YU	Yugoslavia
TV	Tuvalu	ZA	South Africa
TW	Taiwan, Province of China	ZM	Zambia
TZ	Tanzania, United Rep. of	ZR	Zaire
UA	Ukrainian SSR	ZW	Zimbabwe
UG	Uganda		
UM	United States Minor Outlying Islands		

APPENDIX B

NOTES.INI Parameters

This appendix specifies the NOTES.INI parameters that you will need to configure workstations and servers. A few miscellaneous parameters that control the size and positioning of Windows aren't specified. These parameters are operating-system specific and fairly easy to understand when you look in an .INI file.

ACTIONPANEENABLED

Syntax: ActionPaneEnabled=*value*

Description: Specifies whether Notes displays the ActionPane while in Design mode.

1-Display Action Pane

0-Do Not Display Action Pane

Default: 0

Notes UI Equivalent: View | Action | Pane

Applies To: Workstations

ADMIN

Syntax: Admin=*UserName*

Description: Specifies the user name of a server administrator. The name must be in canonical format. For example:

```
Admin=CN=Andrew Dahl/OU=Consulting/O=L3Comm/C=US
```

CN specifies the common name, OU specifies an organizational unit (there can be more than one organizational unit), O specifies the organization, and C specifies a country code (optional).

Default: None

Notes UI Equivalent: None

Name and Address Book Equivalent: The Administrators field in the server document in the Public Address Book

Applies to: Server

ADMIN_ACCESS

Syntax: Admin_Access=*Name,Group*

Description: Specifies the user names and administrative groups allowed to administer this server. Each name should be listed in canonical format. Admin_Access must have at least one entry.

Default: The administrator name specified when installing the server

Notes UI Equivalent: None

Name and Address Book Equivalent: The Administrators field in the server document in the Public Address Book

Applies to: Servers

AdminPInterval

Syntax: AdminPInterval=x

Description: Specifies how often Notes runs the Administration Process. The Administration Process checks for new administration requests every x minutes. See Chapter 13 for detailed information on the Administration Process.

Default: 30 minutes

Notes UI Equivalent: None

Name and Address Book Equivalent: Server

Applies to: Servers

AdminPModifiedPersonDocumentsAt

Syntax: AdminPModifiedPersonDocumentsAt=*time*

Description: Specifies the hour of the day (using a 24-hour clock) when the Administration Process will update person documents in the Public Address Book.

Default: 0 (12:00 a.m.)

Notes UI Equivalent: None

Name and Address Book Equivalent: Server

Applies to: Servers

Allow_Access

Syntax: Allow_Access=*names*

Description: Specifies the users allowed to access this server. Valid entries are server names, user names, group names, an asterisk (*), and wild cards. All names entered must be hierarchical. An asterisk (*) gives access to all users. See Chapter 18, "Administering Notes Security," for full details on using the Allow_Access parameter.

Default: None

Notes UI Equivalent: None

Name and Address Book Equivalent: The Access Server field in the server document in the Public Address Book. The setting in the server document takes precedence over the Allow_Access setting in the NOTES.INI file.

Applies to: Servers

ALLOW_ACCESS_*portname*

Syntax: Allow_Access_*portname=names*

where *portname* is a valid port for this Notes server.

Description: Specifies the users, servers, and groups that can access a server, using the specified port. Valid entries include server names, user names, group names, an asterisk (*), and wild cards. For example:

```
Allow_Access_COM3=*/administrators/L3Comm
```

This example reserves the COM3 port for administrators.

Default: None

Notes UI Equivalent: None

Applies to: Servers

ALLOW_PASSTHRU_ACCESS

Syntax: Allow_Passthru_Access=*names*

Description: Specifies the users and servers that can access this server as a destination server by using passthru. Valid entries include user names, server names, group names, an asterisk (*), and wild cards. If this parameter isn't specified, this server can't be accessed by using passthru. An asterisk (*) gives access to all users listed in the Public Address Book.

Default: None

Notes UI Equivalent: The Access This Server field in the Passthru Restrictions section of the server document in the Public Address Book. The server document takes precedence over the entry in the NOTES.INI file. The NOTES.INI Allow_Passthru_Access parameter is used only if the Access This Server field is blank.

Applies to: Servers

ALLOW_PASSTHRU_CALLERS

Syntax: Allow_Passthru_Callers=*names*

Description: Specifies the servers and users that can cause this server to dial a destination server. Valid entries include server names, user names, group names, an asterisk (*), and wild cards. If this parameter isn't specified, this server can't be used to complete a connection to a destination server by using a dial-up connection. An asterisk (*) gives access to all users and servers in the Public Address Book.

Default: None

Notes UI Equivalent: None

Name and Address Book Equivalent: The Cause Calling field in the Passthru Restrictions section of the server document. The server document takes precedence over the NOTES.INI file. The NOTES.INI parameter Allow_Passthru_Callers is used only if the Cause Calling field is blank.

Applies to: Servers

ALLOW_PASSTHRU_CLIENTS

Syntax: Allow_Passthru_Clients=*names*

Description: Specifies the users and servers that can use this server as a passthru server. Valid entries include server names, user names, group names, an asterisk (*), and wild cards. An asterisk (*) enables anyone listed in the Public Address Book to use this server as a passthru server.

Default: None

Notes UI Equivalent: None

Name and Address Book Equivalent: The Route Through field in the Passthru Restrictions section of the server document. The server document takes precedence over the NOTES.INI file. The NOTES.INI parameter Allow_Passthru_Clients is used only if the Route Through field is blank.

Applies to: Servers

ALLOW_PASSTHRU_TARGETS

Syntax: Allow_Passthru_Targets=*names*

Description: Specifies the destination servers to which this server can connect by using passthru. Valid entries include server names, groups of servers, and wild cards that specify servers. If this field is blank, all servers can be accessed as destination servers.

Default: None

Notes UI Equivalent: None

Name and Address Book Equivalent: The Destination Allow field in the Passthru Restrictions section of the server document. The server document takes precedence over the NOTES.INI file. The NOTES.INI parameter Allow_Passthru_Targets is used only if the Destination Allow field is blank.

Applies to: Servers

Amgr_DocUpdateAgentMinInterval

Syntax: Amgr_DocUpdateAgentMinInterval=*minutes*

Description: Specifies the minimum interval in minutes between executions of a document-update-triggered agent.

Default: 30 (minutes)

Notes UI Equivalent: None

Applies to: Servers and workstations

Amgr_DocUpdateEventDelay

Syntax: Amgr_DocUpdateEventDelay=*minutes*

Description: Specifies the minimum interval between execution of a document-update-triggered agent due to a document-update event, and the next time the Agent Manager schedules that agent.

Default: 5 (minutes)

Notes UI Equivalent: None

Applies to: Servers and workstations

Amgr_NewMailAgentMinInterval

Syntax: Amgr_NewMailAgentMinInterval=*minutes*

Description: Specifies the minimum interval between executions of a new-mail-triggered agent.

Default: 0

Notes UI Equivalent: None

Applies to: Servers and workstations

AMGR_NEWMAILEVENTDELAY

Syntax: Amgr_NewMailEventDelay=*minutes*

Description: Specifies the time to elapse between running a new-mail-triggered agent and the Agent Manager scheduling that agent again.

Default: 1 (minute)

Notes UI Equivalent: None

Applies to: Servers and workstations

AMGR_WEEKENDDAYS

Syntax: AMgr_WeekendDays=*Day1,Day2,...*

Description: Specifies the days of the week that should be considered to be weekends. Specify each day as a number, where Sunday is 1 and Saturday is 7. Agents with the Don't Run on Weekends option selected don't run on the days of the week specified in the Amgr_WeekendDays parameter.

Default: 7 (Saturday), 1 (Sunday)

Notes UI Equivalent: None

Applies to: Server and workstations

APPLETALKNAMESERVER

Syntax: AppleTalkNameServer=*ServerName*

Description: Specifies the server name of the user's secondary AppleTalk server. This parameter applies to AppleTalk network users only.

Default: None

Notes UI Equivalent: File | Tools | User Preferences, Ports panel. Specify an AppleTalk port and choose Options.

Applies to: Workstations and servers

AUTOLOGOFFMINUTES

Syntax: AutoLogOffMinutes=*minutes*

Description: Specifies the number of minutes a workstation can be inactive before the user is logged off automatically.

Default: None

Notes UI Equivalent: File | Tools | User Preferences, Basics panel. Enter the number of minutes in the Lock ID field.

Applies to: Workstations

CDP_command

Syntax: CDP_*command=value*

where *command* can be any of these commands:

- NEW
- OPEN
- EDIT
- SAVE
- CLOSE
- SHOW_ACTIVE_ITEM
- SHOWITEM
- EXIT

Description: Specifies a set of CDP settings to control opening, handling, and closing applications using OLE.

Default: None

Notes UI Equivalent: None

Applies to: Workstations and servers

CertificateExpChecked

Syntax: CertificateExpChecked=*FileName ExpirationDate*

Description: Specifies the path and file name for the default user ID and its certificate's expiration date. For example:

```
CertificateExpChecked=c:\NoteData\User.ID 5/4/96
```

Default: None

Notes UI Equivalent: The Expiration Date field in the Certify ID dialog box.

Applies to: Workstations and servers

CERTIFIERIDFILE

Syntax: CertifierIDFile=*IDFileName*

Description: Specifies the full path and file name for a certifier ID for a server. You must specify the full path.

Default: The location of the certifier ID file, specified when you install the server.

Notes UI Equivalent: File | Tools | Server Administration | Certifiers

Applies to: Servers

COM*number*

Syntax: COM*number=ParameterValue1,ParameterValue2,...*

where *number* is in the range 1-5.

Description: Specifies the settings for a specific COM port. You can specify a value for any of the parameters shown in the following table (in order, from top to bottom):

Required	Driver	Specifies the driver name for this port.
Required	Unit ID	Specifies the unit ID for this port.
Required	MaxSessions	Specifies the maximum number of concurrent connections to a server.
Required	Buffer_Size	Specifies the size of the port buffer in kilobytes.*
Optional	Flags	Specifies flags for logging modem I/O, logging script I/O, hardware flow control, and encrypting network data.
Optional	Modem_Speed	Specifies the modem speed in kilobytes.
Optional	Modem_Volume	Specifies the modem volume and dialing mode.
Optional	Modem_File_Name	Specifies the modem command file for this modem.
Optional	Dial_Timer	Specifies the number of seconds before dialing fails (the connection times out).
Optional	Hang_Up_Time_Out	Specifies the number of minutes this connection can be idle before Notes hangs up.
Optional	Acquire_Script	The file name for an acquire script to run when accessing a server using this port.

*Specify an extra comma after buffer size, but don't enter a value.

B

For example:

```
COM3=XPC,3,15,0,,12302,57600,16,USRSP28.MDM,60,15,COMSERV.SCR
```

This example specifies that the COM3 port uses the XPC driver on COM port number 3, supports a maximum of 15 concurrent sessions, has a buffer size of 0, uses a variety of flags (don't try to set flags using the .INI file; use the user interface instead), has a modem speed of 57,600 kilobytes, uses tone dialing and has the speaker turned off, uses the US Robotics Sportster 28.8 modem file, has a connection timeout of 60 seconds, hangs up after 15 minutes of idle time, and uses the Communication Server acquire script.

Default: Depends on the type of modem you have installed.

Notes UI Equivalent: File | Tools | User Preferences, Ports panel. Select a port name and then choose Options.

Applies to: Servers and workstations

CONFIG_DB

Syntax: CONFIG_DB=*path*

Description: Specifies the relative path and file name of the Statistics & Events database. For example, `Data\Events4.NSF`.

Default: Events4.NSF

Notes UI Equivalent: None

Applies to: Servers

CONSOLE_LOGLEVEL

Syntax: Console_Loglevel=*value*

where *value* is:

0-No information

1-Errors only

2-A summary of the progress information

3-Detailed information on progress

4-Full trace information

Description: Specifies the amount of information to be logged while tracing a connection.

Default: 2

Notes UI Equivalent: None

Applies to: Servers

CREATE_FILE_ACCESS

Syntax: Create_File_Access=*names*

Description: Specifies the users and servers that can create new databases on a server. All specified names must be hierarchical. Valid entries include user names, server names, group names, an asterisk (*), and wild cards. If this parameter isn't specified, all users have the ability to create files.

Default: None

Notes UI Equivalent: The Create New Databases field in the server document in the Public Address Book. The server document takes precedence over the NOTES.INI file. The NOTES.INI parameter Create_File_Access is used only if the Create New Databases field is blank.

Applies to: Servers

CREATE_REPLICA_ACCESS

Syntax: Create_Replica_Access=*names*

Description: Specifies the users and servers that can create replicas on this server. All specified names must be hierarchical. Valid entries include user names, server names, group names, an asterisk (*), and wild cards. If this parameter isn't specified, all users listed in the Public Address Book have the ability to create replicas.

Default: None

Notes UI Equivalent: The Create Replica Databases field in the server document. The server document takes precedence over the NOTES.INI file. The NOTES.INI parameter Create_Replica_Access is used only if the Create Replica Databases field is blank.

Applies to: Servers

CTF

Syntax: CTF=*Filename*

Description: Specifies the international import/export character set.

Default: L_CPWIN.CLS

Notes UI Equivalent: File | Tools | User Preferences, International panel. Select the Import/Export Character Set button and then select a character set from the list.

Applies to: Workstations

DDE_TIMEOUT

Syntax: DDE_Timeout=*seconds*

Description: The amount of time Notes waits for another DDE application to respond to a DDE message.

Default: 10 (seconds)

Notes UI Equivalent: None

Applies to: Workstations

DEFAULT_INDEX_LIFETIME_DAYS

Syntax: Default_Index_Lifetime_Days=*days*

Description: Specifies the default lifetime for full-text indexes for databases on this server or workstation. All indexes that haven't been used for the specified number of days are purged by the Indexer server task.

Default: 45 (days)

Notes UI Equivalent: None

Applies to: Servers

DENY_ACCESS

Syntax: Deny_Access=*names*

Description: Specifies the users and servers that aren't allowed to access this server. All specified names must be hierarchical. Valid entries include server names, user names, group names, an asterisk (*), and wild cards. An asterisk (*) denies access to everyone listed in the Public Address Book.

Default: None

Notes UI Equivalent: None

Name and Address Book Equivalent: The Not Access Server field in the server document. The server document takes precedence over the NOTES.INI file. The NOTES.INI parameter Deny_Access is used only if the Not Access Server field is blank. Be sure to add your deny access group to this field.

Applies to: Servers

DENY_ACCESS_*portname*

Syntax: Deny_Access_*portname=names*

Description: Specifies the users and servers that can't access this server by using this specified port. The port name can be any valid port for this Notes server. All names specified must be hierarchical. Valid entries include server names, user names, group names, an asterisk (*), and wild cards. An asterisk (*) denies access to all servers and users listed in the Public Address Book.

Default: None

Notes UI Equivalent: None

Applies to: Servers

DESKTOP

Syntax: Desktop=*path*

Description: Specifies the location of the DESKTOP.DSK file. If this parameter isn't specified, Notes looks in the Notes data directory for the DESKTOP.DSK file. This parameter is workstation-platform-specific.

Default: None

Notes UI Equivalent: None

Applies to: Workstations

DIRECTORY

Syntax: Directory=*path*

Description: Specifies the root directory of the Notes data tree.

Default: The Notes data directory specified during installation.

Notes UI Equivalent: File | Tools | User Preferences, Basics panel. Select the Local Database Folder entry field.

Applies to: Workstations

DOMAIN

Syntax: Domain=*name*

Description: For a server, specifies the server's domain. For a workstation, specifies the domain of the user's mail server.

Default: The domain specified during installation.

Notes UI Equivalent: For a server, the Domain field in the server document. For a workstation, the Domain field in the user's person document.

Applies to: Workstations and servers

DST

Syntax: DST=*value*

where *value* can be:

0-Do not observe Daylight Savings Time

1-Observe Daylight Savings Time

Description: Specifies whether this server or workstation observes Daylight Savings Time. This parameter affects the time stamp given to documents. If Daylight Savings Time is observed, documents are time-stamped one hour later during Daylight Savings Time.

Default: 1 (Observe Daylight Savings Time)

Notes UI Equivalent: Daylight Savings Time field in the location document.

Applies to: Servers and workstations

DST_BEGIN_DATE

Syntax: DST_Begin_Date=*date*

Description: Specifies the exact date when Daylight Savings Time begins. Specify a date, using dd/mm/year format. If you use the DST_Begin_Date parameter, you must also specify DST_End_Date.

Default: None

Notes UI Equivalent: None

Applies to: Servers

DST_END_DATE

Syntax: DST_End_Date=*date*

Description: Specifies the exact date when Daylight Savings Time ends. Specify a date, using dd/mm/year format. If you use DST_End_Date, you must also specify DST_Begin_Date.

Default: None

Notes UI Equivalent: None

Applies to: Servers

DSTLAW

Syntax: DSTlaw=*startmonth,startweek,startday,endmonth,endweek,endday*

Description: Specifies the exact day when Daylight Savings Time starts and ends. Months are specified using 1-12, weeks using 1-4, and days using 1 (Sunday) through 7 (Saturday). Weeks can also be specified using negative numbers, where -1 is the last week, -2 is the second to last week, etc.

Default: DSTlaw=4,1,1,10,-1,1 (Daylight Savings Time begins the first Sunday in April and ends the last Sunday in October.)

Notes UI Equivalent: None

Applies to: Servers and workstations

EDITEXP*number*

Syntax: EditExp*number=parameter1,parameter2,parameter3,...*

Description: Specifies the settings used when exporting information from a document. The following are valid parameters:

parameter1-Program name and file type

parameter2-The value 0, 1, or 2, where:

> 0-Can't append to an existing file
>
> 1-An option to append is provided in a dialog box
>
> 2-Automatically writes a temporary file if needed to avoid a 64K limit

parameter3-Name of the export routine to use

parameter4-Reserved

parameter5 and up-File extensions used to select a file type in the File Export dialog box.

Default: None

Notes UI Equivalent: None

Applies to: Workstation

EditIMP*number*

Syntax: EditIMP*number*=*parameter1,parameter2,parameter3,parameter4, parameter 5,...*

Description: Specifies the settings used when importing data into a document. The following are valid values:

parameter1-Program name and file type

parameter2-Reserved value. Set equal to 0.

parameter3-Name of the export routine to use

parameter4-Reserved

parameter5 and up-File extensions used to select a file type in the File Import dialog box.

Default: None

Notes UI Equivalent: None

Applies to: Workstations

EmptyTrash

Syntax: EmptyTrash=*value*

where *value* can be:

0-Display a prompt before closing a database

1-Always empty the trash when closing a database

2-Never empty the trash automatically. The trash must be emptied manually.

Description: Specifies whether the trash folder is automatically purged, and when this will happen.

Default: 0 (prompt when closing a database)

Notes UI Equivalent: File | Tools | User Preferences, Basics panel, the Empty Trash Folder field.

Applies to: Workstations

ExtMgr_AddIns

Syntax: ExtMgrAddIns=*value1,value2,value3,...*

Description: Each value specifies an add-in file to use for the Notes server. The file name representing the program is the specified value, appended with a platform-specific suffix. The platform-specific suffixes are:

Windows   _
OS/2 $
Windows NT   N

For example, `ExtMgr_AddIns=Mypurge` would instruct an OS/2 server to look for the file $MYPURGE.DLL.

Default: None

Notes UI Equivalent: None

Applies to: Servers

FileDlgDirectory

Syntax: FileDlgDirectory=*path*

Description: Specifies a default directory for file searches. If this parameter isn't specified, Notes searches the Notes data directory and its subtree. If you specify this entry, Notes looks only in the specified directory.

Default: None

Notes UI Equivalent: None

Applies to: Servers

FixUp_Tasks

Syntax: FixUp_Tasks=*number*

Description: Specifies the maximum number of Fixup tasks that can run on this server. You should never specify more than twice the number of CPUs.

Default: Twice the number of CPUs on the system.

Notes UI Equivalent: None

Applies to: Servers

B

NOTES.INI PARAMETERS

FT_INTL_SETTING

Syntax: FT_INTL_Setting=*value*

Description: Enables full-text searching to work with the Japanese language. When enabled, stemming is turned off, all full-text indexes are case-sensitive, and the stop word file is ignored.

Default: None

Notes UI Equivalent: None

Applies to: Workstations

FT_MAX_INSTANCES

Syntax: FT_MAX_Instances=*NumberOfWords*

Description: Sets the maximum number of words from a single document to be included in a full-text index. The amount of memory required is 10 times the number of words you specify (in bytes).

Default: 100,000

Notes UI Equivalent: None

Applies to: Servers

FULLTEXTMULTIPROCESS

Syntax: FullTextMultiProcess=*number*

Description: Specifies the maximum number of full-text Indexer tasks that can run simultaneously on a server.

Default: None

Notes UI Equivalent: None

Applies to: Servers

KEYFILENAME

Syntax: KeyFileName=*path*

Description: Specifies the path and file name for the server or user ID file.

Default: The ID file for the administrator you specified when installing the server.

Notes UI Equivalent: None

Applies to: Workstations and servers

KITTYPE

Syntax: KitType=*value*

where *value* can be:

1-Workstation

2-Server, Workstation and Server

Description: Specifies whether you're running the Notes workstation or server.

Default: Depends on whether you're running the workstation or the server.

Notes UI Equivalent: None

Applies to: Workstations and servers

LAN*number*

Syntax: LAN*number=PortDriver,UnitID,EnabledFlag,,BufferSize*

where *number* is a valid LAN port number

Description: Specifies information for a specific network port.

Default: This parameter is configured automatically when you install Notes.

Notes UI Equivalent: File | Tools | User Preferences, Ports panel.

Applies to: Workstations

LOCATION

Syntax: Location=*LocationName*

Description: Identifies the current location.

Default: None

Notes UI Equivalent: File | Mobile | Choose Current Location.

Applies to: Workstations

LOG

Syntax: Log=*LogFileName,LogOption,0,Days,Size*

B

Note

The 0 (zero) in the middle of the command is a required placeholder.

where

LogFileName-Full path and file name for the Notes log

LogOption-1, 2, or 4, where

> 1-Log information to the console
>
> 2-Always run Fixup before opening the Notes log
>
> 4-Completely scan all documents in the Notes log when doing a database Fixup

0-This parameter is not used

Days-The number of days to retain documents in the Notes log

Size-The amount of text to be logged for a specific event

Description: Specifies the path and file name for the Notes log, as well as the information to be logged. For example,

```
Log=LOG.NSF,1,0,3,10000
```

This example specifies that the Notes log file is the file LOG.NSF, that all information logged will also be sent to the console, that all log documents will be retained for 3 days, and that the maximum amount of text for a single event is 10,000 words.

Default: `Log=LOG.NSF,1,0,7,8000` (save information for seven days, up to 8,000 words per entry)

Notes UI Equivalent: None

Applies to: Servers

LOG_AGENTMANAGER

Syntax: Log_AgentManager=*value*

where *value* can be:

0-Don't log agent execution events

1-Log agent execution events

Description: Specifies whether the Agent Manager logs the execution of an agent.

Default: None

Notes UI Equivalent: None

Applies to: Servers

LOG_MAILROUTING

Syntax: Log_MailRouting=*value*

where *value* can be:

0-No information is logged.

10-Displays errors, warnings, and major routing events such as startup, shutdown, the number of messages transferred, or a database compact.

20-Includes all information from 10, plus successful deliveries and transfers.

30-Logs all information from 20, plus thread information.

40-Logs all information from 30, plus transfer messages, message queues, and detailed information about documents placed in MAIL.BOX.

Description: Specifies the logging level for MAIL.BOX and the router.

Default: 20

Notes UI Equivalent: None

Applies to: Server

LOG_REPLICATION

Syntax: Log_Replication=*value*

where *value* can be

0-Don't log replication events

1-Log replication events

Description: Specifies whether replication events are logged. If replication events are logged, they are also displayed to the Notes console.

Default: None

Notes UI Equivalent: The Log All Replication Events setting in the advanced server setup.

Applies to: Servers

LOG_SESSIONS

Syntax: Log_Sessions=*value*

where *value* can be:

0-Don't log individual sessions

1-Log individual sessions

Description: Specifies whether individual sessions are logged. If sessions are logged, information is also displayed to the console.

Default: None

Notes UI Equivalent: The Log All Client Events setting in the advanced server setup.

Applies to: Servers

LOG_TASKS

Syntax: Log_Tasks=*value*

where *value* can be:

Yes-Log the server task status and display the status on the console

No-Do not log or display the server task status information

Description: Specifies logging of server task information.

Default: None

Notes UI Equivalent: None

Applies to: Servers

LOG_VIEW_EVENTS

Syntax: Log_View_Events=*value*

where *value* can be:

0-Don't log when views are rebuilt

1-Log view rebuilding

Description: Specifies whether view rebuilding events are logged. If this parameter isn't specified, rebuild events aren't logged.

Default: None

Notes UI Equivalent: None

Applies to: Servers

MAIL_LOG_TO_MISCEVENTS

Syntax: Mail_Log_To_MiscEvents=*value*

where *value* can be:

0-Don't display mail events in the Misc Events view of the Notes log.

1-Display mail events in the Misc Events view of the Notes log.

Description: Specifies whether mail events are displayed in the Misc Events view of the Notes log.

Default: None

Notes UI Equivalent: None

Applies to: Workstations and servers

MAILCOMPACTDISABLE

Syntax: MailCompactDisable=*value*

where *value* can be:

0-Enables MAIL.BOX compacting

1-Disables MAIL.BOX compacting

Description: Specifies whether MAIL.BOX is to be compacted. If this parameter isn't specified, MAIL.BOX is compacted normally by the Compact task.

Default: None

Notes UI Equivalent: None

Applies to: Servers

MAILDISABLEPRIORITY

Syntax: MailDisablePriority=*value*

where *value* can be:

1-The router ignores priorities when delivering messages

0-The router checks priorities when routing mail

Description: Disabling mail priority checking prevents immediate delivery of high-priority mail to different Notes networks.

Default: None

Notes UI Equivalent: None

Applies to: Servers

MailDynamicCostReset

Syntax: MailDynamicCostReset=*minutes*

Description: Specifies the elapsed time between when a server is unavailable and the time that the router will reset its cost estimate for that server.

Default: 60 (minutes)

Notes UI Equivalent: None

Applies to: Servers

MailEncryptIncoming

Syntax: MailEncryptIncoming=*value*

where *value* can be:

0-Don't force encryption

1-Encrypt all incoming mail

Description: Specifies whether all incoming mail will be encrypted, or mail will be encrypted on a case-by-case basis as specified in the individual mail message.

Default: None

Notes UI Equivalent: None

Applies to: Servers

MailLowPriorityTime

Syntax: MailLowPriorityTime=*TimeRange*

Description: Specifies the time of day considered to be off-peak hours. Notes routes low-priority mail only during the low-priority time of day. Times are specified in 24-hour format. You must specify a range. For example:

```
MailLowPriorityTime=20:00-00:00
```

This example specifies routing low-priority mail between 8:00 p.m. and midnight. Notes doesn't deliver low-priority mail if you specify only a single time.

Default: None

Notes UI Equivalent: None

Applies to: Servers

MailMaxThreads

Syntax: MailMaxThreads=*number*

Description: Specifies the maximum number of simultaneous threads that the mail router uses. Notes typically uses 1 thread per port. Raise this number on hubs and mail servers to allow for faster mail routing.

MaxMailThreads isn't used under UNIX.

Default: None

Notes UI Equivalent: None

Applies to: Servers

MailServer

Syntax: MailServer=*ServerName*

Description: Specifies a user's home server (the server that contains the user's mail file).

Default: None

Notes UI Equivalent: The Mail Server field in the person document in the Public Address Book.

Applies to: Workstations and servers

MailSystem

Syntax: MailSystem=*value*

where *value* can be:

0-Notes Mail

1-cc:Mail or any other mail system

Description: Specifies the mail system used by Notes.

Default: The mail system selected during Notes installation.

Notes UI Equivalent: File | Tools | User Preferences, Mail panel. Use the Mail Program drop-down list box to select the correct mail program.

Applies to: Workstations and servers

MailTimeout

Syntax: MailTimeout=*days*

Description: Specifies the number of days an undelivered message can be in a server's mailbox before the message is returned as undeliverable. If this parameter isn't specified in the NOTES.INI file, mail is returned after one day. Increase this number if you are sending mail to a foreign domain or routing a large number of messages.

Default: None

Notes UI Equivalent: None

Applies to: Servers

MailTimeoutMinutes

Syntax: MailTimeoutMinutes=*minutes*

Description: Specifies the number of minutes a message can be in MAIL.BOX before Notes returns the message to the sender. The maximum entry for a number is 1,440 (24 hours). If this parameter isn't specified in the NOTES.INI file, mail is returned after one day. Don't specify both MailTimeout and MailTimeoutMinutes. To specify a time greater than one day, use MailTimeout rather than MailTimeoutMinutes.

Default: None

Notes UI Equivalent: None

Applies to: Servers

Max_Retry_Delay

Syntax: Max_Retry_Delay=*minutes*

Description: Specifies the interval between call attempts when one server attempts to connect to another server.

Default: None

Notes UI Equivalent: None

Applies to: Servers

MEMORY_QUOTA

Syntax: Memory_Quota=*megabytes*

Description: Memory_Quota is used only under OS/2. Specifies the maximum amount of virtual memory that Notes can allocate. If this parameter isn't specified, Notes uses all available memory. The minimum value is 4 megabytes.

Caution

Never use the Memory_Quota setting unless told to do so by Lotus support.

Default: None

Notes UI Equivalent: None

Applies to: Workstations and servers

MODEMFILEDIRECTORY

Syntax: ModemFileDirectory=*path*

Description: Specifies the directory containing modem command files.

Default: The modem subdirectory under the Notes data directory, which was defined during the Notes installation.

Notes UI Equivalent: None

Applies to: Workstations and servers

NAME_CHANGE_EXPIRATION_DAYS

Syntax: Name_Change_Expiration_Days=*days*

where *days* must be in the range 14-60.

Description: Specifies the elapsed time in days before name change requests are deleted by the Administration Process from the Administration Requests database (ADMIN4.NSF). Name change requests rejected by a user are deleted after the specified number of days. If the user doesn't connect to the server in the specified number of days, the name change request is deleted.

Default: 21 (days)

Notes UI Equivalent: None

Applies to: Servers

NAMES

Syntax: Names=*AddressBook1,AddressBook2,...*

Description: Specifies the Public Address Books to be searched when resolving mail routing and group names. A maximum of 256 characters can be used, but you don't need to specify the .NSF extension. Notes only checks the first address book listed when looking for connection, domain, and server documents, and when resolving access control for groups.

Default: Names

Notes UI Equivalent: None

Applies to: Server and workstations

NEWMAILINTERVAL

Syntax: NewMailInterval=*minutes*

Description: The interval at which a Notes workstation checks for new mail, based on the number of *minutes* specified.

Default: 1

Notes UI Equivalent: File | Tools | User Preferences, Mail panel. Fill in the option for New Mail.

Applies to: Workstations

NEWMAILTUNE

Syntax: NewMailTune=*FileName*

Description: Specifies the full path and file name for a .WAV (sound) file to be played when new mail arrives. You must have a sound card and it must be enabled for this value to be used.

Default: None

Notes UI Equivalent: None

Applies to: Server and workstations

NODESIGNMENUS

Syntax: NoDesignMenus=*value*

where *value* can be:

0-Shows the Design menu

1-Hides the Design menu

Description: Removes the Design menu from the menu bar on workstations. Users can't view or change designs or create private views without this menu item. If this parameter isn't specified, the Design menu is included in the menu bar.

Caution

Don't rely on this setting as a security feature; a workstation user can easily edit his own NOTES.INI file to gain access to the Design menu.

Default: None

Notes UI Equivalent: None

Applies to: Workstations

NOEXTERNALAPPS

Syntax: NoExternalApps=*value*

where *value* can be:

1-Disables automatic launching of external applications

0-Enables automatic launching of external applications

Description: Use this parameter to protect against rogue mail messages. Mail messages can include executable applications. If you haven't disabled automatic execution of external applications, applications included in the mail file are automatically executed when the user opens the message. The application may cause data loss or disruption of the workstation. When NoExternalApps is set to 1, the following features are disabled on the workstation:

- ◆ OLE
- ◆ DDE
- ◆ DIP
- ◆ All @ commands
- ◆ @DBLookup (for non-Notes drivers)
- ◆ @DBColumn (for non-Notes drivers)
- ◆ @MailSend
- ◆ @DDE*xxx*
- ◆ Launching of file attachments
- ◆ Subscriptions (Macintosh workstations only)

If this parameter isn't specified, you aren't protected against rogue mail messages.

Default: None

Notes UI Equivalent: None

Applies to: Workstations

NO_FORCE_ACTIVITY_LOGGING

Syntax: No_Force_Activity_Logging=*value*

where *value* can be:

0-Prevents logging

1-Enables logging

Description: Prevents the Statistics task from automatically enabling activity logging for all databases on a server. If this parameter isn't specified, the StatLog server task enables the Record Activity option for every database on the server, which causes 64K to be added to the size of each database. Regardless of the value of this parameter, database activity is recorded in the Database Usage view in the server's Notes log. Because of this, you generally set No_Force_Activity_Logging to 0.

Default: None

Notes UI Equivalent: None

Applies to: Servers

NOMAILMENU

Syntax: NoMailMenu=*value*

where *value* can be:

1-Hide the Mail menu

0-Don't hide the Mail menu

Description: Specifies whether the Mail menu is displayed on a workstation. If this parameter isn't specified, the Mail menu is included. The user's mail system is set to 0 in this case.

Default: None

Notes UI Equivalent: None

Applies to: Workstations

NSF_BUFFER_POOL_SIZE

Syntax: NSF_Buffer_Pool_Size=*value*

Description: Specifies the maximum size of the NSF buffer pool. The NSF buffer pool is a disk cache used to store database updates temporarily before they are permanently written to disk. A large buffer pool can increase performance only when enough memory is available to hold the entire buffer in memory, not in virtual memory. If your server is swapping, specify a low value for NSF_Buffer_Pool_Size. The maximum size for Windows and Macintosh is 16M. Notes automatically changes this parameter, based on the value of the MEM.AVAILABILITY statistic. MEM.AVAILABILITY can be set at painful, normal, or plentiful, and affects the NSF buffer pool in the following way:

Painful-Sets the buffer pool size to 460K

Normal-Sets the buffer pool size to 4M

Plentiful-Sets the buffer pool size to 6M

Default: The Notes server automatically determines this value.

Notes UI Equivalent: None

Applies to: Workstations and servers

B

OS2DDE_COMMAND

Syntax: OS2DDE_Command=*value*

Description: This group of NOTES.INI settings controls opening and closing of files using DDE under OS/2.

Caution

Don't change any of these settings unless instructed to do so by Lotus support. Notes may cease to function if you change this parameter.

Default: None

Notes UI Equivalent: None

Applies to: Workstations

PASSTHRU_LOGLEVEL

Syntax: Passthru_LogLevel=*value*

where *value* can be:

0-No information is logged

1-Errors are logged

2-Errors and summary information are logged

3-Errors, summary, and detailed information are logged

4-All information is logged

Description: Specifies the amount of detail recorded in the Miscellaneous view when using passthru.

Default: 3 (Errors, summary, and detailed information is logged)

Notes UI Equivalent: File | Tools | User Preferences, Ports panel. Choose Trace Connection and specify Log Options.

Applies to: Workstations and servers

PhoneLog

Syntax: PhoneLog=*value*

where *value* can be:

0-Don't log phone calls

1-Record all calls except those that have a busy signal

2-Record all calls

Description: Specifies which phone calls are logged.

Default: 2 (Records all calls)

Notes UI Equivalent: None

Applies to: Workstations and servers

Port_MaxSessions

Syntax: Port_MaxSessions=*number*

Description: Specifies the maximum number of sessions that Notes allows on a specific port. Notes creates at least one session for each active user or server connected.

Default: None

Notes UI Equivalent: None

Applies to: Servers

PORTS

Syntax: Ports=*PortName1,PortName2,...*

Description: Lists the enabled ports in the order that they will be used in the absence of server connection documents. Specify the actual name of the port, such as COM1, LAN0, TCP, as listed in the list of ports in the User Preferences dialog box.

Default: None

Notes UI Equivalent: File | Tools | User Preferences, Ports panel.

Applies to: Workstations and servers

B

PROGRAMMODE

Syntax: ProgramMode=*value*

where *value* can be:

0-Full Notes

1-Notes Mail

8-Notes Desktop

Description: When a user uses Notes with a mail ID rather than a Notes desktop ID, Notes automatically updates this parameter.

Default: 1 (Full Notes)

Notes UI Equivalent: None

Applies to: Workstations

REPL_ERROR_TOLERANCE

Syntax: Repl_Error_Tolerance=*number*

Description: Specifies the maximum number of times a specific error can occur during replication before replication is terminated.

Default: 2

Notes UI Equivalent: None

Applies to: Servers

REPL_PUSH_RETRIES

Syntax: Repl_Push_Retries=*number*

Description: Specifies the number of times a Release 4 server can attempt to push changes to a database on a Release 3 server. Databases on Release 3 servers can be updated by only one Replicator at a time. Second and simultaneous attempts to push changes to a database are denied. If a server is denied push access to a database, it retries the specified number of times once every 30 seconds.

Default: None

Notes UI Equivalent: None

Applies to: Servers

REPLICATIONTIMELIMIT

Syntax: ReplicationTimeLimit=*minutes*

Description: Specifies the maximum duration for a single replication session. If this parameter isn't specified, there is no limit.

Default: None

Notes UI Equivalent: The Replication Time Limit field in a connection document in the Public Address Book.

Applies to: Servers

REPLICATORS

Syntax: Replicators=*number*

Description: Specifies the number of Replicator tasks that can run simultaneously on a server. You must restart the Notes server after changing this value.

Default: 1

Notes UI Equivalent: None

Applies to: Servers

REPORTUSEMAIL

Syntax: ReportUseMail=*value*

where *value* can be:

0-Use the Statistic Delivery API call

1-Use the mail router

Description: Specifies whether the Reporter task uses Mail or its own internal call to deliver statistics, when delivering statistics to another server within a domain. When this parameter is set to 1, the Reporter task logs the fact that it is forced to use Notes Mail.

Default: 0

Notes UI Equivalent: None

Applies to: Servers

SECUREMAIL

Syntax: SecureMail=*value*

where *value* can be:

0-Don't force encryption of all outgoing mail

1-Force encryption of all outgoing mail

Description: Secure mail applies only to workstations. No way exists to force encryption of all outgoing mail from a particular server. Mail sent by a workstation with secure mail enabled is encrypted. Secure mail also causes all outgoing Notes mail to be digitally signed. When secure mail is specified in NOTES.INI, users aren't given the option to sign and encrypt when creating mail. If this parameter isn't specified in the NOTES.INI file, users have the option of signing and encrypting on a message-by-message basis.

Default: None

Notes UI Equivalent: File | Tools | User Preferences, Mail panel. Choose the Encrypt Sent Mail option.

Applies to: Workstations

SERVER_CONSOLE_PASSWORD

Syntax: Server_Console_Password=*password*

Description: This entry is created automatically by a Notes server when the Set Configuration command is entered at the server console. See Chapter 18, "Administering Notes Security," for more details on the Set Configuration Server command. The password is encrypted before being stored in the NOTES.INI file.

Default: None

Notes UI Equivalent: None

Applies to: Servers

SERVER_MAXSESSIONS

Syntax: Server_MaxSessions=*number*

Description: Specifies the maximum number of concurrent sessions that a server can start. Decrease this number if you increase the number of Replicators or mail router threads.

Default: None

Notes UI Equivalent: None

Applies to: Servers

SERVER_SESSION_TIMEOUT

Syntax: Server_Session_Timeout=*minutes*

Description: Specifies the maximum amount of time that a server keeps an idle connection open. When the specified number of minutes elapses, Notes terminates the connection.

Default: (OS/2, Windows NT, Windows 95, UNIX) 240 minutes; (NetWare) 30 minutes.

Notes UI Equivalent: None

Applies to: Servers

SERVER_SHOW_PERFORMANCE

Syntax: Server_Show_Performance=*value*

where *value* can be:

Yes-Displays server performance events on the console

No-Records server performance events to the Notes log

Description: Specifies whether server performance events are displayed on the console. Whether or not this feature is enabled, events are logged. If this parameter isn't specified, events are logged.

Default: None

Notes UI Equivalent: None

Applies to: Servers

SERVERKEYFILENAME

Syntax: ServerKeyFileName=*FileName*

Description: Specifies the server ID file on a Notes server used as both workstation and server. (KeyFileName specifies the user ID for an administrator when a Notes machine is being used as both server and workstation.)

This parameter is ignored on NetWare servers.

Default: None

Notes UI Equivalent: None

Applies to: Servers

SERVERNAME

Syntax: ServerName=*name*

Description: Specifies the full hierarchical name of the server.

Default: None

Notes UI Equivalent: The Server Name field in the server document.

Applies to: Server

SERVERNOREPLREQUESTS

Syntax: ServerNoReplRequests=*value*

where *value* can be:

0-Accept replication requests

1-Refuse replication requests

Description: When this feature is enabled, the replicator running on this server doesn't respond to requests from other servers to push changes during a replication; other servers must perform pull-push replication with this server. If this parameter isn't specified, the server accepts replication requests.

Default: None

Notes UI Equivalent: None

Applies to: Servers

SERVERPULLREPLICATION

Syntax: ServerPullReplication=*value*

where *value* can be:

1-All scheduled replications must be push-pull

0-Scheduled replications occur normally

Description: When this feature is enabled, all scheduled replications initiated from this server must be pull-push. This parameter is generally used in a hub-and-spoke replication configuration to reduce the workload on the hub server. You reduce the workload on the hub server by specifying 1 on all spoke servers.

Default: None

Notes UI Equivalent: None

Applies to: Servers

SERVERPUSHREPLICATION

Syntax: ServerPushReplication=*value*

where *value* can be:

1-Prevents this server from pulling changes from other servers

0-Scheduled replications occur normally

Description: When this feature is enabled, all scheduled replications initiated from this server must be push-pull. This server doesn't send a request to the other servers to replicate back changes.

Default: None

Notes UI Equivalent: None

Applies to: Servers

SERVERSETUP

Syntax: ServerSetUp=*number*

where *number* is:

1-NetWare

2-Windows

3-OS/2

Description: Specifies a server's operating system.

Default: None

Notes UI Equivalent: None

Applies to: Servers

SERVERTASKS

Syntax: ServerTasks=*task1,task2,task3,...*

Description: Specifies all server tasks to be started when the Notes server is started.

Default: Replica, router, UPDALL, stats

Notes UI Equivalent: None

Applies to: Servers

SERVERTASKSAT*time*

Syntax: ServerTasksAt*time*=*ServerTask1,ServerTask2,...*

where *time* specifies an hour of the day, using 24-hour format (0 is midnight and 23 is 11 p.m.)

Description: Use ServerTasksAt*time* to schedule server tasks to start at a specific hour of the day. (To schedule programs, use program documents instead of this parameter.)

Default:

`ServerTasksAt1=Catalog,Design` (runs Catalog and Design at 1:00 a.m.)

`ServerTasksAt2=UPDALL,Object Collect MailOBJ.NSF` (runs UPDALL, Object Collect MailOBJ.NSF at 2:00 a.m.)

`ServerTasksAt5=StatLog` (runs StatLog at 5:00 a.m.)

Notes UI Equivalent: None

Applies to: Servers

SETUP

Syntax: SetUp=*RevisionNumber*

Description: Identifies the version number of Notes software.

Default: This parameter is set during Notes installation.

Notes UI Equivalent: None

Applies to: Workstations and servers

SHARED_MAIL

Syntax: Shared_Mail=*value*

where *value* can be:

0-Shared mail is disabled for new mail delivered to this server. Any currently shared mail is unaffected.

1-Shared mail is enabled for new mail delivered to this server

2-Shared mail is used for mail delivered to this server and for mail transferred through this server

Description: Specifies whether the shared mail feature is used for new mail on this server.

Default: 0 (Shared mail not used)

Notes UI Equivalent: None

Applies to: Servers

SwapPath

Syntax: SwapPath=*location*

Description: Specifies the location of the server's swap file. This parameter shouldn't be used, as the swap file should be specified by using the OS/2 system configuration files. If this parameter is specified, the Reporter server task uses this location for the `Server.Path.Swap` statistic.

Default: None

Notes UI Equivalent: None

Applies to: Servers

TimeZone

Syntax: TimeZone=*value*

Description: Specifies a time zone. Time zones begin at Greenwich, England (0) and move westward. Eastern Standard Time is 5.

Default: Provided during Notes installation.

Notes UI Equivalent: The Local Time Zone field in the location document.

Applies to: Workstations and servers

UPDATE_NO_BRP_FILES

Syntax: Update_No_BRP_Files=*value*

where *value* can be:

1-The Fixup server task creates a .BRP file when it encounters an error

0-The Fixup task doesn't create a .BRP file

Description: Determines whether a Fixup server task creates a .BRP file.

Default: None

Notes UI Equivalent: None

Applies to: Servers

UPDATE_NO_FULLTEXT

Syntax: Update_No_FullText=*value*

where *value* can be:

0-Indexes are updated

1-Indexes aren't updated

Description: Specifies whether the UPDATE.ALL server task can update full-text indexes. If this parameter isn't specified, the UPDALL server task updates full-text indexes.

Default: None

Notes UI Equivalent: None

Applies to: Servers

UPDATE_SUPPRESSION_TIME

Syntax: Update_Suppression_Time=*minutes*

Description: Specifies the elapsed time between full-text and view updates. This parameter is used even if immediate indexing is specified for a database.

Default: 5 (minutes)

Notes UI Equivalent: None

Applies to: Servers

UPDATERS

Syntax: Updaters=*number*

Description: Specifies the number of full-text indexing tasks that can run simultaneously on a server. If this parameter isn't specified, only a single indexer runs at a time.

Note

You must restart the server after changing this parameter.

Default: None

Notes UI Equivalent: None

Applies to: Servers

USEFONTMAPPER

Syntax: UseFontMapper=*value*

where *value* can be:

1-Enables the FontMapper

0-Disables the FontMapper

Description: Determines whether the FontMapper is used to map fonts.

Default: 1 (Enabled)

Notes UI Equivalent: None

Applies to: Workstations and servers

VIEWEXPNUMBER

Syntax:

ViewExpNumber=*parameter1,parameter2,parameter3,,parameter4,...*

Description: Specifies the parameters used when exporting data from a view. The following are valid parameters:

parameter1-The program name and file type

parameter2-The value 0, 1, or 2, where

    0-Can't append to an existing file

    1-An option to append is provided in a dialog box

    2-Automatically writes a temporary file if needed to avoid a 64K limit

parameter3-Name of the export routine to use

parameter4-Reserved

parameter5 and up-File extensions used to select a file type in the File Export dialog box

Default: None

Notes UI Equivalent: None

Applies to: Workstations and servers

VIEWIMPNUMBER

Syntax: ViewImpNumber=*parameter1,0,parameter2,,parameter3,...*

Description: Specifies parameters to be used when importing files at the view level.

parameter1-The program name and version number

parameter2-The name of the import routine to use

parameter3 and up-File extensions used to select a file type in the File Import dialog box

Default: None

Notes UI Equivalent: None

Applies to: Workstations and servers

WINDOW_TITLE

Syntax: Window_Title=*text*

Description: Replaces Lotus Notes on the title bar with the specified *text*.

Default: None

Notes UI Equivalent: None

Applies to: Workstations and servers

WININFOBOXPOS

Syntax: WinInfoBoxPos=*xlocation,ylocation*

Description: Determines the position of an infobox.

Default: 85,193

Notes UI Equivalent: None

Applies to: Workstations

WINSysFontNumber

Syntax: WinSysFontNumber=*value1,value2,value3,...*

Description: All CGM metafiles contain numeric identifiers for fonts. When the FontMapper is disabled, these font numbers are used to map fonts from a Windows system font.

Default: None

Notes UI Equivalent: None

Applies to: Workstations

XPC_Console

Syntax: XPC_Console=*value*

where *value* can be:

0-Hides the console

1-Displays the console

Description: Displays the XPC console that contains modem input/output information, if this information is being logged.

Default: 0

Notes UI Equivalent: None

Applies to: Workstations

XPC_No_Look_Ahead_Reads

Syntax: XPC_No_Look_Ahead_Reads=*value*

where *value* can be:

1-Disables XPC protocol from looking ahead in the Serial Driver's Receive queue to determine if enough data is available to form an XPC packet.

0-XPC look-ahead is enabled

Description: When this feature is disabled, XPC can't look ahead to see if enough data is available to form an XPC packet. Disabling look-ahead results in less than optimal performance, but is useful when troubleshooting.

Default: 0

Notes UI Equivalent: None

Applies to: Servers

XPC_POOL_SIZE

Syntax: XPC_Pool_Size=*bytes*

Description: Specifies the size of an XPC memory pool. You should add 15K to this value for every COM port beyond your sixth COM port. The maximum size of this pool is 1M.

Default: 50,000 (bytes)

Index

X-Z

Add to Your Sams Library Today with the Best Books for Programming, Operating Systems, and New Technologies

The easiest way to order is to pick up the phone and call

1-800-428-5331

between 9:00 a.m. and 5:00 p.m. EST.

For faster service, please have your credit card available.

ISBN	Quantity	Description of Item	Unit Cost	Total Cost
0-672-30907-6		PowerBuilder 5 Unleashed (Book/CD-ROM)	$59.99	
0-672-30909-2		Sybase SQL Server 6 Unleashed (Book/CD-ROM)	$59.99	
0-672-30903-3		Microsoft SQL Server 6 Unleashed (Book/CD-ROM)	$59.99	
0-672-30873-8		Essential Oracle7	$25.00	
0-672-30872-x		Oracle Unleashed (Book/CD-ROM)	$59.99	
0-672-30852-5		Developing Client/Server Applications with Oracle Developer/2000 (Book/CD-ROM)	$49.99	
0-672-30863-0		Teach Yourself Delphi 2 in 21 Days	$35.00	
0-672-30858-4		Delphi 2 Unleashed, 2E (Book/CD-ROM)	$59.99	
1-57521-030-4		Teach Yourself Java in 21 Days (Book/CD-ROM)	$39.99	
1-57521-049-5		Java Unleashed (Book/CD-ROM)	$49.99	
0-672-30783-9		Visual Basic 4 Developer's Guide (Book/CD-ROM)	$49.99	
0-672-30906-8		Lotus Notes 4 Unleashed (Book/CD-ROM)	$59.99	
1-57521-071-1		Building an Intranet (Book/CD-ROM)	$55.00	
1-57521-051-7		Web Publishing Unleashed (Book/CD-ROM)	$49.99	
❏ 3 ½" Disk		Shipping and Handling: See information below.		
❏ 5 ¼" Disk		TOTAL		

Shipping and Handling: $4.00 for the first book, and $1.75 for each additional book. Floppy disk: add $1.75 for shipping and handling. If you need to have it NOW, we can ship product to you in 24 hours for an additional charge of approximately $18.00, and you will receive your item overnight or in two days. Overseas shipping and handling adds $2.00 per book and $8.00 for up to three disks. Prices subject to change. Call for availability and pricing information on latest editions.

201 W. 103rd Street, Indianapolis, Indiana 46290

1-800-428-5331 — Orders   1-800-835-3202 — FAX   1-800-858-7674 — Customer Service

Book ISBN 0-672-30844-4

CD-ROM Install

What's on the Disc?

The companion CD-ROM contains software developed by the author, plus an assortment of third-party tools and product demos. The disc is designed to be explored using a browser program. Using the browser, you can view information concerning products and companies, and install programs with a single click of the mouse. To install the browser, follow these steps:

1. Insert the CD-ROM into your CD-ROM drive.
2. From the Windows 95 desktop, double-click the My Computer icon.
3. Double-click the icon representing your CD-ROM drive.
4. Double-click the icon titled Setup.exe to run the installation program.
5. Installation creates a program group named LNA Survival Guide. To browse the CD-ROM, click the Start button and choose Programs | LNA Survival Guide | LNA Survival Guide to run the browser program.

Note

The browser program requires at least 256 colors. For best results, set your monitor to display between 256 and 64,000 colors. A screen resolution of 640×480 pixels is also recommended. If necessary, adjust your monitor settings before using the CD-ROM.